MY HOME IS WHERE MY HEART IS

MY HOME

IS WHERE MY

HEART IS

The Story of My Life:
An Immigrant from Switzerland

By

Edith Gross Prigge

First Printing, January 1999
First Revision, September 2003

ISBN: 1-58597-223-1

Library of Congress Control Number: 2003114734

A division of Squire Publishers, Inc.
4500 College Blvd.
Leawood, KS 66211
1/888/888-7696
www.leatherspublishing.com

I would like to dedicate this book to my four children. They are my joy, and they helped me unknowingly, through a lot of rough times. Thanks so much, you guys. I wish you and your families lots of luck and happiness. God bless you all.

I would also like to thank Rev. Heins for believing in me and my script. He put the time and effort into printing it, in January 1999. Thanks so much.

And last but not least, I would like to thank Phil Nelson. When I desperately needed a job, he gave me one. And when I needed someone to correct the spelling for my first print, he was there for me. You're my inspiration. Thanks, Phil.

PREFACE

I'm Edith Gross, born in Switzerland in December 1938. I went to school and got married in the Old Country. Then in March of 1968 I emigrated with my husband, Henry, and our four children (two boys and two girls): Edith, 9; Heniz, 8; Lottie, 7; and Reto, 6 years old.

It was my husband's dream to own a farm and work his own land, something that is almost impossible in Switzerland. If having his own farm makes Henry happy, then I'm willing to help him and stand right by his side to make his dream come true.

We worked hard for many, many years, but had to abandon our dream in 1986. That was one of my toughest tasks, to let go of our farm and see everything go on the auction block.

Edith and Heinz moved back to Switzerland, got married there, and now have their own families.

We lost our little eight-month-old granddaughter, "Cassy," in May of 1988.

And Henry passed away in March of 1990. Exactly 22 years after we immigrated into the United States, I took him home in a small box and laid him to rest in the cemetery by the church where he got confirmed, in his hometown, Ebnat-Kappel. He now rests forever in the midst of his beloved mountains.

Lotti and her family live in my old house in Merrill, WI, and Reto and his family reside in Fallen, NV. That leaves me alone to support myself, and even though I work, there are a lot of long, lonely nights. That gave me the idea to write this book and share my life story with you.

God bless you.

1

IT WAS IN Switzerland, December 18, 1938, on a Sunday late afternoon. The snow fell quietly for the first time that winter and covered the world with a sparkling blanket. The Christmas lights tried to spread joy into the eyes and hearts of people, people who were afraid of what the future would hold in store for them. But there I was a bundle of joy in my mother's arms. She just gave birth to me, a little girl whom she named Edith. She said I looked exactly like my dad, and they both were so very proud of me.

Hitler was in command, and war started all around us. My dad was called into the army, to do active duty and defend our country. My parents were poor, and my dad made a commitment to his mother years before he got married, a commitment which he would never break. Because of that, my mother was forced to live with my grandmother and some of my dad's siblings. She had a terrible life, but no shoulder to cry on.

My mother, Paula Wymann (born 1912), lost her dad at the age of 13 (he had throat cancer). Her mother died of blood poisoning one year later, and four weeks after her mother's funeral one of her brothers got killed in a work-related accident. She now was an orphan and had to live with her brother Franz. He was nine years older than she was, but later got married and started his own family.

My mother had to stay on her own two feet, so she rented one bedroom (not an apartment, only a room). Her other two brothers, Willhelm and Josef, were 12 and 10 years older than she was and had their own families. Mom started working at the chocolate factory in Kilchberg (ZH) at the age of 15. That is where she later got to know Berta

Zellweger, and the two became best friends. Berta took my mother home once in a while, and that is how my mother got to know my dad. My dad was Berta's older brother, Jakob Zellweger.

My mother brought me home from the hospital and soon after that had to go back to work at the factory, putting me into the day care center, which the company provided.

I had only one outfit to wear. She picked me up every day after work, took me home, washed the outfit I wore by hand, dried it overnight so that it once again was clean the next morning. There just wasn't any money.

Before I was two years old I ended up in the hospital twice with a bad case of pneumonia. I was not supposed to make it, but I pulled through both times. They tell me that I was walking when I was one year old but could hardly crawl by the age of two, having been sick for so long.

It was on April 6, 1941, my dad was still doing active duty in the military, when my mother gave birth to my brother Heinz. Heinz was born with only one leg. My mother was very weak from all the hard work. She was released from the hospital still having a fever, but she was unable to stay longer because of financial reasons. She brought my brother home but was so weak that she could not nurse him, and they did not send any formula along to feed the baby.

The train ride home from the hospital was uncomfortable, and the walk to the apartment building even worse. It normally was a 30-minute walk, but in her condition it took two hours. It was a big relief when she finally made it home. Nobody was there to help her; everybody was either at work or in the military. She packed the little bundle into his crib and went back to the store to get some formula.

Needless to say, that made her sicker yet. It took only two weeks and she was back in the hospital. The doctors, with the help of antibiotics, got her fever down, but then told her she had contracted TB and would not be able to go home anymore.

They did send her to a TB sanatorium in Davos, but there she got sicker and sicker and developed water in her chest. For many of nights she was wheeled into the bathroom because nobody thought she would survive the night, and the nurses did not want to have her roommates watch her die.

My godmother, who is my dad's sister, Berta, took me in. She and her husband and my parents had a double wedding on July 12, 1938. Her husband, Arthur, was born and grew up in Switzerland, but his mother was a German citizen. Because of that, he wasn't a Swiss citizen either. He had to leave Switzerland and fight in the German army during World War II.

My godmother could visit him a couple of times, but she got the last letter from him just before he was sent to the Russian border. That letter had a drawing on it that I will never forget. He drew on top of the first page ocean waves and a big boat with three masts, the sails billowing in the wind. My godmother always treasured that letter and 50 years later, still had it. She knew Arthur lost a leg fighting the Russians. She heard that he was put in one of those emergency hospitals, but then she never heard from him again.

My godmother gave birth to three boys through the first five years of her marriage, but her blood was an R factor negative; none of them lived for more than a day or two. So she was happy to take care of me. "Gotti," as I called her, also worked in a chocolate factory, and she too had to bring me every morning to the day care center. She wanted to go as far as adopting me, but even though my mother was very, very sick, she did not give her consent for adoption. In the meantime, my grandma took my brother Heinz on, like he was her own child. Neither of us two could ever visit our mother.

At the age of four I got sick again and ended up in the hospital with pneumonia and whooping-cough. My "Gotti" and grandma came to visit me a couple of times, but they could only talk to me through a big glass window; nobody was allowed into our room except the nurses and doctors. Nobody cared about me and the other 11 sick children, who were between six months and 13 years old, and also in my room.

Then it was wartime! It felt like we were not important; we were just a bother to everybody. When the sirens went off to tell us there was another night air attack, the nurses turned our regular light to blue light so that the pilots could not see the hospital. They then locked the door to our room and disappeared to the bomb shelter and left us frightened kids alone. We could hear those heavy, deep-sounding planes fly over us; it felt like the whole hospital was shaking. All of us cried, some screamed, but there was nobody to comfort us.

One time I thought I saw flames shooting up the elevator shaft that was in the building across a small lawn from us. I was just so scared. It seemed to take hours until those planes came back after unloading the bombs over Germany, which was only 30-35 miles away from us. They sounded a lot lighter on their way back, but it still was very scary. I will never, ever forget how frightened I was, and I will remember those sounds as long as I live.

One day my mother sent me chocolate and a nice card with a clown on it to the hospital. It had to be to cheer me up. I could not read the card, but I could feel her close and knew that she still remembered me. The nurse read the card to me and then said, "Chocolate is not good for you." She took everything, never giving me one little piece of it.

After three long months in the hospital, I could finally go home. But I had to live with my grandma and my aunt and uncles from that time on. We had a six-bedroom apartment right by Lake Zurich. There were a total of eight families in that apartment building. The father of one of my playmates got put on the wall and shot. He was accused of spying for Germany. I will always remember his gravestone. It had a beautiful big rose full in bloom, symbolizing the mother, then four little rosebuds for each of their children, and a heavy wooden stem to hold it all up, which was the symbol of Dad; he was there for all of them to lean on. But the wooden stem was broken in half, just like their dad's life.

In my dreams I always felt that is what a family should be — the beauty of a woman, kids that are loved dearly, and a man to be there to support them, not just physically, also emotionally. Our family certainly was not that way.

Even though Switzerland was never involved in the war, we still could feel it almost daily. We lived right across the street from the chocolate factory. That huge building had a flat roof and a big Swiss flag painted on it for the pilots to see that they still were in Switzerland and not in Germany yet.

Almost daily there were the sirens that sent their shrill message out for everyone to hear if the bombers emerged. No matter how many times I heard it, it still was scary. We changed our regular light to blue light immediately and sat quietly around the dining room table waiting for the attack to pass.

Almost all the food in the store was rationed. We had to have ration stamps from the government to buy butter, sugar and most of the other groceries, but we got extra stamps because of my mother's TB sickness. We always had enough food, nothing special, but we never went hungry.

It was a very tough time, but war was not my main concern. I had other things to worry about. I was told my mother would never come home again, and so it was my responsibility to take care of my father and my brother.

I had to learn how to knit. Only five years old and I

had to knit socks for my dad, whom I only saw when he came home on leave from the Army. I also had to knit undershirts for myself. For that I had to use round needles, and there were so many, many little stitches on it; it seemed a never-ending task. My godmother put a mark on my knitting before she left for work and told me how many rounds I had to do before I could quit. She made sure it would take me all afternoon.

On a nice sunny day she allowed me to sit out on our big balcony. From there I could see all the people who enjoyed the beach on Lake Zurich. I could hear their laughter and could see them play games.

My cousin Walter, who also lived with us and was one year older than I (he was my Aunt Ida's illegitimate son), could go and enjoy a swim in the cool lake, but I had to knit because I was a girl. My grandma used to say a woman is on this earth to please a man and to do everything to make life easier for him because he has to work so hard to support his family. And Grandma sure was an example. Women could not take any meat before the guys had enough around our dinner table, and Grandma would not eat at all before everybody was full.

We three kids (my brother, my cousin and me) had to split a bratwurst or hot dog. Only on New Year's Eve would each of us get a whole bratwurst, and that I felt was a very special treat. Our dinner was most of the time almost military style. We kids could never talk, and the adults would always scold us. One would say, "Sit straight," the other one, "Hands belong on the table," or a third one, "Do not make so much noise when you eat." It certainly was no fun. They felt kids had to been seen, but not heard.

****

My grandma did not know any better than that. She had a very hard life, was never loved, and we had to pay for it. She was very strict, but I know deep within my heart she loved us all.

She had to leave her home in first grade. Her dad gave her to a butcher, a good friend of his. There she had to work. She started at 5 a.m. to get the store ready, cut and pack meat so that it could be brought to the customers out there in the country. Eight o'clock in the morning and it was time to go to school, but so often she would fall asleep sitting on the school bench because she was tired from working so hard. But then the teacher punished her for that. She had to work hard through all the school years to support herself. Then in later years if there was money that she earned, her dad was there to take it.

Just as she turned 18, a good friend and drinking buddy of her dad's lost his wife through childbirth. He had three kids and now no longer a wife. My great-grandpa volunteered Grandma. "My daughter Berta could help you raise them kids," he told his friend. Grandma was never asked, but there was no question she had to go there as a maid who did not get paid, but used.

And it did not take long and she was pregnant and had to get married. She worked very, very hard and raised his three kids. Then she gave birth to six children of her own and took in foster kids, besides running a boarding house where the factory workers from the nearby factory could come and eat a hot meal at noon. She did all of that while her husband was drinking and partying with friends and taking life easy.

My dad was born in 1911, but was never accepted by his dad because he looked like my grandma. He had to work hard from little on. Potatoes and other items were hard to come by during World War I, so my dad, as a first-grader, and his mother had to leave their home in the middle of the night pulling a little wooden cart to find places where they could buy eggs, meat, potatoes and other vegetables on the black market, just so that my grandma could feed her family and also the factory workers. Dad's older brother, Ueli, never had to help, just because he was a "spittin' image" of his father.

But when my dad turned 18 and found a job as a carpenter, he convinced my grandma to get a divorce. "We will move to another state," he promised her, "and I will always take care of you and my siblings," never thinking that that could haunt him some day. A divorce in the late '20s, early '30s, was almost unheard of, but she did it and they moved to Kilchberg in the state of Zurich. And this, I think, was the reason why Grandma was so hard on me. She did not know any better. She only knew from her own experience that girls were here on this earth to work, and men are the ones who tell them what and how they want it done.

****

Another year passed. My dad did not know what to do anymore; my mother didn't get any better. But then one of his military buddies told him to talk to this Quaker. If he could not help, there would be nothing anybody could do for her. So my dad got in contact with Mr. Graetzer. The Quaker gave Dad some wine for my mom to drink, just a small glassful, but every day. And he told my dad he would pray for my mother.

The doctors in the sanatorium pumped the water from my mom's chest cavity for days until her heart was too weak to take it, and then would let it go for a week or two until her heart recuperated. But by then she almost drowned in her own water, so it was back to pumping again.

My mom was too weak to get the wine herself, but her roommates helped her and gave her a glass every noon. Two weeks later the doctors got an unbelievable surprise. They were ready to pump her water again, but there was nothing left. It dried up. They shook their heads and could not understand what happened, but were relieved that the battle for her life was finally over. My mother slowly got her strength back.

Edith,
five years old

Edith, 3rd grade.
Heinz, 1st grade.

2

THE WAR WAS over and my dad came home. It was not a big celebration, yet everybody felt relieved and were hoping that life now could get back to normal again.

And then five months later my mother got released from the sanatorium and finally could come home, just to get hurt again. She could not even sit by my dad's side at the dinner table anymore. She was told by my dad's sister Ida and his brothers Henry and Ueli that she was an unfit, sick wife and had no right to sit at my dad's right side. And my brother Heinz did not know her at all, since Grandma raised and protected him as one of her own. My mother was a stranger to him.

It had to hurt her; then she did not know how long she had to live. Nobody thought she would make it for more than a couple of years. My Aunt Olive (Uncle Ueli's wife) died in the sanatorium of TB, and a friend of my mother's whom she got to know in the sanatorium (a young woman who never was as sick as my mother was) died one year after she returned home. There was no guarantee how fast a relapse would occur, and my mother was scared.

She was so alone and a stranger in her own home. I saw her pain, yet I was too small to help her, nor did I know how I could make her feel better. She had to go back to work at the chocolate factory, but it was doctor's orders to take a three-week vacation every year. She had to go up to the mountains to fill her lungs with that fresh, clean air. If my mother went on vacation, visited a friend or one of her brothers, she could only take me along, but never my brother Heinz. Grandma would not allow that.

It was during our first vacation together that she told

me what it means to love a man and to have children. She took a flower and broke off the stem. The stem was the man, the flower was the woman. She said, "I probably will never see you growing up, so I would like to be the one who tells you about the love between a man and a woman. That is something very, very special and precious, and I would never, ever allow you to laugh or make jokes about it."

I still can see us two sitting out there in that meadow all by ourselves, not a cloud in the dark blue sky, and the only noise I could hear was the chirping of the nearby birds, those little creatures that also enjoyed this beautiful day. A butterfly stopped and sat on my shoe. I don't know if he also listened to my mother's explanation, but he surely was pretty. That day made such an impression on me that I never forgot it, and from then on I knew love is more than sex. Love is caring for and respecting another human being's feelings.

My mom came every night to my bedroom to tuck me in and pray with me. And I could talk to her about things that happened during the day, or she would read me a little story. That was the most precious thing in my young life, those few minutes I could spend with my mom. But if she stayed more than 15-20 minutes, then my grandma got mad at me and questioned me the next morning. She wanted to know what it was we talked about that it took so long for my mother to leave my room.

Grandma did not have to hit me or yell at me if I didn't do something to her satisfaction. She just would say: "Boy, you are the biggest slob I ever saw," and I would bend over backwards to do things right so that she would love me, too, not just my brother.

I had to work hard. We had to iron everything, even the bed sheets and the underwear, and then I had to rotate them when I put them into the closet (take the ones that were in the closet out, put the fresh linen in and the rest on top). She was very strict. Nothing was put away with a button or a stitch missing.

Grandma also always cooked for the whole clan and I had to help her. We had a big garden, raised most of our vegetables. We raised rabbits for meat and had chickens, and all of that was a lot of work.

I had to get the eggs and feed the chickens. It was not something I liked to do, especially if they had lice, which was quite regularly. That meant I had to take each chicken in my arm and spray her with a powder, then lock them all out into the fence area, close everything up and burn sulfur sticks in the chicken barn. Boy, that stinks, but the lice were gone for awhile, but for days it felt like those little creatures were crawling up my arms. I know it was only in my imagination, but I could not shake it. I promised myself that I never, ever would have chickens of my own as long as I lived.

Kilchberg, the town we lived in, had the most wealthy people in any town in the State of Zurich. Thomas Mann (a German author) is buried in the cemetery by the Protestant Church in Kilchberg. The poet Conrad Ferdinant Meyer lived in Kilchberg and created beautiful poems. His home is still to this day the way he left it when he died. Even the feather he wrote with is still in the little bottle of ink. Several times I went to visit his house, which they turned into a museum. I was so impressed, and it was so overwhelming that I could almost feel his presence.

Most of my classmates were from very wealthy families. Some of them had maids that had to do whatever those kids asked them to do. My classmates did not have to wear aprons or hand-knitted stockings to school like I had to.

You could really see the difference between rich and poor by just walking into our classroom. One day my cousin Walter (who was in the same grade as I was) and I got into an argument with one of our classmates. She told us later that her mother would come and beat us up, but we did not believe her.

Yet the very next day as we were ready to leave the school at noon, there was her mother waiting for us. Walter and I were afraid. We turned around and locked ourselves in the bathroom. We waited until everything was quiet and then tried to sneak out, but to our surprise the school doors were locked and there was no way for us to get out. Now we really were in trouble. We could not make it home on time for lunch, and that we knew was a disaster. It was one hour later when the janitor came back and opened the doors. We snuck out and ran all the way home. But there was my Uncle Henry ready with his leather belt to paddle our rear ends.

My mother came to my defense and said, "If my daughter has to be punished, then I will be the one to do it." That was the wrong thing for her to say. My uncle turned away from me and told her she had nothing to say, since she was an unfit, sickly wife anyway. He hit her with the belt until she could escape into her bedroom, locking the door behind her.

That night when my dad came home, he was greeted at the door by Grandma and his siblings. They all told him how bad I was and that his wife wasn't any better. Then he went into the bedroom, and there was my mom crying. But he could not cope with all of that, and he knew he made that promise to his mother to always stand by her. That left him no room to emotionally support my mom and me. He said, "Sorry, I cannot talk tonight. I have a meeting to go to," and out the door he went.

My mother was so sad and did not know where to turn anymore. She could see no future. That night she called me into her bedroom. She was already undressed and wore her nightgown. She told me to do the same and then crawl in bed by her. I did, not questioning her. Then I saw the tears in her eyes. On the bedcover was a little white enamel bowl with a thin blue line on top and a sharp kitchen knife in it.

I crawled in by her. She put her arm around me and started talking. She said very calmly: "I will put both of our hands in this bowl so that we do not get the bed dirty; then I will cut your wrist first and then mine. I would never leave you here alone. Don't worry, it won't hurt much. We will slowly lose our strength, and then will fall asleep forever."

I was not frightened, then I knew deep within my heart that my mother would never do anything to hurt me. But yet she taught me to pray every night before I go to sleep, so how could we go to sleep forever without praying first.

I said, "Mama, I know God will take care of us, but let's pray first, just as you taught me."

We folded our hands, bowed our heads and asked the Lord to forgive us our sins and to please watch out for my dad and my brother and to give us everlasting peace."

After we said amen, it was silent for a minute. Then my mother got up, put the bowl and knife away, came back to bed and we both cried ourselves to sleep, but never, ever talked about that night again.

It took months after that before my mother was allowed to eat with us at the dinner table again. In the meantime, she had to cook for herself on a little alcohol burner in her bedroom. Dad was good to her in his own way but did not want to make any waves. He belonged to so many organizations, plus bowling and playing cards, that he had something going on every night. He also taught mountain climbing and loved his mountains. So every weekend from early spring until late fall he was gone.

And then in winter, he favored his second hobby, the stamp collection. Every Sunday he had the whole dining room table full of little pails of stamps from all over the world, the radio turned on full blast so that he could listen to every little detail of the hockey games. We could never talk; we had to be very quiet. We could not even sneeze or cough, or his stamps would fly away and that would get him upset.

But all of those hobbies must have helped Dad to cope with the problems we had. He did not have to talk about it, and maybe that made him feel better. Yet my mother's hands were tied. She was told many times by my grandma or my aunts that if she did not like the way things are going, that she could leave, but without her children. And that is one thing my mother would never do; that would have broken her heart.

I hated Saturdays at our house. I had to start a fire and heat the water in a big kettle down in the wash house and bucket the water into a tub. Then one guy after the other took a bath. One hollered, "Bring me the pants," another one, "Shine my shoes," or "Iron my shirt." My dad had to have his backpack, special clothes and shoes ready when his friends dropped by to pick him up to go mountain climbing.

I had to run all morning, and then after lunch, when they finally all went their merry way, we women, myself included, had to clean house. There were lots of floors that to be scrubbed and waxed and bed sheets to be changed. So often did I ask myself, why did God make women motherly, unselfish, caring creatures and men so demanding and bossy.

It was not just at home, it was hard in school, too. One time my godmother took me to cut my hair. But because we didn't have much money, they made the beautician cut it real short so that I wouldn't have to go back for months. It was so short, I looked like a boy. The next day when I went to school, I put a cap on and kept it on even in the classroom. Yet my classmates figured it out anyway. They laughed at me, pushed me and kicked me. It was months later when I didn't have any shoes to go to school with I had to wear my grandma's black ones, with

1.5-inch heels. Boy, was I the laughingstock of the class. The teacher did nothing to make it any better.

One sunny afternoon in spring the whole class went for a walk in the woods. All the girls picked little yellow flowers called buttercups. We put them under our chin, and if the skin turned yellow, that mean we liked butter. All the girls did it and the teacher helped them. But when it came to me, the teacher said, "I won't help you. You're no good and will never amount to anything anyway," and turned away.

I had to share my school bench with a boy. His name was Peter Ingold, and he was one of a few friends I had. He made me a key-holder out of wood. It was a big red mushroom with white dots and a dwarf sitting on each side of the stem. Below that were little hooks to hang keys on. It was really pretty. I cherished that gift and had it with me for over 30 years.

But most of those rich kids picked on me on the way to school. They ripped my hair, kicked me and called me names. It was that way through all my eight years of school. They could never do it to my brother, he had only one leg (the other one was out of wood), and my grandma walked him to school and picked him up again. She was there for him every day. She never missed a day till he was in fourth grade and old enough, she thought, to go by himself.

There was a widow who lived only a couple of blocks away from us. She came to visit us a lot. She would wait until it was dark outside, and then tell Grandma she was afraid to walk home by herself. So Grandma said to my dad, "Go walk Miggi home," just to get those two together. But no matter what, my dad loved my mom. He walked Miggi home, but did not get involved with her. So Miggi did the next best thing and started dating my dad's brother Henry. Those two got married in the fall of 1947. I really thought that was an answer to my prayers, but I was wrong.

Uncle Henry was a short, stocky man with a big humpback. Most people called him a cripple. But he was Grandma's youngest son, and since he was crippled, her favorite. He could do no wrong.

Yet I only turned six when he started taking me into his bedroom and sexually abusing me. I could not talk to anybody about this. I knew if I would tell my mother she might defend me. But Uncle Henry was the one who beat her once before, and I did not want her to go through that again. Plus he would end up in jail, and we were already one of the lowest-class families in our town.

Now when Uncle Henry got married and got out of our house, all my troubles would be over. But it did not stop. Their apartment was only two blocks away. He still ate lunch with us, since his wife, who was older than he, worked out of town. At least once or twice a week he would tell me, "Go get me cigarettes, or a bottle of beer, at the corner grocery and bring it to my house." My answer was always the same: "No, I do not have time." But Grandma interfered and said, "Kids have to do what adults tell them to do, there are no excuses." Even though I knew exactly what he would do to me, I had to go.

And it hurt. It hurt physically and emotionally. But there was nothing I could do about it, nor did I have anybody to talk to. Why, why do I hurt so bad, yet feel so guilty? Is it my fault? Do I make Uncle Henry feel the way he does towards me? Why can't I change him, make him see how much he hurts me?

He always said to me, "You can never tell anybody what we are doing. Plus, I know you like to do it, too, but if you talk to anybody, then I will punish you and your mother." No, I did not like it at all, but he played with my mind, and in the end I was not sure anymore if it was him or me that did wrong.

The town owned the apartment buildings we lived in, and they decided to remodel them. The apartments got smaller, and we had to look for another place to live, which was not easy for a big family like ours.

I no longer had a bedroom, so I had to live with my godmother again. After she was done working at the chocolate factory, she came and picked me up. We walked to her house, which was about three miles away, and then at 6 a.m. walked back to Grandma's house.

My "Gotti" was good to me. She did a lot for me. If I needed a new pair of white socks for Sunday school, she saw to it that I had them. She went on Saturday afternoon and bought white yarn, started knitting until I don't know how late at night. On Sunday morning when I woke up there was a brand-new pair of white socks to wear.

Or she stopped at the bakery and bought something special, just for the two of us. I could help her bake Christmas cookies. Yes, I loved her, but I also know that it hurt my mother, not being able to come and kiss me goodnight and pray with me. Why did I always have to be the one to hurt the ones I loved most?

But then my dad found a house with a big upstairs apartment, up on top of the hill, across the road from the Protestant church, and about a half-hour away from our old home, so I had to move back home. I was excited and happy to be close to my mother again, and on the other hand was hoping that would get me away from Uncle Henry. But wrong again. It did not even take six months and they moved, too, again only two blocks away from us. And even in those six months he found ways to abuse me.

Uncle Henry worked for the same construction company as my dad, only he could not lift much because he was crippled, so he was the "gofer." He was in charge of the lunch barracks, seeing that there was always beer and snacks for his co-workers. Often I had to take our wooden four-wheel cart and help him move the beer crates from one job site to another.

I knew why it was always me who had to help him,

but Grandma made me go. If I tried to lead the conversation in that direction and hoped she would maybe understand why I did not want to go, she always said, "You are too young to understand and talk about things like that."

But I knew he would do it to me again and again. He put me right on the job site, on the hard, fresh-poured cement floor, not thinking twice how he hurt me. I always got a candy bar or one franc for it.

Thinking back, I was just like a prostitute that he paid for rendering a service. What a terrible thing to do to a child, a child who had no one to talk to, a child who stood alone. What an easy prey for him. My hands were tied and I did not know what to do. I prayed and prayed that God, who is our Savior, would help me, or at least show me a way to get free and away from Uncle Henry.

My "Gotti" got sick in spring of 1949 and had to have her right kidney removed. It was touch and go for awhile, but she pulled through. That's why the doctors sent her to the southern part of Switzerland to recuperate. There the weather is warmer and the air drier.

She met a nice guy there and married him in fall of 1950. I was the only one of our whole family that could go to her wedding. She bought me a pretty dress, and I was so proud. A big bus picked us up at her house and brought us to the church in Rudolfingen, where Karl and his relatives waited for us.

The bus later drove us past some beautiful farms, the cows lying content on the grass. They enjoyed one of the last sunny days that fall, then the leaves turned color, a sure sign that winter was just around the corner. On we went to a nice restaurant on Lake Bodensee, where we had supper. It was a beautiful day, a day I will always remember.

It was in the summer of 1951 when my dad, my mother, my "Gotti" and her husband, Karl, my uncle Henry and his wife, Miggi, together with some friends of theirs, went to "Rimini" in Italy for vacation. Every year that group went mountain climbing, but this year they decided to go some place where the weaker ones, like my mother or Uncle Henry, could go, too. Grandma, Aunt Ida and we kids had to stay home.

I prayed long and hard every night, "God, please help me to get out of that misery and away from Uncle Henry. Please show me a way to get free."

I was almost 13 by now, but I knew I was slowly turning into a woman and could get pregnant, and then what? I did not know where to turn anymore, and Grandma still cut me off as soon as I started on that subject. She just would not let me talk.

It was Monday noon, and they had been gone one week, when the phone rang and I answered. The operator asked if I would accept a collect phone call from Rimini, Italy. I answered, "Yes, no problem."

My dad got on the line. He sounded really sad. I asked him if he wanted to talk to Grandma. But his answer was, "No, you tell her."

He then told me that Uncle Henry just got killed. My Uncle Henry talked a young girl, "Gritli," who would have gotten married four weeks later, into going with him and renting a motorbike. I probably was the only one who could figure out what was on his mind at that time, but I never said a word. Then Dad told me Henry and Gritli drove only one mile down the street when they collided with a semi-truck. Uncle Henry got killed instantly, and Gritli lived only for a couple more hours.

I did not want him dead, but I felt my prayers were answered. I did not have to talk to anybody about my abuse, yet did not have to go through that hurt anymore. I thanked God from the bottom of my heart, but yet felt so guilty. I felt like it was me who killed Uncle Henry through my prayers. Do I really have that much power, to do something like that? I surely was confused.

Both of the caskets were brought back to Switzerland on the train. Uncle Henry and Gritli got cremated the following Saturday, but laid to rest in different cemeteries. I had to go through everything, to the sermon at the crematorium where both coffins were side by side, and then to the final goodbye at the cemetery. I even had to wear the traditional black clothing, but I did not grieve. I felt so guilty, but yet relieved at the same time.

My grandma was a very Christian woman. Even so, she only went to church if a lonely person was buried, or some poor girl got married. She always said the rich ones have enough nosey people by their side so she did not have to go for them. She always told me, "You have to live religion, not show religion. Give to the ones who have less than you do, and never ask, 'What do I get in return?' " And she was an example. She helped any poor soul. The only thing she could not see, I thought, was my hurt.

My dad loved tulips and always ordered bulbs from Holland. Every year around Easter we had a beautiful bed of tulips in any color imaginable in our garden. My grandma cut one armful for me and one armful for her, and then we went to the cemetery and put flowers on every grave that nobody took care of all year. That made me feel so good, but it took me years before I could put flowers on Uncle Henry's grave. Yet, in order to go on with my life, I had to try to forgive him for everything he did to me, and I hoped that God might forgive him, too.

These were my last two years of classes, and I finally enjoyed going to school. The high school teacher came to my home and told my parents they should try to convince me to go on to high school, but I didn't want any part of it. Then that would have meant staying with those rich kids who always looked down on me, and I was tired of that. Instead, I went through seventh and eighth grade. That teacher, Mr. Henke, was my kind of guy. He loved the mountains and went skiing a lot. His face was always brown from the sun. His hair had already turned white. He looked rugged like a mountain that is there for anybody to lean on.

None of the girls in his classroom could wear jewelry, and they all had to wear aprons, just like me. Jnge Scholl shared the school bench with me. Her parents were rich, but walking into our classroom you could see no difference between the two of us.

Mr. Henke taught us how to carve things out of wood. He taught us how to spin yarn and weave our own scarf. We made an insect collection. I caught the most of those little creatures, and I was in charge of killing them with ether and then mounting them. I was quite proud of my work.

My brother could never go along if any of his classmates went on a trip, but Mr. Henke took him along. In my eyes there was no better person than he. He was married at that time and had three children between six and 18 years old. He was my idol. His motivation was, there is nothing on this earth that you can't do. You just have to make up your mind to do the best you can, and then stick with it. I certainly liked him a lot.

Many years later he got divorced and married Jnge, who sat by me in school, and together they had one child. She was 26 years younger than he. That is something I wouldn't have imagined in my wildest dream — Mr. Henke, a rugged nature guy, and Jnge, the nice girl who didn't even want to get her hands dirty. But I guess opposites attract each other.

My birthday was not something that was celebrated at my house. It was one week before Christmas, nobody had money and I was always told, "You get nothing for your birthday, but more for Christmas," which never happened anyway.

I saved myself a little bit of money one year for my birthday and bought two doughnuts at the bakery around the corner and ate them all by myself. But Grandma saw it and gave me a spanking with a leather belt. She told me I should have shared them with my brother and cousin.

My mother, on the other hand, with the little she had, always made something special. I love Swiss cheese, but because our family was so big, we had very little. So my mother gave me a pound of Swiss cheese for my birthday one year and I could eat it all by myself. Next year it was a pudding, and with hazelnuts she wrote a 14 on it for my 14th birthday. It was not much, but to me it was worth a million.

3

ANOTHER WINTER WENT by. I finished school and got my first job in late summer. I was not even 15 when I started my apprenticeship as a clerk in a shoe store in my hometown. That meant for two years I had to work four days a week and go to school the remaining two days.

At work I had to do everything the other two clerks didn't want to do: cleaning, stocking, etc. My boss was very, very strict, which was tough, but I was used to that. It was as if Grandma was behind me once again. But many years down the road I figured out that her being so strict helped me through my whole life.

I had worked for months already when my dad surprised me one night. It was a beautiful fall evening; the sun was just going down when I got off work, and there stood Dad and told me he wanted to walk home with me. We did not go straight home. We went through a small wooded area and sat down on a bench for awhile.

It was a beautiful quiet spot, away from the road, overlooking Lake Zurich. We could see the silhouettes of the mountains in the background. The moon slowly brought his shiny round face up over the horizon. Looking not at me, but at his beloved mountains, Dad started talking: "Tell me, what did my brother Henry do to you? Your mother thinks there was something wrong, but we weren't sure what it was he did." Then he paused.

I looked at him with unbelief. Could I, after all those years, really open up to him and tell him what happened back then? Would he really believe me, or just laugh at me? What if I tell him and he gets mad at me, then I would only get hurt again. Can I really open that door to my heart, or do my feelings get stepped on again?

It took me awhile before I could talk and tell him of all the hurt I had to go through. I had to stop a couple of times and swallow my tears. But finally, after all those years, I could talk to someone. And then to my dad, of all people, he who never ever had time for me or tried to understand my needs. Until now my dad was like a stranger to me who had never shown any interest in my life, but now I felt so close. All I could do was hug him and thank him for listening. He puts his arms around me and held me close. It felt so good to feel loved by my dad, a feeling I experienced for the first time in my life.

I could not finish my two years apprenticeship at that shoe store. The store was sold and I was no longer needed. There was a job opening for a clerk's position in Eglisau, a small, pretty, old-fashioned town. The grocery store was right on the Rhein River close to the German border. I took that job, but I didn't have it good. My bed was in the attic amongst all the items one usually finds in places like that. There was no heat, but that did not bother the mice, which ran right over my bedspread.

I had to work hard, had to have breakfast ready and the store open before my bosses got up, then take care of the store until they were ready to take over. After that, get their two kids up and the older one ready for school and then do the household chores.

The store manager was constantly fighting with his wife, but on the other hand wanted to go to bed with me. He always said, "I have to show them young girls how it is done, that it feels good. I did it to every employee before you, and you should be no exception."

When I got his little daughter ready for bed, he came and gave her a kiss and then also kissed me. But I gave him no chance to get any closer. That was one thing I did not want to do. Yet I could not just leave my job. I was always told that nobody wants to hire someone who won't stick a job out. And I could not tell a future employer that I was maladjusted. Nobody would believe that, coming from a 16-year-old girl.

So I left every Saturday night as soon as my work was done. I took a train and went to my Aunt Berta's house in Toggenburg. She was not really my aunt. Her mother and my grandmother were sisters. Berta was married and had four kids. Their son Walter was my age and became my best friend.

Berta and her husband, Ernest, were in charge of a ski lodge where the skiers could stay overnight, or just stop in for a hot bowl of soup, a hot cup of coffee or tea. I helped all Sunday wherever I was needed, washing the dishes, serving food or cleaning tables. I never got a penny for it, but it made me feel good and I know my help was appreciated.

Walter and some of his friends picked me up at the railroad station late Saturday night so that I did not have to make the two-hour walk up to the ski lodge alone. We had lots of fun together. Sometimes we stopped at a friend's house and had a drink, or even at a bar and danced for awhile. I never drank alcohol because my grandma told me from little on that my aunt "Ida" was drunk when she got pregnant with my cousin Walter. If a girl is drunk, she does not know what she is doing, and that is when it happens. I sure did not want to get pregnant, so I would not drink alcohol.

One Saturday night Walter got drunk. As we walked toward the ski lodge, all he said over and over again was, "Make sure you are quiet so my dad can't hear us, or he gets really angry."

Getting to the ski lodge, Walter opened the door very slowly and stepped into the porch, but stumbled and touched the first pair of skis. They all shifted and one pair after the other fell to the floor, making an awful racket. Uncle Ernst came downstairs and chewed us out royally.

He made us work extra hard the next day, and he had no mercy for Walter's headache.

But my boss did not like it that I was gone almost every weekend. So one Saturday, when his wife was out of town, he made me clean the basement just so that I would miss my train ride. But at nine o'clock that night, as soon as I was done, I left anyway. I was afraid to be with him alone over the weekend. I knew what he had on his mind. I changed clothes, ran all the way to the train station and just caught the last train that night. The train would not take me as far as I had to go, but that did not stop me from going.

It was 11:30 p.m. when we arrived at the train's final destination. I could have stayed in the train, slept on a bench and went on in the morning, but I decided to walk. It took six hours to hike over the snow-covered mountain pass, the moon following me all the way, making the snow sparkle like thousands and thousands of little stars. I saw snow rabbits hop by, and I scared some birds that slept on a twig that I touched. But it was so peaceful, and I felt like I was the only person on God's earth, the only one who really mattered.

The skiers just started to get up that Sunday morning when I arrived at the ski lodge, and nobody could believe that I made that long walk all by myself. I was tired but happy to be with them; they were so good to me, and Walter was my best friend.

I was sixteen and a half years old and got confirmed that spring. I had to buy my own dress for that big day in my life. I only made $35 a month, besides room and board, but I had to support myself. My parents did not have much, and my brother's wooden leg cost them a lot of money. Now that I was confirmed, I could be a big girl and smoke, just like some of my friends did. I bought a pack of "Aiida" cigarettes before I visited my parents; then I wanted to show off.

Just as my father walked into the living room, I lit a cigarette. He took one look at me and said, "You will never be a good mother. A good mother does not smoke," and he went on his way, never taking another look at me. But it hit me, how dare he say that. I surely would like to be a good mother some day. I put my cigarette out, threw the open pack into the garbage and never, in my entire life, lit another cigarette.

I quit my job in Eglisau right after I got confirmed and went to work at a store in Uster. I stayed with my cousin Paula. Paula and her husband, Bruno, were a poor, struggling family just starting out in life. They had one child and they belonged to a religious group called "New Apostolics." Everybody in that religion called each other brothers and sisters. I went to church with them for a couple of times but never became a member of that cult.

Even though it was against their religion, Bruno liked to drink and go with other women. Paula took me along many times to check up on Bruno. We stood behind a tree or a corner of a house and waited until the tavern closed to see who Bruno would take home this time.

It was not easy for me, as I didn't want to take sides. So I quit that job after a year and moved on. I was afraid I would get too much involved in their lives and eventually would get in trouble. Then I would be the one who stood between those two, and I did not want to do that. I felt they would have to work it out themselves. I could not help them.

My next job was in Weisslingen. I worked as a clerk and also lived with my bosses, a family with two daughters. It was a very nice family, and I could be alone with Mr. Steiner for weeks when his wife was on vacation. Not once would I have to worry, not even a dirty remark. They respected me for the person I was and the job I did.

I did not feel good all summer. I had terrible cramps time and time again. Steiners, who were like a family to me, took me to see a specialist, and he said I had chronic appendix attacks and that it was high time to have surgery.

I went home for Christmas of 1956, and then the 2nd of January 1957, to the hospital and had the surgery. Everything went pretty well. The only problem I had, I could not go to the bathroom afterward. The doctor told the nurse to give me a shot of some kind of medicine that makes the bladder work. The nurse put the needle in the muscle in my upper leg, and within seconds I felt a terrible heat take over my body. All I said was, "That shot didn't go to my bladder," and then I was gone.

Hours later when I woke up, there were doctors and nurses all around my bed. The medicine went into a blood vessel and straight to my heart. They thought they had lost me, but I guess my time was not up yet. My guardian angel was watching over me and kept me safe. What would I do without my God's guidance?

I was released ten days later, but the doctor told me to go for two to three weeks up to the mountains to recuperate; my body went through too much stress and I had to get my strength back. So I went to my Aunt Berta and Uncle Ernst's house. I knew they would take me in. They were poor, but their door was always open and they made me feel as one of their own.

It was on a Saturday beginning of February when I had to leave them. I would have loved to stay, they were so good to me, but I had to go back to work. I had no choice. I took the early afternoon train. I had to change trains in Wattwil and wait for almost one hour at that train station for my train that brought me back to Winterthur. So I rested on one of the benches.

The train that brought passengers from Zurich moved slowly into the station. On one of the cars was a window open. Two guys were leaning on it and looked at me. Something hit me and I felt so close to one of them. I felt like I had known him forever.

After the train came to a squeaking halt, the two got out and went to the restaurant to get themselves something to drink. I was very disappointed they did not even say "Hi" to me. But I would not move and stayed right where I was.

It seemed to take forever until they came back. Again I would not say one word. The older one of the two went back to board the train; the younger one came over and started talking to me. I felt like I had a big lump in my throat.

He asked me if I was on vacation. I said, "Yes." Then, are you a secretary? I said, "No." Fifteen minutes later when I boarded my train he knew everything about me, and all I said was yes or no. I stored my luggage away and made myself as comfortable as possible. And all I could think was, how stupid can you get, giving a guy all that information without even knowing his name. Oh, how could I do that!

I was back to work the next day and soon forgot all about that incident at the train station. It was busy at work and had no time to think about personal things, and when I finally could go to bed I was dead tired, still being kind of weak from the surgery.

It was the end of April when I noticed a letter on the desk in the office with my name on it, but with a return address I had never seen before. I opened the letter, and to my surprise there was a picture of the guy I talked to at the train station. His name was Henry Gross. He was a good-looking guy.

I put the picture aside and slowly started reading. He wrote that he had just come back from a weekend in the mountains. He made a skiing trip with some of his friends. He went on to say it would have been a lot nicer if he could have been with me, lying in the sun and him making love to me. I got really mad. Was that all he thought of me?

After a long, sleepless night, I sat down and wrote Henry a letter. I told him that I was very disappointed, and if that was all he wanted from me, then I never wanted to hear from him again.

Just a few days later I got a response back. He apologized and said it was not meant that way, but if I wouldn't see him, then he wanted his picture back. But by then I had second thoughts already and was sorry about my first reaction. I turned right around and wrote, "If you want the picture back, you have to come and get it yourself." And so he did. He called me one evening and said, "I will drive through the town you live in next Saturday and will pick my picture up."

I worked double-time that day. I did not even take a lunch break. I wanted to have everything done before Henry came. I cleaned the store, scrubbed the stairway, stocked all the shelves, and in-between took care of the customers. I was just bubbling over, and the Steiners thought that was really funny. But then when I saw Henry drive in, I got scared and my heart was pounding. I was 18 years old and never had a date yet. It took all my courage to go out of the store and greet him.

He was just a little taller than me, had a rugged, suntanned face and wavy dark brown hair. All in all, he was a good-looking hunk. I could feel my heart jumping two beats at a time, but I was too shy to look at him, so I said very quietly, "Hi, Mister Gross. Here is your picture."

But to my surprise, his response was different than I expected. He said, "I'm Henry, and I would like to invite you to come and have supper with me."

I was scared. He had a car, and I never drove with a man alone in a car, so what if I go with him and he drives somewhere into the woods and leaves me sitting there. What would I do then? But something deep inside of me said, "Go for it! Go!" I overcame my fear and went with Henry.

We drove to Wil, a nice old-fashioned town. He picked a nice restaurant in the old part of town, and I was just in Seventh Heaven. There had been only three or four times in my entire life that I had eaten in a restaurant, and then with a good-looking guy like Henry, and good-looking he was.

We had wienerschnitzel and a glass of wine. And to top it all off, we took a stroll through the old part of town and went window shopping. That was the first time in my life that I was guided by a man's arm. It was like walking on Cloud Nine.

I didn't have to work that Sunday, that's why Henry decided to bring me to his mother's house. And I didn't mind. I was in love, head-over-heels, and I felt that nothing bad could happen to me at her home.

We sat up long that night and talked. It was well past midnight when his mother's head came through the small opening by the door. "Henry, don't you think that girl needs some sleep?" she said. And then, just as silently as she came in, disappeared.

I did not get much sleep even after he left me alone and went to his bedroom. Then my thoughts were running in circles. Could this really be true love? Is that why it feels so good? He is so much more mature than I am. Could he really love me, or does he just play for a while and then dump me? All those questions, and no answers.

Henry had to help move some cattle early Sunday morning so he was not around when I got up. I was scared to face his mother and siblings for the first time all by myself. I took a deep breath and got my courage up. My heart was pounding, but I made it downstairs and had breakfast with them.

His mother was an older lady, had brown hair with just a little silver in it, pulled together in a little bun. She had trouble walking because she had arthritis pretty bad.

Rosemarie, Henry's youngest sister, had a round,

friendly face with red cheeks. She was really nice to me and made me feel welcome.

Henry brought me back to Weisslingen later that afternoon. From that day on, he visited me every weekend and wrote me at least two beautiful letters every week. The minute I got a letter I would find a way to sneak to the back room and read it quick, and then stuff it into my bra. That way I had it always close to my heart. Yes, I surely was in love and on Cloud Nine.

Henry was ten years older than me. He had a very bad childhood. He grew up on a small farm up in the mountains in the Toggenburg Valley. He was only seven years old when his dad died. His mother at that time was pregnant with her fifth child. With the Depression still lingering on, there just was not enough money to go around. Henry was sent to his grandfather, who also farmed. He had to work hard there, make up for room and board. His grandpa taught him how to milk by hand. "You cannot use your forefinger, only the rest of the hand; otherwise, you make them cows hard milkers," his grandpa said.

But Henry was only seven years old and just could not do it without his forefingers. Grandpa took his pocket knife out of his pocket, opened it up, and made four cuts on the end of each of Henry's forefingers and said, "That will teach you not to use them." Henry got no Band-Aid and was sore for days, but still had to milk those cows every day.

He had to get up early in the morning, help in the barn, then go to school and back to do chores again. He didn't have it good at all.

From Grandpa's he came to his Uncle Albert, and there it was worse. His bedroom there was so cold, and the pants were wet from the snow that came all the way up to his hips. He took the pants off before he went to bed at night. In the morning they stood by themselves, they were so icy and frozen. His bedroom was up in the attic and had no heat. It was so bad that the neighbors complained and said to Henry's mother if she didn't bring him somewhere else they would report her to the police.

Henry's dad's older brother, Jakob, helped Henry's mother with the chores on their farm after she became a widow and ended up marrying her. They had one child, Rosemarie, together. But it was not a marriage of love, only one of convenience. Henry's mother told me herself she never loved Jakob, but needed him on the farm.

Henry never took the time to celebrate a birthday, and not even Christmas was important. He could not experience what love really meant. He got out of school at 14 years old and kept on working for farmers, but his wages were sent home to support the home farm and his siblings.

Henry loved to be up in the mountains with the cows during the summer months. He was alone with over 30 cows, milked them and made butter and cheese, and with the leftover milky water fed some pigs. Once a week he carried the butter on his back to town in the valley, then on the way back stopped at the local restaurant to have a glass of wine and sing with his friends.

For two summers he lived in a little shack and took care of over 500 sheep. Every day he had to check the sheep, especially before a thunderstorm. For hours he walked barefoot up to the mountaintop to see if those creatures were okay. He loved to yodel and then listen to the echo. That was Henry's happiest time.

At the age of 19 he left the Toggenburg Valley and started working for a company that builds dams to make artificial lakes. He worked hard, but partied and drank on his days off and did everything to forget his childhood.

I felt so sorry for him and promised myself to give him all the love I'm capable of and to be always there for him, and make him see that he too could enjoy love and happiness. My love for him was so strong and it felt so good, it took over my whole body. I could not even see clearly anymore. It felt like I was wearing rose-colored glasses.

I worked very hard all week so that we could spend every weekend together. Then he was just so great to me, and I loved him so much. I told him right from the beginning that I was abused as a child, but it did not seem to bother him. At least he did not hold it against me, so I thought.

It was the end of July 1957 when my boss and his family went on vacation. Henry brought me home that Sunday night. He stayed with me and made love to me. I was, because of my past experience, very scared. Plus, all I could think was what if I got pregnant. So for me it was a scary experience, but it made him feel good. He kept me in his arms all night.

He left on Monday morning, and I stayed in Weisslingen and took care of the store. I did not feel good one Tuesday morning when I got up, and even worse on Wednesday. Everybody asked me, what is wrong with you, you look so terrible. But I could not answer that question. Then I didn't know myself what it was that made me so sick.

That Saturday when Henry came to see me, he disappointed me for the first time. He took one look at me and asked, "With how many guys did you go to bed last night?"

How could he think that of me? I was deeply hurt, but was taught from little on not to show it if I was hurting. My feelings don't count.

I was nice all weekend, but only made small talk. I could not understand how he could think I would do a thing like that. I loved him with all my heart.

But my worst fear came through. I was pregnant. Two weeks later Henry came to see me again. I told him reluctantly that I was expecting his baby. But to my surprise, he was happy and said right away, "Great, that gives us a reason to get married. Let's go for it." We took the whole weekend to plan our future, and we set our wedding day for October 26, 1957.

The next weeks were hectic. We had to look for an apartment and get everything ready for our wedding. I dried and pressed flowers to make my own wedding invitations.

My parents were on vacation up in the mountains at the time. We went to see them one weekend, and Henry asked my dad if he could marry me, and he told them that I was pregnant. My parents seemed excited and gave their okay. But I did not tell them that Henry mistrusted and hurt me. Then I forgave him already and blamed his mistrust on his bad childhood.

I did not know where the time went, but here it was the day before my wedding. Henry drove me to Zurich to my mother's beautician. She made my hair so pretty, and she also put makeup on my face. She said that that was her wedding gift to me. My cheeks were rosy, my eyes had a little shadow and my lips had a glossy red shine. I myself did not own any makeup, so that was something very special for me. I thought I looked like a princess. I was just so proud and could hardly wait till Henry came to pick me up.

There was a little coffee shop downstairs from the beautician; that's where I waited for Henry. He took one look at me when he came to pick me up and told me to go to the bathroom and wash my face. "I will not take you home with that stuff all over your face, and I will never allow you to wear makeup or lipstick," he told me.

Looking at his eyes, I could see that he really meant what he said and he would get mad if I would not follow his orders. I also could hear my grandma say a woman always does what a man wants her to do. So off to the bathroom I went without one word of complaint. But the tears were rolling down my cheeks and ruined my mascara. I looked in the mirror as I was washing my face, and

I will never forget how pretty I thought I looked. But I never ever in my life wore makeup again.

October 26, 1957 was a beautiful day. Foggy in the morning, but after that sunny all day. When I walked into the church, all my worries were gone. All I wanted was to give Henry all my love. I prayed as I walked down the aisle so proud on Henry's arm that God would please give me the strength so that I could make Henry happy.

It was a small wedding. Only 12 relatives and some neighbors were present, but that did not matter. All that mattered was that we were together.

I never forgot the minister's words. He said that, "Even though we are no longer dating and now became one, we should not get sloppy and think it does not matter anymore how we dress or how we look."

He went on: "It is more important now than ever before to please each other. Then life is long and tough, and you two are the only ones who can make a difference in your lives. And love is the biggest gift anybody can give to another human being."

I had tears in my eyes and my heart felt full of love as I gave Henry my first official kiss.

After the sermon was picture-taking time, and then all of us boarded the small bus that was waiting to drive us through the countryside. It was a beautiful fall day. We stopped at the airport in Zurich for a coffee break and watched the planes for awhile. Then we went on to Bulach where a delicious meal waited for us. We had soup, cordon bleu, French fries and vegetables, and topped all that off with a good glass of wine. Then, after dessert and coffee, on to Sirnach, our final destination.

This is me, in the summer of 1957. I spent a couple of days with my parents.

My Dad and I. We are enjoying a hike in the mountains.

My wedding. Left to right: my brother, me, Henry, my mom, Dad and Grandma.

4

SIRNACH IS WHERE we rented our first apartment. The landlord had a restaurant downstairs, and there we had a couple of drinks and some snacks before everybody was ready to go home.

We only had to go upstairs. Henry told me all along that he would carry me over the threshold on our wedding night. But now, as he unlocked the door, he forgot all about being romantic. He just looked at me, took a deep breath and said, "One dollar is from now on only worth 50 cents, and you better make that last."

Henry was 29 years old, and it was hard for him to share his life and his money, even though he did not have much, with someone else. But I made a promise to myself to do the best I could to make Henry believe in me.

We lived in a new apartment, in a new town where we did not know anybody. We didn't have much money. We could not even afford a radio. But to this day I say that that was the best time in my life. We had to talk together. We had no radio or TV to interrupt us.

On a Saturday afternoon when Henry came home from work we had lunch, then he took a nap and I would sit by him on the sofa and knit baby clothes. At night in bed he would hold me close and we talked, sometimes until the early morning hours. I always folded my hands over his and prayed for us before we went to sleep. I knew, deep within my heart, with God on our side there was nothing that could go wrong. I was so happy and in love. We had nothing, but we had each other and I felt that is all I ever needed.

Our first Christmas was very simple. We went and

cut a little pine tree in one of our friend's woods. I bought a few candles and some candleholders and decorated the tree. I knitted socks for Henry, my dad and my brother, and sewed a skirt for my mother. My parents and my brother came to see us on Christmas Eve and stayed with us for a day. For the first time it really felt like we were a family. At home there were always aunts and uncles around, and nobody could really show their feelings.

We only had a half a gallon of milk and two pounds of bread and no money when my parents left towards the evening of December 26th. We walked them to the railroad station, and my dad bought us two tickets to make it possible for us to visit them on New Year's Eve.

We walked back home and went to bed and only got up to drink some milk or eat some bread. We stayed in bed for five days till the 31st of December. We had no money, could not afford to buy any groceries, and as long as we stayed in bed we did not get that hungry. We were so quiet that the other renters in the apartment building thought we were on vacation.

Then on New Year's Eve we took the train and went home. No matter how bad my childhood was, all of us were always together on New Year's Eve. We had ham, beans and potatoes, and the kids a whole bratwurst for our late supper. And then at midnight after we wished each other a happy New Year my dad washed the dishes. That was the only time of the year that he washed the dishes, and this year was no exception.

I did not want to work in a store anymore because I was pregnant, but there was a job opening in the nearby factory, and I took it. I had no choice. I had to work. We did not have much money, and there was a baby on the way.

The first day at work was miserable. My boss showed me a cabinet where I could hang my coat. My co-workers were not friendly at all, and when I went for my lunch break I found to my surprise that my coat was thrown on the floor. I was assigned a different cabinet, but the same thing happened again. I could not understand why. Nobody knew me personally.

I found out later that they knew I was a Lutheran, and we just moved to an all-Catholic town. That's why they would not accept me. I cried a lot those first months, but I had to stick it out; we needed the money. And eventually they too could see that somebody with another religion could be a good person, too. I worked at that place until the middle of April 1958. Then I expected my first baby the end of April that year.

Henry's favorite sister, Elsa, got married the first weekend in March 1958. Her husband-to-be immigrated to the USA in 1956 and now came home to marry Elsa and take her back to the United States. They had a big wedding, American-style.

Henry was invited, but they did not want me there. I was told that they did not need such a fat pregnant woman at their wedding. (I was eight months pregnant.) Henry was upset and said, "If my wife can't come, I won't either." So we stayed home, and I was proud of him. He defended me and stood by my side. That was really nice of him.

Three weeks after their wedding, Elsa and her husband, Ernst, came to say goodbye. Ernst told Henry that he had a hard time selling his VW car, so Henry asked, "What do you want for it? Our Citroen is old. We might be better off to buy yours."

But Ernst's answer was, "Why should I tell you how much I want for it? You can't afford it anyway."

We still owned the car Henry had before we got married but could not afford to pay for the insurance and license plates during the winter months, plus we did not really need the car. But as of April 1, 1958, we had to pay the fees, since we had to have a car to get me to the hospital. I went to the same doctor who did my appendix surgery the year before. He tested my blood, and we found out that I, too, was R-factor negative, just like my godmother. That got me really scared then; all three of her babies died shortly after she gave birth to them, and I was told this could happen to me.

Henry had to serve in the army for three weeks at the end of March-beginning of April of 1958. Any able man in Switzerland has to go through a 17-week training at the age of 19, and then first serve three weeks every year, later, three weeks every other year. He has to stay in the military service until at least the age of 40.

I was scared to be alone, being nine months pregnant, but there was nothing we could do about it. He had to go. The landlord, who had his bedrooms just above us, also had to do military duty those three weeks, and his wife was pregnant, too, but she was only in her eighth month.

It was on a Saturday, middle of April, when they both could come home again. Early that morning, Grandma Graf (the landlord's mother) came, knocked on my door and asked me to come quick and help her. Mrs. Graf had only one sharp pain when the water broke, and then she could feel the head of her baby coming.

Grandma called the midwife and also needed me to help. The Grafs had their bedrooms upstairs, but the bathroom, kitchen and living room were downstairs where their restaurant was. So I had to carry warm water from the kitchen four stairs up to the bedroom, which was pretty hard in my condition.

Grandma Graf also had customers in the restaurant downstairs, which she couldn't just kick out. I was the midwife's right hand, and the two of us helped the first little baby to get out.

I never saw a child being born before. It was a little boy. He was full of blood and slimy stuff, but his lungs were very good. He screamed as if he were mad at us for helping him come into this world.

Mrs. Graf expected twins, and since she had no labor pains, the midwife made her get out of bed and walk up and down the room, while I gave the little guy a bath and dressed him. I then put him in his crib just in time to help with the second child, another boy.

They both were premature and very tiny. The midwife did not think that they would have a chance if they were kept at home, so she called the ambulance. Just as Henry and Mr. Graf returned from the military, the ambulance drove in to pick the two babies up.

I was exhausted from all that work, yet scared. I was due any day now. But I was also happy and felt good that I had a chance to help to bring them two little boys on this earth. What a great experience! The boys had to stay in the hospital for four weeks, but then were strong enough to come home.

April 24, 1958 was a beautiful spring day. Henry came home from work, we had supper together, and then went for a walk. I felt soon that something was different. I had to rest every few hundred feet. So we went back home, sat around for awhile, and then went to bed. But I could not sleep, my stomach hurt. I woke Henry up at midnight and told him we better go to the hospital, I thought my labor pain had started. We had no phone. Henry had to drive to a phone booth in town to call my doctor. Then he came back to pick me up.

They were ready and waiting for me when we arrived at the hospital a little over one hour later. It felt like everything would go okay, and the nurse said it should not take long then; the baby was already in the birth canal.

Yet one, two, three hours passed, and the doctor and the nurses got worried. The heartbeat got weaker and weaker, but it was too late for a Caesarean. The doctor took some long clamps — they looked like big tongs — and tried to reach the baby's head and pull on it. After trying for awhile, he gave up and explained that he would rip the baby to pieces if he forced it through the canal that way.

The nurse then climbed on top of me and forced the baby through the birth canal. She worked with her knees on my stomach and just pressed the baby out. It was terribly painful, but I would have gone through anything to save the baby.

It was a little girl, but she looked terrible. Her head was long and all out of shape, and she did not breathe at all. They spanked her on her little behind, but nothing. Then they put her in cold, warm, and then cold water again. She made a couple of sounds, but did not want to live. So they took a big oxygen mask, covered her little face completely, put it on her and wheeled her crib out of the room. I could not see her, could not even hold her.

Henry stayed with me through that whole ordeal and supported me. He was great. I do not know what I would have done without him by my side and his calloused hands to hold on to.

But my heart was just aching, and my arms felt so empty. I wanted to hold my little girl so badly. The tears rolling down my cheeks were not tears of joy, they were tears of sorrow. I was so scared I could lose her, and all I could do was pray for the little life I just gave birth to. "Please, God, don't take her away from me." I was exhausted and my face was swollen from pressing so hard.

They wheeled me into my room, which I shared with another woman. It was Friday noon by now and the dinner was served.

On a fancy tray was a silver plate with a cover on it, a cup of coffee and some juice. I did not feel like eating, but was rather curious to see what was under that cover. It was a whole trout, head and everything. It was put together quite fancy, but when I looked at the eyes, that was it; I was not hungry anymore. For some people that might be a delicacy, but not for me and certainly not today.

I could hardly sleep the next night, I was so scared. At 4 a.m. the nurse stormed into my room and had to know how she could reach my husband, since we had no telephone. They said they would bring my little girl, whom we named Edith, to the Children's Hospital to exchange her blood.

It only took a couple of hours, and Henry was by my side, but they changed their mind by then. A specialist examined my little girl and said that she was too weak to have a blood exchange. She probably would die right on the operating table. He felt they should leave well enough alone. My little girl would not live for more than a couple of weeks anyway, so it was not worth it to take that kind of risk.

They never took Edith out of her little bed to feed or bathe her, nor to change diapers. I had to be milked with a little machine; mother's milk was vital for her, yet she was too weak to suck it herself.

The milk I had was enough to feed two babies. My roommate had a little boy, "Beat," but could not nurse him. He was big and strong, and he was fed with my milk, too. She could see her little son every couple of hours, and I could not even hold my baby. She got a house with everything in it as a wedding present, and had company all day long, and her side of the room was full of flowers. We were poor. Henry could only come to see me evenings after work, and there were no flowers.

But all I wanted was my little girl, and that I could not have. I shed a lot of tears the ten days that I had to stay in the hospital, and I prayed a lot. "Please, God, give my little girl a chance. I will do anything you want from me; just don't take her away from me."

I could go to the nursery and peek through the window; the nurses did not allow me to go in, but at least I could see her. Her head was so out of shape, but she had such a pretty little nose. Her whole body was yellow then;

she had a really bad case of jaundice. But in my eyes she was the prettiest baby ever born. Little Edith was the gift I got from God, for all the love I felt for Henry.

It was time to go home. Henry came to pick us up, but he was told he could take me home, but not our baby. "Edith Junior will not make it past the first month, and that would be too hard on your wife," they said to him. Henry told the doctors straight out, "It is either both or nothing; if you keep the baby, you can keep my wife, too."

After they saw he would not give one inch, they reluctantly gave us that little bundle. Edith had from birth a big swelling on her head. It looked like a big ball and had fluid in it. I was told to be very careful not to lay her on that side; then that fluid could go inside, press her brain and kill her instantly.

I was so happy that I could hold little Edith in my arms, finally have her home and be able to take care of her. And even though her head was deformed, she was such a pretty and good little girl. I kept on pumping milk and went every night to the train station to send my excess milk to the Children's Hospital to help another little human being that maybe had no chance to live without my milk.

Weeks passed and Edith cried more and more often. She could not tell me what was wrong, but I felt it was because she had to lay on her right side all the time. Then one day I gave her the bottle at noon, changed her diaper and said to her, "You have to die anyway, why don't I make it easier for you, at least as long as you're here with me."

I shook her little pillow, then gave her a kiss and told her I loved her, and then led her to sleep, but this time on her left side. Over and over again I sneaked into her room to check up on her, because I was scared. The doctors said laying her on her left side could be deadly.

As soon as she woke up, I took her out of her crib. To my surprise, all the fluid was gone. It looked like a little crater, because there was so much skin on top of her head, and the skull looked uneven, but she seemed fine. The doctor could not understand what happened. The fluid went inside her skull, but her body somehow absorbed it. Edith started gaining weight and looking better, not as weak anymore.

She was ten weeks old when I got sick. All that pumping milk was too much for me. I got mastitis, an infection in my breast. I thought only animals could get that, but I guess we are no different.

Henry came home every lunch break, massaged and milked my breasts. He treated me just as he would a cow. It was very, very painful, but it helped, and together with penicillin did the trick.

My parents rented a small apartment up in the mountains where they spent their two weeks vacation in July of that year. They asked us if we would like to come for a week to join them. The clean, fresh air might help Edith get more strength.

Henry asked his boss if he could have off. His boss had nothing against it, so we packed our car, and off we went. But Henry was miserable all week. He never before was on vacation and said that only lazy people would do that. I could never get him to go for a walk with me during the day. He felt everybody could see that he was lazy, and that was just terrible. He would not get out of the house until after dark, when nobody could recognize him. Yes, he loved his mountains and went mountain climbing a lot with my dad, but only on weekends.

We did not like to live above the tavern. It was very noisy. We could hear the guests talk and laugh well past midnight. Henry looked around and found a nice, sunny upstairs apartment in a two-story house in Munchwilen, one of our neighboring towns. So at the beginning of April we moved.

Downstairs lived a family that came from Italy. A very

nice couple, they had one three-year-old son. Mrs. Mazaraty worked at a factory in town, but also was a great seamstress. She sewed until late every night and had customers from far away. A woman could bring her a clipping out of a catalog and she would make a dress just like it. Boy, she was good; she also taught me a trick or two, and we became best friends.

Edith started smiling, then sitting up, and she walked before she was a year old. I was glad she was such a good girl; then I was pregnant again.

We celebrated Edith's first birthday on a Saturday. She was a pretty little girl with a head full of blond curls and always a smile on her face. Two days later, on Monday, I gave birth to our son Heinz. It was a lot easier this time. I had no problems whatsoever. In fact, the doctor who took care of me at the hospital went to school with Henry, so they talked about their childhood and forgot all about me, until only a couple of minutes before the baby was born, a healthy, sweet baby boy we named Heinz.

It was pouring rain the day I could go home from the hospital. The nurse carried the little bundle down to the car. She gave me a hug and said, "I do not say goodbye, only I see you again." Then, "If it pours like this when you go home, that means I will see you again in a year." My response was, "No way!" But I found out later she was right.

Henry joined the yodeling club in town. He was a very good singer and enjoyed it a lot. They had a party while I was in the hospital giving birth to Heinz. I was later told by some of his friends that he took Heidi, the daughter of one of his colleagues, home and spent the night with her. From that time on, Heidi was a regular guest at our house. But her visits stopped when she got engaged a year later.

When I questioned Henry, he said, "No, I didn't do anything," and that was enough for me. I loved him with all my heart and believed in him. But even though the little ones and I loved him, I know he still could not forget his childhood. He always thought he had to prove himself to his family, and I felt so sorry for him.

Many times on a nice sunny Sunday we drove up to the Toggenburg Valley where Henry was born. We drove to a small wooded area. There was a bench where we would rest. Edith crawled in the grass and tried to catch some grasshoppers. Heinz lay on a blanket and listened to the chirping of the nearby birds. But Henry could not see the beauty of nature nor hear anything. His eyes wandered across the valley to the small farm that now belonged to his brother. We could not go there. His brother Walter told Henry: "You're good for nothing, and Edith is just a prostitute from the big city." In Walter's eyes all the girls who did not grow up on a farm were no good and had to be prostitutes.

Walter got married, beginning of April 1959, but I was nine months pregnant with Heinz, and because of that not invited to his wedding neither. Walter did not want Henry near his place; he was afraid Henry could get something from their mother.

Walter got the home farm as a wedding present. He only had to take over the small mortgage that still was on the farm. When we got married, Henry's mother said, "I will give you sheets for your bed someday," but we never ever got them.

Henry would have loved to farm, but it was impossible for us. We had no money, and land is so very expensive in Switzerland. And to know all of that made Henry feel like a loser. But I knew better. Henry was a hard worker and a good human being.

One week before I gave birth to Heinz, Henry's sisters, Martha and Beth, came to visit us. They were on the way home from Walter's wedding. Henry came home on his lunch break, and we had just started eating when they walked in. We had nothing special, but I asked them if they would like to join us. Their reply was, "No, thank you, we just ate at a restaurant in town. We thought you can't afford to feed us anyway." All of that just nagged on Henry, and he was so unhappy, and the hardest part was, I did not know how to help him.

I was busy with my two little ones, and even though I would knit and sew everything they needed, money just did not go far enough. Henry told me over and over again if I would not sit on my lazy butt, we could make a better living and it would be easier for us financially.

I started sewing baby clothes at home for a company at a neighboring town, and later sewed lamp shades, just to make some extra money.

It did not take long and I was pregnant again. Oh, was it stressful! I did not want another baby so quickly, but what could I do? It was hard when I had to see the doctors for me or the kids. At that time someone did not need to make an appointment; you just went to the doctor's office. It was on a come-first, serve-first basis, but only in the morning. The doctor needed the afternoon for house calls. It usually was 10:00-10:30 before I got out of the doctor's office, and it took at least 45 minutes to walk home, pushing the baby buggy with my two little ones in it. We had a car, but I could not drive.

I had to hurry, a lot of times run home to put a hot meal on the table by 12 noon. Henry always came home during lunch hour, and he expected a hot meal, no matter what. I thought I was a good housewife, but it just was not good enough in his eyes. Yet I knew it was not really me, it was his past that bothered him.

Henry did not like the job he had, and that didn't help matters. He worked in a factory where he had to make sprockets for machines. His workbench was right by the window, and it drove him crazy on a nice sunny day. He wanted to be outside working.

So he switched jobs and started working at a gravel

factory. It was a brand-new company, and he was in charge of the department where they wash, separate and crush the gravel. He helped installing that building.

One day when he tried to hook something up, he got hit by 1500 volts. The shock was so strong it threw him right out of the building. The boss picked him up, brought him home and told him to rest so that his heart could recuperate. Henry lay down for a couple of hours, but then went right back to work. He always said, "Being sick is all in your head. If you don't think about it, you can't feel it."

Edith turned two on April 25, 1960. Heinz one year old on April 27, and on May 6th I gave birth to our daughter Lotti. It was on a Friday morning, just before Mother's Day. According to the doctor, Lotti should have been born the end of March, but he told me I was pregnant when I wasn't.

Henry did not want another baby so soon. Money was tight enough the way it was. And I didn't want to go to the hospital, so the nurse there did not have to see that she was right, telling me I would be back in a year. So I got everything ready on my living room table, everything from the bathtub to the diapers and clothing, all covered up with a plastic. But week after week went by and nothing.

The 4th of May the midwife came and gave me some pills to induce labor. She also put a hot water bottle on my back and said that might help to make the water break. But then when she called the doctor and told him that everything was ready, for him to come and continue inducing labor, his answer was, "I think it is too early yet. We will wait a couple more days."

I was crushed and cried when Henry came home for lunch. I just did not know what to do anymore. After talking it over with Henry, I decided to call a specialist. The doctor told me to come the next day and have X-rays taken. He then could figure out exactly how many days, if any, I was overdue.

I traveled to Wil with the railroad early the next morning, but was so disgusted that I walked home. It took me more than two hours, but it made me feel better. I stood for a while and watched the cows grazing in the meadow, listened to the birds twittering; I even saw a red fox with two babies disappear in the nearby woods. Looking at all those beautiful creatures, I felt like my troubles were small and I had no reason to be discouraged.

That night I went into labor, but before Henry called the midwife he started the stove to warm up the apartment, and that brought out the flies.

There are no fly screens in front of the windows in Switzerland. Henry took the flyswatter and ran around the room and over the bed. "I don't want a fly to sit on the little nose of my new baby," he said. It looked funny, but I did not feel like laughing anymore.

The midwife came to my home and together with Henry delivered my baby girl. Everything went well. It just took a little less than four hours and Lotti was born. My other two kids had a long, slender face; Lotti's was round and she had dark hair. She was a Gross if there ever was one. But she certainly was cute.

It was really nice to have the baby at home in my own surroundings, instead of that impersonal, cold hospital room. After I was taken care of and the midwife gave the baby a bath and put her in my arms, she and Henry and went to town to have breakfast. Then Henry also had to go to the courthouse to register our child and to see if we really could name our new little girl "Lotti." If that would not have been legal, he would have changed it to Nelli. I liked neither one of the names, but we made a deal from the beginning that he could pick the girls' names and I would choose the boys' names. So Lotti it was.

One of my neighbor ladies came and helped me with my housework, washed the diapers and gave me moral support. It was tough to have three little ones so close together.

We did not get home to my parents that often, only once or twice a year, but I know that my grandma had cancer and there wasn't anything anybody could do for her. We went to see her in the hospital once, but then her oldest daughter, Anna, decided to take her home.

Anna knew it was only a matter of months until Grandma would die. Grandma lived all those years with my dad; now that it was close to the end Anna wanted her, just to make sure she could get whatever was left, even though Grandma never had much. Grandma always said, "Nobody will ever have to fight over my belongings," and then that was exactly what they did. I did not know how bad it was, as Anna had no contact with my dad, even though they lived in the same town.

It was around 2 a.m. on February 16, 1961. We were sound asleep when all of a sudden I could see someone open the curtain that divided our bedroom and the living room. My grandma walked into our bedroom. She was dressed just as she always was, a black dress with little white flowers and an apron over it, her silver hair combed back and braided in a little bun. She was holding her hand out to me.

I sat up in my bed and was scared to death. But she said very calmly, "Don't be afraid. I only want to say goodbye and good luck."

I shook Henry. I was afraid to say a word. I just stared at her. But as soon as Henry woke up, Grandma was gone. I was just shaking as I told him what happened.

We both were wide awake by now and could not go back to sleep anymore that night. We had no phone, so I could not call home. Then the neighbor lady came in the morning, knocked on my door and said, "You just got a phone call from your mother. She would like to let you know that your grandma passed away early this morning."

No matter what I did that day, all I could hear was

Grandma's voice. What was it she wanted to tell me? If I just had not gotten Henry up, then I would know.

I saw my whole childhood pass in front of my eyes. For years I did not think of the pain I had to go through because of Uncle Henry, but now it was all here again. I never, ever talked to my grandma about it, but now I know without a doubt in my mind that she knew what went on back then, but did not say anything because he was her favored son. And then in her last minutes on this earth she must have thought with all her power if she just could say she was sorry for what he did to me, and those thoughts were so desperate that it made me see her. I will never forget that night. I know now that she loved me in her own way, but her hands were tied. She could not help me. How bad she must have felt all those years.

Three days later we went to her funeral, but even on the open grave was the split between the family visible. Oh, how sad to see siblings on a day like this pulled so far apart! It was good that I had my three children. They kept me busy and helped me to leave my past behind and to hope for a better future.

5

A DREAM is a daring adventure,
A journey to carry you far –
For when you can hold a dream in your heart,
You surely can reach any star.

I HAD SURGERY the following spring. A cyst I had for years had to be removed from my womb. Everything went fine. Henry came to visit me the night after the surgery, but he was different. He was cold and would hardly talk. I had to stay ten days in the hospital, and he was there every other evening, but he just was not himself. Over and over again I tried to figure out what went wrong, but I just could not get anywhere.

It took weeks until he could tell me what happened. Then he finally opened up. As he was walking into the hospital that first day of my stay, an old friend of his came toward him and asked, "What are you doing here?"

Henry told him he was visiting his wife who just had surgery. His friend replied, "Oh, I'm a nurse and I was in the OR when she had surgery," and he told Henry exactly what they did.

Henry was so mad that his friend saw me without clothes and touched me on the most private place, that he blamed me for it. He felt it was my doing. I wanted to show myself off. He said, "You are mine and mine alone. You are my possession and nobody else has a right to see you."

What could I have done differently? I had to have the surgery. But I felt it was not just this incident that made a difference in our lives. It was because we no longer talked together, and I still prayed, but Henry no longer wanted to be included. Where did that beautiful feeling of belonging to each other go? Do we have to give that feeling up when we have children?

But time went on, and the kids and the household kept me busy. One day Henry came home for lunch. He had a fever and was really sick, but went back to work that afternoon anyway.

I felt so sorry for him, took the last little bit of money I had and walked to the store to buy a bottle of wine and some cinnamon sticks. Twenty minutes before I knew Henry should have been home, I made two hot water bottles and put them in his bed, one where his back would be and one by his feet.

Then I cooked the wine and put the cinnamon sticks in it. I knew that was good for a cold and would help him.

I waited and waited. I fed the kids and put them to bed, but no Henry. I was so afraid something had happened. I had no phone and could not call anybody to get an answer to his whereabouts.

I went to bed, but tossed and turned and could not sleep. What if he does not come home anymore? What would happen to my children and me? What if I lost him? I love him so much, what would I do without him?

At four in the morning I could hear something. Henry came home drunk and all jolly and said, "Oh, I thought I had to get rid of my cold so I stopped at the bar and had a couple of drinks."

Even though I was so scared before and promised myself to tell him this time how mad I was and how much he hurt me, I could not do it. I was so happy to know he was okay that I got up and made him some coffee and a sandwich. Then he and my children were all I had and all I ever needed.

We moved again. Henry found an apartment closer to his workplace. And even though they said after I had surgery it was impossible, I got pregnant again that summer.

And that got Henry really upset. We had enough struggles financially without another child. He was mad at me and acted like it was my fault. He said he would not go anywhere anymore with me until I looked normal again. And that it was a disgrace to have four kids in a little over three years.

I could not drive a car, so I always had to walk when I went shopping. People turned their heads when they saw me coming. Here I had one child in the baby buggy, one each side holding on, and one on the way. But my kids were happy, healthy and pretty, and I was so proud of them.

A cousin of mine, Kurt, lived with us at that time. He worked at the same place as Henry and tried to get his chauffeur's license. Those two partied at least two nights a week, but I was not included. I had to be home with the kids.

Henry suffered so much as a child, his brother had a farm and we had nothing, he felt to have another child was a punishment. His brother laughed and made fun of us and said, "If you keep your wife pregnant like that, you will soon need a trailer behind your car to put the kids in."

That really hurt Henry. Why did he always have to get cut down by his siblings? But ten years later, Walter, Henry's brother, had nine kids (one set of twins), so it came back to haunt him. It never pays to laugh at someone else's troubles; what goes around comes around.

I had a hard life, but I would never complain around my parents. I saw them very seldom and it was not their problem; it was mine. I wanted this family and I promised myself I would make it work.

I went to see the doctor who did the cyst surgery the spring before for my first pregnancy check-up, and he said I should not have this child, that it would be too much for me. But I would not allow them to take my unborn baby. I was pregnant and I would give birth to that child no matter what, but they had better see to it that we wouldn't have any more after that.

The doctor talked for a long time to both of us and said that the one who was more jealous should be sterilized. And there was no question, even Henry agreed he was very, very jealous.

Through all the years, if we went to a party or a yodeling get-together, he sat and drank all night and had a good time. I never drank, but I would have loved to dance. I was young, only in the early twenties. Henry was a super dancer and always danced with his sister, Elsa, as long as he was single. There wasn't a dance without those two being there.

Now he was over 30 years old, married and was just not interested in dancing anymore. Once in a while a friend of his would ask Henry if he could dance with me. Henry said yes, but then he hollered at me the whole way home, telling me I acted like a low-life, no-good woman who was ready to jump to bed with whoever I danced with.

Boy, that hurt! I never ever even kissed another man. Henry was my one and only. But I tried to see it his way. He never had anything that was his alone, and so he looked at me as his possession. I never talked back to him or defended myself. I just let him hurt me, since that is what I was taught from little on. Most of the time he knew he did wrong, and then days later showed love and affection again. But "I'm sorry" was not in his vocabulary.

I would melt and forgive him again. How could he know any better, he never saw love at home, and I was everything he had.

Henry was so determined not to have any more kids that he had the surgery done during Christmas vacation. His friends would not suspect anything that way. I was proud of him. I felt that took a lot of courage on his part.

The apartment we lived in was very damp, and the kids were always sick, so at the beginning of January 1962 we moved again, this time only across the road, but it was hard on me. Then I was nine months pregnant, plus I had three kids to take care of. I was glad that I had everything put away and organized before I had to go to the hospital. Even though I gave birth to Lotti at home, the doctor said that it was impossible this time to stay home.

It was January 27, 1962, just before midnight when I told Henry that it was time to go to the hospital. He got dressed, but then said, "I can't leave without breakfast." He got a frying pan out, put butter and a bratwurst in it. He wanted onions, but I didn't have any, I only had garlic. He peeled one little clove after the other, chopped them up and put them in the frying pan, roasted everything, and then enjoyed his meal, while I was sitting there begging him to hurry up.

It was 2:30 a.m. on Sunday morning, the 28th of January, when Henry finally got me to the hospital. The nurse said, "You are so far open it won't take long for your baby to be born." They even got the water ready to bathe the baby, but I had so much scar tissue from the surgery I had the year before, it just would not open any further than 1.5 inches.

They waited and waited. At 8 a.m. they knew they had to do something drastic to save this baby, so they told Henry he should go and eat breakfast somewhere, it would take a while yet.

He went to a nearby restaurant, and there he ran into a friend of his. They started playing cards, and he forgot all about me.

In the meantime, two doctors and at least four nurses tried to get the baby. It was so painful that I wished I could die. My tears were just rolling and I felt so lonely, no hand to hold on to.

The doctor had to go in and strip the opening of my uterus over the baby's head. I do not know how, but they did it, and by 11 a.m. I had my healthy little son "Reto" in my arms. I was so proud, and all my pain was gone.

I think that is the biggest miracle on earth. A mother can hurt so much, but then when the nurse puts that little bundle into her arms, all she can feel is joy. All the pain is forgotten. How beautiful and precious that moment is!

Henry came back at noon, looked at me and our little son, gave me a kiss and said, "It seems everything here is under control, so I could go and visit my sister Martha," and out the door he went.

I think it bothered him so much. There was one more mouth to feed and just not enough money.

There were three other women in my room. They all had company that Sunday afternoon, and here I was all by myself. It certainly hurt, but I swallowed my tears, like so many times before, and was just thankful that I had a healthy baby boy.

It was a nice warm spring day. Henry came home from work. I was just done nursing Reto and the kids were playing in the yard. I was watching them from the window when I saw a boy on his bike come down the side road. For some unknown reason, he did not slow down and turned onto the highway, right into the path of an oncoming car. It threw him and he hit his head on the sidewalk.

Henry called the police and ambulance while I ran out to see if I could be of any help. The head of the boy, who I did not know, was split open and I could see his brain pulsating.

I sat down by the sidewalk, lifted his head slowly and laid it in my lap. He grabbed my hands and, in his pain, squeezed them so hard my fingers turned blue. But I sat with him and prayed, asked God to please give this young boy a second chance and let him live.

The ambulance came, they put him on a stretcher and drove him away. I felt so bad. All I could do was hug my kids and thank God that they were healthy. Days later I heard from the 12-year-old's mother. She told me that her son had brain surgery and that he pulled through. He had difficulty talking and could not remember anything, but he would get better in time. About three months later the boy sent me a thank you note telling me that his name was Richard and that my prayers were answered and he will someday be okay again. Thank you, God, for this miracle.

Henry's job did not work out at all. His boss expected things from him that Henry thought were dangerous. Henry looked around and found similar work in a neighboring state, so he quit his job and made arrangements for us to move again. And Henry was right. The guy who took his job did what was expected of him and got electrocuted three months later.

We moved on June 1, 1962, to Oberluchhofen. It was cold and snowed that day. The grass was a foot high already, but the snow pressed it all down. The day Henry accepted his new job, he was promised a nice apartment, but now that it was time to move, there was no place to move to. His boss found us an old farmhouse which we had to share with some Italians. The kitchen and living room were downstairs, and the two bedrooms were upstairs. Those foreigners, who did not speak our language, were always right there. I could not even sneak into the children's bedroom without them seeing me.

I had to cook on a wood stove that gave me a lot of trouble. It was impossible to start a fire if the wind came from the southeast. All I got then was the kitchen full of smoke. Yet, I had four little mouths to feed, and Henry wanted a hot meal for lunch. If I could not get the fire going before Henry came home, then he would try. And he was an expert at that, since wood stoves were all he had up in the mountains. But so often he had to go back to work with a sandwich in his hand, and I still had no fire in the stove to cook on.

The diapers and all the clothes had to be washed on the washboard and cooked in a big kettle. I had to climb over a fence into the cow yard to hang the clothes on the clothesline. But the cows could walk underneath my fresh washed linen and get it all dirty again. And I had four kids between six months and four years old, and that meant a lot of laundry.

And all four had the whooping cough that summer. It was tough. It was the end of October when we finally found a better apartment. We were told we could move in around the 15th of November, 1962.

Henry's boss asked him if he would start at 5 a.m. on November 2. There had to be enough gravel ready when the trucks drove in at 7 a.m. to get them going. Henry started early two days a week all summer long, but told his boss that it got too cold and that he would not do it anymore. The boss begged him and Henry gave in, but Henry told him he would do it only one more time.

Henry left the next morning at 4:30 a.m. He started the gravel crushers and then took the end-loader to get gravel. But nobody told him that they made a six-yard-deep hole the day before so that they could see what kind of gravel they had underneath. Nothing was barricaded.

Henry drove right into it. The end-loader rolled over and fell into the hole, burying him underneath. The steel roof of the loader was level with the seat, and Henry was squeezed into the little opening around the stick shift, one of his legs sticking out and being caught underneath the metal arm that goes to the loader. But right there the ground was a little lower or he would have lost his leg. What would we do without our Guardian Angel!

Henry was not alone that morning, but his co-worker was from Italy. He saw what happened, thought Henry was dead, and must have gone into shock. He was so scared he jumped in his car and went home, never thinking once to call for help.

The trucks moved in at 7 a.m., but there was nothing ready, no men to be found. The crusher ran, but no gravel.

They went to look for the end-loader, and all they saw was the wheels sticking up in the air.

One co-worker screamed, “Henry is dead!” But Henry used all his power and answered, “I am alive. Please get me out of here.”

They had to get another bigger end-loader from another job site to lift the one in the hole out before they could get to Henry. Nobody thought he would make it.

The bottle of ether he needed to start the machine that morning broke and knocked him out, and we think that saved his life. His deep cuts did not bleed until they got to him; otherwise he would have bled to death.

It was 8:30 a.m. before they got him out of the hole. They laid him in the back of the van and drove him to the nearest doctor. The doctor put a bandage on his skull that was ripped open and his wrist that was cut half off. Then he said, “That’s all I can do for this patient. He belongs in a hospital.” Henry asked the driver to please bring him home to see me on the way to the hospital.

I was in the kitchen making breakfast for our four children when the van drove in. Henry looked so bad I did not even recognize him. Over 70 gallons of oil ran over him. He was black and full of oil from one end to the other.

The driver got out of the van and just stood there and looked at me. It took him quite some time before he could say, “I bring you your husband. He is badly hurt.”

Boy, what a shock! I told the driver to wait. Then I ran to the neighbors to ask them if they would take care of our kids so that I could go to the hospital with Henry. I told them I could not let Henry go alone. I did not even know if he would survive.

As soon as I knew my kids were taken care of, I grabbed a coat and we were on our way.

The doctors waited for us at the hospital. First they sewed his left hand back on, and also sewed together the head wound, which was about six inches long. I stayed with him at all times, as I wanted to see what they did to my husband. The doctor then said to one of the nurses she should take X-rays to see how many fractures Henry had. The X-ray nurse took us into a different room. Then she asked Henry if he could stand up. Of course, he said yes, but then shortly after that collapsed before the nurse had a chance to make any X-rays. I helped the nurse get Henry off the floor and we sat him on a chair.

The nurse then told me, "Oh, there are no fractures. You can take him home." I was really upset and frustrated, but I asked no questions. The only thing I could think was what will happen to us now? Where should I go with Henry?

I called my parents, explained what happened, and then asked if I could bring him to their apartment. At that time we were ready to move into another apartment and there was no way Henry could go through that stress. My parents said yes right away and were very helpful.

Nobody knew until later that Henry had a ruptured kidney, broken ribs, and all the little bones that are in the left wrist were cracked. He got a terrible infection in his wrist and a high fever that lingered for seven weeks. Our family doctor had to come four or five times during the day or at night to give him shots to fight the infection and morphine to help relieve his pain, which was just tremendous. Thank God that at that time doctors still made house calls.

The doctor said so often that if he put Henry into the hospital, they would amputate his hand immediately. But Henry's infection in the wrist just did not get any better. Puss just dripped out of the wound, and I had to change his bandage at least every two hours.

I was glad if Mother took the kids along for a walk. At least that gave me time for a nap. But she couldn't do much more, as at that time she did not feel well either, and four small children were almost too much for her. My mother was so exhausted that she just cried when my dad came home from work late in the afternoon; that made me feel even worse. I felt we were a burden to them.

It surely was tough, and once again I had no shoulder to cry on. Why do I always have to be the strong one? But I did not want to complain. As Grandma used to say, "God will give nobody a cross heavier than they are able to carry."

It was in the middle of December when the doctor said, "I will try one more thing, and if that does not help, then I will have to bring Henry to the hospital and they will take his hand off, no questions asked."

The doctor gave Henry a double dose of pain-killer and then with the help of my dad and me put a cast on Henry's left hand. He made two windows into the cast so that the sores could drain. Then he gave him medication that he just had flown in from the USA.

That was the turnaround. We could see a big improvement in only one week. It was all uphill from that day on, but by now Henry had lost over 40 pounds and was very weak.

There was not much room at my parents' apartment. My four kids slept in my old bedroom, where we put mattresses on the floor. Henry rested on the couch and I had to sleep on the floor beside him, but it did not matter. Henry got better and he was alive. That's all that mattered.

We celebrated Christmas at my parents' house that year. But even though I called Henry's mother the day after Henry's accident and told her how badly he was hurt, there was not one visit or phone call inquiring how he was doing. Not even on Christmas. He was forgotten.

How can anybody hurt one of its own so much, especially a mother her own flesh and blood? I know that Henry was hurting, but I felt even worse. I wished I could have done something to make up for it. All I could do was stand by him and love him.

My brother helped me move into our new apartment, and then whenever I could spare a couple of hours I went and unpacked and got everything in order. It was January 15, 1963, before Henry was strong enough to be moved. I was glad to get out of my parents' house, as I could see that it was too much for my mother to have four small grandchildren and the two of us around. I was anxious to get out of her hair

I did not know how sick my mother was until later. She went to the doctor after we left, and he sent her to the hospital immediately. Her stomach closed up and did not let any food go through anymore, and she also had a growth on her uterus that had to be removed. It was surely tough. How much more can go wrong?

Henry had to have surgery in April to reattach the tendons that were cut in his wrist, and then he hopefully would be able to use the fingers of his left hand again. He could not work all summer, but to give his hand some exercise he took the older two kids along to the woods. He cut brush, and the kids helped him to put that wood together in bundles. In the beginning he could hardly do a bundle a day, but he would not give up. We needed those bundles of wood to heat our home. His hand would get so swollen it was unbelievable. It looked like a big bear claw. The doctors told him he would not be able to use that hand ever again, but Henry knew better. His wrist stayed stiff, but he exercised and exercised until he could use his fingers again, and by fall he went back to work.

We bought our first TV that spring. We could only get two channels, but it was entertainment for Henry, who was not used to sitting around doing nothing. That was the year President Kennedy got killed. We could follow all of that on TV. We did not miss a thing, never thinking that we would live in the USA someday.

Tears were rolling down my cheeks when I watched the President's little son saluting his dad's casket as they loaded it on to the carriage. And Jackie was such a strong woman, just looking out for the welfare of her children. My heart went out to her. But then I think that is a day that most people will never forget. Friends of ours told us to get a lawyer and take Henry's former employer to court, then that big hole would have to be barricaded.

We thought if we just would get a little bit of money for all the trouble we went through, that would be okay. So we got us a lawyer. He sat down with us and listened to our story. Then he told us we should get at least $50,000 out of this deal. "You have to pay me $500 advance, then I will take your case and see what I can do for you."

My parents loaned us the money, to be paid back after a settlement could be reached. But after four months we got a letter and a detailed statement from our lawyer. The $500 was gone, used for phone calls, time spent, etc., but there was nothing he could do for us. He dropped the case, he told us in the letter. We found out later that Henry's former boss took our lawyer out for supper and also built him a new house. Someone along the line got a good deal out of our heartache, but it certainly was not us.

All summer long I sewed baby clothes to help bring in extra money. Reto was a year old by that time. We had a garden to the east side of the house we lived in, so I bought some chicken wire and posts and made a fence around the garden. Then I put in a pillow and some toys, and that was Reto's playground. When the neighbors saw what I was doing, they laughed and said he wouldn't stay in there for long. But I proved them wrong. I put Reto outside in the morning, gave him a bottle, and he stayed out there all day. He drank if he was thirsty, lay on the pillow and took a nap when he was tired, or just watched his siblings play.

Lottie was like his little mother and always by him while the other two played with the neighbors' kids. Thank God I had such good kids, as I had so much work and no time to spoil them.

Then I also went one day a week to clean the teacher's house and another day the postmaster's house, just to make some extra money. But I took the time every night to tuck them in, read them a little story, and then prayed with them, just as I was taught by my mother.

One Saturday afternoon my mother, who by now felt a little better again, came to stay with me over the weekend, while my dad, Henry, and some of their friends planned on going mountain-climbing. I was just ready to cook supper when Edith, crying, opened the door. Tight behind her was the lady next door carrying Heinz in her arms. He was unconscious, as he had just fallen head-first down their basement, which was about an eight-foot fall.

Henry and some of his mountain-climber friends drove in at the same time. Henry took one look at Heinz and then turned around and slapped Edith left and right. I had no idea how that all came about. But before I asked any questions, Jakob, one of our friends, interfered. He gave Henry a lecture.

"You don't even know what happened. How come you slapped your daughter? That was unfair. She did not push Heinz over the railing, it was just a freak accident, so leave her out of this."

Henry's reply was, "It does not matter. If she would not have been at the neighbor's house, this would not have happened, so she deserves to be punished."

They left soon, still arguing. But that was Henry, punish first and then ask questions, instead of the other way around. Yet I had no time to waste; I had to call the doctor, and it did not take him long to get to our house. Heinz came to by then. The doctor checked him out and said, "Your son has a bad concussion and needs lots of rest." Then he went on telling me if I would check his pulse and blood pressure every half hour all night long, Heinz would not have to go to the hospital. But if I should see any changes, I would have to call the ambulance immediately.

I sat with Heinz all night and gave him the medicine the doctor left with me. My fingers glided through his soft, curly hair, kissing him on his once-so-rosy cheeks that now had almost lost all their color. I prayed and prayed and did not sleep a wink that night.

Heinz laid around for a couple of days, but then got better again. Thank God, my Guardian Angel stood by me once again and saved my son.

Henry was back to work late that summer, but I felt it was time that I was looking for a full-time job to help Henry support our family. I applied for a manager's job in Bergun, in the State of Graubunden. It was a grocery store up in the mountains. They sold groceries, some clothing, shoes, also feed for cows and calves, and straw to the farmers.

I took Henry along the day I went for an interview as I felt he could help me and do the feed part. That would get him closer to farmers, as he still missed farming terribly.

The interview went pretty well, but I was so scared my knees were shaking. I was only 25 years old and had four kids and I had never managed a store before. Would they really give me a chance?

But it was only two weeks later when we got a letter from the board's president saying we got the job and they were expecting us by the middle of January 1964. Boy, that was a dream come true!

6

A DREAM is a beautiful vision
That looks beyond what you can see,
Then lifts you and guides you and grows strong inside you
To help you be all you can be.

MY KIDS HAD a bad cold over the Christmas holidays of 1963, and because of that I could not go along as planned to see Henry's step-dad and mother on December 26. But my dad and Henry decided to go anyway. I gave them a bottle of wine to take along as a present for Henry's step-dad, a guy who never was loved, but was only good enough to work and take care of his brother's family.

The first summer I knew him he was up in the mountains with the heifers, but no one would go and see if he had food. We visited him one Sunday and found out that he had nothing to eat for two days. Henry and I went shopping, and I cooked a meal for Henry's step-dad.

When we got together with Henry's siblings the next time, I mentioned it. But Walter's response was quick: "Oh, he is an old man who can't do much anymore. All he is good for is to take care of the heifers, and that is not good enough to spoil him with food."

I could not understand how one can be so cruel. Their step-dad kept the farm going after they lost their dad, and if it wasn't for him Walter might not have a farm now. Even though I would have loved to have him there, Henry's step-dad was not allowed to come to our wedding. Mother said he had to stay home and take care of the animals.

I cut his hair a couple of times because they would not give him the money to go to a barber nor take the time to do it for him. He was not loved at all, just used. Yes, I felt sorry for old Jakob.

Henry walked in the door at his mother's house that day after Christmas on December 26, and the first thing his step-dad asked, "How come you did not bring Edith and the kids along? I really would have loved to see them." Henry told him they had the flu and could not make it.

My dad opened the bottle of wine. They sat around the table and had a glass together. Henry's step-dad only took a couple of sips, then got up from the chair and went to the window. He looked down, and then slowly up the Toggenburg Valley, then turned around, sat back down on the couch, took one deep breath and died right there. Henry and my dad tried to bring him back to life, but there was nothing they could do. He was buried on New Year's Eve, 1963. What a way to end the year!

It was a beautiful day in January when we arrived in Bergun, a small town with mountains all around it. Everything was covered with a big blanket of snow. It felt like the sun was smiling at us, and it made the snow sparkle as if there were thousands of little stars. It looked just like a fairytale town, so beautiful and pure.

The apartment we moved into was really nice, the store on ground level, the living quarters on the first floor. There was one apartment above us where the home ec teacher lived. We had a huge bedroom with a little balcony looking toward the huge rugged mountains. The living room was all paneled with real pine wood, and I had a nice kitchen. I never lived in a place so beautiful, and I was proud of our achievement.

It was scary to manage a store for the first time in my life. Yes, I was a clerk before, but this was different. Henry could not help much. I had to teach him what to do and had to make a clerk out of him.

Everybody in town was really nice and made us feel welcome. Bergun is a small town, population about 250, and then the two neighboring villages, Latsch, with 14 families, and Stuls, with five families, and small farms. Everybody here lived from the tourist industry. The people in town rented out every bed they could just to make some extra money, as there was no other industry and most of the farms are small and not able to support their families.

I started working end of January, with the ski season in full swing. Skiers everywhere, and I was so busy and everything was so new to me I did not know where to turn. We went down to the store at 5 to 5:30 a.m. to get the fruits and vegetables cleaned and looking presentable, then stocked the shelves so that we would be ready to open the door at 7 a.m.

The store was closed daily from 12 noon until 1:30 p.m. That gave me time to make lunch for the kids and us. The older three children could go to kindergarten, but Reto was too small, so I kept him home. We bought skis for all four kids. They could go out of the back door, put their skis on and ski all day. They really enjoyed that. Henry took Edith and Heinz skiing on Sundays, and I went tobogganing with Lotti and Reto.

I had to work very, very hard, but I was proud of my achievement. There was so much excitement and so many things I never saw before. I could sit at my desk in the office and watch the avalanches roaring down the mountain, taking every tree that was in its path along. It sounded like thunder, and I could hear the roaring echo come back from the mountains around us. No matter how many times I saw that, I never got tired of it. It was just so amazing and so breathtaking.

I made it through the first months. It was very tough, but most of the tourists left after Easter. May was a slower month, and we could do all the things we had not had time to do before. I was proud of myself; I was a stranger to that town but yet could increase sales, compared to the year before, in such a short time. It was just great.

The store was closed every Wednesday afternoon and also on Sundays. Henry took me sometimes for a ride on our Wednesday afternoons off. He would drive a little farther up to the mountains where there was a little military shack. We sat there just holding hands and let the sun warm us all the way into our hearts.

We watched the mountain goats roaming around or the eagles soaring in the clear blue sky. The marmots peeked out of their dens and after a while felt comfortable enough to stay out. We watched them play together. We even saw them make hay. One of them laid on its back, the others piled hay on the belly and the one lying on its back would hold on to it with the legs. When it could hold no more, they bit into its tail and pulled it on its back into the den. There were only the sounds of the animals all around us; it was so peaceful.

Henry and I could really enjoy each other and had a great time together. He took me in his arms and held me tight; it felt so warm and comforting. I wished it would always stay that way.

But it was not just fun. There was also a lot of responsibility that rested on my shoulders. Summer came and it got really busy again. The tourists were back, and our little town turned into a city, and with that lots and lots of work.

Sunday was a time to get my sanity back. I got a picnic basket ready, filled it with fruits, fresh bread and "knockwursts."

Henry got the Jeep out of the garage and off we went, the two of us, our four children, and most of the time a neighbor's child or two, crammed into our little Willis Jeep. We had no tarp over it; the wind blew through our hair. We drove over mountain passes, along wild, bubbling rivers, and past thundering waterfalls. We sang together or just enjoyed the beauty of nature.

At least once or twice a month we took the kids to a

little lake way up in the mountains. Henry made a float out of some old lumber and took the kids out on the little lake. Even our German shepherd dog, "Roby," enjoyed a ride on the float. Some mountain climbers that passed by watched us for awhile, smiled at the kids, and then went on their merry way. But otherwise it was just us.

The water was so clear that we could see the little stones on the bottom of the lake. Lotti and Heinz loved to go after the small fish that were barely one inch long, but most of the time they reached too deep and just got some dirt.

Henry gathered some wood and started a fire. With his pocket knife he cut a cross on each end of the knockwurst, then tucked them on a twig so that the kids could get them hot and brown holding them over the open fire. It was just great, and everyone was so relaxed and jolly; I wished those days would never end. But summer gave way to fall, and it got too cold for bathing suits.

Reto got a bad cough that fall. We contacted the doctor in town. He said it was the whooping cough and gave him medicine. But the medicine did not help. No, it got worse. It was so bad that Reto no longer would lay down in his bed when I put him to sleep. He sat where the pillow should be and rested his head on the headboard of the bed. If he lay down, he coughed so bad and could not get any air. He felt like he was suffocating.

I did not know what to do anymore, so Henry packed him in the car one day and drove him down to the valley to see a different doctor. That doctor took one look at Reto and said, "Keep up whatever you are doing now for a couple more weeks and you can put him in a sanatorium. His lungs are full of fluid." He gave Reto different medicine, and within 48 hours we could see a big improvement.

Henry went with the Army Jeep we bought, just before we moved to Bergun, to Latsch and Stuls the following Saturday afternoon. He had to deliver some groceries and calf feed. I closed the store at 5 p.m., took the broom like I always did and started sweeping in front of the store so that it was nice and clean when the churchgoers went by on Sunday morning.

We had a young girl, "Mirtha," that I hired to help me with the housework. She had to give our four children a bath that afternoon. All of a sudden I could hear her screaming out of the girls' bedroom window, "Reto is dead! Reto is dead!"

I threw my broom away and ran upstairs. The only thing I could think was she'd drowned him. Henry just drove in and saw me running. He turned the Jeep off and ran after me. Reto lay on the bathroom floor, still had his clothes on, but was pale and not breathing at all.

Henry lifted him up, ran into the bedroom, laid him on the bed and started mouth-to-mouth resuscitation. I called the doctor, who came within minutes.

The doctor opened Reto's eyelids and could see that he was in deep coma. He said Reto just suffered a stroke, and he gave him medicine right into the artery. Ten minutes later, nothing happened. He gave Reto another shot and said that we should get him to the hospital immediately.

Henry went to get the car. I carried Reto downstairs and crawled into the back seat of the car, Reto in my arms. Henry drove like a maniac, and all I could do was hang on to that little bundle in my arms and pray, "God, please don't take Reto from us; please, please let him live."

We had to drive over a mountain pass. It usually takes two hours to get to the nearest hospital, but not today. Halfway there Reto's muscles started tightening up. He turned blue, and it felt like he would leave us any minute.

My eyes were filled with tears and I had a big lump in my throat as I said to Henry, "You can slow down. This is it. I think Reto is dying right in my arms."

"I will not slow down. I will bring him to the hospital dead or alive," was Henry's answer.

Our doctor called ahead of time so that the whole crew was waiting for us at the hospital when we arrived. They put Reto on oxygen and wheeled him into the trauma center. The doctor there confirmed that Reto just suffered a stroke, but they could not tell us if there was any brain damage. They thought that the medicine we got from the second doctor was too strong for that little guy.

It was Sunday morning before Reto regained consciousness, but they sent us home before that and would not let us see him anymore. They said he had to be kept calm, and if he would see me he would get upset and want to be with me. It was hard to go home and leave my son behind. And just as hard not knowing what the future would have in store for him. But what could I do? I had to follow doctor's orders.

One week later Henry went to visit Reto, but I couldn't. The doctors would not allow it. They kept Reto three weeks and did spinal tests almost daily. They thought it might be epilepsy-related, but that was not the case. Henry even had to drive Reto and another boy, who was in the same hospital, to the University Hospital in Zurich, but they couldn't find anything either.

Boy, was I happy when I finally could get Reto home and hold him in my arms again. But his back hurt so bad he walked around bent, like a little old man; his back was so sore from all the spinal tests. And he now got asthma really bad. Slowly, day by day, he got a little better and soon could play with his friends again, but the asthma stayed with him for years to come.

Our maid went on to a different job, and I struggled between store and household again.

Henry's sister, Elsa, came to visit us that winter. She left Switzerland right after her wedding in 1958 and moved to Ripon in California, USA. She is the one who did not want me at her wedding because I was pregnant with Edith and too fat, so she said. But now that I was a manager of a store and lived in a beautiful mountain area, she came to visit us and was impressed. She could not take enough pictures of the high snow banks that were far higher than our car. She said she did not see that much snow for many, many years. Elsa was Henry's favorite sister, and it hurt him more than anything to see her turn against him. But this time she was really nice.

My brother got married the following summer. He got a real nice girl who came all by herself from East Germany, just before the wall was built. She was first put into a camp, but later came to Switzerland, leaving her parents and brothers behind in East Germany.

Henry and I stood up for them at the wedding, and that meant a lot of work for me. I sewed Lisa's wedding dress and my bridesmaid's dress. My brother is Edith's godfather, so we made her into a little chimney sweeper, a superstitious symbol for bringing good luck. It was a nice wedding on a beautiful, sunny Saturday, and Edith looked so cute. Every place we stopped strangers took pictures of her, and I was so proud she was my little girl.

Henry's mother never cared about us or even visited us. She did not care when our daughter Edith, her first grandchild, was born — never called or sent a little note. Nor did she care when Henry needed her most, after his bad accident in 1962. She had arthritis as long as I'd known her, but by now it got so bad that she could not walk anymore. None of Henry's siblings had time to take care of her, even though they took everything she had. She was their free babysitter and had to help them as much as she could. And now that she was totally disabled, they did not want her anymore, and she did not want to go to a nursing home, so I decided to take her in; I felt so sorry for her.

I put all four kids in one room and gave her the girls' bedroom. It was a nice, sunny room. I put her chair right by the window so that she could see everything that went on outside the store. She could not get in or out of bed by herself, so we installed a bell. She could ring it when I was downstairs taking care of the store to let me know that she had to go to the bathroom or needed something else. It was tough and a lot of work, but she seemed happy and that was most important.

Some of the people in town could not believe that I was so slender, worked so hard and had four kids so close together. So one day a lady who was pretty nosy asked Edith, "How long are your parents married?" because they thought I married Henry with the four kids from his first marriage. Edith's answer was, "I'm eight, and Heinz is seven — that is 15, then Lotti is 6, brings it to 21, and Reto is 4. I guess they are married 25 years already."

That same question was never asked again.

I thought it was pretty funny when different customers came to the store and told me about Edith's answer.

My dad and his friends came once or twice a year to tackle the mountain "Piz Kesch." They came to Bergun by train on Saturday morning and then took off from there by foot.

My mother stayed with my children so that Henry and I could leave, too, as soon as we closed the store that evening, since we both loved the mountains. We hopped into the Jeep, and off we went. Henry drove the Jeep up winding paths and over alpine meadows. It was so steep at times that Henry told me to sit on the hood to make the front a little heavier. There was never, ever someone who drove as far up the mountain trail as we did.

When we finally could get no farther, we parked the Jeep and went on by foot. We only had two more hours to go to get to the SAC (Swiss Alpine Club) House where we met up with the rest of the group. We had a bowl of soup with them, and then went to bed. They aren't really beds, just mattress beside mattress on the floor from one wall to the other. Bedtime is before 10 p.m. Everybody has to be quiet after that. Since mountain climbing is a tough sport, no one should try it if they're over-tired. That could end in tragedy.

It was around five o'clock the next morning when we left the little mountain house we'd slept in. My dad took one group and Henry the other. Dad would never allow Henry and me to be on the same rope; in case one group would fall we both would not get killed together.

My dad, then I and two friends of ours were tied together on one rope, each of us with an ice pick in our hand and a backpack on our back, and off we went, heading slowly up the steep glacier, watching out for the deep snow-covered, very dangerous cracks every glacier has.

The sun rising slowly above the horizon turned the glacier into a sparkling mirror. Once every hour we took a five-minute break to take a sip of water or something to chew on. The best thing is dried fruits. They give you instant energy.

It took us five hours to cross the glacier, and now the last part was a straight stone wall up to the peak of "Piz Kesch." One person at a time, my dad first climbed up while we held his rope around a stone or a safety hook. Then he stopped, put his end of the rope in safety position so that I could climb and feel safe. Slowly but surely we got closer to the top. It was almost unbelievable, but in every little crack along the way you could see some flowers, white, yellow, red or blue. They are really tiny, but ever so pretty.

To climb a mountain is hard work, and so often I asked myself why did I do this. This is way too much for me. But then after an almost seven-hour climb, I was on top. There was not much room to sit down, only two or three mountain climbers at the time could sit all the way on top.

Mountain climbing is like having a baby. It hurts and you're tired and want to give up, but once on top, you forget all your aches and pains. You can't hear anything but the noise of a blackbird looking for some food. As far as your eye can see, nothing but mountains and valleys, and it feels like no place on this planet can one be closer to and respect God more than on top of a mountain.

My daydreaming came to an end when my dad reminded us that it was time to head back. It is just as hard going back down as it is climbing up, but it surely is worth every bit of it. Henry and I did not have to walk as far as the rest of them; we had the Jeep to bring us back. It surely was a beautiful, memorable weekend.

Edith was now in first grade. Heinz, Lotti and Reto went to kindergarten. The native language in Bergun was "Romansch," which is close to Latin. It is called the mother of all languages. So all four of my children could speak that language very well. We didn't have to know it since everybody in town also spoke German, but my children could speak amongst themselves and we would not understand one word.

I had to go twice a year to shows where all the retailers got together to order toys for Christmas, and also shoes and clothing, or, in spring, all the summer items. Henry always came along. On the way home we would stop at a fancy restaurant and eat something very special and just enjoy the time we had together.

All winter long we went at least once, if not two evenings a week, to Davos. It was about a 40-minute drive over windy roads and a mountain pass along a wild stream that was partly covered with ice.

We went to see the ice hockey games. Teams from all over the world played there. We saw the Russians, Czechoslovakia, even USA play there. We also saw Peggy Fleming from the USA win her world title in figure skating. That was on a beautiful sunny Sunday in the outdoor arena in Davos. What a great show!

But it wasn't just all fun. My boss and Henry could not get along together. My boss, Robert, owned the biggest farm in town and had lots of money. He also was the town chairman and kind of like a private banker. He loaned money out to anybody who needed it, but only if he could see that it was to his advantage.

The carpenter, painter and even the lady who owned the drugstore had to borrow money from Robert, so he had them all in his hand. If they would not do what he wanted them to do, he would tell them their loan was due now. That made them shut up in a hurry. They were just like puppets on a string and had to do exactly what he wanted them to do.

Robert's dad, they said, was the same way when he was young. Robert's mother could not take it anymore, so she jumped into the liquid manure tank and committed suicide.

Robert took calf feed if he needed it, never saying a word to us. He also had a key to the store so he could get in whenever he wanted to, and I was responsible for the inventory. Even if we were there, he came in through the back door and read everything that was on my desk, private or business. He felt he had a right to do that. Henry and he argued a lot, and Henry came to the point where he said it's either him or me, but one of us has to go.

Henry had the loaded army rifle under our bed ready to be used, threatening that he would shoot himself. I begged him over and over again not to do it. I needed him and so did the children. They were small and needed their dad, plus their friends in school would tease them if their dad would have killed himself, or if he would end up in jail for shooting Robert.

I was scared. I knew something had to give, since if Henry hated someone there was no reasoning anymore. He told me over and over again that with my knowledge I could have my own store. That way we would be our own bosses.

I checked the paper daily and looked at least at five

stores, but one was old and needed a lot of fixing up, and we had no money. The other one was in the wrong location, but I kept looking. I also wrote a letter to the store's headquarters in Winterthur and told them exactly what went on in this store. They came and investigated and talked to different people in town.

But in the meantime, I found a store I liked in Weite-Wartau. It was a two-family house with a newly remodeled smaller "corner grocery store." We decided to go for it.

A customer of ours, an older man who always spent his vacation in Bergun, knew about our troubles and offered to give us the down payment for that business. The cost was 200,000 Swiss francs ($50,000 at that time; it took a little more than four Swiss francs for one dollar. Today it is 1.20 SF for $1).

The guys who came from Winterthur to investigate Robert's doings in Bergun were done with their work and found out that Robert not only took things at the store, he also was dishonest with his bookkeeping and embezzled money that way. He got charged and was taken to court.

The board members came to us and begged us to stay in Bergun, but we had already bought the house in Weite-Wartau. Plus, if someone did Henry wrong, there was no turning back. Forgiveness is not in his vocabulary.

So we packed our belongings in May of 1966 and moved again. Weite-Wartau is about two miles from the Rhein River; on the other side of the river is the Firstentum Lichtenstein. Lichtenstein, one of the smallest countries in the world, is to this day ruled by a monarch, but protected by the Swiss Army.

I got everything organized and enrolled the kids in school: Edith in second, Heinz in first grade, Lotti and Reto in kindergarten. Now their language was strictly German, which was a big change for them, since in Bergun they were taught "Romansch."

The store we bought was connected with the USEGO,

a warehouse where independents like us could buy everything we needed.

We planned to give away a big shopping bag full of goodies to every customer who helped us celebrate our grand opening. We filled the bags with one pound of coffee beans, a bag of noodles, also one pound of spaghetti and lots of other items. Some of the items we had to buy, and some were given to us by different companies. USEGO was with us from the beginning and put all the figures together. They figured I needed at least 300 of those bags to satisfy all our customers that would walk through the door the first two days.

I scrubbed and cleaned and polished for days and now was ready for that big day, our Grand Opening. But at the end of the second day there were still over 100 bags left. I knew then that our adventure would never work, because they did not show us the true figures. Yet, we bought the business and there was no turning back. But it got worse, not better. It was six months later when someone built a cash-and-carry in the next town, only four miles from us. Now we knew why this neat, newly remodeled store was for sale.

In the beginning only business owners could go and shop at the cash-and-carry (one had to have an ID similar to Sam's Club), but they took their families and friends along and would let them buy under their account also. No matter what I did I could not increase my sales. On Sunday, when the cash-and-carry was closed, then they knew where my store was if they needed salt, sugar or some other small items.

Needless to say, money was tight once again, and Henry had to look for a job elsewhere. First he worked for a construction company, but he did not like it there. Then he started trucking cattle, and that he really liked because he got in contact with farmers again.

We took the kids to the fair that fall, but Lotti moped

around, did not want to go on any rides and complained her belly hurt. Henry thought she only made it up to spoil it for the rest of us.

We went home early and she kept on complaining, so I called our family doctor. He still made house calls and was in our neighborhood at that time. He swung by, took one look at Lotti, packed her in his car and drove her to the hospital. She had a ruptured appendix and had to have surgery immediately.

The first two days were critical, but then she recuperated and was better in no time. Only one week later Edith got tripped by one of her friends, hit her chin on a hydrant and got a deep cut that had to be sewed, and it left her with a scar for life. We certainly kept those doctors busy, but everything turned out okay. I believe my Guardian Angel stood by my side again and spread his wings over my children.

It was late summer, 1966, when I felt a lump in my breast. I went to the doctor, and he put me right away into the hospital to have surgery. He was worried that I had cancer. Catarina, a young girl who worked for us in Bergun, came to take care of my store and my children. I had that cyst removed and, thank God, it was not malignant like the doctors feared.

But the doctors would not do that surgery without my consent to remove my varicose veins at the same time. My legs were just terrible, and I was told if I did not do that surgery my veins in my legs would break open before I turned 35 years old. I felt I had no choice; I had to do it, since I knew I had a long, hard life ahead of me.

To do that surgery they made a cut up by my crotch, then went through the veins with a wire that had a little ball on the end. Whenever they could go no further, they made an incision, cut all the excess vein out and then sewed it back together again. By the time they were through I had 23 incisions on one leg and 19 on the other.

I had to stay in the hospital for one week, but had to have my legs bandaged very, very tight for at least seven weeks.

I was told I could not work during that time. Oh, my legs hurt really bad, but I had no choice, I had to work as soon as I got home again. And, like Henry said, "If you do not think about your pain, you cannot feel it." I had a business to run and four children to take care of.

Catarina left us as soon as I came home from the hospital. She had to go back to work at her regular job. But then she came back five weeks later and stayed with us for two weeks during her vacation.

Henry and I decided to take one week vacation and make a trip, the first time ever that Henry and I went alone on vacation together. We drove through Austria, sat by the lake in "Zell am See," a beautiful little town with a small clear lake surrounded by mountains. We watched the swans glide quietly through the water, leaving ripples behind them.

From there the road took us over the "Gross Glockner." It was just beautiful, the mountains, the glaciers, the wild streams rushing down the mountainside, and the beautiful flowers in any color imaginable.

On to Yugoslavia we went, and we stayed overnight in Rijeka. For the first time in my life I saw oil refineries. We could hardly sleep that night, since the fire gushed out of the refinery's chimney and made the sky light up all night long.

We drove a Volvo station wagon, laid the back seat down, put a thin mattress in it and slept in the car. Soup, coffee or tea we cooked on an alcohol cooker. Otherwise, we lived on sandwiches and fruits.

We took some back roads the next day, drove through Zagreb and Sisak. We saw people in the vineyard. The women picked the grapes, the men carried them in wooden containers which they had strapped to their backs, to a wagon that had a huge wooden barrel on it. They dumped the grapes into the barrel, and two women in black long dresses stamped those grapes with their bare feet. That's how they made their wine. And for the first time I saw a rice field. One farmer worked the rice field with the help of oxen.

Farmers in Yugoslavia still worked with donkeys. One little old lady, all dressed in black with a black bonnet on her head, was riding along the highway on a donkey's back. Henry was amazed. "We have to stop and take a picture of her," he said. When she saw us getting out of the car and walking toward her, she motioned that if we wanted a picture she wanted money for that, so Henry reached in his pocket and gave her a handful of coins.

We did not know how much money it was. We never saw Yugoslavia's money until two days before, but that little old lady looked at the coins in her hand, started hollering in a language we did not understand and threw the coins at Henry. They flew all over the road, and off she went with her donkey. We could hear her complaining and talking to herself for a long time as those two trotted along the long, lonely road.

We saw women washing their clothes in a nearby river, then putting the wet clothes in a wooden tub, which they carried on their heads all the way home to their small shacks. They surely lived differently than we did. I think they had a lot harder, but simpler life than we did.

The second night we spent in a little campground right by the ocean, on the edge of the little town called "Zadar." To stand right by the ocean and see those big waves carrying white crowns come in and slam against the rocks was just overwhelming. As far as my eye could see, nothing but water; what a sight!

The next morning after we swam in the ocean for a couple of hours; we moved on. Not far down the road we had to stop as a flock of sheep crossed the highway, and in one of the little towns they had pigs running loose. Some of them decided to lay their pot belly down in the middle of the road, not paying any attention to the cars.

We decided to stay overnight in "Split," right on the ocean again. What a surprise to see a big U.S. Navy ship come in. The sailors, all dressed in snow-white outfits, stood on the railing, saluting us who stood at the pier.

The mayor of the town was there to greet them and got escorted to the Navy ship after it laid its anchor. They had a party that night, but we could not join them; only a few invited guests were allowed to go on board. Everything was so impressive, and I felt like a little fly standing beside this huge boat from a land so far, far away. Oh, what a story this ship could tell us if it could talk!

On we went the next morning, all the way to "Dubrovnik." Dubrovnik is a beautiful, old-fashioned town that was built on top of high cliffs that reached straight down to the ocean. Palm trees, the blue ocean, big waves with white crowns, it was just breathtaking. We stayed two nights and swam in the ocean all day. I wished it could be like that forever. I missed my children, but Henry was so relaxed and we had a great time together, but I could not stop the clock. It soon was time to head back.

This time we took the highway that winds along the ocean. For hundreds of kilometers nothing but ocean on one side and hills and rocks on the other, not a soul to be seen.

We were almost on the Austrian-Italian border when we heard a big "bang." A bullet hit our windshield. Thank God, it was just by the windshield wiper where the glass is thickest. It did not shatter the windshield. It was just like a drill. The bullet drilled a hole into the windshield, but then got stuck. If it would have gone through, it would have wounded or even killed me, since it was on my side. Oh, what would I do without my Guardian Angel!

We drove straight home, only stopping to get fuel and

something to drink. Henry was really scared. I never saw him that way before.

We made it through another winter, but it just did not get any better. Money got tighter and tighter, and our sales just would not increase. But what was even worse, Henry kept telling me over and over again that he knew from the beginning that this endeavor would not work out and it was time that I should find a way out.

He thought to buy a restaurant would be the way to go. So I applied for a restaurant license, but that is not so easy in Switzerland. The government requires a seven-week course. There they teach you cooking skills, decorating tables and proper settings and lots of bookkeeping. You also have to know which wine goes with which meat and where the grapes grow to make that wine. After seven weeks will be a test, and they expect you to have a 2.5 grade average or better, with 1 being the best. One needs to be able to get that license to run a restaurant.

So off to school I went. I got up at 4:30 a.m., got the store and breakfast ready and the children off to school, then I took the train and went to St. Gallen where they teach you everything you have to know to run a restaurant.

I had no driver's license, so that's why I had to go with the train. The train ride was almost one hour, twice a day, morning and night. But that was good for me. That gave me time I needed to study. Henry stayed home and ran the store.

Those seven weeks were tough, and I was glad when it was over. I had my final tests on a Tuesday. I was so scared and nervous all day and finally could relax when I boarded the train that night for the last time.

I finished third highest in the class with a test score of 1.3, which really surprised me, since I was the only one who never was in the restaurant business. The other students were either waitresses, cooks or bartenders, etc. I could not wait to get home and tell Henry all about my achievement. But Henry was not alone when I got home. His sister Martha and her husband Albert were there. They told Henry that Albert would fly to the USA the next Sunday to look at farms, and maybe buy one.

Those two farmed all their married life, but their lease was up, and so they decided to buy a farm in the USA, which would have been impossible in Switzerland. A 40-acre farm would cost around 600,000 Swiss francs, and they didn't have that kind of money either.

It did not take much to convince Henry that that would be the thing to do, since it was his dream all along to be a farmer. On the other hand, I just completed my restaurant's license with honor. I had a 1.3 on my finals, and I was proud of my achievement. Yet, it seemed that no one else was interested.

But even before Martha and Albert came with their adventurous idea, I had second thoughts of owning a restaurant. Henry felt it would have been a good idea to have one, but he was so jealous of me. What if a drunk got a little too close to me, or said the wrong thing? Henry would get mad. Deep down I knew that would ruin our marriage, and that is one thing I did not want to happen.

So I listened to everything Albert had to say. Then I heard Henry telling Albert, "As long as you are flying to the USA anyway, would you please look around and if you find something reasonable for us, please buy it."

We had mixed feelings after they left us alone that evening since that was something so new, something I never thought of before. We took Albert to the international airport in Zurick-Kloten that Sunday morning and then picked him up again one week later.

Albert bought a 200-acre farm in Merrill, Wisconsin, but told us there were so many farms for sale that it was hard for him to buy one for us. He said to Henry, "You should go look at them and then make your own decision." So I bought Henry a passport and the plane ticket, and he was on his way.

I never forgot that day. My kids and I went along to see Henry leave. Albert drove us to the airport. I watched Henry board the plan, then the plane took off and disappeared in the clouds. My stomach was in knots. I felt like, that is it — gone forever. I will never see him again.

I was really scared and had some long, sleepless nights. I did not hear anything from Henry until the day before he flew back. That was when he told me that he bought a farm. He sounded so happy. His dream finally came through. He would be a farmer and own and work his own land.

I guess that means we had to move again. We were married ten years and had moved seven times (in 1962, three times in one year), but this was completely different.

I had mixed feelings and was really scared to tell my parents what our plans were. So I sat down and wrote them a long letter. I told them that I loved them, but we had made a tough decision. We would leave our homeland and start farming in the USA. I asked them to please understand that if that meant that Henry finally could be happy, then it would be worth it.

My parents never questioned my good intentions, and they were not mad at all. They only said, "Edith, you have to live your life the way you see fit and always do the best you're capable of. We will not be able to help you, but we will pray for you and your family, and we always will be here if you need us."

To the left is the Piz Kesch.

Below, the beautiful view from the top of Piz Kesch.

A Sunday drive with the Jeep — our kids, a neighbor girl and my mom.

Edith's first day of school. Reto is proud of his sister. In the back, Lotti and a friend.

By himself Henry built a float. Reto jumping in the lake.

Reto, Heinz and Lotti — each has an itch.

The store I managed in Bergün ...

... and the store we bought in Weite-Wartau.

KANTON ST. GALLEN

Auf Grund der abgelegten Fachprüfung wird der

FÄHIGKEITS-AUSWEIS

zur Führung einer

Wirtschaft mit Alkoholausschank

erteilt

Frau Edith Gross-Zellweger

von Kappel SG

St. Gallen, 23./24. Mai 1967

Volkswirtschafts-Departement
des Kantons St. Gallen
Der Regierungsrat:

Prüfungs-Kommission
für das Gastwirtschaftsgewerbe
Der Obmann:

Buchdruckerei Flawil A.G.

My diploma from the restaurant management school.

7

A DREAM is a door to tomorrow,
A secret reflection of you.
A threshold that leads to a wonderful future
Where nothing's too good to be true.

I TOOK HENRY'S mother in again that fall. It was tough, but that was the least and maybe the last thing I could do for her. She was with her sister for awhile, but now returned to us, since there was no other place to go except the nursing home, and there she did not want to go. It surely got hectic around our house, but I hung in there.

There were a lot of other things that had to be taken care of. I wrote a letter to the USEGO and told them we would leave Switzerland in March of 1968, if they would please help me. But they did not even answer my letter. They felt it was not worth it. We could not leave. We had no money and were stuck. A month later I wrote them again, this time a certified letter, asking them to please help me, but no response.

Henry got a small monthly pension for his stiff left hand that he had since his accidents in 1962, so we took a lawyer and he asked workmen's compensation if we, instead of monthly payments, could get a one-time settlement. Workmen's compensation does not like to do that, but after a couple of meetings gave in. We got 22,000 Swiss francs (a little over $5,000). And $5,000 was our down payment for the farm, so at least we had that money together. One less headache.

Each of us needed a visa to be able to immigrate. I had to get them at the USA Embassy. But before we could get the visas, we had to see a doctor, a doctor that was recommended by the USA Consulate. We had to have our chest X-rays taken. The doctor told us those X-rays had to be put in big yellow envelopes and sealed by him and could not be opened until we went through customs in Chicago.

The doctor took the children's X-rays first, then mine, and at last Henry's. As soon as Henry stood by the X-ray machine, the kids stood by the doctor's side and asked if they could see it, too. The doctor asked them, "Why, what is so great about this?"

Their reply was, "Mommy always tells us that a little child's heart is pure and white, but every time we lie we will get a black spot on it. So we would like to see how black Dad's heart is."

The doctor laughed and told them, "I can't see any white on your dad's heart anymore. But you kids have to realize that Dad is a lot older than you and went through a lot in his life. But if you guys are always honest, then your heart might stay pure forever."

We also needed the required shots, so we all had some rough weeks with fever and feeling lousy. And then was picture-taking time. We needed them for our passports. So many things that had to be done, it was just unbelievable. Every time I turned around there was something else that had to be taken care of.

The USEGO still did not believe we would move. Henry owned the house. I owned the inventory in the store, and I had the contract with the USEGO. But selling our store was almost impossible. Who wants to buy a little corner grocery store? They are out; the big supermarkets are in.

So in January I decided to have a total liquidation sale, and then after that Henry could try to sell the house. I applied and got the okay from the government, starting February 15th I could get rid of everything.

I had a big sale lasting two weeks, selling everything all the way down to the shelves. I did not spend a penny of that money and sent it all to the USEGO to pay part of my loan off, since that was the company that did lend me some money to start my business. It was just so strange that even now they would not respond. Not a phone call, nothing. Yet I still had a contract with them.

Henry's aunt came to pick up my mother-in-law just before February 15, 1968. I felt bad to see her go, but I just did not have the time anymore to take care of her. Plus, we had to sell all our furniture and all my appliances, and after ten years of marriage, one accumulates a lot.

We even sold all our skis, since we thought we would never see snow again. What a mistake, since northern Wisconsin has a lot of snow, but how could we know?

My dad made us two wooden boxes 1.5 yards by 1.5 yards so that I could take my nice china, the feather beds and some other special souvenirs along. We also packed some of Henry's sister's goods into our boxes, and then shipped them by boat.

I had health insurance from little on, but did not know if we could get some in the USA. Every year at least once I battled with strep throat, and the doctors said all along I should have my tonsils removed. So I decided it was high time to do it, as long as I still had insurance.

I went to the hospital and had the surgery. Three days later, when Henry got me home, the police were waiting for me. They locked my store up and took my passport away.

"But why? I can't understand," I asked. They were cold and not helpful at all. All they told me was that I had to appear before the judge the following Friday.

I was so scared and had no idea what I did wrong. Boy, there were some long, sleepless nights. What went wrong? What did I do?

But Friday came and I went to court. The judge took me into his private chamber and told me, "The USEGO is very angry that you gave that store up. They know that they can't do anything, but they will try to make it as miserable as possible for you."

I knew that after someone files for total liquidation it is illegal to buy anything from any wholesaler. The USEGO said I did, but I could prove to the judge that that was not the case. I know the law and I did not break it.

The judge was very helpful, and gave me my passport back. I was in tears by now and asked the judge what he would do if he was in my shoes.

He replied, "This is off the record and I could get in trouble for it." Then he went on, "You got your airplane tickets for next Thursday, the 21st of March, so go straight from here to the travel agent and see if you could leave before that."

I was so thankful I could have hugged him, and yet so scared at the same time. I walked straight down the road to the travel agent and told him I wanted to change our departure date. He found room for all of us on Monday's flight. I put those new airplane tickets and my passport in my purse and home I went, quickly packed the rest of our belongings and then took the train, since we had already sold our car, and got my family to my parents' house. I could hardly sleep that night.

Two long days and two sleepless nights followed, but Monday morning finally came. I got my children up and ready, then packed our last suitcase. Nobody said much, and I felt guilty seeing the sadness and hurt in my parents' eyes. My dad ordered a big taxi to bring us to the airport. But just before we were ready to leave, the phone rang and my dad answered. It was a representative from the USEGO who called, and he said to my dad, "We know when your daughter is leaving and we will stop her at the airport. We will not allow her to leave this country."

I was just shaking, not knowing if my family would have to go alone on this long trip into an unknown world. And what would they do to me, put me in jail?

We made it to the airport and got checked in. I was

constantly looking at every person behind me. My brother and his family also came to say goodbye and to morally support my parents. Everyone was crying. My mother was strong until now, but now she fell to pieces. And my children cried not knowing where they were going and also with the knowledge that they might never, ever see Grandpa or Grandma again.

Lotti was Grandpa's favorite, and he told her a lot about other countries, but especially about Africa, because it was his dream to visit the Serengeti National Park some day. So he told Lotti that the natives there only wear straw skirts. Lotti, seven years old at the time, cried because she did not want to walk around half-naked, not realizing we were going to North America, not Africa.

I felt like the minutes turned into hours, and that waiting got to me, but I had to be strong and show no fear for everybody else's sake. It came loud and clear over the loudspeaker, "We are now boarding the plan taking passengers via Montreal to Chicago." One last kiss and a big, desperate hug to all our loved ones. One more time we had to show the passports and airplane tickets, and on board we went. We stored our belongings away and then patiently waited for takeoff. All I could do was pray.

Then when we finally got off the ground, I felt like a stone was lifted off my shoulders. The USEGO did not know of our decision to take an earlier flight. It was such a relief to leave all of that behind. But I was also scared, since I did not know what the future had in store for us. And that was a good thing.

The plane was packed with passengers. Most of them were tourists and spoke English. One older lady came and talked to us in German. She asked if we were immigrants. I answered, "Yes." She looked at me and said smiling, "Do not worry, you did the right thing. You will never again have to work as hard as you did in your old country." She made me feel good, but, oh boy, how wrong she was!

The plane stopped in Montreal for one hour, then went on to Chicago. We arrived in Chicago about 2 p.m. and then had to wait till 6:30 p.m. to board the small commuter plane that took us to Wausau, Wisconsin. The kids were tired by now, all that excitement, and Switzerland is seven hours ahead of Chicago time, so it was way past their bedtime.

Reto, six years old, had a backpack and on his shoulder a wooden milking pail that Henry got from his yodeling buddies as a goodbye present. As soon as we had to wait someplace in the airport, Reto took the pail from his shoulder, turned it upside down, sat on it and right away fell asleep. I said, "Come on, let's go." He got up and walked, but as soon as we stopped again, back down on this pail he sat. So many people took pictures of him. To them he looked so different. He wore leather pants and had little golden four-leaf clover earrings in his ears.

We finally could board the small plane that went to Milwaukee, Green Bay, Appleton, with final destination Wausau. When we left Switzerland on March 18, 1968, it was a warm spring day, the tulips peeked out of the ground already, and the birds chirped in the trees. My girls wore pretty blue, short-sleeved dresses. Now in Wausau it was cold and ice raining. But even colder than the weather was the welcome we got.

Hans, a Swiss farmer who immigrated four weeks earlier, and Ted Reinhard, the guy who sold Henry the farm, waited for us at the airport. Ted told us before we even got our suitcases that we could not get the farm we bought. "The farmer, Leslie Weber, will not move off the farm," he said. And Hans, who did not even know us, said, "You have to have money to start something here, and the little bit you have gets you nowhere."

It was like someone hit me over the head with a hammer. What now? I had four kids to worry about. They had to have a home and had to be able to go to school. Henry and I did not say one word, just looked at each other, stowed all our belongings in the two cars, and off we went. Ted and Hans drove us to Henry's sister's farm. Martha and her family would not arrive until Thursday night.

Their house was not lived in all winter. It was cold and damp, and nobody even knew how to start the space heater. Ted had put one double bed into every room, beds he got for nothing when the Merrill Hotel burned down the fall before. But he charged us $25 apiece. All we had was a frame and a mattress, no pillows to lie on and nothing to cover up with. And it was so, so cold.

We put the two girls in one bed and the two boys in the other one and covered them up with our coats. Henry and I just cuddled and tried to keep each other warm and give each other comfort.

It was a long, lonely, scary first night in the USA. The kids got up early the next morning, but there was nothing to eat, not even a bread crumb. Neither Hans nor Ted gave it a thought to leave some milk or bread for the children. Hans was Martha's next-door neighbor, so Henry walked up to their farm to see if he would drive us to town to get some food. We had no car, nor did we know where the town was, but our children were hungry.

Hans was an only son. He had three sisters. The older two sisters stayed behind in Switzerland. His younger sister, Maya, came along. His parents just rented a farm overseas, but they had some money. So they decided to help their only son getting started on his own farm in the USA.

Hans' parents came with him to Merrill to help him and his family get started on their new farm. The parents, together with their daughter, Maya, later returned to Switzerland.

Henry knocked on their door. Hans came out and said to Henry, "My dad and I will drive to town soon. We will go and look at some machinery. You want to come along? We will drop you off at the grocery store, but we won't have room for your children." And Hans' mother told Henry, "And don't even think that we will be your free babysitter."

So off we went, leaving our children all by themselves in a strange place and an unknown country. I wanted Henry to go alone, but his response was, "I cannot understand English and do not know what groceries to buy." But then neither did I, but I knew something had to be done. Those kids had to eat.

Hans dropped us off at the Red Owl grocery store and told us he would pick us up in a little while. Into the store we went. It certainly looked different than the ones we were used to. The bread felt like cotton, the butter was salted, even the meat cuts looked different. But we had to eat, so we bought bread, cereal, potatoes and some fruits.

It took awhile to get it all together, but we did it, and through the checkout we went. We never before saw someone bag the groceries for a customer and bring them out to the car. In Switzerland you do that yourself. We packed our goodies into our big handbags that we had along. There was no question everybody in the store could see that we were strangers.

We stood outside the store and waited and waited. It was so cold and windy, and my throat was still sore from the surgery I had just two weeks ago. Hans and his dad did not show up. I was scared. Where are my children? We did not even know our address.

About half an hour passed. We were so cold we were shivering. Then an old man walking on a cane stopped, spoke some High German and asked us if we were lost. He said, "I got time. I can drive you home. Where do you live?"

But Henry and I just looked at each other. We did not know where we lived. The old man did not give up and said, "Get in. I will drive you to Ted. I know him and he will tell us where we have to go."

It was so scary to get into a stranger's car, but we had

no choice. We had to do something. He did just as he said, stopped at Ted's and then drove us to Martha's house. There the children greeted us at the door. They too were scared and they cried, since they had no idea if we ever would come back to them.

We thanked that little old man, whose name was Louis Tesch. Ironically, weeks later, we moved to our own farm, and Louis became our next-door neighbor.

The kids were so hungry and ate those sandwiches I made in no time. I could not cook a meal since there was only a wood stove to cook on, but no wood nor pans to cook with. So we borrowed an axe from a neighbor and went to Martha's woods to gather some firewood. We had to carry it home, since we had nothing to drive. Yet it got the kids tired enough so that they could sleep that second night.

The next morning came and we could not even make coffee. So Henry got hold of Ted, asked him for a small tractor and a wagon. We had to get more wood, since the only stove there was a wood stove.

We also drove the tractor to town to get us at least some pots and pans, cups and plates, since the items we packed up in the wooden boxes and had sent here from Switzerland by boat would not get here for at least another three to four weeks.

We also had to have some pillows and blankets. All of that kept us busy and did not give us much time to feel sorry for ourselves. We knew we had to get going, if only for our children's sake.

Thursday, March 21, 1968, Martha and her family arrived. I took that day to scrub the house from one end to the other, since I knew that Martha would be very, very disappointed. When Albert traveled to the USA the summer before and bought the farm, he took pictures of a beautiful kitchen with an electric stove, refrigerator, and even a freezer and a nice dining room set. He brought those pictures back to Switzerland, and Martha was all excited.

She showed those pictures to everybody and dreamed all winter long of her beautiful kitchen.

Albert asked Ted at the time of the closing if everything stayed the way it was now. Ted said, "Yes, of course." But then Mr. Kienbaum, the seller of the farm, asked Ted if Albert wanted to buy the kitchen appliances. Ted told him, "No, just take everything along. They have enough money to buy new things." Now this was the evening Martha and her family arrived from Switzerland. I was done cleaning, had the house warm and supper ready on the shaky old table, when Ted and Hans drove in with them.

Her four kids ran straight into the kitchen and then behind came Martha. She had a suitcase in her hand, but she dropped it as she stood in the doorway, disbelief painted all over her face. This was not the kitchen she dreamed of. She felt she was at the wrong place.

But then Ted explained that he thought that she'd rather have new appliances. It was a good thing that Martha was tired; I think otherwise Ted would have been thrown out the door. But we all sat down for a hot meal, talked for awhile, and then went on to bed.

On one hand, I felt really sorry for Martha, but on the other hand, felt good that I could ease her pain at least a little bit by having the house warm and the beds ready.

Ted picked Henry and Albert up the next morning and took those two to town. They went car shopping. We were used to walking. My parents in Switzerland never owned a car, but here, walking to town for groceries was way too far.

Those two guys came home with a large, light brown Mercury car. Henry and Albert went to buy the car together, but when it came to paying, Albert said, "Sorry, but all the travelers' checks are in Martha's name, and she is not here to sign them." So Henry ended up paying for it. It was only $500, but all we had was $2,000 to our name, and the $500 made a big dent into our pocketbook, as we had four children to support and no income yet.

Martha's barn needed repair. The block stone wall was ready to collapse. So, since we did not have a place of our own and had to be thankful to live with Martha, Henry went to work. He got trees to jack the upper part of the barn up, knocked the stone wall out, and then built a new block stone wall. The whole east wall had to be replaced. Martha and Albert went to buy cows right away. It did not take a week and they shipped their first milk, and because of our help had an income almost from day one on, unlike us who worked for nothing.

Henry, our four children and I had to sleep in the same bedroom. We had the two double beds that we bought from Ted and all our suitcases under the beds. Yet Martha's house had five bedrooms and they only needed three. But our kids had to go to school, and because of that we had no choice but to stick it out. All of us were so frustrated with everything that happened the last couple of months that no one could think straight anymore.

I felt like a cheap maid. Henry, Albert and Martha went to the barn at 6 a.m. I had to get their three and my four kids up, feed them breakfast, and see to it that they all got on the school bus on time, which sometimes was not an easy thing to do. Little Martha was too young for kindergarten, so she stayed home.

Then I had to clean the table and get breakfast ready for Henry, Martha and Albert. They were hungry when they came in from the barn. While eating, those three talked about what went on in the barn, never including me in their conversation.

One morning they talked about a cow just having a calf one hour ago. Yet, I never saw an animal born and I would have loved to see it. For them it was nothing special, they had seen that so many times already. They never thought of letting me know about it so that I could watch that calf be born. It hurt and was very hard for me, but I had to keep it to myself. I did not want to make it any harder on Henry than it already was. All I had to do was cook, wash and clean, and keep the children in line.

Martha's kids could ride with their dad on the tractor; they were used to that from Switzerland. My boys never sat on a tractor and would have loved to take a ride. Martha never allowed my kids to ride on their tractors. But I think Martha's disappointment had a lot to do with her actions.

All winter long Martha took courses and learned how to weave baskets so that she could decorate her new home. And now everything was so different. Yes, it was tough all around for everybody involved, not just for me.

Henry took Martha and me shopping one day. We bought groceries. No more bread; we baked our own bread by now, but we needed vinegar. Two days later when I made potato salad with, so I thought, vinegar, everybody spit and sputtered. It was apple cider and not vinegar.

We also bought something, or at least so we thought, that looked like extract that we could mix with coffee. That's what we did in Switzerland to stretch the expensive coffee and still give it its dark color. That little package hung right by the coffee. When we opened it at home, we found out that it was some kind of powder to clean the coffee pot and not something you add to the coffee. But how should we know? We could not speak nor read one word of English.

Werner Schmid, who immigrated from Switzerland one year before us, came to visit us one Sunday. He wanted to see how we were all doing. We told him that Ted had the $5,000 that we gave him for the down payment, but we could not get the farm we bought and did not know what to do.

We bought the farm from Ted, so we had to give him the down payment. Ted in turn bought that same farm just hours before he sold it to us, from Leslie Weber, but never gave Leslie one penny. That's why Leslie did not move and we in turn could not get the farm. Leslie wanted $19,000 and Ted sold it to us the same day for $24,000. So the $5,000 down payment was only Ted's profit. Werner told us that Ted is known all over town as a dishonest person. Werner made us understand that if we did not get a lawyer we would never get our money back.

Martha had the idea that we could ask Ted to put our $5,000 toward their farm, and Henry could be their hired man. But we immigrated to this country to own our own farm, and I certainly did not want to be a maid for the rest of my life.

Werner gave us the name of a lawyer, Tom Sazama. He said that that was his lawyer and he thought he was pretty fair. Werner called Tom Sazama and made an appointment for us, but otherwise, and with good reason, wanted to stay out of our confrontation with Ted. And since we did not speak any English, he asked Clarence Kienbaum if he would be our translator. Clarence, too, had German ancestors and still spoke fairly fluent German.

So off to Tom Sazama's office we went. Yes, Clarence spoke German, but I felt he did not translate right. It was not his money and his life that depended on the outcome of this. So I tried, with hand and eye contact, to make Tom understand that to have our own place was very important, especially for Henry. Tom promised to look into it and to do the best he could, but he couldn't make any promises.

It was a couple of days later when Clarence came with a representative from the social services. They explained that since we had four children and no income, we would be eligible for assistance. They told us to come into the courthouse on Thursday afternoon. So Henry drove Martha and me to town, and into the courthouse Martha and I went, Henry waiting outside in the car.

We had to stand in line and wait. Then when it was

our turn, they handed us a box with two big cans of peanut butter (we never had peanut butter before, did not even know what it was). We also got beans, pork in cans, lard and some cornmeal. I never felt so humiliated in my life as I did that day when I walked out of the courthouse. Did we really stand that low that we had to get handouts? I'm used to working hard and, no matter what, always supported myself and my family. No, this is not for me.

As I packed the food into the car, I told Henry that I would never, ever go there again. If he wanted it, he would have to go himself. Martha got assistance for at least a year, but I never stood in line to get handouts again.

We had to go back to Tom Sazama, this time with Ted. Ted would not budge an inch. He said it was not his fault that we did not have more money. The $5,000 we paid him as down payment was only his profit on the farm and he didn't want to give us anything back.

Tom shook his head with unbelief, but then said, "There is nothing I could do about it, and you probably will lose everything." We felt terrible when we left Tom's office that day, and sure did not want to drive back to the farm.

We got into the car and drove east on Highway 64. About six miles out of town was a little rest area with a bench. That's where we stopped. We sat on that lonely old bench, letting our tears freely flow. Where can we go from here? Almost out of money and no home for our children. Who would hire us? We can't even speak English.

But then I got myself together and said to Henry, "Yes, we feel lost, but as long as we are together as a family, there is nothing anybody can do to us. Love and determination will overcome all those barriers."

Henry put his arm around me and kissed me. After daydreaming and building air castles for an hour or so, we gave each other a kiss and promised ourselves we would make it. No matter what, nothing will stop us.

We went back to the car and slowly drove to Martha's

farm where our children were waiting for us. Looking at those happy faces, I knew we had no choice. We had to go on.

Martha taught me how to make bread, and we needed a lot of it. At least every third day we had to bake. And we had only a ringer washer, and there were a lot of clothes to be washed for four adults and eight kids. It seemed that was all I did, wash, clean, cook and bake — a never-ending task.

Easter, a day to celebrate, but without money there is not much we could give our children. Martha had real nice neighbors. Mr. and Mrs. Erich Paul, and their two daughters felt sorry for us, so they colored eggs, bought some candies, and made eight Easter baskets, one for each of ours and Martha's children. And they gave us two chickens and told us to butcher them so that we at least had chicken for Easter.

They gave so freely to us, it was like my grandma used to say, "You have to live religion, and not just show religion." Pauls sure did that. I truly appreciated it and was thankful that the children had an Easter basket. But Martha took one look at the chickens and said, "No, we will not butcher them. They can lay eggs for a while yet." And that was all there was to it.

So our Easter meal was potatoes and vegetables and no meat, but so what, at least we did not go hungry. Grandma's saying also was, "Hard bread is not hard, but no bread is hard."

As I grew up, I was always told if you have to work hard, you have to eat right. My grandma was an example and she was never stingy. But I sure learned different from Martha. Even though they milked their own cows, I could never get more than one gallon of milk per day for the house, and that did not go far with eight children.

We were already one month in the USA when Ted called and said he and Hans would pick us up on Wednesday morning and show us a farm. My hope of owning our own farm perked up. Maybe there was a future for us after all.

They drove into the yard around 10 a.m. Henry and I went into the back seat of the car, me holding on to Henry's rough hand for moral support, and off we went. We drove north on Joe Snow Road, crossed Highway 64, and went north on County Highway E.

It was only five miles from the highway, but it seemed a lot farther to me. There, one mile in on Mail Road, was a small, hilly 80-acre farm. Nobody had lived there for the last two years. The paint on the house was almost gone, and the bare, gray wood showed. It had no furnace, only an oil space heater. It was a small house, no stove, no refrigerator, not even one closet, and the roof was leaking.

The barn was not much better. It had 12 stanchions to tie cows on and two stalls for horses. The manure gutters were full of water because the roof was leaking also. No barn cleaner, but a big manure stack right behind the barn and one of those manure buckets that had to be pulled up and then pushed out on a railroad-like track.

It sure looked grim, but Ted told us in no uncertain terms that if we buy this farm today, he would give us back $2,000 of the $5,000 we gave him as a down payment for the original farm deal. But if we do not sign the papers today, he would keep all the money.

Henry and I talked it over. But we also knew we had no choice. Our children needed a home. So we said okay, we will buy it.

They dropped us off at Martha's and told us to make sure to be at Tom Sazama's at 2 p.m. that afternoon to sign the papers. So Henry and I drove to town determined to take Ted's check, but then not to buy the farm, instead just take the $2,000 and leave town, go south and make a new start somewhere else.

But it did not work out the way we planned. Ted made

the check out right to the real estate person. He must have figured us out. So we had no choice. We had to get that small farm. It sure was not our dream farm, but I guess it was better than nothing.

Edith turned 10 years old the 25th of April, and that was the day we moved onto our own small, hilly 80-acre farm. Martha and Albert went to town the afternoon we left their farm, but we packed the little we had and now finally could move to our own place. It was nothing fancy, but it was ours.

I took a small pitcher of milk along, since we had no cows yet, but I should never have done that. Martha got really mad, and they would not talk to us after than for many, many years. She said it was because of the milk, but I think it was because they lost their help.

Henry went to ask Martha why they were mad and would not talk to us anymore. But she told Henry off, chased him off her land and told him to never come back again. She said, "Henry, you will never amount to anything, and your children will someday pay you back for all the trouble you caused."

That hurt Henry so much. We had such a small farm, no machines and cows yet. No matter how hard I tried, his hurt would not go away. It made him so determined to be a big farmer some day that he could not see how he hurt us on his way there. He said, "I will show her and my other siblings that I can do it, too."

But I could not understand it. Why can't we all live together in peace? Life is so short and life's road so rugged that every smile and every praising word would make it so much easier for everybody around us.

Erich Paul and Clarence Kienbaum knew of somebody who sold a dining room, and also a bedroom set. It was not much, but then it only cost us $25. Erich took his pickup truck and brought it to us and they helped put it up. Then we had coffee and some cookies together. As we ate, they both laughed and said, "That bed is so old, it probably will collapse when you climb in it."

They left a little after nine, but I was scared they would stick around and peek in, since we had no curtains on the windows. I turned all the lights out, then got undressed and slowly crawled into bed. Nothing happened, but then when Henry crawled in, too, the bed fell down in the back and went up in the front. One of the legs broke off.

So we got up again, got dressed and Henry went to the little old shop. He found a piece of old wire and wrapped some around on each of the four legs. We tried it again, and this time it worked. We slept in that bed every night for the next ten years.

Clarence came around a lot and took Henry to implement dealers to check the machinery out, and then also to farmers to look at cows. The first Saturday that we lived on our farm was an auction, and those two went there. Thorp Finance Company was in charge of it.

Henry talked to Mr. Peterson, who also spoke a little German. He was the manager for the Thorp Finance Company, a really nice, understanding, older man. He let Henry bid on and buy a total of 12 cows.

We didn't have that kind of money, but through Thorp Finance we only had to pay one-fourth down and could pay the rest in monthly payments. Yes, that interest is higher than a regular bank, but there was no other finance institution that would lend us any money. As soon as they knew we bought through Ted, bankers would not even talk to us anymore. So Henry bought our first 12 cows and paid a total of $3,200, and we only had to pay $800 down.

Henry brought the 12 cows and the newborn calf home late that afternoon. One real pretty, small black cow gave birth to a heifer calf only a half hour after Henry bought her. That had to mean that our luck was turning now, and I named that calf "Heidi." We had Heidi for a little over 14 years and she gave us a lot of good offspring.

I never milked a cow, never was even close to a cow before, but I tried to help Henry that first night. He also bought one Surge milk machine at that auction to make milking easier. He didn't want to milk all those cows by hand. Yet, he did not know too much about that milk machine himself, but eventually he figured it out. Yes, they were not the best cows. Most of them had mastitis and gave very little milk, but they were ours and I was so proud of them.

Willi, one of our countrymen, walked into our barn that night. He was looking for a farm that he could buy, and he was at the same auction as Henry, and because of that knew that we bought some cows. He sure was no comfort.

Willi made nasty remarks and told us, "Those cows should be shipped to the butcher shop. They are no good and I would have never bought them, but then one has to have money to get good ones, and I guess you guys don't have much." That was really not what Henry wanted or needed to hear, but it did not bother me. I was determined to make a go of it.

We carried the milk to the milk house, then put the milk through a strainer into cans, cooled them overnight with running, cooled water, and then brought them to town the next morning. No milk plant would drive that far out for that little bit of milk, but we could bring the milk to the Page Milk Company, putting the cans in the trunk of the old Mercury car Henry bought just weeks before.

Our first milk check, which was for the milk we shipped on April 30, 1968, was $4.28. It was not much, but I was in Seventh Heaven. We finally had a milk check, an income, and it could only go uphill from now on.

We had 12 cows now, but could only milk nine cows with the milk machine, since the vacuum line didn't go any farther. So three had to be milked by hand. I had to learn how to milk from day one on. Henry always had something going on, or Clarence took him somewhere.

It was so hard for me to milk the three cows by hand, and with every stroke of milk I pulled out, I promised myself, if Henry walks into the barn now I will scream at him and tell him that it wasn't fair to leave me do the barn all by myself. It was just too much work for me alone. I was not used to that.

But Henry knew better. He would never show up until I was done with all the barn work and the milk house was clean. He knew that I would not say anything then. I felt the work was done, no use to holler at him anymore, it wouldn't help anyway.

But, looking back, there would have been an easier way of milking the three cows. I could have let out three cows that were already milked, and then tied the other three in their place. That way I would never have had to milk any one by hand. But I guess that was too easy. Henry said the three are milked by hand, that was it, and I did not question. I was so dumb and didn't understand anything about farming back then, so I did whatever I was told.

I just loved the place we lived on. It was not much of a farm, but we owned it and I felt so proud. I could watch the little cottontails hopping right up to the house and nibbling on anything they could find. The deer were looking for food close by the barn, and there were so many beautiful birds, real small yellow ones that looked just like the canaries my parents used to have. And then the blue jays, my favorite birds.

For the first time in my life I saw a skunk. They are pretty, black animals with a white stripe on their back, but boy, their smell sure makes your eyes water. And then at night, the fireflies. I could not believe how they can sparkle, just like little stars. It felt as if I lived in a fairyland. But the one thing I could have done without were the mosquitoes. They are terrible little creatures, and it seemed they came by the millions, especially in the evening. Yes, we have mosquitoes in Switzerland, but not that many. There we never had screens in front of the windows.

Henry went with Clarence to see different farms and here and there bought a cow or two, all financed through Thorp Finance. So slowly but surely we got more milk and it got to be too much to take to town. The milk plant offered us 20 cents more per 100 pounds of milk if we would buy a bulk tank. PCA (Production Credit Association) finances the tanks, we were told, and all they take as payment was the extra 20 cents. We felt that was a good deal and bought a 250-gallon tank.

From then on we carried milk to the milk house and dumped it into the strainer. From there it went into the tank and got cooled right away. Then Tom came every other day with his big truck and sucked the milk out of our tank. Boy, what an improvement! We really were modern now. No farmer in Switzerland has a milk tank like ours.

Our first used tractor was an Oliver. We also bought an old two-bottom plow. Henry tried to plow, but the plow just did not go into the ground. The ground was stony and very, very hard because that part of our land was never plowed before. So Henry made me sit on the plow for hours, just to make the plow a little heavier. But after we were done with the field, I could not sit on a chair for days, my butt hurt so bad.

After the plowing was done, stones had to be picked. There were many, many stones. And, again, Clarence picked Henry up daily to look at things to buy. It was silly, since we had no money anyway, but it seemed that did not bother those two. That left me picking stones for many, many days all by myself, and I was not used to working so hard, and in the fresh air all day long.

Yet, that gave me time to daydream. Why did we do this? What if we would not have left our homeland? Would it be better? Tears rolling slowly down my cheeks made my eyes cloudy. I rested for awhile, sat down and let nature take over. There was a chipmunk looking for food close by. A deer brought her little fawn through the brush and into the open meadow to feed on the light green, young grass. Birds were singing and the swallows were building a nest in one of the small, rundown barns. I asked myself how could I be sad with so much beauty all around me. I dried my eyes, got up and kept on picking stones.

Our house, the barn, our cows and me milking.

Edith, Heinz, Loti and Reto try their luck with the barrel.

Lotti holding the dog, "Debby"; Reto on the pony and Heinz holding on to it. The kids did not have much to play with on the farm, but they seemed happy.

Heinz with a kitten. Lotti has the cat. Reto thinks the dog needs glasses, too.

8

Count each blessing,
not each tear.
Count on God's love
to be near.

LOUIS, OUR NEIGHBOR, came with his two horses and a wagon the following weekend and helped us. Henry, our four children and I picked stones, while Louis drove the wagon. Louis was crippled already. He had hip and knee joints replaced. Because of that he had a hard time getting on the wagon. Twice he fell off, right between those two big horses. He just said, "Whoa, whoa, whoa," grabbed their tails and slowly pulled himself up. It was just so amazing, not one of those horses lifted a leg until he was back on the wagon and told them to get going.

We got done picking stones that day. I sure thought that was it. But we had a rain for the next two days, and after that Henry dragged the field again, and there were just as many, if not more, stones than before. There I went again, picking stones. I never complained to my parents or told them in my letters how tough we had it. I told them only of the beauty of nature all around us, and that I wished my dad could be here with his camera. But after three weeks picking stones, I wrote in one of my letters that if this keeps up and I have to pick stones like this, then I could build the Swiss mountains right in my back yard.

The field was finally ready to be planted, but we had no corn planter, nor could we afford one. So Henry went to our neighbor, Eddie Hass, and asked him if we could borrow his corn planter. Henry tried the little bit of English he learned so far, but Eddie, who also has a German background, looked at Henry and said, "I think you would be better off speaking in German, so I might be able to understand." There was no problem. Eddie helped us out so that we finally could plant our corn.

Heinz, who just turned nine, had to step in and do hard man's work right from the beginning. He had to hook the corn planter up for Dad, but got caught by one of the hydraulic arms. It ripped a piece of meat out of his handball right behind his right thumb. His dad looked at it and said, "You're so stupid it is pathetic. Now this will teach you to be more careful next time."

There was not even time for a Band-Aid. We had to load the corn on the wagon and get going. But that is the way Henry was taught when he was a child. That is what his grandpa did to him, and now he does the same to his son. Yet, deep down, I could never understand that; if something hurt you so bad, then how could you do the same thing to another human being, especially someone you love?

Edith, Lotti and Reto could not help with the field work more than picking stones, so they were home all day long by themselves. We went and bought a TV for $30. We did it for them, but it also helped us a lot. That is how I learned most of my English. As long as I could see the facial expression, I could figure out what they were saying.

The Beverly Hillbillies, Gomer Pyle and Green Acres were my favorite shows. The woman (Zsa Zsa Gabor) in Green Acres said she could only drive a "prndl" car, which I now know is an automatic car, and it shows P for park, R for reverse, N for neutral, D for drive, and L for low, which makes "prndl"; and she was right. We had a car just like that.

I loved country western shows and could never get enough of them. Some of my favorite singers were Loretta

Lynn, Anderson, Porter Waggoner, and especially Johnny Cash, with his song "Detroit City," where it says "if you could read between the lines." That always brought tears to my eyes, since at least every other week I sent a letter home, and I was so glad that my parents could not read between the lines. They would never have believed what their daughter had to do. We never saw baseball or football played before, but even Henry got into those sports on TV.

Henry bought more cows. One of them was pretty close to calving. I watched her very closely, as I wanted to be there when she gave birth since I never saw an animal born before.

One afternoon I was home alone and she started calving. I sat by her, rubbing her back and talking to her. "Don't worry," I said. "I stay right here and I will help you." Every time she pressed, so did I. I was so emotionally involved, as if I would give birth myself.

I do not know how much time passed, but the water broke and two tiny hooves came out. I was holding onto them very carefully, and every time she pressed, I pulled. The calf slipped out. I took some fresh straw, dried the calf a little, and then pulled it up to the cow's head so that she could start licking it. The cow stood up and seemed to feel no pain, but I had such a terrible stomach ache from all that pushing I could hardly stand straight.

Yes, I was so overwhelmed at how independent that little calf was. Within minutes it tried to stand up, and an hour later felt around to find the udder to get some fresh milk. It is so unbelievable — we have to nurse a child for almost a year until it tries its first steps, and a calf can do it within one hour. What an experience that was!

The Merrill school system was a big help, and I'm very grateful that they cared so much. The school bus came all summer long, three days a week, and picked the children up. They were taken to a greenhouse, a TV station, and a grocery store. There they taught them English right on the spot. One teacher, Mrs. Ranke at Scott School where most of the new immigrants went to school, spoke some German. She was just great, and a very, very big help. I'm truly grateful to her.

We needed a mower and a baler to make hay, so Henry went to Midland Co-op one day and found something that was not too expensive. The Credit Union had a small office in the same building and they financed it for us, or we could never have gotten it. We were simply out of money.

Soon it was time to cut the first hay. Our tractor ran good as long as we did not have to use the power takeoff. But when we hooked the mower and the crimper up, then we needed the power takeoff. Once around the field and we had to fix it. The clutch for the power takeoff just would not hold together. I had never driven a tractor, but I sure learned how to take this one apart.

The sickle on the mower was mounted onto the side of the tractor, but it was old and could not be lifted up anymore at the corners. There was only one way out, at least in Henry's perspective. I had to run behind the mower, and when Henry got to the corner, I had to lift the sickle up so that he could take the corner without getting off the tractor. He could let it down using the hydraulic. And then, off to the next corner we went. I made many, many miles running around the 40-acre field.

The grass was dry enough to be side-raked. Henry told me, take the tractor and the side-rake and rake the hay, but make sure the rows are straight. I answered, "How can I? I can't even drive the tractor." But looking at Henry, I knew he meant every word he said.

The tractor was running when I sat back into the seat. Henry said, "Look, this is the brake," and then from the ground shifted into second gear, and off I went. I screamed, "I can't do it. I can't do it. I will jump off!" But Henry's eyes were cold, and something told me I'd better stay on it.

It was tough. My heart was pounding and I was so scared that I would not do the job to Henry's satisfaction. But I got it done, and then was kind of proud of myself, after I took one last look at those fluffy, pretty, straight rows.

The next day we started pressing the dried grass into bales. Henry never made hay that way before either. At their farm in Switzerland, the haying was done differently. The guys cut the grass by hand with the sickle, then the women raked the hay. The guys then put the loose, dry hay into bundles and carried them on their backs into the barn. Here it wasn't done that way. Henry was told by Willi and Hans that the bales had to be very, very tight.

He hooked the tractor to the baler, then the baler to the hay wagon, and off we went. After we arrived at the field, Henry told me to drive the tractor so that the baler could catch the rows. He said, "Make sure you look back to the wagon and check if I can keep up."

I tried very hard, yet I just could not do that. As long as I looked straight ahead, I was okay, but as soon as I looked back to see how he was doing piling the bales, my hands turned the steering wheel and I would drive a row or two farther over. I just couldn't stay at a straight line. I simply could not follow the rows. It would not work the way it should have.

Henry got mad, jumped off the wagon and stopped the tractor. He said, "If you're so stupid and can't even stay with the rows, then you go on the wagon and pile the bales and I will drive." I was ready to cry, but on the wagon I went, without saying one word.

The bales were so heavy I could hardly lift them, let alone pile them. So every time Henry could not see it, I loosened the press a little and the bales got lighter and lighter. I was pretty proud of myself. I had half the wagon loaded already. Then Henry took a corner and gone were the bales. They were so loose that almost all of them fell off the wagon. And that did not go over well at all, and I heard some choice words.

We had to take the baler twine off the bales and send the hay through the press again. "Those bales have to be hard as a rock," Henry said.

What a job! My tears were rolling. "Why can't I do things right? Why do I have to get Henry angry all the time?" But I had to get on the tractor and try to drive along the rows again, and this time it worked a little better. I saw a hawk soaring in the blue sky. Oh, how I wished I could be him, just flying away from all my troubles.

We drove the hay wagon home. Edith, Lotti and Reto had to help unloading the wagon. Henry and Heinz piled the bales. It was a hard job for the kids, but I was sure thankful for their help. If it wasn't for my children, I would have given up. Farming was a lot harder than I ever imagined, but there was no turning back. We had to keep on trying and do the best we can.

The girls had to learn how to cook and keep the house clean. It was not always easy, and sometimes they quickly stored everything away. Clean or not clean, all the dishes went into the cabinet when they saw me coming up from the barn. But somehow Mother always found out and made them do it over again.

Henry surely knew his cows and reacted to every need of theirs. If he could hear one noise at three, four, five o'clock in the morning, he jumped out of bed to see what was wrong, and I had to be right behind him. I was not used to work outside, and I was so tired. So often when I milked in the morning I leaned my head against the cow's warm stomach and closed my eyes just for a minute or so to take a catnap. But I had to listen for Henry's footsteps, since if he had caught me sleeping I would have heard a word or two.

We were so busy that we had hardly time to go grocery shopping. Every time I asked Henry if he would please take the time and drive me to town, his answer was always the same. "I got no time today. There has to be something in the kitchen cabinets that you could use to make another meal."

But there just was nothing left. So one day I sat in the car. My heart was pounding, but I turned the key and started the car, put it in gear, and off I went. I left the children at home, since I thought should I get into a wreck, then at least it was only me that would get hurt.

I took all the back roads, and as soon as I saw a car come toward me, I drove out to the soft shoulder and waited, let the other car pass and then proceeded. Thank God, the IGA store was on our end of town. What a disaster if I had to drive all the way through town!

I got my groceries and returned home in one piece, without even a scratch on the car. I tried again and again, and it got easier as time went on.

The car was not running right, and Henry had to fix it all the time. Then one Sunday morning on the way to visit Willi Rusch he did not see the car coming over the hill, the brush in the ditch covered his view, so he ran into the side of the oncoming car. A good thing his English wasn't good, since the lady driver of the other car screamed at Henry, but he did not understand a word she said.

The police came and made out the report. The policeman asked Henry for proof of insurance. Henry showed him the slip that the car dealer gave him when he bought the car, but that was not for the insurance. That only stated that if something goes wrong with the motor for the first three months they would give us a 40% discount. But how should we know? Nobody in Switzerland gets a license plate without proof of insurance. The car dealer ordered the license plates for us, and so we thought the insurance was included.

A couple of weeks after Henry's accident we got a certified letter saying we owed this lady $900 for damages, plus pain and suffering $900, which we did not have, but if we did not pay, Henry would have to surrender his driver's license, and that got him scared. He still drove with his Swiss driver's license.

We went to Tom Sazama again to see if he could help us. It took only one letter from him and the bill got reduced to $350. Even that was tough, but we had to pay it. It also said that we had to take the driver's test and get a Wisconsin driver's license within the next 30 days. That meant a lot of studying, especially on Henry's part.

Henry also decided to sell our car and buy a better one. Our new car no longer was an automatic. Now it was a stick shift. That's what Henry always drove before, but for me it was a brand-new ball game. This time Henry gave me driver's lessons. He made me parallel park or park on the hill by the courthouse. It was just so hard and he was so strict. I ended up in tears almost every time we drove together. One time I put the car in park and got out of the car. "I will walk home. I will never drive with you again," I told Henry. But deep down I knew I had to try again, since I wanted my own driver's license.

Two weeks later we went for our test. Henry, because he was driving for so many years already, could do it all in one day. I had to take the written test first, and then ten days later the driving test. Henry could hardly read English, but the guys who did the testing were very helpful. They let me translate the questions into German for Henry. Without their help, we could never have done it. But we both got our driver's license after the first attempt. Thank God, one more obstacle behind us.

The baler, a machine we needed to press our hay, just did not hold up through all the hard work it had to do. We were constantly fixing something. First the needle broke that brings up the twine. When that was new, the board that pushes the hay over broke. After we fixed that, then the rest did not fit anymore. And it was hard to get parts because it was such an old machine.

So one day I said to Henry, "We cannot go on like this; if we really wanted to farm we have to have decent equipment. Go see if you can get something reasonable that can do the job for us."

So Henry went to the Midland Co-op and bought a brand-new New Holland baler. It was late in the season and we could by the baler with only the trade-in off the old machine and the balance interest-free until April 1969. I had no idea how we would pay for it then, but at least we could get our crops in now and worry about the rest later.

The dealer also had a brand-new Allis Chalmers tractor, a "One-Seventy," with about 50 horsepower for $4,800. The same deal, no payments until the following spring. I figured as long as we go in debt anyway, why not go all the way, since we had a lot of field work to do yet. We had to spread the manure. That was very important, since that was the cheapest fertilizer we could have. And all the fields were in desperate need of it. The next day Henry started working with his brand-new toys, and he was just in Seventh Heaven.

Willi Rusch found a farm just a couple of miles from us. He started farming here, leaving his wife and children behind in Switzerland. Willi had only one arm. He lost his left arm in an accident in the factory he worked at while still in Switzerland.

It was very hard for us to start farming here, and it had to be even harder for Willi. Willi had a lot more money than we had, but he was an invalid, so everybody felt sorry for him. All the neighbors came and helped him make hay.

Then he stopped by us one day and said that all his furniture he had shipped here from Switzerland arrived. We never could have shipped our furniture here. We needed that money for our plane tickets. He had the money, but needed the help. So he asked us, if we would please come and help him. For many nights we went to Willi's place after we got done in the barn. We unpacked everything. I washed and folded all the clothes and put them in the dressers. I could imagine how hard it must be for Annemarie, Willi's wife, to come here to an unknown world with five young children. I felt I had to make it as easy as possible for her. Annemarie and her children arrived on July 28th, and because of all our help they could feel right at home.

The first of August is Switzerland's Independence Day. Werner Schmid invited all the Swiss to come to his farm and celebrate this day, together with his family. We made brats on the grill, had potato salad, beer and soda. Werner made a big bonfire and all of us sat around it and sang.

It was a beautiful clear summer night. The stars spread their magic all over us. We sang songs we learned in school, songs from our homeland, the mountains and the sunny meadows. Henry yodeled and for just a couple of hours it felt like home.

All summer long every time my dad and our friends overseas went mountain climbing they sent us a postcard. They wrote a little note and everyone signed the card. But that got Henry so upset. He would not even read the card. He felt they did it in spite, just to get him upset. Henry was so homesick and missed his mountains so much, but we did not have enough money to go back. And, no question about it, pride stood in the way, too. He never could have gone back to our homeland, showing everybody that it did not work out for us, and then, listening to his siblings saying, "We told you all along, you amount to nothing."

Why did it have to be so hard to be accepted as the plain, good, hard-working person he was? Why was it that only a dollar sign seemed to prove how good you are?

In Switzerland Henry always said, "If I just could farm, that is all I ever want, and I would be happy for the rest of my life." Now he had his farm — not the best one, but it was a farm — and now he missed his mountains. He was hurting so bad, and I felt so sorry for him. But I could not help him at all. I only could stand by his side and try to do the best job I could.

The children were back in school, and the leaves started turning into so many beautiful colors. It was a sure sign that old winter was just around the corner. We were almost done with our field work. The corn had to be chopped yet, but we had no chopper. Eddie Hass said they would do it for us. It was not that much, only a little over two acres, and the cows got through the fence a couple of times and stamped some of the corn down.

Eddie's two boys came one Saturday. They both had a hangover, and each of them wanted the easiest job. So Tom gave in and said, "Okay, I will unload." That meant Brian had to chop the corn. But Brian drove round and round the field while Tom took a nap sitting by the silo. We got a whole two silo wagons full of corn off that field. For us it was better than nothing. But Tom and Brian never forgot that day. Brian thought he had one over Tom. He could take it easy driving, but he had to drive all afternoon while Tom could sleep by the silo.

Whenever we had some time through the summer, we worked on the barn, ripped the horse stalls out and added stanchions so that we could have more cows, and we needed more vacuum line for the milk machine, as I sure didn't want to milk by hand anymore.

We bought a Montgomery Ward cement mixer. I had to shovel sand, gravel and cement into the mixer and mix it. Heinz had to wheel, wheelbarrow by wheelbarrow full, into the barn, and Henry poured and leveled it. It was hard work, but it was worth it. We could never have gotten the money to pay someone to do that job for us.

We had, like so many times before, little or no money. Often late at evenings I sat on the cement step by the front door looking at the buffalo nickel that was cemented into the 1.5 foot by 2 foot cement plaque just below the step. The buffalo nickel symbolized that whoever lived in this house never will run out of money. No matter what, they will always have that nickel. Me, daydreaming as I eyed up that buffalo nickel, wished it would multiply. I did not want much, just enough money to get through that long first winter. But those dreams did not become a reality.

The feed mill was looking for some seasonal help, so Henry decided to go to work for them. He had to start at 7 a.m. That did not leave him much time to help me with the barn work in the morning, but he made around $80 a week, and that paid for the food and a lot of other things we needed.

The kids also had to be on the school bus at seven, and after that I was on my own to milk the cows, clean the milk house and then the barn. We had no automatic barn cleaner. There was a track that was mounted to the ceiling, a bucket with wheels hanging on it, and a chain to let the bucket down. I let it down to the floor, took the fork and filled the bucket with manure, then hoisted it up and pushed it out of the barn, and dumped it into the manure spreader.

It took me two or three attempts, if the wind was strong from the east, to get lined up with the spreader so that I could run up the 25-foot-long, 2-inch-thick board. Sometimes I made it halfway up, slipped off the board and then had to start all over again.

It was a tough job, and there was lots of manure, since by now we had 30 cows and 12 calves. Most of the time it was around noon when I got back to the house, tired and hungry. I made myself a hot cup of milk, put a teaspoon of instant coffee in it, and cut myself a couple slices of homemade bread, and sat down on the chair. But so often I fell asleep while eating, just dropping my head right on the dining room table. I still was not used to all that hard work.

A little black cow had a calf one Saturday morning. Everything went fine, or at least so I thought. But the cow would not get up. After hours of trying, we called the veterinarian. His secretary said the vet would be there shortly, so we waited and waited. Another hour and no vet. Henry got impatient, took the car and drove to town to go and see if he could find him. But while Henry was gone, the veterinarian came, checked the cow and told me, "She has milk fever, and she needs liquid calcium right into her blood veins."

I had to help him, and I watched every detail. By the time Henry came home, the cow was on her feet again. The next time a cow had milk fever, Henry said, "You saw how it is done, you do it. You know we can't afford the vet."

And so I did. It was scary for the first couple of times, but I knew how much the veterinarian charged, and we sure could not afford that. In time I got pretty good at it. We always had the bottles of calcium on hand from that day on. I said so many times, if I could be young again I would become a veterinarian. It is so rewarding to help the animals and make them feel better again.

My children did well in school. In fact, Edith, who was in third grade when we came to the USA, made one-half a year in fourth grade and then was put into fifth grade for the second half of the school year. English came easy to my children, since they were taught Romansch in Switzerland, and the schools in Europe are ahead in mathematics.

I wanted to get involved in the school, too, since I wanted to know how my children progressed, so I joined the PTA. Soon after I became a PTA member that fall, they elected a new board, and I, out of all people, was voted in as secretary. How could I, I hardly speak and I sure couldn't write in English.

But everybody said there is only one way for you to learn how to write, and that is to take this job. I had a lot of support from my daughter Edith. With the help of my dictionary, I wrote what went on at the meetings, and then

Edith corrected it for me.

We had a benefit dance for the Scott School PTA the following spring. In my next report I wrote how successful the dance was. When Edith corrected my spelling, she almost fell off the chair laughing. "What is so wrong?" I asked. Her reply was, "You spelled successful 'sexesful.' "

It is easy for her, but so hard for me to learn a new language. In German if I say a word slow, I can spell it out with no problem, but not in English. It is so much harder. But we came to the USA out of our own freewill, and so we have to learn how to read, write and live the way they do here. And that is a promise I made to myself. At least I will try my best.

We had records with Swiss music on it, but no record player to play them, nor could we afford one. But then one week before Christmas we got a big package from my parents. What could that be, I thought. Henry opened the package, and to our surprise there was a portable record-player.

We had no idea that Edith wrote a letter to my parents, telling them how homesick her dad was and how much he would love to listen to the records. So they gave us the biggest surprise ever. Nothing could have made Henry happier than to be able to listen to his yodeling records.

Christmas was here, but I had no money. Heinz and Reto got a tree out of our woods, and Edith and Lotti decorated the tree with the few lights and Christmas ornaments I got and some of the chocolate ornaments Grandma sent from Switzerland. I bought four bags of different kinds of candy, opened them up, mixed them, and then made four bags again, and that was all our children got for Christmas that year. I told them that they always have to remember, the biggest present of all is that we are healthy and that we all can be together.

We got invited to Willi Rusch's for Christmas Eve. Willi and his family are Catholic. The hospital in Merrill is

Catholic also and was built in the early 1920s by nuns who immigrated from the Monastery Ingenbohl in Switzerland. The nuns felt sorry for Willi and his family and started a collection in church. Willi got three turkeys, two hams, cans of fruits and vegetables by the cases. It was just unbelievable.

Their five children each got a huge stack of toys, but they would not give a single toy to my children, after everything we did for them. Willi even got a nice big rug for his living room, but he did not like the color, so he used it to cover up his tractor. We had no rug in our living room, and I would gladly have given him a couple of dollars for it.

I was not jealous, but to see all of that waste was awful. It was especially hard on my children. They could not understand why Rusch's children got so much, and they only got a small bag of candy. If I had known that before, we would not have gone to Willi's to celebrate Christmas Eve.

Breitenmosers, Roths, Haltinners and us, all new immigrants also, belonged to the St. Paul's Lutheran Church, and there they did not have a collection for us, which was fine, since it was a small country church, and most of the younger couples struggled themselves. But it proves once more that if one gets too much for free they get spoiled and do not appreciate the little things in life anymore.

My parents wrote in their Christmas letter that they would try to call us on New Year's Eve. I could hardly wait to hear their voice again. But it started snowing the day before, a wet, heavy snow, and it snowed and snowed. The telephone wires got heavier and heavier. I hoped and prayed that they would at least hold up until after the important phone call from our homeland came through. And my prayers were answered. At 5 p.m., just before we went to the barn, the phone rang. In Switzerland the New Year had just begun, since they are seven hours ahead of us.

It was the first time since we left our homeland that

we could talk to my parents, and it sounded as close as if we called our neighbor. We did not talk long, since each and every one of us wanted to say a few words. They wished us lots of luck for the future, and that is something we sure needed.

The board of the vocational school decided to give all of the new immigrants a chance to learn English. They hired Otto Bacher to teach us the language and a little about the culture. Otto, an immigrant himself, was a man in his early 70s, a retired school teacher. He was 11 years old when he and his family immigrated to America, the land of the greatest opportunities.

We took advantage of that chance to learn English and met once a week with some of the other immigrants. Otto was a great guy. He took us to the "A&W Drive-In" to have a root beer float, something I never tasted before, but really liked; or he took us to a restaurant where he taught us English right on the spot. He held up a fork and asked, "What is that?" — then a spoon or a cup. The other customers who stopped in for a late snack got a kick out of listening to us trying to speak English. It was tough, but Otto did not give up and had a lot of patience. Thanks, Otto. You were great!

The snow was melting slowly and the sun got warmer. I had the cows out every day all winter long. They were always quick to come back into the barn. But now that it got a little warmer, they stood around and let the sun warm their backs.

It was the end of April and Henry no longer went to work at the feed mill. He had to get the machines ready. Then it was soon time to start with the field work. We also had to find a bank that would give us the money that we owed on the tractor and the baler. So we went to the PCA (Production Credit Association), a farmer-owned lending institution, and they now were willing to help us. What a relief that was!

One day we were just done eating lunch when the phone rang. It was Eddie Hass. He asked Henry to come right away to help him to get Willi out of the silo. Willi's silo unloader got stuck, so he went up to the silo, telling his five-year-old son to push the start switch when he told him to, and then wait until he hollered again to press the stop button. But after the little guy started the unloader, he wandered off and forgot all about his dad. Willi tried to pull the running unloader to the center, but then slipped with one foot and got caught in the chain. He screamed and screamed, hoping his son would turn the loader off, but his son went into the house.

It was a good thing that Willi wore heavy Swiss army boots that choked the motor off, but not before it took his pants and all the meat on his left leg off. It went all the way down to the bone.

He yelled and yelled until his wife Annemarie, who was about eight months pregnant at the time, could hear him. But she was in no condition to crawl up the silo to see what happened. She ran to the phone and called Eddie and Eddie called us.

Eddie and Henry went there and crawled up to the silo chute to get Willi out, while the ambulance waited to get him to the hospital. Willi was in tough shape, and Annemarie was to have a baby in four more weeks and unable to take care of the cows.

But what could be done? We knew somebody had to help. Henry offered to milk their cows until Willi could take over again, which meant my children and I had to take care of our cows, and by now we had 32 cows of our own. It was tough for all of us.

One week after Willi's accident, Mr. Nollan, who financed Willi's farm, stopped at our farm and told Henry that he should get everything ready for an auction. Willi was behind in payments, and now, after this, for sure unable to farm. But Henry would not do such a thing. He told Mr. Nollan, "There will be no auction as long as Willi is in the hospital. Whatever you do after he comes home is up to you. But for now I'm in charge of this place, and nothing will be sold." Mr. Nollan accepted Henry's decision and no longer interfered.

Annemarie gave birth to her son, Willi Junior, while Willi Senior was still in the hospital. I drove Annemarie to the doctor and wherever she had to go. I also took her to the different bankers and let them know that it was impossible for her to make some payments now, but that they would take care of all that as soon as Willi got back on his feet again.

Eddie and some of the other neighbors came and plowed Willi's fields and planted the crops, while Henry had to do our field work in between. It was tough, but it all got done. Willie was in the hospital for seven long weeks, but now could come home. He had to walk on a cane for quite some time.

But Willi was not home more than a week when he told Henry that he wanted to look at a 200-acre farm by Gleason, and Henry should drive him there. He said he was thinking of buying a different farm, yet he could not even make the payments on the $55,000 farm he had, and the one he looked at was almost $100,000. I could never understand the logic behind it. What was even worse was that Henry started thinking we should have a better, bigger farm, too.

So we went to look at farms, a 200-acre farm by Edgar. The house wasn't good either. It had a newly remodeled barn, but the farmer wanted all the money up front, and we did not have that kind of money. Then we looked at one by Deerbrook, a beautiful house with fireplace. The barn was not too bad, but the land was kind of low and wet. Henry would not go for that.

All summer we went at least once a week to look at a different farm. Then we checked on a farm out by Marathon City. It was a real nice place, and the farm couple even offered to sell the farm on land contract. They were about Henry's age, but just inherited a lot of money. That was why they wanted to sell the farm and just take life easy.

Henry was excited, and even I thought that might be the thing to do. But we asked them to give us a little time to think about it. We went home and back to work, but that farm was on our minds, all we talked about.

One week had passed when that same farm couple came to visit us and wanted to know if we had made decision yet. I still see them driving into our yard. They got out of their car and looked around. Then the missus looked at me and said, pretty stuck up, "And this you call a farm?"

She could have slapped me in the face, it would not have been any worse. I was so proud of what we did to this place. For her to come here and cut us down that way was not right. I made up my mind right then and there not to buy their farm. Even if they had given us their farm for free, I would not have wanted it. They had to be cold human beings to hurt somebody else's feelings that bad. Henry was still interested, but told them that he will give them an answer soon.

Henry and I went later that day to check out one of our corn fields. That is when I told Henry that I would never sign the papers to buy that farm; that woman hurt me more than she would ever know.

I also told Henry that if we would take the time we spent looking and talking about other farms and turn that into productive time and improve our farm, we would be better off and money ahead. We could never sell our farm and did not have the money to buy another one, so what was the use to even think about it or dream of a bigger place?

Fall was here again and Henry had no time anymore to look at farms. He went back to work at the feed mill.

Hans got his feed there, too, and he said to Henry one day, "You're just a moonshine farmer. You can never stay farming and working through the day. It will not work." That really hurt Henry.

But three years later, after Henry quit working at the feed mill and stayed home to farm full-time, Hans ended up working there. Once again it shows what goes around comes around.

Grace Hass talked me into joining the Homemakers' Club. She said that was the best way to get to know most of my neighbors. I knew I had to get out, as my English still was not too great and the cows didn't speak the new language, so I agreed to go with her.

Grace took me along to a planning committee meeting for our spring Husband and Wife Party. I volunteered to drive, since I had to go past her house anyway. It was about 10:30 p.m. when we got back. We sat in the car and talked awhile before she got out. She knew that I didn't have it easy and thought if she told me a little bit about her life on the farm it might make me feel better.

We were still talking when a cattle truck drove up and the driver got out. In a broken English he asked if we could tell him where Willi Rusch lived. He had to deliver a couple of cows.

Curious, I asked him for his name. He said, "Julius Bach," and that he was Swiss, just like Willi. "I'm Swiss, too," I said, and told him my name, and then gave him directions to Willi's place, which was only a half a mile to the east. Then I said goodnight to Grace and went home.

The next morning Martha (Henry's sister), who did not talk to us since we left them, called. Now that Willi put her up to it and she thought she could hurt Henry again, she had the nerve to interfere in our lives again.

I was in the milk house washing the milk equipment when she called. Henry talked to her, and then when he came down to the milk house was angry and slammed the door. "Why," I thought, "what did I do wrong now?"

He asked, "Who was in your car last night? You said you were going with Grace. Instead you were seen parking with a guy."

I told Henry exactly what happened, but he did not believe me. He was jealous by nature, and that was gas on his fire. But I knew I did nothing wrong, and I felt I had to prove it. So I got Julius' telephone number and called him. I did not tell him why, I just said, "Since we are countrymen, I would like to invite you and your family to come for a visit and have lunch with us next Sunday."

"We have no other plans and will gladly accept your invitation," he replied.

The closer it got to Sunday, the more I was upset. I would not let anybody know how bad I felt, but it sure nagged inside of me. I felt dirty, I guess, because of my childhood and what my uncle did. The only man who ever mattered in my life was Henry. Then why does everybody think I'm after every man that crosses my path? Why can't I get free of that feeling? Why does my past have to haunt me all my life? How could Julius talk about me like that? He doesn't even know me.

We went to the barn early that Sunday morning. I hurried to get the milk machine washed and the barn cleaned. I got the children ready and drove them to church so they could attend Sunday school. I did not stay and listen to God's word that day. I went back home to get dinner ready.

Going to church here was not the same as it was when I was a child in Switzerland, and I missed that a lot. Fifteen minutes before the church service starts in Switzerland, the bells start ringing, telling everybody it is time to rest and listen to God's word. That beautiful sound from the bells carries all through the valley, and if you want to or not, it makes you feel good. I used to walk to church and listen to the sound of the bells, and it made me feel like God was talking to me, and then when I sat down on that church bench, I was ready to accept God's word.

Here I had to hurry to get the barn work done, then get all four kids ready and hurry to church. By the time I sat down on that church bench, I was exhausted and not ready at all to really listen and understand what the minister had to say. All I wanted to do was take a nap. And today it would not help at all. My mind was preoccupied, so it was better I kept busy.

At 11:30 I picked my children up by the church. As we came back and drove into our yard, so did Julius and his family. I did not want to spoil anybody's appetite, so I waited until after dinner. Then I asked Julius straight out, "What did you tell Willi?"

He did not understand what it was I wanted to know from him, so I asked again. To find out he told Willi that night that he saw me and that he was glad to find someone that late at night who could give him directions, and especially someone who spoke his language. Julius did not tell Willi that there was a man in my car, he just said that I was parked in one of Willi's neighbor's yard. Julius did not know Grace Hass.

Yet everything we did for Willi, he made up this big, stupid story. Willi did not call us, he called Martha, and she could not wait to give Henry the newest gossip. It is beyond me how people can get pleasure out of hurting others. But I guess that is something I will never understand.

Julius, his wife Erika, and their two little girls, Patricia and Claudia, stayed all afternoon, until it was time for them to go home and do their chores, since they farmed, too. We became best friends, friends for life. They were always there when we needed them, the only true friends we ever had.

Another couple we became friends with were Hubert and Martha Wick. They also came from Switzerland, but about six months before us. If Henry felt blue and down in the dumps, then we went at night, after we were done with barn work, and drove to Huberts, played cards with them all night. Around midnight, Martha, who is a great cook, put one of her special meals together. Meat, noodles or potatoes, vegetables and homemade bread, then cake or ice cream for dessert. Many times we did not get home until daybreak, just in time to go to the barn.

Yes, Wicks are hard-working, great, plain people, and can make anybody feel at home. But then when Martha got pregnant with her fifth child, Henry made some nasty remarks, just as his brother did when I cxpected Reto, and that made Hubert mad. We still stayed in contact with them, but the friendship was not the same anymore.

A couple of months after Julius and his family were at our house, we went to visit them one Sunday. It was a nice, sunny day, and I truly enjoyed the 40-mile drive through the rolling farm country, watching the cows in the pastures enjoying the fresh grass. The fields had a green tint already.

Julius had a real nice farm. He gave us a tour, and we had a great afternoon together. After living in the US for so long already, Reto, our youngest son, just did not feel at home here. It was like he was homesick, but homesick to where? He was too young to understand.

Julius' dog had puppies. They were about five weeks old, so cute, fat and funny. There was one dark, skinnier one. It was the runt of the litter. That whole Sunday afternoon Reto sat on the steps by the porch holding this little puppy in his arms. We were ready to head for home when Reto asked, "Julius, could I please take this puppy along?"

"Of course," Julius answered, "but be good to her."

It was a female and Reto called her "Debby." That was Reto's turnaround. It was his little dog and he felt he had something to love and live for. Debby was with us for 14 years.

Eddie Hass did custom work with some of his farm

equipment. He chopped the hay and filled silos in the whole neighborhood. But two of his boys were still in high school, and the oldest one, Dick, had to enlist in the army and was sent to Korea with his troops. So Eddie didn't have much help and asked Henry if he would ride the tractor for him. Henry gladly accepted, since that meant we could fill our silos cheaper. We had just built a 16' x 50' silo and tore the old wooden one down, so that came in handy.

I had to help everywhere and work like a man, and Eddie made it even worse. He told Henry that Margrit (Hans' wife), who is shorter than me, would be on the hay wagon and pile the hay bales eight rows high, and she got in the silo and leveled the grass that they blew in. So in the silo I had to go, as Henry chopped the grass and Eddie blew it up into the silo.

I was in the silo all morning, and then as those two had a beer, I got the lunch ready. I just had time to store the dirty dishes in the sink for the girls to wash after they came home from school, when I was told to get back into the silo. It is not an easy job and wore me out.

Years later I found out that Margrit was not in the silo all day; she only went up there in the evening so that the half-dried grass settled evenly overnight.

It was on a Saturday. I felt so sick and had high fever, and a bad case of the flu. The kids had to go to catechism that afternoon. "Mom, would you drive us there?" they came and asked. "No, I can't. I feel so sick, please go and ask your dad if he would get you there," I replied.

But it did not take long, and I could hear Henry hollering, standing in front of the milk house. "Go tell your mom if she is so lazy, stays in bed and will not help me with all that work I have, then I will not drive you to catechism neither."

Before the kids came back to the house, I got up, got dressed, started the car and drove them to the church. Henry was just so unreasonable sometimes.

Another winter passed and spring work started. We still had only one tractor, and because of that decided to buy a four-wheel drive Jeep pickup truck. And since we needed it to do farm work, we had them put a power take-off on right away.

A new four-wheel-drive Jeep with the power takeoff included was at that time only $3,600. It was a great idea of Henry's. Then we used that truck to spread manure and to pull silo wagons home, and unloaded the silo wagons with the same Jeep.

Our fields were far apart, two miles to the west or three miles to the south, so that Jeep came in very handy. But it got our former landowner mad.

We bought our farm on land contract and still owed Brosowskis a little over $5,000. Mrs. Brosowski called me one night telling me, "I want my final payment."

I could not understand what she meant, but then she made it real clear and said, "If you had the money to buy this new truck, then you can also pay us off. You should have painted your house a long time ago, and for that you should have used Pittsburgh paint. But you are just a bunch of no-good low lifes, since if you were decent human beings you would not have had to leave your homeland. Only scum comes to this country, and we do not want them."

I was taught from little on to respect my fellowmen, and especially anybody older than me. But that night I lost my cool. I said to her, "Mrs. Brosowski, your name alone proves that either you or your parents came from the old country. Then they must have been bad, too, just like us. To my knowledge, only Native Americans are true Americans. All the white people immigrated at one time or another."

That made her even more angry, and she called her lawyer, Tom Sazama, who was also our lawyer. We had to see him early the next morning at 9 a.m. Mrs. Brosowski talked and talked. We couldn't, nor did we have to, say anything.

But then Tom told her that as long as we pay our payment, which was $65 per month, on time, she could do nothing, even if we made a cranberry farm out of that place, as long as we do not devalue the property. And the paint on the house was gone already when they bought the farm, so why should that be their first priority?

She was not happy at all leaving Tom's office, but there was nothing she could do to us.

Tom's office is right next door to the Lincoln County Bank, so we left Tom and went straight to the bank to apply for a loan, and as long as we needed that money, we asked them if we could add a building for the heifers. We would like to build a 48' x 64' Wick building to the south of the barn. The cost would be $4,200.

The loan officer saw no problem, and we got the money ten days later and paid Brosowskis out. What a relief, to finally have her out of our hair. Brosowskis had the little Jersey cows, and she always complained our Holstein cows ate too much and made too much manure. She also wanted to see curtains on my porch windows, but I had no money for things like that. So now she no longer could tell us what to do.

The new addition we built was open to the east and connected in the north to the existing barn. Henry built a bunk feeder along the west wall. We could have the heifers out there and also the dry cows.

They always had feed. But after the first winter we saw that that did not work out too well. It was too cold for the cows, their bags just could not develop enough, which, in turn, made the cows not produce to their fullest potential.

Henry helped Eddie fill silos again, and he really liked it. This way he got to know our neighbors and could work with them.

One day they were at Norm Krause's farm filling their silo with corn silage. Eddie and Henry were invited to eat lunch with the Krauses. Henry came home late that afternoon and could hardly wait to tell me all about his lunch experience.

"We had corn on the cob," he said. "I did not know what to do with that cob on my plate, so I waited till everybody else ate, and then chewed on the cobs just like the rest of them."

He didn't want to look stupid, and they did not know that he had never seen someone eat corn on the cob before. In Switzerland we only eat the corn as corn meal. I bought sweet corn, too, the next time I went to the store, and all of us got to like it.

Palm Sunday, 1971, a nice sunny day. The snow was almost gone. The soft, young, light green leaves stretched themselves towards the sun and gave the brownish, dead pastures a spring-like look. Some birds sat in the close-by tree and sang. A couple of them even looked for a companion. And the butterflies glided in the cool spring breeze.

Our daughter Edith got confirmed that day. I sewed a pretty pink dress with short sleeves for her special day, so I was glad that the weather wasn't too cool. Bachs and Wicks came to our church up on the hill and witnessed as Edith became a member of the Lutheran religion. The St. Paul's church is only a small country church, and most of the members are farmers. We had a party at our house after church, a real nice afternoon among friends.

Bob Hass, a nephew of Eddie's, got confirmed, too, that day, but it was not a happy day for him. His dad, Herold Hass, had been killed two weeks before in a logging accident. Herold left an empty spot in all of our hearts, but yet we all have to learn that the happy and sad times are part of all our lives and sometimes go hand in hand.

The fields were planted again, and it was time to make hay. We rented more and more land, which meant more and more work. After we built the silo, Henry told all of us that we didn't have to make so many bales of hay next year, which meant a lot less heavy lifting. But then he rented more land, and we were right back to square one again. I don't know what I would have done without my children. They were a big help. They worked very hard.

One day I came home from the field, just drove into the driveway, when one of the fan blades on the tractor broke off. That meant the water in the radiator no longer got cooled, so I no longer could drive it. It would take a day or two to get it fixed, yet there was hay out there that had to be baled.

Henry went to the PCA and also stopped at the Midland. Three hours later they delivered a brand-new Allis Chalmers 180 for $6,400. Unbelievable how easy it was all of a sudden to get the money for machinery, now that they know us.

We had the Allis Chalmers 170 tractor at the Co-op for the 100-hour checkup, and had them do the oil change at the same time. They also fixed the fan blade. It only took two days and we had the tractor back. "You could go and cut the grass over at Mutz's," Henry said.

I liked that job now, so on the tractor I hopped and off I went. But I just drove into the hayfield when the tractor started sputtering. What now, I thought, but kept on driving. Just a couple of hundred feet and the motor sounded terrible. That's when I saw that the red oil light is lit up. What could that be? They just did an oil change.

I turned the tractor off, stepped down and to my surprise saw oil dripping. I checked where it came from. There was no plug in the oil pan. I lost all the oil. I followed the oil trail and found the plug laying on the soft shoulder on the road. It must have shaken loose on the bumpy road and then fell out, just as I turned into the field.

I knew I could no longer drive the tractor, so I left it there and walked the three miles home.

After Henry heard what happened, he screamed at me: "You are the stupidest thing that walks on this earth.

Why can't you see things like that? Why couldn't you listen to the sound of the motor and turn it off as soon as it sounded different. You're just so stupid. This tractor is ruined forever, can't be fixed anymore. Now we have to get a different one and that costs money. If we can't make it farming, then it is all your fault. You break everything."

I was in tears and at first did not know what to do anymore. But then I got myself together and called the Co-op. They came, picked up the tractor and fixed it. I later argued over the bill. I felt it was partly their fault. They should have checked if the plug was in right before they poured the oil in. They in turn told us we should have checked it before driving it. So we ended up splitting the bill. That same tractor ran for 19 more years, and I did not sell it until 1990.

The crops were good, and all in all we had a pretty decent year. Henry went one more winter to the feed mill to make some extra money.

Heinz got confirmed in the spring of 1972. It was a sunny, but cold Palm Sunday. We still had a lot of snow, but the house was warm, and Bachs and Wicks again spent the day with us. Even Henkes, some neighbors of ours, stopped in. We sang and played cards together, and for at least a couple of hours we forgot all our troubles.

We now had 45 cows and only 36 stanchions. The dry cows had to stay outside in the steel building. I could hardly wait until spring came round, since Henry told me all winter long that I fed them cows too much, and that we would run out of hay before spring. But I just could not see that the cows could stay in top production if they were hungry. And if they do not produce to their capabilities, that means less milk check, which in turn means I can't pay the bills. It is like a never-ending rat race.

Whatever leftover hay the cows had in the morning, I fed to the heifers and they ate it to the last crumb. So there was none wasted. The cows produced really good, but, yes, the hay mow got smaller and smaller and the pasture still looked dead.

My eyes wandered every day through the fields as I stood by the sink washing the dishes to see if I could find a sign of spring. It seemed to take forever.

But then the warm sun slowly turned the washed-out brown grass into a soft green meadow. The swallows came back and made nest beside nest on the old wooden barn wall. The birds started singing, and the deer brought their fawns out to the meadow to nibble on the fresh young grass.

But the best sign that spring finally was here to stay were the frogs in the nearby pond. They came out by the hundreds, and one had to croak louder than the next one. It was beautiful to sit on the steps in front of the house in the evening after the chores were done and listen to the frog concert. Sitting there daydreaming I used to think nobody on this earth had a prettier place than I had.

We plowed the fields and planted the crops. And now the grass was ready to be cut. Henry bought a chopper last winter, so from then on we filled the silos ourselves. Eddie still did custom work, but there were so many farmers that wanted him, and Eddie himself had more and more land and more cows. We could not wait for him anymore. If the grass gets too old, it loses protein. And protein is very important. It makes the cows produce better, which means more money.

By now we had two tractors and the Jeep, but still an old haybine that constantly needed fixing. So Henry had this glamorous idea and bought a self-propelled haybine. I did not see the machine before they unloaded it in our yard. Boy, what a surprise! It had no steering wheel, only two handles which one has to pull or push to make the machine turn. It was no problem for Henry, since bulldozers are driven the same way and he drove them in Switzerland. But for me it was different. It was a completely new ball game. Now that I finally knew how to drive a tractor, he bought this machine that didn't even have a steering wheel.

I didn't say much all day, but as we milked the cows that night I said, "Henry, how can I drive this machine without a steering wheel. Besides, it is so big I'm scared just to sit on it."

That was not what Henry wanted to hear. He got really mad and told me, "You are so stupid it is pathetic. All other women have no problems driving a machine like that, but you are just so dumb it's unreal."

Henry is just like my grandmother. He knows which button to push. Grandma used to say I was a "slob," and I bent over backward to do things to her satisfaction. And it is the same now. I worked so hard to make Henry love me, but something always comes up and I'm at square one again. I did not say much anymore that night.

Henry had to go to town the next day. As soon as he left, I went outside and started the haybine. My heart was pounding as I sat high up on that machine. I tried to make it go and slowly drove up and down the driveway. For hours I went 100 feet one way, then 100 feet the other way. By the time Henry came home, I knew how to drive it, and I was proud of myself. But in his eyes there was no praise needed. He expected that from me, just like my grandma used to.

A typical day on the farm: the alarm goes off at 5:15 a.m., but it is so hard for me to jump out of bed right away. I like to lay there just for five or 10 more minutes and snooze a little. Five-thirty and time to go to the barn. Henry gets dressed and is out of the door in no time. I have to have a piece of bread with butter and jelly, even if I have to eat it on the way to the barn. I just need something in my stomach or I'm dragging my butt all morning.

The silage and grain I had put into the manger the night before, so in the morning we just open the door and let the cows in. Each of the cows has a name and her own stall. This way they all get always milked at about the same time. Henry is pretty strict that it is every 12 hours.

He and I milk the cows. After we are done, we let them out and clean the barn. We had no barn cleaner yet, and still had to do that job by hand. After the milk machines are washed and the milk house is clean, we get the silage and feed ready for the evening milking.

And then we finally get to eat breakfast. But we don't have much time to sit around. Quickly off to the fields.

I go out and cut the grass with our new haybine, and that is truly a great machine. Before with the tractor and the mower, I always had to drive over the grass to get the first couple of rows, and now wherever I drive, it cuts. Someone who does not love farming like I do by now maybe thinks I'm crazy. But when I'm done cutting down one of the fields, and then take one last glimpse over it and see the rows lying there so nice and straight, that gives me an indescribable satisfaction of a job well done. Nobody has to tell me I did a good job. It just makes me feel good. But I think it does not matter what one does in life. If one loves what one is doing and does the best he can, then one has to be happy.

Henry is still home and gets the chopper, the silo blower and the wagons ready. At noon he picks me up for lunch, and we will have a sandwich or a bowl of soup together.

After lunch, Henry starts chopping, while I drive the wagons home and blow the half-dried grass into the silo.

The school bus drops the kids off at 4 p.m. Five o'clock and Reto and I will get the cows into the barn. It makes me feel good when the cows are all tied up, so content, and have big heavy bags full of milk. That milk is as good as gold.

Reto washes the cow's udder and gets them ready for me to hook the milk machine up. Reto tells me stories all through milking. By the time we are done, I know everything that went on that day. I truly enjoyed the time I had alone with Reto.

Henry, with Heinz as his helper, will finish the field work and fix whatever broke down through the day. The girls have to cook and do the housework. At 8-8:30 p.m. we will sit down at the dinner table and have supper together, and by then it is almost bedtime. Yes, the days are long, but also rewarding.

9

EARLY THAT SUMMER I did something I never thought I would do, but I just could not stand it anymore. No matter how hard Heinz and I tried, we just couldn't do anything right. All I heard was other women can do this or that, why can't you? Heinz worked like a man, yet he too was called stupid and lazy, good-for-nothing.

Henry was so unhappy and frustrated that he could not see the beauty of nature all around him. All he wanted was to prove himself worthy to his siblings, yet hurting us along the way.

I got a catalog in the mail from "Bauer by Mail," a company out of Germany, but with a warehouse in Minneapolis, Minnesota. That company wanted to get customers together and planned a trip to Germany to show their store off. The trip was $240 per person.

I saved money left and right so that I could buy two tickets and go home. I did not want to stay here anymore; if I can't do anything right, then it wasn't worth it. Henry did not know why I was going on that trip. I just told him I would take Heinz and go home.

I worked hard all summer to get the crops in before we were leaving. I would have never gone without Heinz, since, to me, he was more like a friend than my own son. If I broke something, I could say, "Heinz, can't you fix this quick before Dad sees it," and most of the time he could. He was my rescuer so many times. But I also covered up for him so he wouldn't always get scolded by his dad.

The first and second crops were good that year, and all stored away. All that was left was the oats and the corn. We borrowed a pull-type combine from Elmer

Stevenson, a neighbor of ours. I hooked the combine up to the tractor, and off to the field I went.

That stupid old machine overheated all the time. I was in a hurry, since I wanted to get done. I opened the radiator to add some cold water, but I opened the cover too quickly and burned my arms from the hot steam that escaped. How stupid of me!

I put my arms in cold water for awhile, but then back on the tractor I went and combined the whole field. Henry came with the truck to get the oats, but I did not tell him what I did. I did not want to be called stupid again, and I knew I would leave for Switzerland in a couple of days and then would have time to heal my arms.

Mrs. Smith had a daughter who was stationed in Germany. I talked her into coming along on that trip, and so she did. She took a friend of hers along. Our tour started in Chicago. Erika Bach volunteered to drive us there, since she had a girlfriend that she had not seen for a while and lives in a suburb of Chicago.

It was so hectic all summer, and I was so disgusted that it didn't bother me to leave Henry behind that morning. The only hard thing was to say goodbye to my children. But I was determined to go home, find a job and a place to live for me and my children, then come and get the other three kids and move back home to Switzerland.

Mrs. Smith was never out of the country and was so excited that she talked all the way to Chicago. That was good, or I might have turned around then already.

We met with the rest of the group at the O'Hare airport. It took eight hours to fly with the Lufthansa to Nuremburg. That gave me a lot of time to think.

I could not believe myself. How could I do that to Henry? How could I leave him with all that work? How terrible of me! And how could I even think of leaving him forever? His siblings are against him, and if I'm gone, then he has no one anymore, and life would be empty for him.

How could I ever let myself go that far?

But there was no turning back anymore.

We landed safely at Nuremburg, and from there we went by bus to the hotel, which turned out to be an old castle. It was September, and the rooms were cold. They had white painted whales and an old wood stove in the corner, but no wood to heat the room, nor would I have tried it. I would have been afraid to burn the place down.

After checking in, we got escorted to a real nice restaurant where the mayor from that town had a delicious German-style supper waiting for us. After the meal was entertainment. The square dancers and singers entertained us way past midnight. Later that night when I lay in that strange, cold bed all by myself, I felt lonely and I missed Henry so much. I knew then that I really, truly loved him and could never leave him.

The next morning after breakfast we went and toured the huge department store, "Bauer by Mail." I bought a few souvenirs for my family, and then went back to the hotel. I was so tired and wanted to get to bed early that night since at 5 a.m. the next morning Heinz and I had to board the train that took us home to Switzerland.

It was a long train ride. It took over six hours. Three older people sat in the same compartment. They must have known each other since they talked about different young people by name.

"No one wants to work hard nowadays. The young people think they have to have everything that we have, but do not want to work for it. And commitment is gone nowadays. No one wants to stay together anymore. As soon as the road gets rocky, they leave."

I listened for a long time, but then got kind of fed up. I was still young, only 32 years old, and I gave up my family and my homeland to make Henry happy and worked very hard. So I asked them, "Do you want to be without a washing machine? You know how to wash by hand. You must have done that years ago. And why do you need a refrigerator? You did without it before. I gave up a lot, and love my husband, so please don't cut all the young people down. There are some your age that are lazy, too."

They had to agree, and we had a real nice conversation the rest of the way.

Then, as we slowly drove into the Zurich train station, I saw my parents waiting for us, and that made me forget all my troubles. It felt so good to see them again. I did not tell them why I took this trip; I just told them that I missed them.

My sister-in-law, Lisa, gave birth to a little girl, "Susan," (their third child) that morning, so we went to see her in the hospital. Heinz and I stayed with my parents and just took it easy.

I promised myself the first thing I would do was to see my mother-in-law. So two days after we arrived in Switzerland, my mother, my son Heinz, my brother's two girls, Irene and Regula, and I took the train and went to Wallenstadt. From there we took the bus.

It was a beautiful trip. It went up steep winding roads along the majestic mountains that already had their tops covered with snow.

The bus had to stop for a farmer who brought his cows down from the mountain meadows. He and his helpers were all dressed up in their white embroidered short-sleeved shirts, red vests with silver buttons and brown pants, black shoes with silver buckles. They yodeled all along, and the cows walked behind them.

The cows have head pieces made out of paper roses tied between the horns and huge bells around their necks. That beautiful sound carried way down to the valley. Some of the farmers have to walk eight to ten hours until they get to their home farm

But it is a beautiful picture, the guys and girls, the cows, the high mountain, and below us the Linth Valley. I thought of Henry. He would have loved to see this, since that is what he used to do in his late teen years, take care of the cows up in the mountains. But they are all past us now and the bus keeps going, slowly climbing the steep road.

The sanatorium where Henry's mother lives now used to be a TB sanatorium. My mother was there, too, when she had TB many years ago. But since TB declined, they turned that place into an old folks home. Heinz and I went to see Mother, while my mother and my nieces took a stroll through the nearby woods.

Henry's mother shared her room with one other woman, but that one had Alzheimer's and did not know what she was doing anymore. Right outside the bedroom was a big balcony, and we went out there to sit down. The view was just gorgeous. We could see all the way down to the valley. But it was also sad. All those old people up here were like prisoners. There is no town within miles. The roads are steep, so they can't go anywhere. Most of the old people are forgotten. Here I sat with my mother-in-law on a beautiful sunny day, and we could reminisce for awhile.

I saw that she had her suitcase beside her bed and asked her if she was going somewhere, and she was quick to reply, "I stayed with Beth, my oldest daughter, before I came here. But Elsa from California came for a visit, and those two and their families went on a vacation trip and couldn't take me along, as I can only walk on a walker. So Elsa brought me up here and promised me that Beth will come and get me later. That was months ago. That is why I got my suitcase packed, so that I'm ready when they come to take me back."

As we sat there and talked, the nurse came and handed Mother a letter. It was from Beth. Mother's hand trembled as she ripped it open. In her eyes I could see a glimpse of hope. "I bet you they're going to tell me now when they come to pick me up," she told me, smiling. But her smile froze and she got sad, the tears slowly rolling down her cheeks as she handed me her letter.

Beth just asked how she was doing and told her that they just moved into a smaller apartment and no longer had room for her. Oh, how sad! That means she has to stay here until her days on this earth are up. I took her in my arms and gave her a big hug; that was all I could do for her. If I could, I would have taken her along to the States, but that was impossible.

We sat with her for a little while longer, but I felt terribly guilty as I said goodbye and had to leave her behind late that afternoon. She looked at me, her eyes filled with tears, begging me, "Please help me."

Yet there was nothing I could do for her. Henry's mother raised six children, lost two husbands, and now even though she is still alive, she is all alone up here on this mountain, and already forgotten.

My mother sat under a tree on a bench waiting for us. We boarded the bus and then the train, and back to her house we went, but there was not much said on the way. I felt so bad for Henry's mother. My thoughts were wondering, "Will I end up that way someday. God, I hope not."

Mrs. Smith and her friend came to visit us in Switzerland, and together we made a bus trip over some of my beloved mountain passes. They were scared, since they'd never before driven such windy, steep roads. But I enjoyed every minute of it. It was so pure and beautiful.

Those two spent the night with my parents, and went the next morning by train back to Germany, but not before my dad could give them some of his homemade clear whiskey. They wanted to taste every drink my dad had, and after a while got pretty jolly, but it could not hurt them. They just had to crawl into bed.

One week was gone already, and I was so homesick. I missed Henry so much. We went shopping one afternoon and then made supper and waited for my dad to come home from work. My parents lived in an apartment building on the third floor.

I sat in the living room when I could hear someone coming up the stairs. I knew right away that it wasn't my dad. I could never figure out why, but my stomach knotted up and I got real scared. Something told me that whoever was slowly making his way up the stairs could make trouble for me.

I whispered in my mother's ear, "If they ask for me, I'm not here." I took Heinz with me and disappeared into the spare bedroom. We crawled under the bed and lay very still, me having my hand over Heinz' mouth, just to make sure that he did not make any noise.

And I was right. It was a representative from the USEGO, together with a lawyer. I heard them say, "We know your daughter is here, and we will get her this time."

My mother's answer: "She is not here right now. She went to visit a friend." But they did not believe her and wanted to see her apartment.

My heart was just pounding and my palms were sweating. I was so scared I could not move and prayed that Heinz would not give me away.

My dad came home from work and got the two sidetracked. Dad wanted to know what gave them the idea that I was home. Their answer was, "Someone who lives in the same town in the US as she does called and said Edith was on her way to Switzerland. They would not give my dad any names.

"Sorry," my dad answered, "but she is not here right now."

The guys were very nice to him and talked for awhile, but then left. The USEGO has seven years to appeal the judge's decision from way back in March of 1968. After that the case is closed forever.

Heinz and I crawled out from underneath the bed, but stayed in that room until it got dark. My dad brought us some food while they sat at the dinner table, just in case someone was watching them from a nearby apartment building.

A little after 9 p.m., it was dark by then. I took Heinz and sneaked to the basement, opened the window and climbed out. We walked at least five miles that night and met up with my dad in a remote area.

My mom and dad rented a cab. They picked us up and drove us to my brother's house. Early the next morning we got up, had a quick bite to eat and then left for Germany. We had to show our passports to the border patrol, and I was scared, my heart was pounding, my hands sweaty. I felt like a criminal, yet I never did anything wrong. And who hated me so much in the USA that they had to give the USEGO all that information? How could someone do that?

But we made it across the border. Once in Germany I no longer had to worry. My parents, Heinz and I stayed in a nice motel in the Black Forest for the last three days of our vacation, then took a train back to Nuremburg where we met up with the rest of the group. One last hug and a kiss, the tears were flowing.

My parents stayed at the airport until our plane took off. I know it was not any easier for them this time than it was the first time. I felt so bad that I had to put them through all that heartache, yet I was glad to get out of Europe.

I know now Switzerland will always have a special place in my heart, but it is not my homeland anymore. My home is where my heart is, and that now is in the great land of possibilities, in the good old USA.

The plane took us over England, Canada, down to Chicago. The pilot just told us that we are flying over Lake Superior towards Ashland. Then only a couple of minutes later the pilot came on the air again. Loud and clear was the message, "Please put on your seatbelt immediately and follow the stewardess' orders."

Our stewardess stood by the emergency exit, the phone

in her hand. That alone was a scary sight. Then we were told that because of the weather and the heavy traffic, they had to fly farther north than normal, so they are short on fuel. What a scary thing to tell us: 34,000 feet up in the air and short on fuel.

It was so quiet in the plane you could hear a needle drop. Everybody was hanging onto their seat or a loved one. It was one of the longest hours in my life. But O'Hare Airport was in sight, and over and over again we were told that we might make it. The airport is informed and an emergency alert. The closer to the ground we got, the better I felt, and when the wheels touched the runway, I was relieved.

One passenger was so eager to get out that the minute we got on the runway he got up, even though we were warned not to do that. But he did no more than get out of his seat when the plane stopped. It was such a sudden stop that it almost flipped the plane over. That passenger flew down the aisle.

We did just touch down onto the runway when we ran out of fuel, we were told. A tractor had to come and pull us into the airport. As we waited to get out, the gentleman who sat beside me said, "I'm traveling back and forth to Europe at least once a week for the last ten years, but this never happened to me. That is the closest I ever came to death."

Everybody was relieved when we finally had solid ground under our feet and stood in line to go through customs. There we met Julius, who was ready to drive us home. We got a couple of miles out of the city, and the two ladies in the back seat fell asleep already. All the excitement, plus the seven-hour time change was too much for them. I was too wound up to sleep. Plus, I had to tell Julius everything that happened to us. I told him that I had plans to leave Henry, but that I now know how much I loved him and that I would never again want to be without him.

Just about 50 miles from the airport Julius drove over a deer that just got killed by the truck ahead of us. It screwed up the steering on his big Buick, but we still could drive home.

It was just past midnight when we dropped the two ladies off and then only had a couple more miles until I could be together with my family again. I asked Julius if he would like to come in and have a cup of coffee with us, and he said, "Yes." I started my coffeemaker up, then took Heinz upstairs and put him to bed. Edith, Lotti and Reto were asleep, but I kissed them, told them I missed them and was glad to be home with them again. Then I went to say "Hi" to Henry, who also was in bed, sleeping already. I gave him a kiss and a hug, but he was cold.

Not giving in to that cold feeling, I asked him if he would please come and have coffee with Julius and me, but he was not interested at all. He answered, "It's time you come home. If you would have stayed just a couple more days, I would have left the farm and moved on. So drink your coffee with Julius. I will not get up anymore."

I swallowed my tears so Julius did not have to see how disappointed I was. Why do I do this over and over again? Why do I make Henry so angry? The whole two weeks overseas I missed him so much, could hardly wait to come home and feel his arms around me again, and now he does not want anything to do with me and blames me for everything that went wrong those two weeks. Isn't that why I left in the first place?

But I pushed my thoughts aside, had some coffee and a piece of cake with Julius, cake that my girls baked especially for me. They wrote on it, "Welcome home, Mami." That made me push all my sadness aside. I know at least my children were glad to have me and Heinz back, and I felt that if I worked hard, eventually Henry would come around, too. It took a couple of days of pouting on Henry's part, but then everything went back to normal.

We joined the German club, and that got us at least once a month out of the house and together with friends who spoke our language. Henry still was a great yodeler, and we two started singing together. We sang on the Oktoberfest or at the Mardi Gras. It was lots of fun and I truly enjoyed it.

We also still went once a week to English class, but we no longer had Otto as our teacher. Now it was Mr. Justus. Otto had a stroke and ended up in a nursing home.

We were the only Swiss immigrants who still went on to improve our English. The others were no longer interested in learning how to read or write in English.

Mrs. Justus taught us, and also young women from Thailand, Korea, and Shanghai. I wanted us to become US citizens as soon as possible, and I felt English was very important. Being involved in all the activities got us through another winter.

It was the 22nd of March when Henry's brother Walter called and said that their mother was close to the end. It was almost seven months now since I had seen her, and she still was at the same nursing home and no one had time to visit her. I think she was lonely and just gave up.

Walter told Henry that a nurse called him and said that they have to come soon if they would like to see her alive. Henry and Walter talked for awhile, and Walter promised to go see Mother and keep Henry informed.

I tried to convince Henry that night to fly home and see his mother one more time, talk to her and maybe make peace with her again. But he felt it was not necessary. "Walter said he will call if it gets worse, so I wait," was his answer.

I could not understand him. I felt the longer he waited, the slimmer was his chance to see his mother alive. And I was right. Three days later we got the phone call that she passed away. I went and got Henry a ticket, and 24 hours later he was on his way home.

The whole way to the airport he pouted. Farmers were

in the field everywhere planting oats and corn. We hadn't even started with field work yet; that was why it was so hard for Henry to leave. This was the first trip back and now for such a sad get-together. Henry's sister Martha did not go, since she just gave birth to a little boy, "Norbert," and made plans already to go home later that year.

My parents picked Henry up at the airport, took him to their apartment and went with him to the funeral the next day. The casket was still open, and Henry saw his mother for the last time. It was at the open casket where he got hurt again. His sister Beth walked up to him and asked, "How come you came so quick? Could not wait to get your hands on Mother's money, ha." But that was not on Henry's mind at all. How come they have to hurt him so much? My dad and Henry's Aunt Settli took him aside and sat with him in church and also at the meal afterward. He could not even sit at the same table as his siblings.

How sad! How can a family get split apart that way? Yet there is nothing more important than family ties. Nothing on this earth, not money or other earthly possessions can make one feel as good as a hug from a loved one.

My brother drove my dad and Henry two days after the funeral to Henry's mother's home to talk to Walter and maybe make peace. But even that effort turned against him. Walter did not allow my brother or my dad to come into the house. They had to park on the road and stay in the car.

Henry was escorted into the living room and then told that there was nothing left. Mother's money was all gone, and the house that still belonged to her will now be Walter's, too. He said to Henry, "You can go back to the States now, and don't ever think there is a penny left for you."

It sure was a very sad trip home for Henry. He wished he could fly right back, but he had to stay there for two weeks, since that is how we booked the flight. It was not a pleasant vacation for Henry. He was happy to come home to us, and all of us were glad to have him back.

We had our share of troubles, too, while he was gone. My kids helped me as much as they could; yet they also had to go to school. It was a beautiful day end of March when Henry left, and most of the farmers had planted their oats and corn already. But then, two days later, the weather turned and it rained for two weeks straight. I was glad that we could not plant as early as some of them. Most of their fields drowned out and had to be replanted.

Lotti got confirmed that Palm Sunday. Heinz and I went to the barn early that morning, but everything went wrong. We had a cow calving that got us behind, and then as I was in a hurry to clean the barn (we still had no automatic barn cleaner), the bucket that I just filled with manure pulled up and tried to push out of the barn, crashed to the floor, and one of the wheels busted in two. I was almost in tears.

Henry would not be coming home for another week, and the barn had to be cleaned. Heinz tried to weld it. It was cast iron, and he could not do it. But there was no time to stand around. Lotti had to get to church. We got all washed up, put our Sunday clothes on, piled into the car and off to church we went.

Julius, Erika and their two girls were waiting for us when we arrived at the church. They were the only so-called "family" we had at that time, and I will always be grateful for their friendship.

Julius came after church and fixed my manure bucket, but the manure could wait. This was Lotti's day and we celebrated it as such. Her favorite food is pizza, so to the Pizza Hut in Antigo we went. It was pouring rain, but that could not dampen our spirits. We had a nice afternoon together. It was late that night when I got done in the barn. I was tired, but I was happy knowing that our third child now also was a full-fledged member of the Lutheran religion.

Left: Edith's confirmation, Palm Sunday, 1971.

Below: Heinz and Henry, confirmation, Palm Sunday, 1972.

Above: Lotti, Palm Sunday, 1973.

Right: Reto, Palm Sunday, 1975.

10

IT WAS MEMORIAL weekend when my parents came to visit us. They flew into Chicago, and I drove to the O'Hare Airport to pick them up. It was a long, scary trip (310 miles one way). I had never driven in a big city before, but I was anxious to show them how good we have it, and that gave me the courage to make that long trip all by myself.

It was past midnight when we got back, but everybody was still up and made Grandpa and Grandma feel right at home.

For the first three days I let them adjust to the time change, and then took them on a trip out west. I had never driven that far before. We went to Minnesota, then South Dakota, stayed in Mitchell, where we toured the Corn Palace. A great thing to see, the huge pictures out of different-colored corn.

From there we went on through the Badlands and stayed overnight at a motel there. To sit on flat land, on top of those high cliffs, watching the sun go down is a feeling I can hardly describe.

The next day up to Mt. Rushmore. What a sight! My dad could not get enough pictures. He was just so overwhelmed from the beauty and all the open space. Switzerland is only about 200 miles from east to west border, and not even that much from the north to the south, and here we can drive for days and still be in the same country.

We saw for the first time in our lives antelope roaming the meadows and mixing in with the beef cattle. We sat and watched the prairie dogs; they're so neat and quick to peek out or drop into their dens.

Dad got out of the car to take pictures of a buffalo herd. The bulls started making that awful noise and stamped their front hooves into the dirt. It was scary, and I told my dad, "I will leave if they attack, and you better see to it that you can jump onto the trunk of the car." But even though they seemed to be mad at us, they kept their distance.

The most breathtaking sight was to see an elk carrying his antlers so proud on his head, walk out of the woods into the open meadow. I was so overwhelmed I got goosebumps. My dad was in Seventh Heaven.

But it was time to head back. Henry needed me, since we hadn't planted our corn yet. We would have made it home that Saturday, but we ran into very bad weather in Minnesota. It was like driving into a wall. We couldn't see anything anymore. But there was a truck stop and motel just a couple of miles down the road, so we decided to spend the night there. We did no more than check into our room when the phone rang. How could that be? Nobody knows we are there.

It was the desk clerk telling us to stay put for further news. A tornado was sighted. Oh, how lucky we were that we stopped. We would have driven right into it. My guardian angel was by my side again.

I could hardly sleep that night. I knew Henry expected us, and he gets mad if I'm late. Plus, we traded our Chevy Belair in for a brand-new Matador only two weeks before my parents came. Henry told me before I went on this trip out west that I would bring that car home with dents because I wasn't a good driver. I did not even get a scratch until now. What if the heavy wind damaged our car? Henry would never believe that it wasn't my doing. But I was lucky again; nothing happened and we made it home safe.

Our neighbor, Louis Tesch, took my dad fishing a lot. They both enjoyed each other's company. Dad got up early every morning, walked through the fields and took pictures of the birds, butterflies, white-tail deer, and he even saw a fox family. As a nature lover, he was just in Seventh Heaven with all the open space he had here. Their four weeks went fast, and I drove my parents back to Chicago for them to return to Switzerland.

It was a long and lonely drive to Merrill, but once back on the farm I did not have time to feel sorry for myself. The hay was ready to be cut and the silos had to be filled. We were busy from early morning until late at night.

I sent in the application for our US citizenship. We decided to immigrate to this country, and it was important to me to become one of them. We had to have two witnesses who would swear under oath that we are decent, law-abiding human beings. We asked Eddie Hass, our friendly neighbor, and Mr. Monka, the principal from the Scott School where our children went to school, if they would vouch for us. They were honored, since neither of them had any idea what it takes to become a citizen of the United States.

It was late in September 1973 when we had to appear before the circuit court judge to get tested. Henry and I had to be alone in a room with the judge to take the test. I was asked by the judge if I ever belonged to a communistic party, the terms of the president or the senate, and what the name of Wisconsin's governor was. Then I had to write a sentence, "Today is a beautiful day."

Henry told me later he had to write, "I like food," but he wrote food with only one "o", so the judge made him write, "I'm a good boy."

We both passed and that made me feel really good. Now we had to wait until November 16, 1973 to get sworn in.

I was so proud to become a US citizen that I decided to have a citizenship dance and invite all our friends. That is my way of saying, "Thank you so much for all your help." The girls and I made the invitations. I bought little patriotic stickers (Liberty Bell, the Statue of Liberty, etc.), glued them in front of the invitations and wrote in fancy letters "God Bless America." Everybody thought that was so neat.

Dewey Schwoch, the president of the Holstein Breeder Association, got up at the annual meeting and said, "I got an invitation in the mail the other day that brought tears to my eyes. We are in the middle of Watergate and have nothing but negative thoughts of this country, and here is a family that came from Switzerland. They are so proud to become US citizens that they will have a dance. And they can still say, 'God Bless American.'" Everybody got up and we got a standing ovation. It made me feel so good. Henry, the children and I had to sing for them later that night, and I was so proud of my family.

The closer we got to our big day, the more Henry complained. Why do we have to have this dance the day that we get sworn in? That is stupid and we do not have time to do the chores. We could have made that dance a couple of weeks later. But we get sworn in on the 16th of November, and not two weeks later. There was nothing that could make me change my mind. Plus, I ordered a three-man polka band to play for us, and I had made the reservation at the Legion Hall, of all places. That was one time Henry could not make me feel bad.

We went to the barn early that day. We had to be in Wausau at the Marathon County Courthouse by noon. Some of our friends were already waiting for us. Phyllis Reinhart, the daughter-in-law of Ted, who got us to this country, pinned corsages on my girls and me, and a carnation for Henry and the boys. The teachers from Scott School were present and brought the fourth and fifth graders along. That is maybe the only time in their lives that they would see someone they know becoming a US citizen.

The courtroom was full, and more than half of the people came to witness us taking our oath, one of the proudest days in my life. It is an indescribable feeling when the cadets march in with all the flags, holding them with their white gloves, and then standing in line saluting while we are taking our oath to become good, productive USA citizens.

It was so quiet you could hear a pin drop. I had a lump in my throat and my heart was pounding 90 miles an hour as I said: "I pledge allegiance to the flag of the United States of American, and to the Republic for which it stands, one Nation, under God, indivisible, with liberty and justice for all."

Julius and Erika were there with us. They got sworn in, too. Then each family received a letter from the White House signed by the President, Richard Nixon, and a neatly wrapped package with an American flag in it given by the Republican Party.

There was only one thing I could never understand. After I unwrapped our gift, there was a little rubber band holding the rolled-up flag together. Underneath that rubber band was a sticker, and on there it said, "Made in Korea." We just became citizens of the United States of America and are proud of it, yet the flag we were given was made in Korea. Something here is definitely wrong. If we can't make flags in this country, then at least take the sticker out before you wrap it and give it to a new citizen.

The Women's VFW Auxiliary had some snacks ready after the ceremony, and we got a lot of hugs and kisses. But then we had to hurry home to get the chores done, to be at our dance at 8 p.m.

Henry complained the whole way home, how stupid it was to plan a dance the same day. But I was determined and happy, and I would let nothing make me feel bad.

The kids helped get the cows fed and milked, and we were done in time. We changed clothes again and drove to town to celebrate with our friends, now that we are one of them.

The band played the first dance especially for Henry and me. He danced with me. Dancing in his arms made me feel on Cloud Nine, and he looked so happy and very proud.

The dance hall was packed with friends, and everybody was so relaxed. Never ever before did one of them go to a citizenship dance, but everybody thought it was a great idea. It was past midnight when the last of our guests left. Henry gave me a hug and a kiss and said, "That was really a great night, and that meant more to me than the most expensive present. Thank you." Yes, Henry can be romantic, too; it just won't happen too often.

Edith and her best friend Sally love to dance, but did not spend much time on the dance floor that night. We invited Henry's friends from the feed mill to come and celebrate with us, and one of them was Brian Schulz. That was the night Edith fell in love with Brian, who two years later married Edith. From that day on Brian became a regular guest at our house.

It is kind of scary seeing your children dating. It makes you feel old. Looking at them, I asked myself, "Did I really do with my life what I set out to do?" Yes, I did, I told myself. I had a great family and well-behaved kids, at least so far, and I think that is the greatest accomplishment anybody can achieve.

But, US citizen or not, we had to get back to work to support our family. Edith was a cheerleader and also a candy-striper. As such, she did two nights a week volunteer work at the hospital, and that meant a lot of running on my part.

All four of my children were also involved in 4-H. They participated in different projects. Reto took cattle to the Fair, and Heinz helped him, but then Heinz also tried his talent in woodwork and small engines. Edith, Lotti and Reto took baking, and the two girls also were busy sewing. And they were good at it, especially Edith. She was a perfectionist. She ripped something open three, four times until it was right, where Lotti felt as long as it looked good on the outside, then it was okay. No one had to check the inside of her garment. That is how different siblings are, even if we raised them the same way.

I taught all four of them to sing, and they got blue ribbons two years in a row for their performance at the 4-H competition. All in all, I was very busy.

My parents came again for four weeks vacation the summer of 1974, but this time flew into Mosinee, only one hour from here.

My dad worked in construction all his life, and that came in handy now, since we just decided to add 64 feet to the north of the old barn. Henry dug the hole with the bulldozer that we bought the spring before, and then my dad helped pouring the foundation. Together they also laid the block stonewall. There was hardly time for Henry to take care of the cows, so that became strictly Reto's and my job. Thank God for my girls; with my mother's help, they cooked for us and kept the house clean.

One morning Edith came to the barn and said Reto was crying; he had a terrible headache. I was just done with milking, told Henry I would finish the milk house later, and ran to the house.

Reto rolled on the floor, he was in so much pain, and he also had a fever. I called the doctor and told him, "I think Reto has spinal meningitis, can we come and see you right away?" But Dr. Karoby answered, "I don't think it is spinal meningitis. That is rare nowadays. I think he has a sun stroke. It was very hot yesterday. Give him aspirin and make vinegar soaks, and then call if it isn't any better by tomorrow."

I said okay, but I knew that was not what it was. My dad thought it was because Reto ran into the cord they put up so that they could lay the block stones straight.

I did as the doctor told me, made cold vinegar soaks

and calmed Reto down, and then went to finish the milk house.

One hour later Reto's temperature was higher yet, and he could not put his chin down to touch his chest. I knew there was something definitely wrong, and I called the doctor again. "If you won't take the time to see Reto, then I will bring him straight down to the Wausau Hospital," I said. "Okay, bring him in. We'll check him out," he replied reluctantly.

I drove Reto to the Merrill Hospital where Dr. Karoby waited for us. He took one look at Reto and called in a specialist from Wausau. Reto's fever shot up to 106. The nurse tried to put a needle into his veins for the IV, but the vein in his arm collapsed. They quickly put him into a rubber suit and laid him on ice to get the fever down. Dr. Karoby cancelled all his afternoon appointments and did not leave Reto's bedside until after 11 p.m., not until he was sure that Reto was stabilized. He was afraid that they would lose him.

It was just as I thought, spinal meningitis. But I was told to keep it quiet so no one would know, because this is very contagious, he told me. And no one except you can visit Reto during the next days.

I sat all night with Reto. The medicine started taking effect toward morning, and I could see him improving. Another one of those close calls.

I was tired as I drove home that morning, but so thankful that God did not take Reto from us. Once home there was no time to relax. There was work that had to be done. But daily I took a couple of hours to be with Reto. He had to stay in the hospital for ten days. We all were so relieved when we finally could take him home again. Then that was his second close call, and he was only 12 years old.

Thanks, Guardian Angel. You stood by my side again.

My dad worked hard to get the barn walls up, and even on the morning of his departure helped to set the

48-foot-wide crossbeams. Henry tied a tree to the bucket of his bulldozer. Heinz, only 14 years old, stood on the west wall and I stood on the east wall. My dad tied the crossbeams onto the beam and Henry lifted them up. Heinz and I had to straighten them out and see to it that they were exactly two feet apart.

It was a tough job, but got done, and I had to hurry to get my parents to the airport on time. A good thing that I only had to drive to Mosine, about a one-hour drive from here. My mother got all upset and worried that they would miss their plane, but we made it, and it was good there wasn't much time for long goodbyes. A hug and a kiss and on board the plane they went.

Henry nailed plywood onto the rafters, and then at last the shingles had to be put up. And that was Heinz's and Reto's job.

Then the second crop was ready to be cut and pressed into bales. Henry showed Heinz and Reto how to start the roof, and then it was all theirs. Those two boys, 14 and 12 years old, shingled that whole roof. The addition was 64 feet long and 47 feet wide. Yes, it was a lot of work for the boys. If they got mad at each other, they threw each other off the eight-feet-high roof, but all in all they did a great job.

Our county agent came one day to investigate. He checked with his yardstick to see if the shingles were straight, and he could not find anything whatsoever wrong with the job our boys did. Yes, my children had to work hard, but they also learned a lot. We could never afford to pay for someone else to do the work. Thanks, guys. I love you. You are the greatest.

To get to our farm, one has to drive on Highway 64 west out of Merrill just two miles, and then turn on County Highway E north. About 1.5 miles in on E, just as you get over the hill, there is a nice farm with a neat, white, two-story house on it. It has a nice lawn in front and looks just so lovable. Every time I came over that hill on E, I thought to myself I would like to own that farm someday and maybe retire there.

Bob Mutz, a real estate broker, came to see us early summer and told us that there was a 200-acre farm for sale just two miles from us. "The farmer just signed the papers and I will list it tomorrow, but I thought I would give you the first chance," he said.

"Two miles from here? Where could that be," Henry asked.

"Elmer Stevenson's place," he replied.

Boy, that was my dream farm. We had just added more cows and Henry was looking for more land.

Farming is like a wheel that can't be stopped, unless you stop it yourself. You want more income. That means you need more cows. But more cows need more feed, so you need more land. Now the workload is too big with the small machines. The barn has to be bigger to house new cows, and you need more silo room to store the feed. So you build more silos, add to the barn and buy bigger equipment, which costs more money. Then you have to have more cows to get more milk check to be able to pay the extra bills. And you start all over again. One has to come to the point where he says that's it. I just have to do with what I have.

Every time we bought something new, Henry seemed happy, and I thought now we have it all. But it did not take long and something else came up, and again we were short on cash. So now it is this farm. Yes, it is my dream farm, but the cost is $74,000 — $74,000 we don't have— and I don't want it that bad.

Henry felt we could not go wrong, paid $500 down and signed the contract. Bob went to see a bank in Wausau about financing the farm, and within a week that farm was ours.

Now we had to milk more cows, then we had one more

payment, and more cows meant a lot more work. Elmer Stevenson and his wife retired and moved off that farm. For the first year we rented the house out. Later Edith lived there and then Lotti. (Lotti bought the house and eight acres of land from me in 1994.)

The children had to go back to school, and that meant winter was right around the corner. Field work had to be finished, corn chopped, fields plowed and manure spread. And in between, we kept on working on the inside of our addition.

After the kids got home from school, they had to change clothes and then help us. The girls cooked and cleaned house. I mixed the cement with our Montgomery Ward cement-mixer. Heinz pushed wheelbarrow by wheelbarrow into the barn, and Henry poured and leveled the cement. Reto had to get the feed ready and let the cows in the barn and then put the milk machines together. Reto and I milked, while Henry and Heinz kept on with their cement work.

Those were long, long days, but the job got done, and before the first snowfall we had the barn full of cows. We now had 64 stations (64 cows) and still cleaned the barn by hand, which was hard work, but that was my job. Like Henry so many times laughingly said, "A man should never have more cows than his wife can handle." And so I did.

Because of all the work on the addition, it got late fall and the corn was not chopped yet, but the fields were wet. Then it rained a lot that fall. Henry tried to chop it with the tractor, but got stuck in no time. So he went home and got the caterpillar, put it before the tractor, and told me to get on it. I had to pull the tractor, chopper and wagon.

I did a lousy job, since I had to look back to see that Henry stayed straight with the corn rows. Plus, the caterpillar has no steering wheel either, only two sticks. If I just pulled a little too much on one stick, we moved over and Henry missed the row of corn. Then I corrected too much and he drove over the corn. There were a lot of choice words used and tears that flowed, but the corn got in and that was most important.

I still was a member of the Homemakers Club and belonged to the Ladies Aid at St. Paul's Church. I was Scott School PTA secretary from 1969 to 1974, and now could retire, only to get involved in the Women's Auxiliary for AMPI (American Milk Producers, Inc.) Together with other farm wives, I promoted dairy products, something I thought was vital if we wanted the dairy industry to improve. We went to Madison, our state's capitol, to testify, and wrote letters to our legislators.

Yes, I kept busy. The winter went fast and gave way to spring, and the field work started all over again.

Reto got confirmed that spring. He was the last one of our children to become a full-fledged member of the Lutheran religion. Henry's nephews, Albert and Urs, were in Reto's class, but because I was in the church basement getting Reto ready, Martha did not come downstairs, so I pinned the carnation on Albert's and Urs' robes. We are in church, so how can hate be part of us?

That morning was the first time I had trouble praying, "Our Father, Who are in Heaven ... forgive us our trespasses as we forgive those who trespass against us ..." How can we pray this and yet have so much hate in our hearts? We are all humans. We all make mistakes and should be able to forgive each other. Hate was never part of my life, and I guess that is why I will never understand where someone else is coming from.

Again, Bachs helped us celebrate the special occasion. Yes, it is good that we have holidays like this so that we can relax, if just for a few hours, since with our workload we find less and less time for enjoyment.

A good thing that Reto was confirmed then; just a couple of months later we got kicked out of that church. I refused to put money into the envelopes that were given to us by the church every month. Henry's sister Martha and Breitenmosers went to the same church. End of the year we got a booklet showing us how much money each individual member gave through the year. I felt very strongly that that was no one's business. That is only between me and God.

I went to church almost every Sunday, gave each of the children a quarter or more to put into the hat, and I gave a dollar. That was at least $3 per Sunday, multiplied by 52 weeks equals $156, and that was all I could afford at the time. But it was not good enough, and the minister, together with some board members, sent us a letter. They didn't even hand-deliver it. They wrote us we were no longer welcome in their church. Didn't Jesus talk to the poor people also, and kept them in his care?

In 1975 we remodeled the free stall barn (the steel addition to the south) that we built in 1971. Since we were shipping grade A milk we couldn't just build the way we wanted to. We needed a permit. Once again I had to make a blueprint and sent it to Madison. The gutters had to be the right depth and the cow layers the right length, and we had no problem. They accepted my blueprint the first time I sent it in. Everything had to be okayed by the Department of Agriculture. I sure had a lot of different jobs. It was a good thing that I watched my dad when I was a teenager so I knew how to do blueprints.

We closed the east wall and put stanchions in, and now, finally, an automatic barn cleaner. Since money still was tight, we just bought the barn cleaner, and Henry and I installed it. We sat for hours by the corners and tried to figure out how it worked, how the curves had to be cemented in so they would hold up.

The barn was now 200 feet long with 92 stanchions to tie on cows. We also had heifer pens and calf stalls; all in all, room for 170 head of cattle.

Our barn cleaner was about 400 feet of chain that had

to be pulled by one motor, which meant a lot of pressure. I was scared when Henry said, "I will push the button now and see if it runs." But it worked, no problems whatsoever. Boy, we sure can be proud of ourselves. We achieved great things. That barn cleaner made my life a lot easier, but now we had 92 cows to milk, and then all the calves to feed, so I still did not run out of work.

We also put up two Harvestore silos that year, a corn unit and a hay unit. Now that we milked so many cows, the milk tank got too small. We needed a bigger tank, and that meant a bigger milk house

We did not build the Harvestores ourselves, a crew came and did it for us, but everything else was done only by our family. Henry was the carpenter, welder and electrician, besides all the other jobs on a farm. He was really happy and proud of his achievement, at least for a little while.

Reto got terrible headaches again early that spring. I took him to see Dr. Janowiak, and he transferred Reto straight to Wausau to a specialist. That same afternoon we had an appointment with Dr. Stanko in Neurology. He did different tests on Reto and then put him the same afternoon into the Wausau Hospital.

"Reto has terrible pressure in his head. I think he has a brain tumor," Dr. Stanko told me. "Reto might have to have surgery, but not before we know exactly where the tumor is located."

What a shock! Will it never end?

I stayed with Reto for awhile that afternoon, but then had to go home to help with the chores. Henry was just crushed when I told him what the results were. The next day at 8 a.m. I had to be at the hospital again.

Dr. Stanko took me into a small room, and there on the blackboard he drew exactly what they were going to do. Every day from then on we met at the same time. He would explain everything and answered any of my questions. They made a small incision by Reto's crotch, then went through his artery all the way into the brain, and put dye in it. Then they strapped him into a big chair and turned him every which way. The dye went to a certain point, but not any farther.

When they brought Reto back into his room, he had to lay on his back very still with a sandbag over his cut, to make sure it did not bleed, or he could have bled to death.

Four days later they did it again. This time they put tiny radioactive balls into his brain. All along Dr. Stanko explained what they would do. Reto was such a good sport, even though he still had terrible headaches.

Dr. Stanko told me on Good Friday they now knew where the blockage was, and Reto would have surgery on Monday afternoon. I was so scared. Brain surgery. Will he ever be the same again, or will he lose his memory, I asked myself.

It was a long Easter weekend. All of us went to see Reto that Easter Sunday, and we all wished him luck and told him we would pray for him. His eyes looked sad when we left him, but he swallowed his tears. And I felt so bad, not being able to help him.

We milked the cows and went to bed early that night, since I knew I had a long day ahead of me. I was tired, but could hardly sleep. It must have been almost midnight when I finally fell asleep. That is when my grandma came again. She walked into the bedroom just as I saw her the night she passed away. A smile on her face, she said, "Don't worry, Reto is going to be okay. He will not have to have surgery tomorrow. But Edith will," she said.

Just as I did once before, I woke Henry up. The minute he was awake Grandma disappeared, never finishing her sentence. It haunted me for years. Every time Edith was sick, I thought maybe that is it. Maybe that is what Grandma wanted to tell me.

I could hardly wait to get to the hospital the next morning. There stood Dr. Stanko with a smile on his face. "Reto will not have to have surgery," he told me. "Reto had a blockage, and for some unknown reason it disappeared last night. His headaches are gone."

I gave Dr. Stanko a big hug, and all I could say to myself, "Thank you, Grandma. Thanks so much. You just made up for all the hurt you caused me."

I knew it might sound odd to strangers, but I told Henry that night what happened. Long before I knew, what Grandma told me came through, or Henry would never have believed me either. Maybe that was my grandma's gift to me for all the pain I had to go through as a child. I never, ever saw Grandma again after that. I love you, Grandma. Thank you. May you rest in peace now.

Our progress from 1968-1975.

84TH CONGRESS, 1ST SESSION,
HOUSE DOCUMENT NO. 225

Pledge of Allegiance to the Flag

★

I pledge allegiance
to the flag
of the United States
of America
and to the Republic
for which it stands,
one Nation *under God*,
indivisible, with liberty
and justice for all.

You are cordially invited
to help us celebrate our
becoming citizes of the
U.S.A.
The dance is from 9:00-1:00
Nov. 16, atthe Legion Hall
Merrill, Wis

The Henry Gross Family
RFD 4, Merrill

We made invitations to have our friends come to our naturalization celebration.

THE WHITE HOUSE
WASHINGTON

Dear Fellow Citizen:

I extend to you a warm welcome to citizenship of the United States of America.

George Washington, the first President of the United States, once said this to his fellow citizens: "The name of American, which belongs to you in your national capacity, must always exalt the just pride of patriotism..." By your free choice you have become a citizen of this country; the name of American is now yours.

As an American, you now share not only the rights of all Americans but the common heritage which has always called forth the "just pride of patriotism". As an American, you now have the opportunity to engage in the most rewarding activity of free men: full participation in the democratic process of a self-governing people.

Our constitution begins with the words which we all know: We the People. We, the People, your fellow citizens, by birth and choice, salute you, because on this day you have become a most valued citizen of the United States of America.

Richard Nixon

November 16, 1973.

THE UNITED STATES OF AMERICA

CERTIFICATE OF NATURALIZATION

No.

Petition No.

Alien Registration No.

·ORIGINAL·

Personal description of holder as of date of naturalization: Date of birth December 18, 1938 sex Female; complexion Fair color of eyes grey-brown color of hair Brown height 5 feet 7 inches; weight 136 pounds; visible distinctive marks None

Marital status Married Country of former nationality Switzerland

I certify that the description above given is true, and that the photograph affixed hereto is a likeness of me.

(Complete and true signature of holder)

STATE OF WISCONSIN
COUNTY OF MARATHON } ss:

Be it known, that at a term of the CIRCUIT Court of MARATHON COUNTY held pursuant to law at WAUSAU, WISCONSIN on NOVEMBER 16, 1973 the Court having found that EDITH GROSS then residing at ROUTE #4, BOX 252, MERRILL, WISCONSIN intends to reside permanently in the United States (when so required by the Naturalization Laws of the United States), had in all other respects complied with the applicable provisions of such naturalization laws, and was entitled to be admitted to citizenship, thereupon ordered that such person be and (s)he was admitted as a citizen of the United States of America.

In testimony whereof the seal of the court is hereunto affixed this 16TH day of NOVEMBER in the year of our Lord nineteen hundred and SEVENTY-THREE

Seal

Clerk of the CIRCUIT Court.

By ________ Deputy Clerk.

IT IS PUNISHABLE BY U. S. LAW TO COPY, PRINT OR PHOTOGRAPH THIS CERTIFICATE.

DEPARTMENT OF JUSTICE

Edith Gross' Certificate of Naturalization.

11

SPRING 1975. EDITH still is dating Brian. She is going to be in 12th grade in fall and quite a young woman, who had a part-time job as a clerk at the local drugstore. She had no support from me about sex education, since I was so busy with the barn that I didn't have much time. Plus, when I had my children there were no birth control pills. We just went by the calendar, which turned out to be wrong every time. And then before I had Reto, Henry had surgery and we no longer had to worry.

So that was one subject I did not know much about. Edith got help from her future sister-in-law, Charleen. Charleen took Edith to see a doctor in Athens. Edith told me that night as I kissed her good night that she had a prescription for birth control pills and asked if I would pick them up for her the next day. I felt bad that my daughter had to go to someone else to seek help. I should have been the one to tell her what to do, yet I had no experience, but at least I could buy her the pills.

Edith did not feel that good the next couple of days and went to see our doctor for a checkup. Dr. Janowiak promised her he would call the next day around noon to give her the results. We were eating lunch when the telephone rang. Edith went to answer the phone. She did not say a word. Her face turned pale and tears started slowly running down her cheeks. I knew right then, without even asking her, what that meant. Edith was pregnant.

She later had to tell Brian. They talked it over and decided to get married. They set their wedding day for August 16. That was only two months down the road, so that meant a lot of planning, but it also was fun to go and look at wedding and bridesmaids' dresses. Edith and I could spend a lot of time together to plan her wedding, and that felt good. The last couple of years Edith drifted away from me. Many of times she told me, "You don't love me. You never have time for me. We do not even spend our Sundays together the way we did in Switzerland. All you and Dad see is work, work and more work. On Brian's side they enjoy life. They spend weekends on the lake."

Yes, she was right, at least with part of her frustration. We did not take time for the children like we did before we moved to the USA, but I still and always will love her, and someday she will understand that. But for now it hurts as a mother to feel that you failed. Now that we together could plan this wedding, we got closer again.

From the beginning, Brian's mother, Ada, volunteered to pay for the supper at the wedding. "You can't afford it anyway, and we have lots of relatives, where you have no one," she said. "I got a lot of flowers in the garden and you can make a bride's bouquet out of them. I know you don't have the money for flowers," she offered.

But my answer was simple: "If I can't afford the flowers for my daughter's wedding, then there will be no wedding. What if we have a storm that ruins your garden just days before the wedding, then what?" I was not mad at Ada. It was nothing new to me. She was not the only one who made us feel like we were the poorest family in town. So we just didn't ask her anything anymore and made all the plans for the wedding ourselves.

It was a beautiful Saturday. All the preparations were done and we were on our way to church. I got butterflies. My daughter getting married. Does that mean I'm old now? But who cares? I'm proud of my girl all in white. She looked just like a princess.

Ada (the future mother-in-law) was at the church already and told me that they would seat some of their relation on the bride's side, since we have no one. Slowly but surely the guests arrived. I could not believe my eyes. There were so many, many of our friends. The bride's side of the church was full in no time. Boy, that made me feel good.

Julius and his family and Hubert and his family were seated in front as close relatives. But the bench right behind Henry and me was empty. We reserved it for Martha (Henry's sister) and her family, the only true family we had.

Martha and her daughter Inge came to church, but they went upstairs and sat in a pew. That hurt. This was Edith's day and at least, for her sake, they could put their differences aside. But I guess that is the way the chips fall, and nothing I can do about it.

Gretel Fischer, a good friend of ours (she immigrated from Germany) told Martha after church that it wasn't nice for them to go upstairs and, through the empty bench below, show the whole congregation that she and her brother can't get along. This was Edith's and Brian's day; everything else should have been overlooked. Yes, it hurt, but we are used to that by now.

After the service we had a chicken and ham dinner in the church basement. We did not have much time to sit around, since we had to hurry home. The cows had to be milked, and we did not want to miss the wedding dance later that evening.

The dance hall was packed. Brian's dad, who left his family when Brian was just 16 years old, attended the wedding. There was a lot of tension, and after a couple of beers it flared up. Sandy, Brian's sister, started arguing with her dad. I went to them and told them, this is Edith's and Brian's day, if you want to argue, then do that tomorrow, but I will not allow you guys to fight tonight, or I will have you kicked out of here. And they did quit and got out of each other's way. It was a great, happy evening.

Edith and Brian could move into my dream farm house,

the one we bought two years ago, just about three miles from home. That is where we had the after-wedding on Sunday afternoon. Boy, if I could get married again, I would do it here. Edith got so many, many beautiful presents, it was unbelievable. I could count my presents on one hand. But I am happy for her. Our present to her was one year free rent.

Edith finished school and became a mid-year graduate. She graduated with a gold tassel, in the top 10% of her class. What an honor! What a great job! I'm so proud of you!

Lotti was in 10th grade now, but she got in with the wrong crowd and got in trouble.

One morning I was milking when I got a phone call from the high school. "How sick is Lotti? I heard she had a deadly disease. Do you want a tutor to come to your house and help her?" someone on the other side asked.

"What do you mean deadly sick," I asked. "Lotti goes to school every day."

"No. For three weeks now we get a phone call everyday that Lotti is too sick to come to school," that lady told me.

"Lotti goes to school every morning on the bus and comes home with the bus every night. There is nothing wrong with her," I argued. The lady apologized for getting me upset and promised to investigate.

At 2:30 p.m. that day Henry and I drove by the school to see what was going on. And sure enough, there was Lotti getting out of a car with other girls and guys and then standing in line with the rest of the students waiting for the bus.

But when she saw her dad, she quickly went into the school to her guidance counselor and told him, "My dad will beat the shit out of me. I'm afraid for my life. Please put me in protective custody."

They got her overnight into a foster home, and made

an appointment with the judge for the next morning. At 9 a.m. we had to appear in court. We had to get up early to be able to make it to town on time. All along I told Henry not to say one word, since if he is upset he says anything that comes to his mind, not thinking clearly anymore. "Just stay calm and let me talk," I said.

We got into the judge's chambers, and there was Lotti with a social worker and the judge waiting for us. It was tough to sit there defending yourself against your own daughter.

First the social worker talked. She gave us that big lecture, how to raise children, and then told us, "You have no right to punish your child, since she also has rights, just as you have. We have to see that their rights aren't violated."

Then the judge gave us his viewpoint. And Henry did not say one word, even though I could see that he was ready to explode. The judge asked us, "What do you have to say to all of this?"

"Lotti did wrong," I started. "She went to school every day for the last three weeks, but never was in school, called in sick every day, which meant she was lying, something I can't stand. So she deserves to be punished in some way. I can see that beating her will not help, but she has to be punished, nevertheless. And if you, as judge, tell me I can't punish my own daughter for the bad things she just did, then you can have her. I don't want her anymore."

The judge looked at me, nodded his head and said, "Yes, you are right." And, turning to Lotti, he went on. "Lotti, you have two options. Either you go home and obey your mother's rules, or I put you into a home where all the dopers are, with their brains fried. That would teach you a lesson. It is your choice. Now, what do you want?"

Lotti looked at me, took a deep breath and answered, "I guess I will take the lesser of two evils and go home."

Thank God it turned out the way it did. But I also

knew where Lotti was coming from. She has a lot of Henry's personality, and they clashed often through the years. Even if Lotti did not deserve it, she got punished. I remember one night not too long ago. Lotti was babysitting for Weavers and came home around 10:30 p.m. Henry never asked where Lotti was, and I did not say anything. I thought he knew. Lotti came in through the front door, and before she knew what happened she got slapped left and right on her head. "That will teach you not to whore around," Henry said.

I was stunned. What triggered that, I asked myself. But before I could respond, Lotti looked at her dad and said, "Your hitting me did not hurt at all, what really hurts is you not loving me. I'm almost 16 now and you never gave me a hug or a kiss, and not once did you say I love you. That hurts all the time, not just today." And upstairs to bed she went, letting Henry stand there.

Henry and I talked long that night and I tried, like so many times before, to make him understand that the kids need his love.

"But I put food on the table and clothes on their backs, isn't that love enough? And I will not kiss the boys because they are boys, nor will I kiss the girls, since if I kiss a girl that means I want sex from her, and I sure would not touch my own child."

Yes, for that I'm truly thankful, but I still could not understand that he could not see the difference between kissing his own daughter or a woman. But I'm not in his shoes, and tried so many times before to make him see that the kids needed his love, but it did not sink in then, and sure won't now.

Henry knew he did wrong, but "I'm sorry" is not in his vocabulary, so I stood up for him again and made the children understand that all of this comes from his horrible childhood.

That is why I know what Lotti's logic was, but neither

of us said one word to the judge. Sometimes one has to see the whole picture before one can understand and is able to judge. Yet, we are all responsible for our own actions and there are no excuses. Lotti did wrong this time.

Fall gave way to winter and all the animals kept us busy. And we were excited, as we expected our first grandchild.

It was on February 3rd; I had to go to the dentist. I had an overbite all my life, and for some time already had a sore behind my top front teeth. The dentist was worried it could turn into cancer and recommended to pull all my teeth.

So I drove to the dentist and he pulled all my upper and lower teeth, cut my upper gums open and chiseled the damaged bone out. That was when Brian walked in and told me that Edith just gave birth to a baby girl. They named her Jessica. My mouth clamped wide open, I could not even say "Congratulations," but I felt very proud. Boy, I'm only 37 years old and a grandma already.

The doctor finished his chiseling, then sewed everything together and put the new dentures in, gave me pain pills and said, "See you in four days. You have to keep the plate in or it swells up too much," were his last words, and on my way I was.

I had to stop at least every mile, I felt so sick and it hurt so much, but I made it. Once home, there was work that had to be done, cows that had to be milked and no time for pain.

Edith had a Caesarean and had to stay five days in the hospital, but we went to visit her. What a great feeling to have a healthy, beautiful little granddaughter in my arms. Jessica had a cute round little face, but most important, she had all her toes and fingers. What a great gift from God!

For the last four-five years I told Henry I would like to adopt a small child. I had my children so close together and was still very young, plus had to work hard, I didn't have time to enjoy them. No longer could I cuddle a baby, and my arms felt so empty. I'm more mature now and would like to have one more child. Not a baby, just a young child.

But I could not get Henry to agree, so I left well enough alone. Thank God now I have a grandchild that I could baby-sit for, and that will make up for it. Edith stayed home for seven weeks, and then went back to work. That left me with little Jessica, and I loved every minute of it. We became best buddies.

Reto had a wrestling tournament in Minocqua. Henry, the girls and I went to watch Reto wrestle. And he needed us for protection. Reto was a great wrestler and a good-looking guy, and the girls were after him like crazy. They would not even let him rest between matches. He had won every match so far, and only had one more to go. So we all went to the cafeteria and had a bite to eat.

We got interrupted when we heard a strange voice come over the loudspeaker. "Would Henry Gross please come to the announcer's table." We saw a policeman waiting for us as we walked up there. What does he want, I asked myself. Maybe someone made a dent in our car.

But then my heart skipped a beat and it felt like someone just dumped a pail of cool water over me when I heard the policeman say, "Your son Heinz just got shot."

"Got shot means he is dead," I replied.

But he had no answer. He helped us find a telephone and got the phone number of the hospital. He even dialed the phone for me since my fingers were so shaky. Please, God, don't let him die, I prayed, as I listened to the ringing in the phone.

Then a nurse answered and told me, after she knew who I was, that I had to talk to the doctor. "What does that mean, did we lose him?"

Then the doctor came and told me that Heinz lost two

fingers and part of the third one; otherwise, he was okay. But they could not do surgery without our okay.

"Is it good enough if I sign a statement with this policeman here saying that I allow you to do the best you can," I asked. And it was okay. The policeman even volunteered to escort us to the hospital, but Henry felt we could do it, as long as he alerted the police station so that we do not get stopped for speeding.

Henry drove like crazy and no one said a word. He dropped me off at the hospital, and then went home with the others to do chores, since Heinz was supposed to have the cows fed before we came home. As they walked into the living room, there laid the bloody gun. Blood everywhere — on the phone, on the rug, and the fingers were splattered all over the room. Henry, not knowing what happened, took the gun and slammed it over the table, which broke the gun in two.

I stayed at the hospital through the surgery and waited until the early morning hours when Heinz was out of the anesthesia. That was when I got to know the facts. Heinz saw a crow sitting in the tree and figured that she was a good target. So he got the gun and aimed, but the crow flew away before he had time to pull the trigger. Dad taught him never to shoot if you don't have a target, and he didn't. He put the gun down and went back to the house. He put one foot on the chair and the gun on the knee to unload.

Henry also taught him to always put his hand over the barrel when he unloads the gun so that the bullet doesn't jump too far. Heinz did that, too, but something did not function right. A .22 caliber has like little clamps that hold the bullet, and they did not release as the bullet came back. It made a spark and the bullet exploded in the back of the barrel. Thank God Heinz had his hand over it and not his face. It could have killed him. The splinters from the bullet were visible in the ceiling for many, many years.

Heinz had to stay a week in the hospital, but then recuperated quickly. Thanks, Guardian Angel, for saving my son.

****

My children, one by one, are going, and we no longer have help. That gave me the idea to put an ad in a Swiss farm paper. "Help wanted on a farm in the USA with the chance to see the country." I figured, one could work and live with us, and then between hay and second crop we would give him our car and he could travel the States for two to three weeks. I thought that was a fair deal.

We had a lot of applications, and it was hard to pick without seeing them or being able to talk to them. But I picked Hans Ueli Moser, and it was a good choice. He was 19 years old and a very hard worker.

Henry cleared ten acres of rough pasture land. There were stones to pick, big stones; it took weeks. It was hard work, but not once did Hans Ueli complain. We gave him our car for two weeks to take a trip. Since his English wasn't the greatest, he took Heinz along, and together they went all the way to New Mexico, Grand Canyon and California. Hans Ueli was very impressed and truly enjoyed the trip.

Lotti dropped out of school and worked in the kitchen at South of the Border, a Mexican Restaurant. Her friend, Vicky, had no place to stay, so she moved in with us. It was not too bad in the beginning, but then they stayed out until the early morning hours, slept till 11 a.m., got up, ate breakfast, then locked themselves into the bathroom for the next two hours, and out the door they went again.

"Lotti, you can't do that," I said. "I can't sleep worrying. You have to be home by midnight." No matter what time I went to bed, I could sleep like a rock, but then, as if my body had an alarm clock, I woke up at midnight and could not sleep anymore.

I could hear a car coming up the road. "I hope it turns

in. I hope it is Lotti." But no, it went past again. I just lay there in bed. I was afraid to even turn, since I had to make sure that Henry didn't wake up, because knowing that Lotti was not home that time of night really would have gotten him angry.

I warned Lotti more than once, "Lotti, one more time and you will have to leave this home." But nothing seemed to make a difference.

Then one Saturday morning, after another sleepless night, I waited till Lotti and Vicky came downstairs. I blocked Lotti's way and said quite calmly, "Lotti, the car keys, please, and there is the door."

Lotti looked at me and knew I meant every word I said. She handed me the keys without saying one word, grabbed Vicky's arm and dragged her out the door. They walked across the lawn to the street, put their thumbs up in the air, and within five minutes someone stopped and took them along.

That was one of the most awful things I ever had to do. I stood by the kitchen window and saw them leave. I cried so hard and felt like someone just ripped a part of my heart out, but I would not go out there and ask them to come back.

I know no matter how much it hurt, I had to let her go. She was just like a young bird. I had to give her wings and let her fly. She had to fall, so she would learn to pick herself up again. I realized that is the only way she would learn.

I did not see nor hear from Lotti for three months. She helped people she knew with housework, babysat, and did all kinds of things to support herself. Years later she told me, "Mom, that was the best thing you ever did for me, to kick me out. I would never have changed if you had given in."

We only want the best for our children. Then why do we have to go through so much heartache, as we see them go, one by one.

****

My parents came to visit us again. My dad remodeled the old part of the barn and Reto helped him. Heinz worked for a neighbor who was building a log cabin. My dad could never understand that we had so much work at home, and Heinz goes and helps for little or nothing somewhere else. I could see it, but did not want to make any waves, and so kept quiet.

Heinz was not one to defend himself. If someone thinks he did wrong, then so be it. But he said once to my dad: "Our neighbor doesn't pay me much for helping neither, but every night when we're done working he says, 'Thanks for your help. Great job.' That is something I never, ever hear at home. Here I can do ten things right, no one says one word, but then I do one thing wrong and all hell breaks loose, and I'm tired of that." And on his way he went, not even waiting for my dad to respond. Yes, I could understand where he was coming from. We were buddies, and for too long already had to cover each other's mistakes.

One example: one day I baled hay on Louis Tesch's land. I was low on diesel and sent Louis to get me some. He came back with two five-gallon cans. I dumped them into the tank, and off I went to get the baling done before milking time. But the tractor just did not have the power that it had before. "What went wrong?" I thought to myself, but kept on pressing the bales.

Once I was done, I drove home just in time to get the cows into the barn to milk them. As Henry helped tying on the cows, I mentioned the tractor. "It just doesn't have power anymore." Boy, that was the wrong thing to say!

"What did Louis bring you," he asked.

"I don't know. I told him to get me diesel, and when he brought it, I just dumped it into the tank," I answered.

"Didn't you smell it? Couldn't you see he brought you gasoline and not diesel? Now the tractor is ruined and can never be fixed again. All the money it will cost us to get a new one…" and on and on he went.

Heinz heard the conversation, went and drained the tractor, flushed it out and filled it with diesel, started it up and it worked like a charm, and we had that tractor for 14 more years. I was really lucky that Heinz could fix it.

One other time Henry and Heinz went up to the silo to chop some ice off the wall, then came down without closing the last door. I went to the barn that afternoon, not knowing what they did, since no one was around. I started the silo unloader. The first load came down fine, but all of a sudden I heard an awful racket. I quickly turned the unloader off and climbed up the silo chute.

What a disaster! The unloader chopped part of the wooden door up and bent the iron bars that were needed to hook the door in. "What do I do now?"

I took the door out and exchanged it with the one farther up, straightened the off-centered unloader out, and then fed the rest of the cows.

As soon as Heinz walked into the barn, I told him of my troubles. He took the door and hid it, to be fixed later. If Henry would have seen it, it would have been awful, but that is just the way Henry is.

I didn't want my dad to know all of that, or I would have made Henry look bad, and I did not want that, since he did not know any better. That's what Henry had to go through as a child. But that's why Dad did not understand why Heinz would rather work for free for someone else than at home.

My parents left the end of June and took Edith and Brian along. That was Edith's belated wedding present from my parents. They wanted to show them Switzerland. And Hans Ueli left us, too. He had to serve in the military overseas. He flew back the 2nd of July. Now we were alone again, with so much work. But we got all our crops in and the plowing done before the first snowstorm hit.

In 1977 Edith changed her job and started working for Dr. Janowiak, and she really liked that. We had another Swiss guy who came and helped us on the farm, and my parents, my dad being retired now, came to stay with us for the whole summer.

Edith and Brian took them up north fishing on weekends. They also went to Wisconsin Dells, saw the water ski show there, and then went on to the House on the Rock. My parents sure liked that.

I did not have much time for them anymore, we had too much work, but I was glad that Edith showed them around. That was the last summer my parents spent with us. They never came again after that.

The summer went fast. Reto and Heinz went back to school, and that meant hurry up with the field work, since winter was just around the corner.

Reto was in wrestling and was really good at it. There wasn't a match that he lost, and even though he was only in ninth grade, he could participate in varsity matches. We were very proud of him and would not miss a match. Henry came along to all the home matches, but if it was out of town I had to go alone.

After school wrestling was over, he tried out for free-style wrestling and made it all the way to the State championship. The final competition was in Wisconsin Dells. I had to get up early, get the chores done quickly so that I would make it on time to see him wrestling. Reto won every match, and the last two guys in his weight class gave up when it came to the round robin. "Reto is going to win anyway, so why bother?" they said. I was proud of him. That win gave him a ticket to go to Nebraska to try out for the Junior Olympics.

I could not go along, since there was too much work at home that had to be done. A friend of Reto's from Merrill got under the first three in his weight class, and so also had a chance to go to Nebraska. His parents took Reto along.

Reto did not make it into the top three there. He had too many other things on his mind. The girl gymnastics team was at the same location for their tryouts. The girls were more important to Reto than wrestling, and there was no Mom to keep him going.

He also went to Chicago that fall and participated in an international free-style competition and made fourth in his weight class. A great achievement!

For us there was just so much work, and Henry still was homesick. All along, every time we bought a bigger, newer machine, or more cows, he was happy for awhile, but just as a child with a toy, it gets old quickly and they have their eyes on something else.

Henry went to the PCA one day to finance a "cultypacker" we recently bought. They had no questions, just said, "No problem. You can have the money."

I prayed so often that the loan officer just would say no once; that would make Henry quit buying, since getting bigger and bigger in farming is just like a wheel — after it rolls, you can't stop it anymore. You want more cows so that you have a bigger milk check. But then you need more feed and to take care of more land you need bigger machines. And to pay for all of that, you need more cows, and the cycle starts all over again.

I was so tired of that. Can't we be happy just with what we have? Why do we still have to prove to Henry's siblings that we can achieve great things? And I still get told I'm stupid and lazy. So I said to Henry one day, "I've had enough. You can have everything we have here. I'll get me an apartment in town and I will look for a job. All I need is a car to get to work."

But Henry didn't want any part of that. I had Jessica in my arms and stood in the bedroom crying. "I really will leave you this time. The kids are old enough, and you can make it on your own. I'm tired of always being put down. I was only quiet so long so that the children didn't know how bad it was."

Henry reached for the Swiss army rifle that stood in the corner of the closet. It was loaded. He cocked it and held it just one inch from my temple. I could feel the cool iron on my temple.

"One more step and I will shoot. If I can't have you, no one else will get you neither," he said.

I was scared to death. If only nothing would happen to Jessica. I slowly backed up, Henry following me, but I forgot that the playpen was behind me and I fell backwards into it. But even as I fell, I would not let Jessie out of my arms. With my weight, I flattened one side of the playpen.

When Henry gets mad, it is like something snaps, and he does not know what he is doing, and there is no reasoning anymore. But seeing me fall brought him back to reality and he put the gun down. "Please don't leave me. I can't live without you," he begged me.

I was so tired of hurting that I didn't even cry anymore. I felt numb. And I started thinking, what if he really would have killed me, and then him. What would happen to my children? Would that rip them apart? No, I can't leave him, and if only for their sakes I have to stick it out. They still needed me, and I know that if Henry is desperate enough he would do a stupid thing like killing us both.

Why does life's road have to be so bumpy?

I gave him my word that I will stay and we will try it one more time, but I will never forget that feeling, and I never want to be so close to death again.

****

Again we had a young guy from Switzerland that summer to help us.

Henry spread manure all winter, but got stuck so many times that he decided it was time to build a storage facility. He dug a 12-feet-deep 100' x 70' pond, then dug a trench to the barn and laid pipes all the way to the liquid manure pressure tank we just buried there. The bottom of the pit got blacktopped. It was a lot of work, but Henry did a great job, and once again without any outside help. The greatest thing was I could let the barn cleaner run and fill the pressure tank, then close it like a pressure cooker and hook the air hose up to it. The air pushed the manure out to the pond. It was just so easy, and I loved it.

That fall I had trouble with my throat. My right side swelled up over and over again. It looked like I had the mumps. So I went to see the doctor. "You have a stone blockage in one of your glands," I was told. "That stone blocks the saliva that goes into your mouth and that makes the swelling."

They tried to dissolve it; it did not work. Then they made a cut under my tongue, but that didn't work either. So surgery was the next best option. After all the tests were completed, they scheduled the surgery for the end of February. But Henry didn't feel well all winter either. He had something like morning sickness. I laughed and told him every so often, "If you were a woman, I would say you are pregnant." I finally convinced him to see a doctor.

Edith called two days later and said, "Dr. Janowiak wants to see you both today." That did not sound good at all, but she could not give us any specific reason. That was all she knew.

So we made the trip to town. Dr. Janowiak sat down with us and told us that they found a growth as big as a pea in Henry's bladder. It should be removed immediately, but there was not much more that he could tell us.

"I'm scheduled for surgery in a day," I replied, "but the week after he could come in."

"That's okay," the doctor answered.

Edith drove me to Wausau that Wednesday, and Thursday I had surgery. Henry did not feel well and had all the cows to milk; that's why he had no time to come and see me. I had no reason to complain or feel sorry for myself. I just had to look at my roommate and then count my blessings.

My roommate had a cold a couple of weeks before and just took some aspirin, but still went to work. Then one day she collapsed. They rushed her to the hospital where they found that the cold she had made her brain swell up. She lost all her memory, did not know when and how to go to the bathroom. But what was even worse, her husband was there every day, and her children came to see her regularly. They brought photo albums, hoping that that might bring some of her memory back, but nothing. They were all strangers to her.

That woman was a few years older than I and she just celebrated her 25th wedding anniversary a couple of months before, and now she couldn't remember anything; didn't even know her husband.

I tried to talk to her and she would respond, but only to things that just happened. Everything from the day before was gone. Oh, how sad, and here I am feeling sorry for myself! I saw that woman years later. She was still the same, having no idea that the person taking care of her was her husband. I really had to count my blessings.

It was Sunday, and Henry came to take me home. Even though I was weak, I had to start working right away, knowing well that in three days Henry had to have surgery. He had to be in the hospital Wednesday noon to get ready for his surgery.

Thursday I got up early, and Reto helped for a while until he had to go to school. I finished the barn, took a shower and had a quick bite to eat. Then I had a 9 a.m. doctor's appointment in Wausau. They had to take my stitches out. It was past 10 a.m. when I left there, and I hurried to the Merrill Hospital to see how Henry was doing. I did no more than walk into his room; Henry was not there yet when Dr. Mayersack came in.

"Where in the hell were you? How inconsiderate of

you. Your husband just had cancer surgery and you are nowhere to be found," he said.

I felt like he hit me with a hammer. "Cancer!" No one told me that that is what Henry had. I replied with a shaky voice, "I got here as soon as I could. I had surgery myself not even a week ago and had the stitches taken out this morning. But before that I had to milk 90 cows."

It did not seem to sink in. The doctor was still mad at me.

It took hours before they wheeled Henry into his room — long, lonely hours for me. What would I do if he was dying? Could I keep on farming? What if I have to quit? Where would I go? What would I do? All those questions and no answers.

A nurse wheeled Henry into the room, put him in his bed and covered him up. I could see that he had a catheter and a bag hanging down. Dr. Mayersack made another appearance. He was still upset with me when he told Henry, "You have bladder cancer. We put a balloon into your bladder so that it can't collapse. Some test samples got sent to Madison to figure out how deep into the bladder wall the cancer has gone. It will take about five days for the results to come back, and if the test isn't good, we will remove your bladder and see if we can save your kidneys."

Henry, his eyes filled with tears, just listened. "Please tell me, how long do I have?" he then wanted to know.

"No promises," the doctor replied. "If you make it past the first five years, you have a pretty good chance."

I sat with Henry for a while longer that afternoon, but my heart was heavy, yet I had to be strong and cheer him up. It was not until I drove home that day that I could let my tears free flow. I felt so sad. All those dreams — is that the end of them?

But I had to dry my tears up quickly before I got into the house. I didn't want to get Reto upset. He was home from school and waiting for me. I had to tell him his dad just had cancer surgery. Reto and I went to the barn together, since the chores had to be done, no matter what.

Reto walked into the middle of the barn. Our cows have their heads toward the middle, and they all looked at him like, "What do you want?" He patted one on the head, his eyes filled with tears. He said, "Now that we got it all together, now Dad has to get sick. What if he dies, do we lose all of this?"

I gave him a hug and promised him, "I will do my best, and if we stick together, we can make it, and nothing will stop us." But deep down I was not sure if that really would work.

I went to see Henry daily, and the nurses were just great. They tried to cheer him up. It was not until Tuesday that we knew that the cancer did not get into his kidneys yet. What a relief! He had to stay eight days more, and then he could come home, but had to take it easy. But that did not matter. We still had him with us, and that was most important.

Henry's best childhood friend, Hans, from Switzerland, asked if his son Andy could come and work for us in the summer of 1979. And then a girl who was related to Andy wanted to come for two months to see how we farmed. "Great," I said. "At least we have help."

And then only one month later Annekather, who was an employee of mine in Bergun and through all those years stayed in contact with us, wrote that she knew a young farmer who would like to get first-hand experience how we farm in the USA. Since Henry needed to take it easier, we decided to take them all.

At that time Heinz lived in town and worked for an implement dealer as a mechanic. Lotti lived in Tomahawk. And Reto got in with the wrong guys. Drinking parties were more important than anything else.

Reto was still good in wrestling, and a lot of people

came to the matches only to see Mike Man and Reto wrestle. That got to Reto's head. Plus, one of the not-so-famous wrestlers, who was a year older, got Reto all the beer he wanted. Reto, just like our other three kids, got a car after his 16th birthday; each of our kids got a car. We emptied their savings account before we left Switzerland and used their money to start our endeavor, and now was payback time. We made the down payment on a new car, and then each of them had to work to pay the rest off, and Reto was no exception.

But he hadn't had his car more than two months when one of his drinking buddies said, "Let's skip school today and go for a drive." Reto thought that was a great idea. "Let's go to Tomahawk and see my sister Lotti," Reto said.

But Lotti was not home, so they drank elsewhere. Reto felt he was too drunk to drive his car home and let his friend drive it. Only his friend had never driven a front-wheel-drive car before. He came too fast into the curve and flipped the car three times. They flew eight yards up into the air and took the branches right off a tree. It took over 200 feet until they landed in the ditch.

I was in the barn already wondering where Reto could be when the phone rang. "Your son Reto is in the ambulance on the way to Tomahawk hospital," the nurse told me. "We will call you when we know more."

"How bad is it?" I wanted to know.

"We don't know," she replied.

I called the police, but the only information they could give me was that Rod's Wrecker picked up the car, so I called them and that made me feel even worse. They told me, "The car looks so bad, it is unbelievable that there are any survivors." I was just sick to my stomach.

Heinz came home to see how we were doing. I told him what just happened, and he said, "Just do your chores. I will go and see what goes on, and if it is bad, then I will call you immediately," and off he went.

No wonder my hair is turning gray so quickly. If it is not one thing, then it is another.

Heinz came back later that night and brought Reto home. Reto's friend ended up in the Wausau Hospital, as he had a deep cut above his lips and the lower part of the nose ripped off. God, I'm glad no one got killed. How could that even happen? Reto was supposed to be in school. Reto was all banged up and in pain, but not too badly injured. He straightened out for a couple of weeks after that, but then went right back to drinking again.

There is no guy on this earth who had more accidents than Reto. With our Volvo, he rear-ended a lady who all of a sudden decided she needed gas and turned just in front of him. He drove our four-wheel-drive Jeep up the curve-guard when he fell asleep at the wheel early one morning. He ran into a lady in town who did not stop at a stop sign. It was unreal.

Reto, instead of helping us at home, worked for an out-of-town company harvesting beans. There he could work till 3 p.m., and then drink for the rest of the day.

Reto was not old enough to drink, so one day he and his buddy came home half drunk and went upstairs. I called the police, since I had had enough. I wanted Steve, who was of age, to get away from Reto. But they must have overheard my telephone conversation, sneaked out the window and disappeared over the roof. When the policeman came, those two were gone. And by the time they found them in town they were sober again.

Steve, Reto's drinking buddy, talked him into enlisting in the Navy. "We would make good money, and it would be lots of fun," he told Reto. And so they both went to the recruiting office in Wausau and took their tests. Reto's test was tougher, because he did not graduate from high school yet, but he was smart and already had letters from colleges that would have loved to have him as a student. He passed the test with flying colors.

Then the recruiting officer came to our house. He needed our consent, since Reto was not 18 yet. Henry did not say one word, signed his name on the dotted line and then disappeared into the barn. Like always, if something bothered him he crawled into his shell. And it truly, truly hurt him to see Reto, our herdsman, enlist in the Navy. Heinz is gone, and now Reto is leaving, too.

Henry built this farm up so that his boys someday would be proud of him and take over the farm. So often through all those years I told Henry, "Your children will only remember the love you give them, and if you do the best you can, they will always be proud of you."

My parents never owned a house or a car, they were just plain simple workers, but through all those years I was proud to say they are my parents. And it will be no different for our children.

But Henry wanted to stand up on that pedestal so that the children always have to look up to him. And now he could see that pedestal crumbling in the sand. It was sad to see his hurt, but that is something he has to work out himself. I could not help him.

I was glad I had those guys from Switzerland. Plus, we had a lot of laughs with them. Regula, the girl from Switzerland who came to stay with us for two months, was my housewife. And she did it by the book. Monday is washday. Tuesday is ironing day. Wednesday shopping and mending day. Friday was cleaning day. She used to lock the doors so none of those inconsiderate guys could get her fresh cleaned floor dirty with their barn boots.

And Sunday she went to church, and she walked, even though we lived seven miles out of town. Our dog liked to tag along; that's why she tied him up before she left. Andy and Martin, our two farmhands, waited until she got over the first hill, then untied the dog and he ran after her. Ten minutes later Regula came back holding the dog on the collar and tied him up again.

One day she made a roast and mashed potatoes, but no gravy. Those guys complained through the whole meal. The next day she made pork chops and spaghetti, and a big bowl of gravy. I thought it was funny, but did not say much. I had enough on my mind the way it was.

Lotti told us that she was pregnant and would get married to Larry Hess on September 22, 1979. That was only three months away, and there was a lot of planning that had to be done. The wedding dress, bridesmaids' dresses, the church, the hall and the invitations, but Lotti did a lot herself, and so made it easier on me.

It was the end of June when Regula returned to Switzerland. I sure missed her, since now I had to do all the housework myself again, plus the fieldwork and milking.

One day I was cutting hay all morning. Around 11:30 a.m. Henry came and picked me up. It was lunchtime. The guys were hungry so I'd better get going. As I stood by the hot stove heating up some soup, I listened to those guys. They sat at the dinner table enjoying a cool beer. I do not know anymore which one started the conversation, but one asked, "Can you see the bean stalks in Edith's garden?" The other two started laughing and replied, "No, I can't see anything. All I see is weeds!" and on and on they went.

I did not say one word, since the garden was my project. My garden always looked good in spring, but during haying season I had hardly any time to work on it. After nine at night, when everybody else was taking it easy, I usually went to weed the garden. But my workload had gotten so big by now that I just did not find the time anymore. And those guys relax while I'm preparing their lunch, and then they have the gall to laugh about my garden. Not one of them ever helped me.

Lunch was ready. We ate, and then I quickly returned to the haybine to finish that one hayfield. It was just a little after 4 p.m. when I got done. I took one last glimpse over my fresh cut grass, all those rows laid out nice and straight, so homeward I went with my machine. As I drove the three miles to the farm, I could hear those guys laughing about my garden. I thought to myself, I will fix this problem once and for all. So, as I drove into the yard, I steered straight through the lawn and into the garden. I let the sickle head down, started the sickle up, and cut my whole garden down. Never again would someone have to make fun of me, and I never planted a garden again.

The corn was planted and cultivated, the first crop in the silos, and even part of the second crop was baled when Martin left us at the beginning of August. He had to go home to be best man at his sister's wedding.

It was almost time for Reto to enlist. Reto told us all along he was going to have a big drinking party before he had to leave, but the closer the day came the more he changed his mind. The Sunday before he had to leave, he took us two, his sisters, his brother, his girlfriend and her mother out for a Sunday brunch at the Hoffman house.

He told us, he had changed his mind and wouldn't have a drinking party, because he realized that after he was gone, his drinking buddies would forget him in no time, but his loved ones would always be there for him. I was so happy that he realized that I could have cried. How quickly reality hits. Reto, I love you, and may God always watch over you!

Lotti and I drove Reto to Milwaukee the following Tuesday. All the way there we made small talk, since Reto, I think, felt just as bad as I did. We stayed in an old hotel right downtown. I could hardly sleep that night there was so much noise in the hallway, plus my thoughts were going wild. What will happen to Reto? Will he have to go to war? I had sat so many hours already by his bedside praying for his life, and now he might give it away in the Navy. It was just so scary.

At six in the morning a stranger knocked on the door.

It was time for Reto to get his checkup, his haircut, and then change into his Navy clothes.

We saw Reto one more time for just a few minutes. There were newly enlisted guys all around him, and no way could I give him one more hug or a kiss. He stood there as if he had to convince me, "I'm a big boy now. I have to be tough," but I could see in his eyes that that was not easy for him.

One more time we waved, and then went on our journey back. A good thing Lotti's wedding would be in a little over a month. That gave us something to talk about and kept my mind off leaving Reto behind. Lotti and Reto were best buddies when they were little, and now he couldn't even participate in his sister's wedding. But I guess that is life. We can't always have what we want.

****

The weeks went fast, and here it was, Lotti's wedding day. Henry walked Lotti down the aisle. Just by the last bench she stopped, and a lady started singing, "Thank you, Dad, for everything you did for me. Even if I didn't always show you how I felt, I truly love you."

I could not hold my tears back anymore. Lotti, out of all of my children, the biggest troublemaker, to have picked a song like that was unbelievable. She gave Henry a kiss to seal that song, and then took Larry's arm.

The minister talked from his heart. He tried to make them understand that it is easy to get married, but that it takes a lot of work to keep a marriage together. And, boy, do I know that feeling!

After the sermon was picture-taking time, and then off to the dance hall, where the supper waited for us. Bachs and Fuellemans were with us. Again, we had to hurry home. The cows had to be milked, and we did not want to miss the dance.

Andy, Henry and I had the chores done in no time, and back to the dance hall we went. Henry still was a great dancer, and that night asked me more than once to dance with him, and I felt so proud and warm, being led by his strong arms.

It was past midnight when the band packed their things together. Some of our friends had to have one last drink on us, but Henry, for some unknown reason, did not drink at all. He only had two drinks all night. He was so calm and caring.

We paid the bill and walked outside, and so did the rest of the group. "Since you paid the bill, we will let you lead the path," they laughed, "and we will follow you." And off we went, down Highway 51 toward Merrill. We got to the last curve, just before town, when we saw a car come toward us. "My god, that guy drives right off the road," I said. And that is the last thing I remember.

That guy came from town and did not realize there was a curve. He was out on the soft shoulder when I said that. But the gravel made him realize he was off the road and he corrected his steering wheel, only he over-corrected it and came across the road and hit us head-on, then slipped to the side of our car, took the doors and everything on the driver's side off, and then went on and hit Werner Rusch's car behind us. The impact on our car was so powerful that as he left us it threw us into the ditch.

As soon as we came to a standstill, I came to and screamed, "Henry, are you okay?"

"Please don't touch me," he answered, almost crying in pain. "Please leave me alone."

My next thought was Andy. He was in our back seat. What if something happened to him? How could I call his parents in Switzerland? I turned around and asked, "Andy, are you okay?" He looked at me and down he went. He passed out.

All the ones who drove behind us had stopped and came running to see how we were. Henry could hardly breathe, and the bone in his left arm stuck out of the tuxedo sleeve. Lotti left earlier and drove to Tomahawk to get a pizza and sober Larry up before they got to their motel room in Merrill, so now she was behind us. From far away she could see the flashing lights. "The lights are from my parents' car," she told Larry. "I know the Volvo lights."

I was out of the car when the ambulance drove up, and I ran around like a chicken with the head cut off, but I had to see if someone else got hurt. I felt no pain. I was in shock. Lotti walked up to me still wearing her wedding gown. She took my head and pulled it to her heart and said, "Oh, my God, Mom. Oh, my God."

Henry was strapped onto a stretcher, and Andy, still unconscious, in the other stretcher. Everybody told me to get into the ambulance. "Why? I'm not hurt."

But they forced me to sit in the front by the driver. That was when my head started hurting and I realized that I took the rearview mirror off with my head, went into the windshield and had a deep cut over my right eye. The left eye got cut by glass from the windshield, and all of a sudden I had a pounding headache.

Lotti and Larry drove to the hospital right behind us. Oh, how terrible Lotti's dress looked! My face had a lot of cuts from all the glass, and I was bleeding when Lotti hugged me. My bloody face was painted onto her wedding dress.

The doctor took a scissors and cut Henry's sleeve off. "No, no," he said, using all the strength he had, "that tuxedo is rented."

"Don't matter," the doctor replied.

They took Henry and Andy for X-rays and had already sewed my wound when I heard through the police scanner that they got the guy that did that to us. He was drunk and on drugs, lived just around the corner from where the accident happened. He hit his head on the steering wheel, but then walked out of his car. When our friends saw that he was okay, they all came over to us to check if they could help. That is when the other driver disappeared and went home to bed. It was a 22-year-old guy who borrowed the car from a neighbor. He had no insurance, no job, and owed back child support. Yes, a real loser.

Henry was scheduled for surgery the next morning. They had to put a screw into his arm. He also had seven broken ribs on his left side. Andy came to in the meantime but had to stay for observation.

The doctor told me I had to stay, too. "No way. I have to go home. No one knows which cows to milk and how to feed them." They saw how determined I was and released me early Sunday morning. Lotti and Larry drove me home, but I was hurting really badly. There was not one bone in my body that did not ache.

They took no X-rays of my neck, but I found out years later that I went home with a broken neck. I could have died or been paralyzed, yet never got a penny for it.

Larry's parents were there to help me in the barn, but they were never close to a cow before, and I hurt so badly I could hardly bend down and did not want to talk or even show them how to do things. I just wanted to be left alone.

Before I went to the barn, I called Julius. He could not believe it when I told him what happened to us. "We went straight to the barn when we got home and are almost done."

"I will be there to help you right away," he answered. Thank God he is coming. At least he knows how to milk.

He called Schneider's dispatcher, the company he drove truck for, and told them, "I have to have a couple of days off. I have to help my best friend out." And so he did. He stayed for three days and helped me do chores.

I felt terrible after the chores were done that Sunday morning, but asked Edith to please drive me back to the hospital. I wanted to be there for Henry when he had the surgery. Edith stayed with me at the hospital while Lotti prepared for the arrival of the guests that came to the after-wedding. Henry's surgery went well, but with all those broken bones he was in a lot of pain.

I could not call Reto since he was still in boot camp, but volunteers from the Red Cross did it for me. A lieutenant went and got Reto straight from the exercise field so that he could call home and talk to us. Oh, if I just had him here now to help me.

Henry had to stay in the hospital two weeks, while Andy was released the following Monday. That is when the nurse found out why Andy was unconscious when they brought him into the hospital. Andy cannot stand the sight of blood. When he saw my face all full of blood, he passed out. He was not injured at all, only some scratches on his left ear.

Andy stayed with us for three more weeks, but then he too had to fly back to Switzerland, which left me alone with all the work. Henry came to the barn, but could not help me at all. His ribs bothered him and he had a cast on his left arm. But Edith was in the barn at 5 a.m. every morning and helped milk the cows. Then we had breakfast together, she took a shower and went to work, and I went to clean the barn and did the rest of the chores. I don't know what I would have done without her help.

The guy who hit us had to go to court. He got a ticket for crossing a double yellow line, drunken driving and leaving the scene of an accident. But then the judge said, "He did all of those things because he was drunk, so he only got a fine of $175 for drunken driving."

How unfair! He had no job and I had so much work and was alone. Why couldn't the judge make him work for me? This guy had no insurance so the State wanted $50,000 from him to pay for our doctor and hospital bills and our car, which was a total loss. If he does not pay, he has to surrender his driver's license, which he did. But then two months later, with the help of his dad, he filed for bankruptcy. Everything was forgiven. He got his license back and we got nothing. Oh, how unfair! I went through so much pain and he got off scott free. And I had to work so hard while he enjoyed life.

Reto graduated from boot camp in October, and since Henry could not work anyway, I got him a ticket to fly to California and be there for Reto. So off to San Diego he flew, and from there he went to visit his sister Elsa. Henry and Reto had some great days together, and that was good. I think it helped both of them emotionally.

I had Jessica with me. She was my helper. Jessica sat by the calf pens singing to them while I was milking. She was with me when I put silage out, constantly clambering along. It was great to have her by my side, even if it only was for entertainment.

It was only October but we already had snow, and it was cold, while Henry sat in California by the pool, enjoying the warm sun. But that was good for Henry. It will help him heal, hopefully inside and outside.

12

CHRISTMAS 1979 PASSED, and a new, hopefully better year begins.

Heinz tried for more than a year to get into the Air Force as a mechanic. He was a mechanic at the local implement dealer, and he was a good mechanic. The farmers really liked him. He passed all the tests at the recruiting office and was accepted. But then they saw that he had two fingers missing from the accident he had as a 16-year-old boy when the gun malfunctioned. From then on they gave him the runaround. No one had an answer and would tell him why they did not want him. Typical bureaucracy.

He even went so far as drawing his left hand on a piece of paper and sent it to the Pentagon. But no luck. His dad always told him if he welded something, "No one would hire you in Switzerland, you're doing such a lousy job." And now he was not good enough for the Air Force either. That really must have hurt.

Heinz was no dairy farmer; he was a mechanic through and through, so he dared his dad and went to Switzerland to look for a job. My dad took Heinz to the Toggenburg Valley where Henry grew up. Heinz applied for a job there. Since he had no apprenticeship with diploma as a mechanic, the implement dealer was skeptical and made a deal with Heinz. "I will hire you. Your grace period will be three months," he said. "If I do not like your work ethic, I will let you go. But, if you don't like it here, you're free to leave also." Heinz accepted, and within six months was foreman. He sure could prove his dad wrong.

My dad and Heinz became best buddies and went mountain climbing together. Yet, Heinz was homesick. He missed the good old USA and would have loved to come back. But since everyone teased him before he left this country, "Oh, you will be back by Mom in no time," he suffered through it, just like his dad did in the USA. Why does one have to hurt so much to prove a point?

Henry could not work all winter. His arm did not heal. He had too many broken bones, and his body could not produce enough substances to mend the bones. Then in April they took bone out of his hip and put it into his arm. That was when the doctor said to me, "You have way too much work. You need help."

"What can I do," I asked.

"We will get Reto out of the Navy," was their reply.

The Red Cross, two doctors, a lawyer and a friend of ours wrote letters to the Pentagon. I had to write one, too, telling them why I needed Reto at home. In May we got an answer. They would give Reto an honorable discharge because of our hardship.

What a relief! Even though he had to work at the recruiting office in Wausau every afternoon until all the papers were finalized, he was a lot of help in the mornings. How grateful I was to all the people who helped me to make this possible. God bless you all.

On February 19, 1980, Lotti gave birth to a healthy baby girl. They named her "Bobby Jo." Lotti, too, had to have Caesarean. The water broke on Sunday, but she had no labor pains. Then by Tuesday the doctor knew he had to do something to save this baby.

Larry, my son-in-law, got a speeding ticket on the way to the hospital for driving 45 in a 35-mile zone. He told the police officer, "I just got a phone call that my wife has to have surgery, so I did not watch my speedometer closely enough."

"That is a pure excuse," the police officer answered, and made Larry wait until he got the ticket written.

Larry said, "Please hurry up. I have to get there."

The officer replied, "If you aren't quiet pretty soon, I will haul you in and put you in jail."

Larry told me about the mishap, and I called that same police officer later that morning and told him that was not nice. But he was nasty to me, too.

"You could have called the hospital and checked it out," was my argument.

"We do not have time for stupid things like that," was his answer.

I was not mad that Larry got a ticket, he was speeding, but I was mad the way it was handled. So I called the police chief and told him what happened. "You do not have to give me an answer now, but please would you look into this," I asked. It did not take more than an hour or so and I had an apology and the ticket was dropped.

Five days later Lotti brought her cute little round-faced baby girl home.

Martin came again that spring, and I was so glad. Since he was a farmer, he knew what to do. Edith's marriage wasn't that great anymore, but she still tried to keep it going. In July she wanted to take a trip with Brian, and so that it would be cheaper for them, take Martin and another Swiss guy along. The two could pay for the gas, she thought.

It was all set and they would leave on Friday. But Brian came home from work that night and said, "I have no money to go on vacation."

"What did you do with your vacation pay?" Edith asked.

"I just spent $700 for new golf clubs," was his response.

Edith was so frustrated and did not know what to do anymore. "Okay, then there will be no vacation, but my mom babysat free all this time while I was at work, so we at least will take her and the others out for supper," she told Brian.

"Okay," he replied.

All of us went to Tomahawk to a fancy place. Some of

them ordered shrimp and fancy drinks. "Would you please go and pay," Edith said to Brian just before we were ready to leave.

"But I have no money," was his answer.

Guess who ended up paying — Mom and Dad. And Dad was really furious, and I could not blame him. Edith had thoughts long before, but now knew their marriage would never work.

Brian wanted to be a professional bowler, but could not find a supporter. He asked us for support, but I told him that it would be foolish of me to finance his hobby. Our daughter Edith would have to work and raise a child while he would travel all over the country.

Brian bowled every night in winter, besides snowmobiling, which cost money, and in summer it was bowling, golfing and baseball. All in all, he never had time for his family, so Edith filed for divorce — nothing ugly, just split and get on with life. She still worked for Dr. Janowiak, and could live in our house. She helped a lot on the farm and made up for her rent payment.

Yes, our children make mistakes, just like everybody else's, but they have to learn to get up again when they fall, and then go on with their lives.

Early that spring I told Henry, "I will go home to visit my parents this summer. And I will go no matter what. Are you coming along?"

"No, of course not," was his answer. "I can't see why you have to spend all that money."

I did not reply, as something deep inside of me told me, "Go for it."

At the beginning of July I asked Henry again, "I go and buy my ticket today. Are you coming or not?" He hesitated, but then told me to get him one, too. And then the 14th of August we flew back to Switzerland. For the first time since we left in 1968 did we go home together.

I hadn't seen my dad for two years, but I could not

believe my eyes when we stepped out of the plane. He looked sickly to me, his skin yellowish-brown, and he'd lost a lot of weight. Yet he tried to convince me that nothing was wrong.

Dad had something planned for every day. At six in the morning he woke us up. "Let's go," he said. He took us up to the Schilthorn. That cable car was built especially for the movie "007." Once on top we had lunch at the restaurant. We could sit at the table and not move at all, but the floor turned. Within one hour while we were eating a delicious meal we could see every mountain around us, the whole 360 degrees. It was just gorgeous.

Dad ordered some soup, but after two or three spoons could not get anything down any more. I could see that he was really sick. But still he said, "No, nothing is wrong."

We stayed at a hotel in Wengen, and the next day took the train up to the Kleine Scheidegg. Henry felt just like at home. The cows were grazing in the light green mountain meadows. Some of them wore bells, and that sound carried for miles between the mountains, then came back as an echo. It really felt like home.

We boarded the cog-wheel that would drive us up to the Jungfraujoch. We went from 6,400 feet above sea-level to 12,400 in a little over 30 minutes. The small train circled its way up through the mountain. Twice it stopped and everyone had to get out and walk to the huge window they built into the rugged mountain. From there we could see down to the valley.

The small towns looked just so peaceful. It was beautiful. The farther up we got, the thinner the air. That is why they make you get out and walk, so the heart can adjust to the huge difference.

Once on top we could see mountain peaks all around us and just below the huge Aletsch glacier. And that brought back old memories:

My dad and Henry went mountain climbing one day. I

only had two children at that time. My mom and I stayed in a little cabin. Those two guys told us that they would be home before dark. The sun went down and it got late. 10 p.m. and they still were nowhere to be seen. We got so scared. Mom cried — what if we lose them? What would happen to us? We could not go to bed, since sleep was the last thing on our minds. But we also knew that we had to wait until morning to call a rescue team and see if they would go and find them. It was just so scary.

Then at 2 a.m., all of a sudden I could hear some noises. I ripped the door open and there stood my dad and Henry, holding each other up. They were so tired and had nothing to drink or eat for so long that they couldn't even talk. I made them some tea and warmed up a bowl of soup and that helped a little.

Later they told us that they had to climb through new snow, and then got caught on the edge of an avalanche, and that's where they lost their backpacks. I took their shoes off and helped them to bed, and was just so glad to have them back.

Now, standing up here at the "Jungfraujoch" looking down at the glass-clear, bluish mirror-like glacier that they had to cross that day, all of those memories came back as if it happened yesterday.

But enough of my daydreaming. Those times are past. We went to the restaurant and had some coffee, and soon it was time to head back down. It was a great, memorable day.

The next day we went over the St. Gotthard to the southern part of Switzerland. We took a boat ride on the beautiful deep blue "Laco Maggiore." My dad paid for everything. It was as if he wanted to show us Switzerland and its beauty one more time and make us see the pretty flowers, the meadows and the rugged mountains through his eyes.

The vacation went way too fast, and it was time to

head back to the farm. But I made Dad promise before we boarded the plan that he would see a doctor, even though he still insisted there was nothing wrong.

Once back home I had no time to dwell too much on Dad's condition as there was work that had to be done. I still was involved in AMPI, and also was a member of the Wisconsin Women for Agriculture, or WWA. Martha Rusch, the president for the local chapter of the WWA, and I, as treasurer, made arrangements to go to the American Agri Women Convention in Hershey, Pennsylvania. We decided to drive there, stop in Madison and take one other member, Anna, along. The convention was the first week in November. If we left early Sunday morning we could easy make it there the same day.

Friday before the convention I got a phone call from my mom. "Your dad is in the hospital," she said, "and they only give him four more weeks to live."

"Can't be! Why?" I questioned.

What should I do now? My dad told me when I left Switzerland in 1968, "Never come home for my funeral. Remember me as I was when you saw me last." And Dad always stood by his promises.

The doctor told my mom not to talk to Dad about dying, unless he started the subject. Yet Dad thought he could not talk because it would be too much for Mom, but they both knew that it was close to the end. Dad asked my mom daily, "Did Edith call?" But not once did he say, "Please tell her to come home. I would like to see her one more time."

I was crushed when I heard the bad news and told my mom that I would think about it and see what I could do. I could not sleep that night. What should I do? How could I help him? The next day I decided to call my dad in the hospital. I asked him how he was, and just made small talk. Then, just like a sideline, I said, "Oh, by the way, Henry and I planned a trip to California before Christmas, or what do you think? Maybe we could come home one more time. Would you like that?"

"Oh, it would be great to see you again," he answered. It was like he was afraid to ask, but waited for this question for a long, long time.

The kids talked Henry into coming along with me, so I went and bought two tickets. I thought I should cancel my trip to the convention, but Edith convinced me that I was no help at home, having so much on my mind. It would be better for me to go and be with other women. That would keep my mind occupied.

So Martha and I left Merrill at 4 a.m., stopped in Madison where we met Anna, had breakfast, and then drove straight through to Pennsylvania. In Indiana I got a speeding ticket; otherwise, everything went fine. I drove all the way and was really tired when we pulled into the parking lot at the motel in Hershey at 10 p.m. We drove 1,004 miles all in one day.

It was nice to get together with women from all over the USA, and all kinds of farming backgrounds. But I could not shake it, I was constantly thinking of my dad.

Wednesday night they had a banquet to mark the end of the convention. Martha even got an award. But I went to bed early, knowing we had a long trip back to Wisconsin the next day. It was late Thursday night when I lay in my own bed again. The next day I had to pack again, pay some of the bills and get ready, since we would have to leave for Switzerland on Sunday.

We arrived in Switzerland on Monday morning, and the first thing we did was visit my dad in the hospital. "I would like to come home," he begged, his eyes just glued to mine.

"Give us a little time to rest. We are very tired, because of the time change and the long trip. We will get you the first thing tomorrow morning," I promised.

Tuesday morning at eight he was ready to go home

and could hardly wait until we came to pick him up. He looked terrible, just skin and bones. His skin had a brownish, yellowish color, since he had liver cancer. Four years before they took part of his stomach out that was cancerous. It must have spread already, but no one detected it.

Dad has such bad convulsions that his whole bed was shaking. If he got one of those attacks, he couldn't even talk anymore, so we installed a bell for him right by his pillow that he could press and alert us. It was so sad to see this once so strong man deteriorate to nothing, a man who had mastered almost every obstacle and was such a hard-working human being. But none of us said a word about dying.

He wanted to go for a ride and stop at a restaurant one day. I gave him my arm to hold on to, but before he walked into the restaurant he let my arm go and tried to walk in straight so no one could see how sick he was. Yet all heads turned as he tried to sit down, and even though they were strangers, I could read in their eyes what they thought. He looked like Death was walking in in person.

Then another day he wanted to go and see a friend of his, who also was something like a natural healer. My aunt had to drive us there. She was so scared. "What if he dies on the way, what do we do then?"

"Don't worry, he is so determined that he will make it," I tried to convince her. And he did.

That friend told my dad, "Just hang in there a little longer. Your headache will be gone soon. I will pray for you."

Then, on the way home, Dad tried to convince us that everything would be fine. "See, my friend told me I get better and my headache will go away soon," he told us. But we all knew that is not what his friend meant. And still no one said one word about dying. What a lie we all live. There is so much that could be said. Time is running out, everyone is hurting, but no one talks.

Saturday, November 22, a mountain climber friend of Dad's came and visited for a while. Dad told him, "Edith is such a good daughter. She takes such good care of me. She deserves a new, beautiful Swiss chalet-style house, and as soon as I get better her mom and I will fly to the USA and I will build Edith her dream home. Don't you think that is a great idea?" he asked me.

"Yes," I said, but my heart was aching. I knew that he would never be able to do that for me. What could I do, Dad was still in denial and was hoping for a miracle. How sad, to forever lose those unspoken words, words that maybe could have helped to heal some wounds.

Sunday morning Dad had two convulsions in one hour, and he felt really sick. He was not able to leave the bed, could not eat nor drink. It was just awful. All of a sudden he broke down. "Please call all my siblings, and even Ueli, my brother, the one I did not talk to for years. I would like to say goodbye." I could no longer hold my tears back and had to give him a hug.

One by one came, and one by one spent some time alone with my dad. My son Heinz stopped by. My dad and he had become best friends through the last year, but today Dad had nothing to say to him. He just looked at Heinz, his eyes filled with tears, and said, "Take care!" To see this young 21-year-old grandchild who had his whole life ahead of him while his time was running out was just too much for my dad.

Then it was my turn to be alone with Dad. "Please forgive me for not being the father you deserved, and for not seeing what you went through because of my brother," he told me, holding onto my hand. He talked about things that I had long forgotten, but they still were vividly in his mind.

At last he wanted to spend some time with my mother alone. I think that is the hardest single thing I ever had to do in my entire life, to say goodbye to my dad.

The doctor came all along three or four times a day and gave my dad morphine shots, and in between the town nurse came to help us. She was a real nice lady who was familiar with death. She gave me a book to read from Mrs. Kuebler-Ross, *Encounter with Death,* and it gave me a lot of insight into the feelings of someone who sees his end coming.

The doctor came late that afternoon and gave dad another shot. Dad quickly fell asleep, and my mother lay right beside him. Monday morning when he woke up he could no longer talk. His sister Ida walked into the bedroom. Dad threw his hands up into the air and made animal-like sounds. But we all knew what it meant. He didn't want her to see him like that. He wanted only Henry, my mom and me around him.

If he was in too much pain, then Henry and I carried him out to the bathtub and he could soak in a vinegar bath, which seemed to relieve his pain. My mom sat on the toilet watching him so he would not drown as he dozed off every so often. With his eyes he could make my mom aware that he wanted to go back to bed.

Dad no longer could eat or drink. If he was thirsty, I gave him a wet washcloth to suck on. A man who worked so hard all his life now has to be taken care of like a newborn baby. There was always something that had to be done, and Henry and I were glad if we got one hour's sleep at a time. But if I could make life easier for my dad, then it was all worth it. And maybe some day, when I'm that far, one of my children will be there for me.

Thursday morning Dad got blisters on his feet. The doctor explained, as we stood outside the front door, that that meant his feet were dead already but his heart was still strong. He could not tell us how much longer it will take. He also told us to never talk in front of Dad about things like that, since even though we think he is in a coma he can still hear.

Dad's bladder and intestines gave up, and I had to wash and change him almost every hour. I kept the washer going night and day.

My mom, Henry and I sat with Dad all day Friday and saw him slowly fade away. Then at 4 p.m. he took his last breath. We folded his hands and prayed with him and then closed his eyes forever. With tears slowly running down my cheeks I whispered, "Goodbye, Dad. I love you. May God now take you in his arms."

I called the doctor, and he told us to go to the courthouse and sign as witnesses to Dad's death. That was hard for me to sign my dad's death certificate, but not nearly as tough as saying goodbye the Sunday before.

Yes, it is a sad day when you have to bury your dad, but seeing him suffer so much was even harder. A once so proud man, a man who stood on so many mountains peaks with a spirit that seemed unbreakable, being in so much pain and having to be taken care of just like a child is a lot harder.

The undertaker came early that night with the wooden casket. They carried Dad out after dark when the neighbors no longer could see everything. I put fresh pajamas on him and bought some carnations and put them between his folded hands before they took him away. He was to be cremated and laid to rest just a block down the road in the Protestant cemetery right by the church.

We couldn't sleep that night either. We still listened for Dad's needs. It was especially hard on my mother. She had lain by his side all this time and still could hear him breathe, even though his place was empty now. The next morning I packed a suitcase and we went to see my brother. Maybe if we get away from everything, we get over it.

The funeral was on Tuesday, a crisp, snowy day beginning of December. I let my thoughts wander as the minister had his sermon by the open grave. I saw us two sitting on that lonely bench as I could open up to my dad for the first time. I saw us sitting on our beloved mountain peak, the "Pi Kesch," saw him holding Lotti, his favored granddaughter, on his lap. All of that will now be a memory. "Thanks, Dad, for everything." I really was glad that Dad no longer had to suffer, and I had to thank God for finally giving him peace.

Afterwards we had a nice meal at a nearby restaurant, and that was one opportunity to talk to some family members I had not seen for 20 or more years.

We stayed two more days with my mother, but then had to go back to the farm. It was very, very hard for me to leave her behind. I felt so guilty. What did my parents ever do to me that was so bad that I have to hurt them so much? But I had to go. I had a family and a job to do.

No one thought that my mom would make it long. We all felt she would follow Dad quickly. But she fooled us all. It is now 1996 as I'm writing this book, and she is still living alone in a small apartment, taking care of herself. And even though we are thousands of miles apart, we are now closer than ever. She calls me at least every two weeks and talks for hours. Yes, it is expensive, but if it makes her feel better spending her money talking to me, then more power to her. I love you, Mom, and would do anything to make life easier for you.

Our son Heinz, my brother, his wife Lisa and my mom took us to the airport. One last kiss and one more "Love you all," and on the plane we went. The goodbyes get harder and harder, and it seems to hurt more and more every time. But I took a nap on the plane on the way back, and that seemed to make the time go faster. Lotti picked us up at the airport. It was a long day, but it felt good to walk back into the warm, smelly barn. They did a super job while we were gone. We did not lose a cow nor a calf, and not even the milk production dropped. Great job, guys!

****

Henry felt we needed a different bull and went to Van

Der Geest, the local cattle dealer and found one he liked. They bought that bull the 12th of December, 1980, and a week later two cows aborted their calves. Some of the calves got the diarrhea and died. It was unbelievable. We never had a big vet bill; we always took good care of our animals, and now this.

The vet came and tested the cows. "They have BVD," he told us. "More of your cows will abort. You have to watch them very closely."

We had just bought a three-week-old purebred bull calf for $500, and on New Year's Eve he got the scours. We did not know that if we give the calves milk from a cow that has BVD, even if she does not have symptoms, that they will die, too.

Henry was so frustrated and blamed me for it. "If you would have watched that new bull calf closer, that would not have happened. That is $500 out the window. You are just too careless."

Henry stayed with that bull calf all night. Every hour on the hour he gave him some tea with brandy. I did some housework, then at midnight I went back to the barn, but there was no way that I could even talk to Henry, let alone say "Happy New Year." He was just so mad at me and the whole world.

I went back to the house, fell on the bed and cried. If this is how we start a new year, after everything we just went through, then I never wanted to see another one again. I was just so depressed and wished I could be where my dad is now. Then at least my pain would be over.

But it is not that easy. I lay in my empty bed, my pillow soaking wet from my tears, and I prayed, "God, please help us. I can't take any more." I had to think of the saying I heard once: "When you're at the end of your rope, remember to hang on to your faith and look upward!"

The bull calf was dead before the sun came up on New Year's morning. BVD was also too much strain on cows that just had calves, and they would die. It was terrible. We must have gotten that sickness into the barn through the bull we got from Van Der Geest.

All in all, we lost six cows, 18 aborted their calves, and at least 30 calves died. Plus, the vet bill was tremendous. Over $3,000, and that is only medicine, and we treated the animals ourselves. Never again did we get a new animal from anyone into our barn in winter. That is a lesson to be learned.

****

Martin went back to Switzerland, and so did Edith. Edith and Jessica stayed with my mom, and Edith got a job at a local grocery store. Martin and Edith dated already when they still lived here, but Edith wanted to be sure she did the right thing this time.

Martin told her that he would like to marry her, but wanted to wait another year and work for us throughout that time, but he was a Swiss citizen and could not get a permanent visa, only a tourist visa. So for Martin to be able to come here on a long-term basis, he had to get married. That is not right. He had $10,000 in his bank account and a job with us, and he can't get a visa. Yet from the underdeveloped countries they can come without a red cent to their name, and we support them. So to make a long story short, Edith and Martin had to get married for him to be able to stay here.

It was April 24, 1981, when they exchanged their wedding vows in Switzerland. We could not be with them since we had cows to milk and could not just leave. Reto had to help on the farm, and Lotti had no money to fly there. The only one who could be with them was our son Heinz, and he was Edith's and Martin's best man. After the wedding, they applied for the "green card," but it took them more than a month to get all the papers ready to legally come back to the States.

Larry, our son-in-law, just couldn't find a job he liked,

and Lotti was on his case all the time. "We will not live from hand-outs and take from the government, like your parents always did. Get a job," she told him.

Larry heard at the Job Service Office that they were looking for help in Tulsa, Oklahoma. So he, his brother John and two of their friends went to Tulsa to investigate, and within two days all four of them had jobs. Larry came back up to Wisconsin. Lotti and he packed their belongings and off to Oklahoma they went.

It was on a Saturday, early in the afternoon, when they came to say goodbye, but Henry didn't want any part of it. He walked into the machine shop and let them stand there. Henry was still mad about the money he gave to Larry's brother John. Henry co-signed a car loan for him two years ago, and then after the car was trashed, John never paid another penny to the bank. I took the loan over because Henry was on my case for months already. It made Henry feel better that my name was on that delinquent loan now, even though it made no sense, since no matter what, the money to pay for the loan came from the farm anyway.

But now Lotti and our little granddaughter, Bobby Jo, were leaving and we did not know if we would ever see them again, and Henry would not even say goodbye. How sad. I hugged them and kissed them and wished them good luck. Oh, how goodbyes hurt!

I watched them drive off and then went into the house, threw myself on the bed and cried. I felt so lonely. Heinz gone, Edith gone, and now Lotti; and Henry still can be so cold. What does it take to make him see the light?

Reto plowed the fields for the first time in his life that spring. As a boy he always was with me and took care of the cows. He knew every one of the cows by name and could easily say which heifer belongs to which cow. Where Heinz did the field work, he never was good in the barn, he was not interested, but he could fix anything from a wristwatch to the biggest tractor. Heinz is gone for good, and now Reto had to do all of the outside work.

And he worked hard, yet Dad was constantly checking up on him. "Martin can do this, or that, so much better," was all Reto heard. Every so often Reto told his dad, "Then get Martin to do it. I will get a job somewhere else and move on."

Reto did not take Dad's scolding too seriously. Since he was in love, that kept him preoccupied. He got to know Lisa at the recruiting office where he had to work every afternoon until he had his final Honorable Discharge papers. She was a senior at Wausau High School and came to work at the recruiting office a couple of hours a day. She wanted to drop out of school, but we gave her a home. She could drive Reto's car to school, and because of that promised us that she would finish school.

Reto was in love head over heels. One night Lisa went to a 4-H meeting. It was almost midnight and she was not home yet. Reto paced the floor. He woke me up. "What should I do," he asked me. "I don't even know where to look for her."

I felt sorry for him and got up. And then, smiling, told him, "Now you know how I felt the many of times you did not come home." We sat and talked for a while until Lisa returned.

It was in June when Martin and Edith, the newlyweds, came back from Switzerland. They settled down in our other house, where Edith lived before, and Martin came to farm with us, just in time to make hay. We were so glad to have all that help.

Our house was in terrible condition. Through all the years we put every penny into the barn and nothing whatsoever into the house. I could never understand why the weatherman says, "It's raining outside." Everyone has to know it is raining outside, and not inside, I used to think. But now I know it can rain inside, too. We had to pull the bed away from the wall since the water ran down the wall in little streams if it rained. The roof was leaking. Henry just took a 4'x 8' sheet of plywood and put it against the wall so that the water could run behind it. But then even Henry figured it was time to buy a new house, if we wanted some of our kids to stay and farm with us.

Henry contacted the representative of Wick Buildings, and we ordered one of those prefab houses. We even picked the color for the carpets, and the price was not too bad either. For a three-bedroom home, with a full basement: $47,000.

My thoughts were to move over to the house where Edith lived and let the newlyweds live in the new one. That way I could take life a little easier and would not have to get up in the middle of the night if a cow comes fresh (has a calf). That would be Martin's job then.

But interest rates skyrocketed. We had to pay almost 15% interest on the money we borrowed for the cows and machinery, and I could not see going more in debt now. I felt that the payment would get too high and decided to wait with the house until the interest rates came down a little. But then, when the interest came down, so did the milk price. The milk price bottomed out. We got almost $15 per 100 pounds of milk, but within six months it dropped below $10 per 100 pounds. And with that kind of a milk price, it was impossible to build a house. So we stayed in the old house and Edith and her family three miles away in our other one.

I heard a Swiss singing group that toured the US. Switzerland's Independence Day is the 1st of August, and it is celebrated just like here, with speeches, bonfires and fireworks. But Switzerland is a lot older than the US. The first three states there became independent over 700 years ago (1291). So every year around the first of August there are groups that come to the States to entertain the Swiss clubs.

We have a friend in Detroit who belongs to the Swiss

club there, and he gave me their names. I contacted that group in Switzerland and then signed a contract with them. They were all amateurs who spend their vacation and come here to do what they like best, sing about their homeland. I was told they would stay with us for three days, but I was responsible to find volunteers who would house them for those three nights, plus they needed $1,000 for their performance. I had my work cut out now. But it worked out just great, I had them all placed in no time. In fact, I had more volunteers than I needed.

I sat many nights at my kitchen table drawing posters, since I had no money to have them printed. Sunday afternoons Henry and I drove all over the country to hang them up. I made arrangement for those Swiss people to entertain at the fair grounds the night before the Fair opened, and the next night at the dance hall at Les and Jim's.

Jim said, "I usually closed during the Fair, but I will do you that favor and stay open for that one night, but I don't think you are going to have a big crowd." That got me scared. What if it flops? But it was too late to chicken out. The deal was done.

That group was beyond anybody's expectations. The youngest yodelers were twin girls only eight years old. The first night at the fairgrounds we had people from all over the country. They came by busloads, and the grandstand was packed.

The next day we brought them all to the farm for a picnic. It was just great. They sang and played the Alphorns, and we had such a good time. At 8 p.m. that night they had to entertain at Les and Jim's. Jim thought there wouldn't be many guests. He opened the doors at 6:30 p.m. and by 7 p.m. there wasn't an empty seat available.

I had a lot more than the thousand dollars left after I paid all the expenses, but I gave everything to them, since most of them were young, struggling families, just like us. I had the satisfaction of doing something no one else around here would have ever tried. Needless to say, it was a great success, something people will remember for a long, long time to come.

Lisa and Reto got engaged and talked of a June wedding. I could see for months already that that would never work between those two, but how can you make someone that is on Cloud Nine see that?

Now, with Lotti gone, we had an empty apartment over at the other house. "Reto," I said, "since you guys get married soon anyway, why don't you move into the apartment that Lotti left? I'll buy you a TV as an early wedding present. You have your bedroom set, and we have a used kitchen table. Wouldn't that work?"

"Oh, yes," he replied, all excited. "We will move next weekend." And so they did.

The following Monday after we got done in the barn, I asked Reto, "Don't you want a bite to eat with us?"

"No, Lisa has supper for me," he answered. Reto is a wholly hubby-type person, a dreamer, and he hoped Lisa had a candlelight dinner ready for him. But when he got home and asked, "What do we have for supper," the answer was, "Check the refrigerator." That was the last thing Reto expected to hear, but he hung in there.

One night as we milked together, he asked if I would come along to pick out wedding invitations. "The mother of the groom usually does not go along," I said.

But he went on, "I think that is a very special day, one commitment closer to being married. Please come. I will take you all out for supper afterwards." How could I say no to that?

He picked me up and together we went to Wausau. Lisa's mother was there already. We started going through the books. One half hour later, Lisa and her girlfriend walked in. "Sorry we are late, but we had something to do," was her excuse.

Reto gave her a kiss, and said, "It's okay."

It took us quite some time to go through all the books. We narrowed it down to five cards already when Lisa said, "Sorry. We have to go. I have something I have to take care of."

I could see in Reto's eyes how disappointed he was, but like I would have, so did he say nothing. A hug and a kiss, "See you later," and Lisa was out the door.

Before we made the final decision, Lisa's mother was gone, too.

Reto and I ordered the cards, and then went out to eat by ourselves. That was when Reto opened up.

"I don't know what's wrong with me," he said, "but I thought all of those decisions would be a lot more romantic. Lisa does not cook, she makes herself something to eat and then sits in front of the TV. Or she tells me she ate before she came home. There is just no closeness anymore. Maybe I'm wrong, but it bothers me."

"Reto, those are all little stones. But then after you are married, those little stones turn into big stones, and someday you can't stop them from rolling over you, and that will split you two forever. So think about it, and do not rush into something you regret later," I told him. It is so hard for a mother to see the kids get hurt; yet there is nothing I could do about it except to let them know that I would always be there for them, should I be needed.

Reto dropped me off at my house and then went home. He talked it over with Lisa later that night, and they decided to stay engaged but postpone their wedding and for now to cancel the invitations.

It took only two weeks and Lisa brought a boyfriend home to stay with them. Three weeks later she gave Reto her engagement ring back and said, "I will move back home," only to break into the house a couple of days later to get the ring back, after she figured out how much money she could get for it.

Lisa still had her purebred horse with us. Reto told

her, "The ring for the horse, or no deal." Lisa's dad got Lisa a lawyer, and then the lawyer came one Saturday morning and brought the ring, and in turn picked up the horse. How sad to have to go through all of this, and not even be married.

Henry and I got into a big argument over that stupid ring. After Reto picked out the ring, he took me along one day and wanted to know if I thought he made the right decision. It was a real pretty white gold band with a big diamond. I was not supposed to, but I saw the price. Yet I felt it was no one's business how much Reto paid for it, since it was his money.

Henry could not understand what this big thing was about a wedding band until Reto told him what he paid for it. Then all hell broke loose, because I knew all along how much it was but did not tell Henry.

"What an idiot," he said, "paying that kind of money for a ring. This is okay after one is married for some years and knows that it works out, but not if one just gets engaged and doesn't even know if you're going to make it."

"We are married almost 24 years, and I still have the original wedding band that only cost $8. Do you still have your doubts about our marriage? You never gave me a diamond, but I guess that is okay, too," was my reply, and I walked away.

But Henry was mad at me for days because I kept the price of the ring a secret, and there should be no secrets in a marriage was his reasoning. I guess it depends how one looks at it. I felt it was not my business to interfere. Henry never really trusted anyone, and that only added fuel to the fire. But it was too late for me to change it.

Reto was hurting pretty bad for awhile after Lisa left him, but then got on with his life. He went to his cousin Albert's wedding and got to know another girl, and they had a nice weekend together, only she was ready to leave for Florida to stay with her aunt.

Reto was getting restless and felt that since he can never measure up to his brother-in-law Martin, maybe it would be better to move on as soon as all the fall work was done. And so he did.

I got all his clothes washed and packed neatly into the trunk of his car. Then he took his dog "Semi" and put him in the back seat. A quick hug and a kiss, and down the road those two went, leaving me, feeling lonely and hurt, behind. Reto, my baby, the one with whom I spent so many hours sitting by his bedside worrying about him, is now gone forever. This is it. From now on Henry and I will be all alone for the rest of our lives.

When my kids were teenagers and all at home fighting, I said so often, "Thank God when you are all gone some day and I have my peace and quiet." Now they are all gone and that peace did not feel like peace to me. No one came home anymore asking, "Mom, what's for supper," or, "Mom, is my shirt clean?" And, boy, does that hurt, to have four kids so close together, watch them grow for 20 years, and within two years they are all gone. Yes, I know mothers have to give their children wings so that they can learn to fly, and then let them go, but it is still a deep wound in a mother's heart, one that never completely heals.

Granddaughter Jessica, my big helper.

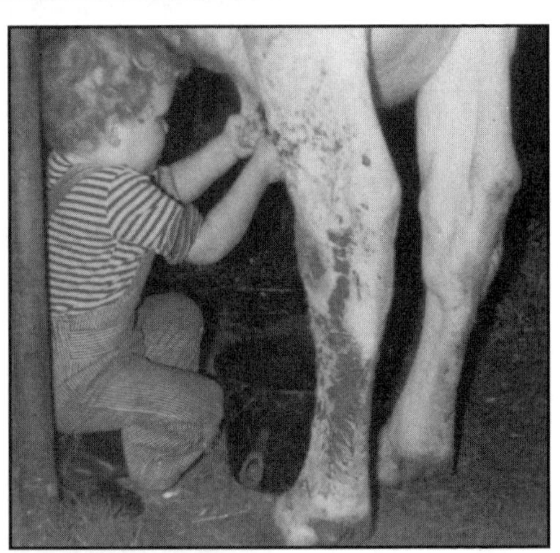

Jessica wants to milk the cows by hand now; then Grandma gets done quicker. Great job, Jesse!

Granddaughter Bobbi Jo, "I can feed the calves for you, Grandma." Thanks, Bobbi!

13

I KEPT BUSY, and with Reto gone more work was on my shoulders again. I also was very involved in AMPI, and Wisconsin Women for Agriculture. Joyce Trapp and I put together two slide presentations, one for the milk group and one for the meat group. We took those slide presentations to the schools and had great success. I took all the pictures and Joyce put the words to them.

The milk group was easy for me since it showed what a farmer has to do to get that refreshing glass of milk on your dinner table. A dairy farmer has to be a herdsman, a veterinarian, a machinist, a bookkeeper and a mechanic. He has to know the soil, and a lot more.

I wanted to show everybody how much Mother Nature and God's influence have to do with farming. A farmer has to pray that the cows won't get sick and the calves will grow, that it is not too wet in spring to plant. Then, please God, don't let the new seedlings freeze. Let it rain enough so that they can grow and don't dry out. And please don't let it get too wet so that we can get our crops in on time. Yes, I think there aren't many professions closer to God's grace than a farmer.

The meat group took a little more running on my part, but I learned a lot about other sectors of agriculture. What it takes to raise a turkey and get it to the market. The turkeys have to be de-beaked the first day the farmer gets them so that they can't hurt each other, and then after that have to be very closely watched and kept in the exact same temperature for weeks. The farmer I visited had thousands and thousands of turkeys. It takes a lot of tender loving care to get that lean great tom turkey on your dinner table for Thanksgiving.

I learned more about the sheep and beef business, and also about those so-called dirty pigs. They aren't dirty at all. In fact, they are a lot cleaner than a lot of other animals. They will not lay in their own manure, as a cow does. Yes, they wallow in mud, but that is because they have no sweat glands so mud cools them down. Yes, to do those two slide presentations was a great experience for me. I was very proud of our achievement, and we got a lot of publicity out of it.

I went to hearings on wetland preservation. I was involved with the Chamber of Commerce and the Ag Board, and some of us went to Madison to the State's capital to testify. That is an experience I will never forget.

Marie Skic, two of her friends and I decided to testify for "no inheritance tax between spouses." That was a subject that was close to my heart, since we immigrated into this county and Henry and I together worked so very hard to get the farm to where it is now. So, with the existing law, should I die, everything goes to Henry and he pays no inheritance tax. But should Henry die, nothing is mine. I will get a trustee appointed and he will make all the decisions on the two-thirds of our assets that would belong to my children, if they aren't of age yet. And I have to pay inheritance tax for my one-third. Not a bed sheet or spoon is mine. How unfair!

The big day was on a Tuesday. The Sunday evening before Marie called me. She wanted to make sure I didn't forget it. We decided when and where we would meet. Then Marie said, "I have go. I think someone is knocking on my door."

"Okay. See you Tuesday morning bright and early," and we hung up.

My daughter Edith called me the next morning from work and told me that Tony, Marie's husband, passed away the night before. The knock Marie heard while she was talking to me was her husband in the bathroom falling as he had a heart attack.

I thought, this is it. I have to go alone, and then asked Henry's sister Martha if she would like to come along. But no, Marie called me Monday evening and told me, "It is more important for me now than ever before to get that law changed."

So I picked her up on Tuesday morning, stopped to get her two friends, and we were on our way to Madison. We met some of our friends there, and one woman after the other testified, telling their stories, why they were for or against "no inheritance tax between spouses."

Then it was my turn. I told them how we came to this country, how hard we worked to get where we are now, that Henry had cancer, and what would happen to me should he pass away and they did not change the law by then. We are a team that works together, and should one pass away then it should all go to the partner. But the deceased spouse should be able to will his or her part to the children to make sure that should the surviving spouse remarry, that the children later don't walk away empty-handed. But the surviving spouse should be in charge of everything until he or she wants to give it up or passes away, too.

I could see in the assemblymen's eyes that they could understand where I'm coming from. I told them I worked too hard to not be considered part-owner of our business. It was quiet in that big, otherwise so hectic assembly room, and I had to swallow my tears a couple of times, telling this big audience how much heartache we had to go through to get to where we are today.

After me was Marie's turn. Marie lost her oldest son in a car accident, her youngest son through leukemia, and now her husband through a heart attack. She started talking:

"I probably have the best reason of anybody to testify. My husband passed away on Sunday evening, and after we are done here we have to hurry home, since I have to make it to the showing. But I worked so hard side-by-side with him, and now all of that should go to me without me paying that awful high inheritance tax."

I got goose bumps as she went on with her testimony. It was so quiet I could have heard a pin drop to the floor. The assembly men and women were stunned as Marie gave the rest of her presentation.

But we could not stay all the way to the end and listen to the rest of the women testifying. We had to hurry home, since it is 160 miles between Madison and Merrill; I had to speed all the way. Surprisingly, I did not get a ticket. I unloaded the other two ladies in Wausau and then drove Marie home. She quickly ran in the house, freshened up, then came back and I drove her to the funeral home, where she met up with the rest of her family We made it just in time. The first visitors had already arrived.

As I lay down in bed that night, I thanked God for my blessings and my at least partly healthy family. Heinz was still living in Switzerland and had not yet gotten over being homesick. He missed the good old USA, but since he was of age and healthy, he was forced to do the initial 17 weeks military duty there. All of us are dual citizens. The US and Switzerland have an agreement so that we can be citizens of both countries. Heinz lives in Switzerland under the US passport; even his children can become US citizens as soon as he registers them at the US embassy in Zurich.

Heinz did not like it at all in the military. All his colleagues were three or four years younger than he, and he thought it was a waste of time, since he will be back in the States in a couple of years anyway. The only highlight was that he had a girlfriend, "Uschi," he could visit on weekends.

Heinz later got engaged and planned to get married in October. Uschi and Heinz did not want a big wedding.

We couldn't get there anyway, and Uschi was pregnant by now, so Heinz felt it was better just to go to the Justice of the Peace.

The closer the wedding day came, the more Heinz knew that that was not the right thing to do. On the morning of their wedding day, he took a long walk and tried to figure out what was right and what was wrong with their relationship. And he felt there were definitely more wrongs than rights, and it would be a lie if he were to go through with it.

He went home and told his bride-to-be that he could not marry her. "I will always support you and the baby, but it will not work between us." Uschi was very disappointed, but stayed with Heinz at least another couple of months, and then moved on. Their little girl, Tamara, was born on my birthday, December 18th. Uschi called me and told me what had happened. I got so mad at Heinz I could have strangled him.

A couple of days later I talked to Heinz on the phone, but he did not defend himself at all. But then he never did that before, so why start now? If one thinks Heinz did wrong, then so be it, and this time it was his mom who doubted his judgment. I was not there, so how could I know?

Henry and I visited nursing homes and church groups showing them our slide presentation from Switzerland, and we sang and yodeled together. Even though Henry gets older and went through some rough times, his voice was still as beautiful as ever. And those people could never get enough of his singing. What a great gift! We could make some of the very lonely old people smile, even if it was just for a little while.

****

February 1, 1982, and Edith gave birth to our grandson, Martin, a cute, dark-haired little guy. Edith no longer worked for the doctor. She was a full-time housewife and mom now. And that meant no more babysitting for Jessica.

Yes, Edith and her family only lived three miles from us, but it was for Henry and me almost harder to let go of Jessica than of our own children. Jessie was my little girl, and wherever I went, she went. Hours and hours she sat with me on the tractor or on the haybine. She was in the barn with me and sang to the calves, and now, if it really goes well, I maybe see her once a week.

Yet, I knew I had to let go. Jessie was Edith's child, and Edith had a new family now, and they had to get to know each other. And Martin was a great dad. He would have done anything for Jessica. But that did not help matters. Deep down it still hurt something terrible. For me, it was another loss, but as I learned in later years, it was just as hard for Jessica.

July 7, 1982, Lotti gave us a grandson named Tyler. She knew she had to have a Caesarean section again, and asked me if I could come and stay with her for a couple of days. Because of Edith's and Martin's help, it was possible for me to go. I took Jessica along, and together we drove straight through to Tulsa, Oklahoma where Lotti lived.

Lotti was in terrible pain as I picked her up at the hospital three days later. When the doctor gave her a shot into the spine to numb the lower part of her body, an air bubble entered the spine and that gave her an awful headache. But there is nothing anyone can do. That air bubble has to work itself out.

I stayed three more days and then packed Bobby Jo and Jessica into the back seat of the car and took them both back home so Lotti had only to worry about her newborn son and at least could get some rest.

My trip went pretty well, but about 60 miles from my home we got into a terrible thunderstorm. Bobby Jo cried because it was so dark. Living in the big city, she never saw a street without street lights, and with the thunder and lightning, she got really scared. I had to drive and had no time to hold her close, but Jessica took her into her arms and told her, "Don't worry. I'm right here. I will hold you close; that way nothing can ever happen to you." How neat, this six-year-old girl being a little mother. Thank God we made it home safely.

Bobby Jo loved it on the farm, especially in the barn. Whatever I did, she was always just a step behind me, her hands in her back pockets, walking down the barn while I was milking, nothing but talk, talk, talk. She was just so much fun.

Four weeks later Lotti and Larry drove up to Wisconsin, baptized little Tyler in the same church, and by the same minister as they got married. They stayed a couple of days and then took Bobby Jo along back to Tulsa.

****

I was invited to participate at a class reunion that fall. That was a good opportunity to see what goes on in Switzerland and to see my new granddaughter. I bought myself a plane ticket and flew home.

My mother and I went to visit Uschi and my granddaughter, Tamara. That's when I got the real picture, not from Heinz, from Uschi.

"I'm from a poor family. We never had money," she told me. "Heinz made good money and gave me the whole paycheck. I was supposed to pay the bills, just like he saw you do it. Heinz only took some lunch money out. On the other hand, I could not handle money and blew it all. When I left Heinz, he was four months behind on his rent payment and had a lot of other bills he thought were paid. I see now why he did not want me anymore."

Now I finally understand why it got that far, and I admired Heinz for his courage. It took a lot more guts to say NO on their wedding day, rather than to go through with their plans.

Heinz is a US citizen, and as such he could have left Switzerland and come back to the United States. Because they were not married, he would never have had to pay child support. But again he stood up and did the right thing. "I will stay until my child is of age and at least financially support her," Heinz said, knowing well that the way the Swiss law is written he will never be able to see Tamara, because he was not married to her mother, since under the Swiss law if one is not married but fathers a child, he has to pay child support, but has no right whatsoever to see the child. I was proud of my son, who stood up and said, "I made a mistake and I will pay for it, no matter what."

Yes, my trip to Switzerland was a real eye-opener. First Heinz's troubles, and then I went to my class reunion. I was almost 45 years old by now and had never seen my classmates since I left my hometown as a 15-year-old girl. A lot had changed in that time.

The girl, Inge, who shared the school bench with me did get married to our teacher, Mr. Hugo Henke, and they had a 14-year-old daughter together.

When we went to school under Mr. Henke, he was married and had three children. He was 30 years older than us, and a good-looking guy. He loved to mountain climb and ski, and he always had a brown complexion. The hair on his temples had turned gray already. To me he was like a dad who understood my problems, or at least so I thought.

Now, so many years later, it felt different. He is 75 years old, still rugged-looking, and married to a woman who is even one year younger than I. As a child, I thought that there wasn't anything Mr. Henke could not handle, and that he would always be fair. On the other hand, I went through a lot the last 30 years and look at life differently. I always stuck to my commitments, and now I felt that Mr. Henke would not do that. I think he is a Casanova who takes advantage of others and would do anything to get what he wants, no matter who he hurts on the way.

Boy, images sure can change.

Mr. Henke had a speech after we had supper the evening of the class reunion. He thanked everyone for coming and reminisced for awhile. Then he looked at me and said, “I’m sure glad to see you, Edith, here amongst us. You can be proud of your achievement, since when you were 12-13 years old I never thought you would amount to anything, knowing the background of your family.”

Everybody clapped, and for anyone else it might have been a compliment, but not for me. I was crushed. I looked up to my teacher, did not go to high school because I wanted to be in his class. The rich ones could not wear jewelry, there was no difference between rich and poor, and I admired Mr. Henke for it. I always thought he respected me for what I was and not for what some of my family members were doing. But now I found out that he did not take me seriously and thought because my Aunt Ida, who lived with us and had two illegitimate sons, I was going to be the same someday.

I put a smile on my face and played along with the rest of them all evening, but I wished I had never gone there. I had it tough through all my school years because we were poor. I was never accepted by the teachers. Mr. Henke was the only one who made a difference in my life. I put him on a pedestal and looked up to him, and now he shattered my dream. If someone just knew how words can hurt. I was really glad to live so far away from all those unpleasant memories. I was glad to get back to the States and work side by side with Henry.

****

Another summer gave way to winter, and Henry and I slowly got used to being alone, but I could feel that it nagged on him. He was homesick and emotionally hurting again. And what once was a great relationship between Martin and Henry slowly deteriorated. Martin, when still in Switzerland, went to school to become a farmer, and now wanted to try new things that he learned some years ago. Yet Henry was from the old school and felt nothing should be changed. Martin: "We should buy more hybrid, better corn to plant." Henry: "It is my money, and we always did it with the cheaper one. Why change now?" And I was in the middle once again. But, nevertheless, we made it through another summer.

Edith and her family flew to Switzerland two days before Christmas to see Martin's family. That left the two of us all alone. We would have had enough work on our own farm, but Arnold, another farmer, asked Henry to pump his manure pit.

"My pit is full. Please come and empty it for me," he begged. And Henry could have said no.

On December 24, early in the morning, Henry went there and pumped manure all day while I had to do the chores alone. It is hard work, and especially on a day where most everyone goes home to visit their loved ones. And here we are, all by ourselves. What a sad, lonely feeling. But I did not want to be a nag, and cooked ham and green beans for supper, just for us two. Then how could I be sad? Henry worked hard, too, and maybe he needed to work to take his mind off things and not dwell and get more homesick. All I said as we sat down and had supper together, "I don't mind to work alone, but from the money you made today, we maybe could buy something special."

Henry replied, "Arnie told me that he is broke right now, because of the Christmas season, so he could not pay me. Don't worry. We'll get our money, if not before, then at least in the spring when he needs us again" I thought to myself, I hope you're right. But then in spring when it was time to pump the pit again, Arnie said real proud, "I don't need you this spring. I do it by myself. I borrowed Eddie's liquid manure tank." So we never, ever got our money. It was a good thing we did not know that as we sat down and enjoyed our Christmas Eve dinner.

Edith and her family came back from Switzerland the 2nd of February. Henry and some other delegates went to an AMPI meeting in Madison that day. We had light snow flurries as they left in the early morning hours, but it quickly turned into a blizzard, which did not allow them to come home that night. They stayed in Madison, and Edith was stranded in Chicago.

I was all alone, and it was just terrible. Late afternoon I shoveled myself a walkway to the barn. I could hear the wind whistling and blowing the snow against the barn window. It was warm in the barn, and the cows were content.

I should have stayed there all night, but I was hungry and tired. It was after 10 p.m. when I got done with my chores. I could not even get out of the milk house door anymore. I had to climb up to the hayloft, take the back door and slowly stump my way around the barn and up to the house.

I was dead tired and the house was cold. We had no furnace, just a wood stove in the basement, and the fire in the stove went out hours ago. I was too tired to start it again, so I took a glass of milk and a piece of bread and went to bed.

At 4 a.m. the next morning I got up and shoveled myself back to the barn. As soon as I was done with the chores, I tried to get the tractor going so that I could plow. But we always drove the tractor forward into the barn, and there was no way that I could back it out without getting stuck, so I took the shovel and shoveled enough to back the tractor out and turn it around.

I was sure glad when I finally could sit on it and start plowing. The road had to be opened, since the milk truck had to be able to pick my milk up or my tank would run over.

I also had to take care of Martin's pigs while they were on vacation. But I could not feed them the night before because of the snowstorm, so today I had to go. I plowed myself the whole three miles to Edith's house, and just as I got there, the county snowplow went through. If I just would have waited a little longer, I would have had it a lot easier.

But I still had to plow Edith's driveway to get to the pig barn. I was just done as a car drove in and they dropped Henry off. Thank God I had help again. I was so tired, since it is way too much work for one person.

Once back at the farm, Henry checked the roof on the south addition and found out the weight of the snow busted at least eight rafters. Boy, thanks, Guardian Angel; you saved me once again. That roof could have collapsed under the heavy snow and I could have been crushed while milking the cows. I sure was lucky.

****

The only way I could keep my sanity was to stay involved in WWA and AMPI, and through them I was put on a speaker list, which gave me a great opportunity to let the public know about the heartaches and struggles an immigrant and a farmer has to go through.

I spoke at a NTC Farm Banquet at a Christian Women's Day, and the Homemakers Convention. It took me days to prepare the speech, but it came from the bottom of my heart, and I always had a great response. I loved every minute of it. I drove as far as Baraboo, Wisconsin, to be a speaker. The title there was "Lord, Help Me Hang In There." And I sure was the one who had to think about that every day of my life. Sometimes the rope felt very fragile, but I hung in there. Henry came along and we yodeled together, something he was just so great at.

Our chapter of the WWA helped with the preparation for the Alice in Dairyland Pageant, held in Wausau in the spring of 1985. Henry and I were asked to entertain. We dressed up in our original Swiss costumes and sang the night the new Alice in Dairyland was crowned. That was a great, memorable evening.

I decided to run for school board, and was on the ballot for the April 5th election. I got interested a long time ago as my children went through school, but never had the time since if I decided to do something and took a job on, I wanted to do the best I could. Now I felt was my time.

Before I put my name on the ballot, I asked Henry if it would be okay with him if I took that job. "No problem," he answered. "That would be great if you could do that." But then when I went around to hang posters and went to speak at PTA and other meetings, he changed his mind. I got too much into the spotlight, and he got no recognition. That did not go over too well. I guess he is not the only man who wants to keep his wife at home and not in the public eye. But I did not give up. I said yes, and now would go for it.

Yet I was somewhat disappointed. After all the work I put in it, Henry went to bed early the night of the election, even before the 10 p.m. news came on. "I don't have to stay up. You won't win anyway," he said, and went to bed.

Yes, I did not make it. Tom Sazama, who was our lawyer and ran for this third term, beat me by 11 votes. All three incumbents made it again. I did not win, but it gave me great satisfaction to know that I almost beat Tom. Yet it hurt that Henry had so little confidence in me. But life goes on, and I will get over it.

Martha Rusch and I attended a seminar, "Agriculture in the Classroom," in Lincoln, Nebraska, put on by the U.S. Department of Agriculture. There were some real good speakers from all over the USA and I learned a lot. It was only 4 p.m. when we left the convention hall on a beautiful late afternoon. "We could drive halfway home," I said to Martha, "and then get a motel," and she agreed. So we took a bite to eat and went on our way.

It was gorgeous to drive past the cornfields while the sun was slowly setting in the west. At 9 p.m. we stopped to have a cup of coffee and a piece of pie, and homeward we went.

Martha soon dozed off, while I was determined to drive home so that I could help with the milking in the morning. I had missed three milkings already and I knew I was needed. It was 4:30 a.m. when I dropped Martha off at her farm, and then drove the last 10 miles to our farm.

I was the first one in the barn that morning, but after milking those 90 cows, I was done for, ready to go to bed. Somehow those meetings always perked me up. No matter where I went, I always came home enthusiastic and full of energy, ready to make a difference in our lives. I did not always succeed, and sometimes it faded quickly.

One day I came home from a WWA meeting all excited. I unbuttoned my blouse and my pants as I turned into Tesch Road a quarter-mile away from home. Then I parked the car, ran into the house, dropped the clothes and slipped on the barn clothes, buttoning it as I ran to the barn. That night as I walked into the barn, all the cows were bellering. It was past seven and they had nothing to eat, nor were they milked yet. When I dropped Martha off a little bit earlier, her husband walked out of the barn, all done with chores. He was ready to sit down with Martha and listen to her tell him what went on all day. But not at my farm. "Henry! Henry, where are you?" I hollered, but no answer. This is ridiculous, I thought to myself. The first thing I have to do was feed those poor animals.

I took the silo cart and wheeled it out to the silo house. There was enough silage down, so why weren't they fed? I filled the cart once, fed every cow a little to get them to quiet down, and then went back to get more. Now that the cows were calm, I could hear Henry holler, "Get me out of here." That's when I almost had to laugh. I don't know if it was because I was so angry with Henry, or because I felt he had it coming, but there was no time to figure it out. The cows needed feed and had to be milked, and it was late.

Henry was mad that I had gone to a meeting and left him home alone, so he went up to the silo and watched the silo unloader throw the silage down the chute. I do not know how long it took him to realize he could not get down anymore. First, he got a pail of silage into the silo house, but since he then did not turn off the unloader, the silage couldn't go anywhere but up the chute. He packed it tight, the whole 30 feet up.

When he finally realized what had happened, he unplugged the unloader, but the silage in the silo was too far down to climb up to the opening that would have gotten him down on the outside. Yet it was just impossible to get down through the inside chute. He had to stay up there until I was done feeding. I had a lot more silage than I needed. The silage in the chute was so packed it was almost like cement, and it took me quite some time to get it opened so that Henry could climb down again. I did not say much all through milking, and he must have felt foolish.

Why does he have to get so mad all the time? He goes places and I have to do it alone. No one feels sorry for me. But what is the use of arguing? The work had to be done. It was late that night when we finally walked out of the barn and could go to bed.

****

Summer gave way to fall once again. The leaves turned into so many beautiful colors and the nights got longer and colder, a sure sign that Old Man Winter was just around the corner. The cows do not produce that great if they're cold, so like every fall before, we started keeping them in the barn overnight. But something went wrong. The milk production dropped day by day, and I could not figure out why. We did not change their feed, so what is the problem?

The first thing I did was scrub the mangers. Since the cows, through the summer, eat most of their feed out in the pasture, some mold might start to grow. That didn't help, so I shaved their backs, bellies and tails, brushed them and looked for lice. But that wasn't the problem, either. They were clean. What else could it be, I asked myself.

If a cow slows down her milk production, she will not get it back to full capacity anymore, even if the problem is corrected. The farmer then has to wait it out till the next lactation; or, in other words, until she gives birth to a calf again. If one or two cows drop their production, a farmer can overcome that. But the whole herd, that is almost too much. Yet I still could not figure out what the problem was.

My last resort was the drinking cups. The water might be stale. I took a bucket and started scooping the water out of the drinking cup, and then took a scrub pad and scrubbed them. As I had my hand in the water, it felt like little shocks going through my hands. I went to the second cup. That same thing happened.

"Henry, I think there is some electricity in the cups or in the water," I said to Henry and Martin. They both laughed at me and thought I was so petrified that I was losing it. "I can feel it in my hands," I insisted. Henry couldn't feel it at all, so he put his tongue on the cup. "No way. There is no electricity. You are dreaming," was Henry's response. But one hour later as I sat down to eat breakfast, I could still feel the tingling in my hands.

I called Dave's Dairy Supply. Dave installed our pipeline; he should be able to figure this out. And he stopped in the same afternoon. Dave hooked a little ammeter up to the water line, and there it was. The needle went as far as it could go, and that was 6 amps. Come to find out, our hot water heater shorted out and put electricity into the water. A cow can stand a maximum of one amp. Every time the cows wanted to drink and put their noses into the drinking cup, they got a shock, so they just would not drink anymore. A cow needs about a bathtub full of water a day, and without water, they can't produce milk.

That same afternoon we installed a new water heater.

Thank God, the problem was licked. But, needless to say, we lost a lot of money that winter, since none of the cows came back up to full milk production until they had a calf again. It is unbelievable how many things can go wrong on a farm, and how much it will influence a farmer's income.

****

Mother's Day, a cool, cloudy day. Schneider's needed their manure pit pumped, and so Henry went. "Please don't go. It is Mother's Day and I don't want to be all alone," I begged, but without success. Martin went out of the barn early that morning to bring Edith roses for Mother's Day and treat her for breakfast. I was all by myself. I cleaned the barn and the milk house, and then went up to the house. I was pretty disgusted.

We were invited for supper at Edith's. Henry should be back by the time Martin and I are done milking so we could go there together, but here I was, all alone Sunday morning, and on Mother's Day of all days. What should I do with myself so that I don't go crazy?

I could do bookwork. There are bills that have to be paid. So I made myself breakfast, and even though it was May, it felt cool in the house, at least too cold to sit down and go through my books.

I went to the basement and started the woodstove. "I'm so lonely, and if no one cares, at least I want to be warm," I told myself, and then went upstairs and lay down on the couch. I'm tired and deserve to take a nap. The bills can wait. It is Mother's Day. Or I at least could nap until the house was warm. I took the feather bed that we brought along from Switzerland and cuddled up on the couch. It didn't take long and I fell asleep.

All of a sudden I could hear some funny noises. I reluctantly opened my eyes. What I saw woke me up in a blink. The flames were shooting up from the basement and danced before my living room window. One jump and I was up, ran to the phone and called Edith. Jessica answered. “Please tell your dad to come immediately,” I screamed; and hung up.

I had a pan full of water in the sink. Not thinking clearly, I ran outside with that pan in my hand and threw it onto the fire, and then ran in for more. It did not take long and Martin was there to help me. Together we got the fire out, but not before we ripped some siding panels off and made the basement window bigger.

There was a big pile of sawdust just in front of the basement windows, since we sawed wood all week; that pile of sawdust looked like the Yellowstone Park. Out of every little gap came smoke. I had no time to put shoes on. My socks had holes and my feet blisters, but, thank God, we got the fire out.

Like I said before, we had no furnace, just a wood stove in the basement and a hole in the living room floor for the heat to come up. My house had no decent chimney, so Henry took a stovepipe, made a hole in the basement window, and then took the pipe up the outside of the house. He put old rags around it to fill the holes.

I was pretty mad being alone on Mother’s Day, and put more wood in the stove than I should have. It overheated and started the rags on fire. That’s what I get for getting mad. God punished me.

We later laughed about it. Michael Knab, our insurance agent, asked me: “You live in such an old, ugly house and always said if it burned down, at least you would get a new home. Now that it burned, you put the fire out. How come? You would have been better off taking what you want to a safe place and letting the rest go.” I don’t know why, but all I could think was, I can’t lose all those memories I have in this house. I have to save it. But I will always remember that Mother’s day.

Ag Women Donate

Members of the Wisconsin Women for Agriculture, Mar-Lin Chapter, presented a slide show and tape to MAPS Superintendent Thomas Strick last week. President Edith Gross (left) and secretary Rosemary Eckardt present "The Meat Group" to Strick in the photo above. The show will be used to promote good nutrition in Merrill area schools, according to Gross. . . Foto News.

Merrill Area Public Schools

PINE RIVER ELEMENTARY SCHOOL — *TEL. 715-536-6101*
ROUTE 6 — *MERRILL, WISCONSIN 54452*

Thomas L. Strick, Ph. D.
District Administrator

Mrs. Virginia Kohnke, Principal

April 9, 1983

Dear Mrs. Gross,

On behalf of the students in grades 4-6, thank you for sharing the slide program about the meat group. The information presented and the question and answer period which followed was valuable to them. The Wisconsin Women for Agriculture are to be commended for their effort in developing programs of this type.

Also, thanks for the ice-cream treat which proved to be a great afternoon "dairy break."

Sincerely,

Virginia Kohnke

Virginia Kohnke

Newspaper coverage of our slide presentation on the meat group, and letter of appreciation from the school district.

Section 2, Page 4 MERRILL SHOPPER & FOTO NEWS • M

Gross Honored

Edith Gross, Rt. 4 Merrill received special recognition for her outstanding service in agri-business promotion at the Lincoln County June Dairy Breakfast last Wednesday, June 1. Edith and her husband, Henry, operate a 440 acre dairy farm in the town of Harding where they settled after immigrating from Switzerland in 1968. She is currently state vice-president of the Wisconsin Women for Agriculture and president of the local Mar-Lin Chapter. She is also currently the president of the AMPI Women 11-B. She is the mother of four children and the grandmother of five. Edith is shown here receiving her plaque from Bob Bloechl, representing the Agri-Business Council Board of Directors. . .Foto News.

July 7, 1982

Dear Editor;

July 1st was a big day for us women, because a very important law went into effect; no more inheritance tax between spouses in the State of Wisconsin.

Now is your time to do something about a will and the way you own property. If you own property in joint tenancy now is the time to change it.' Joint tenancy' means the property is half yours and half your husbands, but neither of you can will your half to your children. If your surviving spouse should remarry and his second spouse outlives your spouse she or he gets everything and your children nothing. You can change it to 'tenancy in common.' This means each of you still owns half but you could will part or all of it to your children. Which means your spouse could still be in charge of your half until he dies, but it will go to your children upon his death, as stated in your will. Through this action you may save a lot of inheritance taxes your children would have to pay.

Talk to your lawyer or just go to the Register of Deeds office and pay a small fee to change this. There used to be a gift tax charged when a husband gave his wife over $100,000. - (once in a lifetime) but this is also no longer in effect. But all you then need is a simple will.

So now is your time. Do something about it. Wanting to change this has nothing to do with divorce. The divorce laws were revised a few years ago. Upon a divorce everything is divided fifty-fifty anyway.

Some important people and lawyers are afraid that if our legislators see the impact that this law has financially on our state they may change it back.

So if you wish to change it do it as soon as possible or you may find out you are too late!

Wis. Woman for
Agriculturist
Edith Gross

Recognition for agri-business promotion, and my letter to the editor about Wisconsin's Marital Property Reform Law.

Page 6—The Daily Herald, Wausau-Merrill, Wis.

Gross is candidate for School Board

Herald photo

Edith Gross

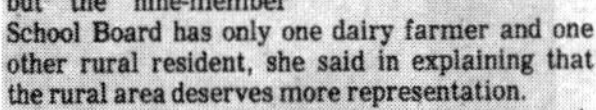

MERRILL — Edith Gross, Route 4, Merrill, is among five candidates in the April 5 spring election for three seats on the Merrill Area Board of Education.

Mrs. Gross, 42, and her husband, Henry, operate a dairy farm of nearly 600 acres in the town of Harding.

About 60 percent of the property tax money needed to operate the school system comes from the rural area, but the nine-member School Board has only one dairy farmer and one other rural resident, she said in explaining that the rural area deserves more representation.

She is beginning her second term as vice president of Wisconsin Women in Agriculture, has been the group's state education chairman for four years, and is current president of the Mar-Lin Chapter. She was district treasurer of Associated Milk Producers Inc. Women in 1976-80 and has been president since then. In addition, she was secretary of the Scott School PTO from 1971-75.

A native of Switzerland, she received her schooling and technical training there. Mrs. Gross came to the Merrill area in 1968 with her husband and four children. They became United States citizens in 1973.

Mrs. Gross' photo appeared inadvertently in Friday's Daily Herald in connection with another story.

Don't need ERA

EDITOR: In answer to the ERA letter from June 26, 1981:

After thinking and studying ERA for years now, I still cannot see why we need ERA. Could the main problem not be solved in another way? For example "equal jobs-equal pay."

I am a farm wife and got more than my share of equal job opportunities. I have to work hard 365 days a year, but even on the farm there are some jobs a woman can't do. For example, I will never be able to lift as much as a man, no matter how hard I try.

I am proud to be a woman and would never want to be equal to a man. Is it not nice if your man takes you out to a nice restaurant and opens the door for you, maybe even takes your chair out so you can sit down first? If you get to the car and it's raining he lets you get in and he gets wet.

All these nice little things which I treasure so much would have to go if ERA comes through.

I can see that the difference in Social Security payments for women and men can create a problem. I won't say it has to be that way but I am sure the Social Security law could be changed, and as more and more women will get equal pay it changes by itself.

If you like to be equal to a man, it is your privilege. We are in a free country, but please don't change the law for those of us who still like to be a wife and mother!

Equal job opportunities would be nice and are needed but if you apply for a job and the owner of that company (a man) will not hire you because you are a woman, he still wouldn't hire you after ERA is passed. You could then take him to court and the law would be on your side but do you think you could work for someone you just beat in court?

We as mothers have to help change the thinking of our boys so they will, when they are men, see us as equal partners.

No law on this earth can change the many male chauvinists.

EDITH GROSS, Merrill

Explains views on ERA

EDITOR: Todd Marten, I am sorry if I offended you and other ERA believers. I did not want that. I simply stated my viewpoints.

I have been a farm wife for the last 13 years. Before I worked first as a clerk in a store and later as a manager. I am also a naturalized American citizen, but maybe that makes me in your eyes even less qualified to talk about ERA.

Nevertheless, I will answer you and won't even get radical. I know ERA is for "equal jobs-equal pay" and I agree with that, but ERA will have a lot more consequences than that.

If we are equal to men we have to go to the armed forces also and cannot refuse to be drafted. What would happen in wartime if the women would have to go too? Who would take care of our children, our future generations which are the backbone of a great country?

If you look at the changes in the last 10-15 years, a lot more women have top positions and many even earn more than their husbands. That all came without ERA. But our thinking changed. If a woman these days would like to go to work and a man takes care of the household, that is fine. Each individual has the freedom to do what he or she likes best.

Watch TV when the sexes compete against each other. We should not say the sexes, no, they are two persons competing against each other (in 100-meter swimming, 1 mile run, etc.). If we can be equal why do we need special points or a head start, all of which penalizes the guys.

In the job force there are also a lot less women going out for specialized top jobs, than guys, but if a girl really wants to do it she can get there. We have women training to be astronauts.

Todd, I really hope you understand just a little better how I feel, and if you have such strong feelings for ERA, good for you.

That proves my point, if all men would think like you and look at us as equals, we would not need ERA.

EDITH GROSS, Merrill

I ran for the school board, and wrote to the editor about the Equal Rights Amendment.

May 11, 1984

Dear Edith,

I'm sure I speak for all present at last night's meeting when I say, "It was a most pleasureable presentation." You can certainly be proud of what you and your husband have accomplished and better yet you tell others. Your "speech" is one of the best that I've heard, entertaining yet informative, humorous in parts as we can relate yet serious, truly enjoyable.

Perhaps you don't realize it but you've no doubt also passed on the "art" of yodeling to your children. A great gift indeed and one which you and your husband do beautifully.

I extend our thanks, on behalf on our chapter, for being our guests and speakers. We pray that you have continued success, your faith has made you wise beyond your years, and we hope that you shall reap the rewards for all your labors.

Sincerely,

Sherl Albers

Secretary, Eagle Bluff Chapter, WWA. Sauk County

I was a speaker, and to end my presentation with a light note, Henry and I yodeled for the Wisconsin Women in Agriculture, Sauk Center.

Lisa Hoesly

Dear Mrs. Gross,

I'm sorry this note took so long to write, but I certainly wanted to thank the Mar-Lin Chapter of Wisconsin Women for Agriculture for the time and effort they spent to make the Alice finals the memorable four days that they were. I especially enjoyed hearing you and your husband sing at the night on the farm. I look forward to seeing you again at the state Convention, and please pass my thanks on.

Sincerely,
Lisa Hoesly
1985 "Alice"

I helped Lisa Hoesly in her successful 1985 bid to become "Alice in Dairyland."

14

THROUGH WWA WE put together stress management meetings. Every week we had one in a different township. Farmers and their families could come and talk about their frustration, and we told them about ours and what we intended to do about it.

Doreen, one of our WWA members, bought her parents' farm after she got married. That farm is over 100 years in the same family, so there was a lot of pressure that rested on Doreen's shoulders. But they, just like us, had some bad luck, and the terrible farm economy did not help matters, so they got foreclosed by their bank and had to sell out. That by itself was tough to swallow, but then Doreen's husband turned against her, divorced her and blamed her for all the troubles they had. Yet she did the best she could and was a very hard worker

Mary Jo's husband had a heart attack. He survived but has to take it easy now, and that is easier said than done on a farm.

So we all were experts in going through stress on a farm, and because of that we had a good turnout wherever we went and our meetings were a success. It was very rewarding for me, and if I only could make a difference in one lonely person's life, then it was worth all the effort.

Every year they have a party in Colby, Wisconsin, where they honor the Farm Wife of the Year, a farm wife living in the state of Wisconsin who did something to make a difference in the farming community. My daughter Edith put my name in in 1980 and 1982. I made second place both times.

The first time, Audrey Sickinger, a good friend of mine,

made it. She started farming as a young girl and later got involved in farm legislation. She went all the way to Washington to testify on behalf of us farmers. Audrey was also on the National Dairy Board, and for many years, state president of WWA. All in all, a super girl. It was a special honor to be runner-up behind such a great, caring human being.

The second time Marie Skic won, and she too is known nationwide through AMPI. She was on the board for the North Technical College, and state president for VFW. So I was just a little thing compared to them, but to have great ladies like them as friends is something very special to me.

****

June Dairy Month is always kicked off with a dairy breakfast. I was so busy that I did not believe that I had time to go that year, but Edith insisted. "You guys always went, and we have company here from Switzerland and they would like to go, too. Please don't spoil it for them." Martin's brother, Walter, and two of his friends were here from Switzerland. "Okay," I said. "Dad and I will come too."

The banquet hall at Les and Jim's was packed and the breakfast was good. Every year they honor an outstanding FFA member, a young farm couple, and they also give an award for someone who did outstanding services in agri-business promotion. I was wondering who was going to get that award this year. Most of the time it is some businessman.

I sat straight up so I could see everybody really good. Bob started speaking, and all of a sudden it hit me, and I quickly slipped down in my chair. He is talking about me, I thought to myself.

Edith, Martin and their friends all smiled. They knew it all along, that is why they were so determined to get me there. I got over the initial shock and accepted that award with pride. Edith certainly knows how to keep a secret.

Yes, it truly was an honor to get that award.

Reto went from working in Florida, where his new relationship quickly deteriorated, on to Lotti's in Tulsa. There he worked for the same company as Larry. But it was not what he wanted, and he moved on. California was his next goal. He stranded in Tracy, where he was a milker at a huge dairy farm. His off-days he spent at his aunt's house (Henry's sister Elsa). That is where he got to know Brenda, a good friend of his cousin Heidi. Brenda is a great girl with a level head on her shoulders. Her parents got divorced, and she learned as a 12-year-old girl to stand on her own two feet and also stand up for her little sister. Her mother quickly got remarried and took the girls to the East Coast where she made a new home with her husband.

But Brenda did not like it at all and called her grandpa to please give her the money for two bus tickets so that she and her little sister could come back to Nevada. Brenda's grandma is a full-blooded Shoshone Indian, a neat, nice lady. Brenda's grandpa is a tall blond, blue-eyed, great-looking guy with a mustache. He looked like the guys in those western movies.

Grandpa sent her the tickets, and Brenda, as a 12-year-old girl, took her 10-year-old sister and made that long bus trip to the West Coast. How courageous on Brenda's part.

Brenda and Reto fell in love and planned to get married in a couple of years. Reto switched jobs and went to milk at a farm in Minden, Nevada. Brenda moved with him, and that's where we met her for the first time. Henry and I flew to Reno and stayed with them for a week. They took us everywhere, to Virginia City, where Brenda went to school in her early years. It was an interesting old town. Brenda showed us where her parents one week apart got remarried. It is a bar with slot machines. If you walk through the saloon and all the way to the back door, there is a little chapel. It was just unbelievable how easy they make it to make a commitment for life. One can go from saying "I do" right back to gambling.

On the way back from Virginia City we saw wild horses roaming in the prairie and nibbling on the sage brush. The first time in my life I saw wild horses, and it was breathtaking.

Reto and Brenda also took us to Tahoe. It felt almost like Switzerland in the midst of all those mountains. They took us to a midnight show. The entertainer was Barbara Mandrell. I always liked her singing, but seeing her in person was beyond anything I had ever seen before. But the week went quickly, and it was time to go home, but the memories will linger forever.

Brenda and Reto came to visit us in August of 1983. That was when Brenda asked me if I would come and help her find a wedding dress. "I really would like something that would please Reto, and I know that if you like the dress, so will he." What an honor for a future daughter-in-law to put so much trust in me.

Martin's mother never went wedding dress shopping, so she, Brenda, Jessica and I went to Wausau and had a great time looking at the beautiful dresses. We found one we really liked, and it fit Brenda to a T. Even Jessica got a pretty, long pink dress for Reto's wedding. Yes, it was one of those great days that make you feel glad to be alive.

****

I was called for jury duty that fall, and I thought I'd get through without having to serve once, since there were a lot of drunken driving cases and no defense lawyer wanted me for that, not after the experience I had at Lotti's wedding. For the sixth time I appeared all ready, and went home not getting all the way to the jury bench.

The following day I had to go again. This time they needed jurors for a murder trial, and I got on it. That trial took a whole week. We went to the farm where the killing took place, listened to the mother of the victim and also to the two who were there at the time of the killing.

A young girl, Sue, had Mr. Roggenbach as a boyfriend, and he fathered her child, but those two quickly went separate ways after the baby was born. Only she fell in love with Mr. Helt, who moved in with her. But Roggenbach was jealous and wanted to see his child. He also was violent when he drank. So one morning the end of May, Sue ran into Roggenbach in town. He told her to leave Helt because he still loved her. She told him she loved him, too, and they made love together. Sue then went home. But Roggenbach, in the meantime, called Helt and told him that Sue and he just made out. So when Sue came home, Helt was mad at her and threw her on the garage floor and hit her. After she convinced him that she didn't love Roggenbach and only loved him, those two made up. But Roggenbach went on a drinking spree that evening, and at 1:30 a.m. he stopped at Sue's doorsteps demanding to see his baby. Sue went outside to talk to him, but what can one do with a drunk? She could not calm him down.

Helt, in the meantime, carried the baby to the basement and called Sue's parents, who lived on the other end of the 40. Then he took the gun and loaded it. He stood by the kitchen door when Roggenbach stormed in to the porch yelling and screaming, "I want to see my baby." Roggenbach wanted to grab the gun. That was when Helt pulled the trigger and splintered Roggenbach's collarbone. One of the splinters ripped one of his arteries close by his neck. Roggenbach turned around and walked to the pickup truck just as Sue's parents arrived. There he collapsed and bled to death. I was kind of mad at Sue. She really was the one who was at fault.

Jurors couldn't discuss the case until they started to deliberate. Nine of the jurors made a decision the first 10 minutes we deliberated. "If a stranger comes to my door in the middle of the night, I would shoot, too," was their explanation. There was no doubt in my mind that Roggenbach also was at fault, but Helt did not use reasonable force, in my opinion. Helt wrestled Roggenbach to the floor once before at a previous argument, and now Roggenbach was drunk and had no gun and Sue's parents were on the way. I felt Helt could have stalled him for awhile; and two of the jurors agreed with me.

But as hour after hour passed, one by one gave in. I did not want Helt in jail for life, but he did not use reasonable force and should get punished for it. After six hours of deliberation, I gave in, too.

We went back to the courtroom and the judge read the verdict. Then the district attorney stood up and said, "Oh, I guess we win some and we lose some. So what." That got me even more upset. I took jury duty seriously, and it is my duty as a citizen to see that justice is served, and the district attorney took it as a sporting event, where the better one wins. I will never forget that experience.

Years later Helt became a regular customer of mine, and every time I saw him I thought to myself, "A good thing that you don't know that I would have put you, at least for a couple of months, into jail so that you would have to think what you did." But he didn't know, and that was good.

****

It was beginning of December. Martin went home early that night. Edith had a meeting to go to. I went once more behind the cows, scraped the manure down and shook the straw a little. I was almost at the end when I saw a baler twine in the manure gutter. I could not leave that there, since that is a no-no as we have to pump the liquid manure out of the pit in the spring. Those strings could wind around the propeller of the pump and plug it up. So I bent down, just as I always did, but before I knew it, I slammed into the calf pen. It went so fast I didn't even know what happened. A cow that otherwise never lifted a foot got spooked and kicked me straight into my face.

I got up, finished the last two cows, and then went to the house and lay down. Within 20 minutes my face was so swollen that I could not see out of either eye, my lips were swollen and ripped, and my nose hurt.

Henry looked at me and said, "You're so stupid. After all these years and you still don't know that you do not bend down behind a cow." But Jessica, as a little girl, fell in the gutter once behind that same cow and the cow did not lift a foot.

I could not go to the barn the next morning. I simply could not see. My neck hurt, plus the pressure in my head was almost unbearable. After the swelling went down, both my eyes turned black and blue, and for weeks I wore sunglasses if I had to go somewhere.

Lotti and her family came home unexpected for Christmas that year. We went shopping at the mall one day. Henry, Larry, Lotti and I walked from store to store, when a little old lady whom we never saw before stopped. She nudged Henry in the side, smiled at him, and laughingly said, "You really did it to her," pointing at my still black-and-blue eyes. We all got a good laugh out of that one.

****

The winter went fast, and we had to hurry with spring planting, since Reto's wedding was set for June 2, 1984, and we surely did not want to miss that one. Heinz came home from Switzerland to be Reto's best man. Heinz did a lot for us in the few days he was here: put new brakes into the manure truck. He could see that it got to be too much for his father, and so he fixed whatever needed it most. Then on Tuesday I packed the suitcases, and as soon as we got done milking that night we drove off. Henry, Heinz, Jessica and I went on that long trip to California. While one was driving, the others dozed off, and then we switched. We only stopped for food and gas.

Near Kansas City where Highway 80 turns off was an

accident, and we had to watch carefully where we were going, and because of that missed our turnoff. So we went all the way down Highway 70, and through Denver.

The second night at around 8 p.m. we filled the tank and ate supper. Heinz drove a little bit longer, but then got tired, so just as we drove onto Highway 50 I volunteered to drive.

It was a long, long, lonely drive through the desert, no house in sight. The sun came slowly up over the horizon. It was a beautiful morning, but I didn't feel that great, since the needle on my gas gauge went lower and lower and no gas station as far as my eye could see.

There was a sign "Gas," so I made a little detour, but the gas station was vacant, just an old rundown building. So on I went, but I woke Heinz up. "What should I do?" I asked. He pointed to the left. "There is a trailer home and a gas station." We stopped. There was another car waiting, a young couple with a little baby. But on the door of the trailer was a sign: "We will not be open before 10 a.m. Please do not disturb." That young woman was almost in tears. "We have to wait here. We can't take a chance with our little one," she said.

But Heinz decided to try it. We had no idea how far it was to the next town, and it went uphill over the Austin summit. It was scary. The needle was on empty. But we made it up to the top, and then Heinz just coasted down the winding road, the car motor turned off and hoping and praying that the brakes would hold. After about 50 miles of sweating, we made it to a little tavern that sold gas. They charged almost $2 a gallon, but we did not care. At least we got gas.

The owner of that gas station had his binoculars close by and told us that he could watch the cars coast down from the summit and knew they had to stop by him to get gas. "This is a lonely place, but a good business," he told us. After a cup of coffee to calm our nerves, we went on to

Reno where we met Brenda and Reto.

Lotti and Larry, who drove in from Texas where they now lived, were also there. Two classmates of Reto's flew in to Reno. Henry and I rented a motel room in Reno after being on the road for over 40 hours. I needed a shower desperately, and definitely some sleep. Henry, Jessica and I went to bed while the rest went gambling. At 1 a.m. they came back and crashed on the floor in our room. Then at 5 a.m. we all got up and drove to Stockton, California, where we had breakfast, and then on to Manteca.

It was Friday by now, and Brenda had to get the last details straightened out. I had her wedding dress in a box in our trunk, and that had to be pressed.

Edith, Martin and Martin Junior flew in that evening. We hired someone to milk the cows for two days so that they could be with us. Edith was eight months pregnant at the time.

Saturday, a beautiful day. We went to church early and helped Brenda to get ready. But where was the veil? Brenda left it at her friend Stacy's house so that Reto would not see the veil, but Stacy, who was a bridesmaid, forgot to bring it along. What now? It is a 30-minute drive and the family and friends were in the church already. Brenda made some phone calls and found someone who went and got it.

Reto got scared, not knowing what was going on. He thought Brenda maybe changed her mind. But then, with only a ten-minute delay, everything else went on as planned.

I was proud of my son, standing in front of the church by the altar. On the other hand, I could feel a sting in my heart and a few lonely tears ran down my cheeks, knowing that my baby, the one I prayed for so many times when he was deathly sick, now starts his own family. One sure can be happy and sad at the same time. And from the bottom of my heart, I wish Reto all the luck and happiness on earth.

The greatest joy was to have all my kids together. Even Henry's sister Elsa and her family joined us. On Sunday was the after-wedding. We relaxed all day by the poolside. Martin and Edith flew back to Wisconsin.

We stayed one more night and left early the next morning. Again we drove straight through and were back on the farm late Tuesday night, dead-tired from the long trip. We drove because the plane tickets were too expensive, or so I thought. But I would never, ever do that again. To drive that much in one week and have a wedding in-between is no fun at all.

****

Edith gave birth to a little girl, Heidi, on July 16th that year. She was busy with her household and had a big garden. But the best part was, she cooked for all of us, if I worked in the fields. It was great to be able to just sit down and enjoy a meal and not have to first cook it.

But the distance between Henry and Martin got bigger and bigger. What didn't make matters better was that Martin, just like Henry, was homesick. As long as Martin wasn't married, he had a return ticket in his pocket and that was his security. But not anymore. Plus, when he came here as our son-in-law, milk prices were good. We even ordered a new house to be built on the farm later that year. They could have moved into the new house and we would have moved into theirs. But interest rates were skyrocketing and we decided to wait until they came down. But then when the interest rates came down, the milk price bottomed out. So Martin could see that farming wasn't as rosy as he thought it would be, and that nagged on him, too.

It go so bad between Henry and Martin that Martin asked me which field to plow, then I had to ask Henry, go back to Martin and give him the answer. Here I was again, in the middle. I got so fed up that I went to the feed store, told the crop specialist there how many acres I wanted to plow, what I wanted to plant, and asked him how much seed and what kind of fertilizer I needed.

I also took Edith out for lunch one day that spring and told her to take a long look at her dad, and then think what she really wanted for Martin. "He will end up unhappy just like your dad if you don't make any changes," I told her. "Do not feel obligated and sorry for us. If you guys want to start new somewhere else, then do so. And if you decide to move back to Switzerland, then so be it. I will keep the farm going, and if I can't anymore, I will sell everything, but I can't go on like this, being constantly ripped between your dad and Martin. So please think about it long and hard, and then tell me when you make a decision."

Edith and I both felt bad, but knew something had to give. Martin got in contact with his old boss in Switzerland, and he told Martin he would take him back anytime. Martin also told me so many times that his family was so much closer, they cared for each other, something he can't see in our family. But the grass always looks greener on the other side of the fence. Yet when you get to the other side, the green grass dries up quickly and turns brown and ugly. So, slowly but surely, they came to the conclusion to go back to Switzerland.

On May 31, 1985, Brenda gave birth to a little girl, Sierra, and we went to visit them for a week in September. They lived in Watsonville, California now. We spent one day at the ocean just lying in the sand, and another time they drove us along Highway 5. It was a great week. Reto worked now for PG&E, the Pacific Gas and Electric Company. He was in the midst of his apprenticeship. It will take him a total of four and a half years to be a #1 lineman. Yes, my children had a tough childhood, but it made them the great, determined human beings they are now.

But once back home, knowing that Edith and her family would be moving back to Switzerland ripped Henry apart. That was the end of him. Henry just didn't want to go on. His body collapsed. He had rheumatoid arthritis and farmer's lung. It was plain and simple — his body said, "I worked long enough, I don't want to go on anymore."

I had to get him in and out of bed and drive him to Marshfield to the doctor. He was unable to drive a car. For weeks he could not do anything but lie in bed. The neurologist told him he had to take up to 25 aspirins a day. "That will kill him," I said to the doctor. But his answer was, "No, it won't. And if Henry feels a humming in his ears, then he has to cut back until the humming stops, and then slowly increase the aspirin intake again."

It was sad to see that once so tough, rough man deteriorate. And no matter how hard I tried, I could not cheer him up. All those years I told Henry he should show his children he loved them, then they would always remember the good times. But his response was simply the same: just wait, they will come home crawling and want the money from the old man. And now they are all going their own ways, and not one begs for money. We did not have much anyway, but that destroyed Henry.

I still was the corporate area woman for AMPI, still fighting for better farm prices. I had an opportunity beginning of November to go to the American Agri Women convention in Phoenix, Arizona, an all-paid trip. Knowing that that would be the last time that I could go, and Martin and Edith promising they would take care of the farm and Henry, I made reservations and decided to make that trip. It was great to get together with farm women from all over the USA with all kinds of farm background.

There were a lot of great speakers, but one speaker was especially inspirational to me. Her speech was titled "There is Life Beyond Farming." She had examples from farm wives who called her, sometimes in the middle of the night, because their husbands were on the end of the rope and were thinking of killing themselves. She tried to talk them out of it, and make them understand that there is more to life than worldly possessions. And that is something that hit home. Wasn't I in a similar situation?

The other women who came along would sit together afterwards, but for some reason I could not. I felt sad and lonely and did not really know why. Then on Thursday morning when we waited for our cab that had to bring us to the airport, I was told by the desk clerk that my daughter tried to get hold of me.

We had the final awards banquet the night before, and so I got to my room later than the other nights. And now the cab was here and I had no time to call either. But as soon as we got to the airport, I called home.

Edith told me that her dad collapsed twice the night before. She wanted him to go to the hospital, but he refused. "Your mom don't care about me anymore or she would not have left me here alone while she is having a good time in Arizona. She did not even call last night. So if I do not matter to her, then I'd rather die," Henry complained. Edith was terrified and worried, but she could not get hold of me and did not know what to do.

When I got home later that evening, I told Henry that I did not call every night because we do not have that kind of money, and I was only gone five days. Oh, it was so tough to understand Henry, and I did not know what to do anymore. Yet I could not burden Edith and make leaving harder on her. I had to go through this alone. Henry was hurting so bad. But looking back, I think it was just because he could not cope anymore. It was too much for him.

In the beginning of December Henry begged to get a waterbed. "Maybe then my joints won't hurt so bad," he said. But I didn't want any part of it. "I don't like to get seasick while sleeping." I laughed. Yet I could see his pain and decided to give in.

Edith and I went to look at waterbeds and bought one for Christmas. Martin helped me to remodel the bedroom a little, to make the floor stronger and the wall sturdier, and in came the waterbed. I was so tired from all the work that it made no difference to me. I could sleep, waterbed or not. Henry, on the other hand, the one who wanted the waterbed, had a hard time getting used to it and slept the first week in the recliner anyway.

It was so tough for me over the holidays and to celebrate New Year's Eve. I had to look into a new year that once again would bring a lot of changes. But life goes on and I will somehow survive.

****

Martin, Martin Junior and Heidi would be leaving us in the beginning of February and move to Switzerland. Edith and Jessica will pack the household goods, clean the house, and ten days later join the rest of the family. What would I do then? Henry sick and no loved ones within 1,200 miles, yet a farm to take care of — 90 cows that had to be milked and 60 calves and heifers to raise. What a job! But I was the one who told Edith to do what she felt was best for her family, so I had no right to feel hurt. Once again, like so many times before, I asked God to stand by my side and help me to get through this, even if it is only one day at a time.

Henry's left leg was swollen and he felt very sick, and Edith and her family had a lot of company the night before Martin left for Switzerland. We two alone, all we had left was each other.

As I came up from the barn the night before Martin's departure, Henry had convulsions. He shook so bad that the whole bed was shaking. With tears rolling slowly down his checks, he told me, "That is my night. I just saw my whole life pass in front of my eyes, and I know I will leave you, this time forever."

"You can't do that. I need you. I will call the ambulance," I told him, with tears in my eyes.

"No, please don't. My joints hurt so bad. If you bring

me to the hospital, they will lay me on one of those hard mattresses. I could not stand that. So please, let me die right here in my waterbed, right here by you," Henry begged.

I sat sobbing on the bed for a while, holding onto his hand. Again I begged, "Please let me call the ambulance." But he did not think he could make it to the hospital, and just wanted to die right here in his familiar surroundings. I paced the floor and could not ask anybody for their support. What on earth should I do? Edith had friends over for their goodbye party and I did not want to spoil that. Plus, I really didn't want them to feel guilty that they made the decision to move back to Switzerland.

I cried and asked myself, "Why, why do I have to suffer so much?" But then I could hear my grandma say, "God will never give you a cross heavier than you can carry." And mine right now was very heavy, and I did not know if I could go on. It was way past midnight when I finally lay down and fell asleep.

I hired a young man to help me conquer my big workload. Martin did not come to help me milk that last morning of his stay in the USA. I was just done with the milking and went to the house to see how Henry was doing and to make some breakfast when Martin came to say goodbye. He left the kids at home, since he figured that was not something he wanted them to see.

Henry's convulsion eased off, but he looked very weak and could not get out of bed at all. Martin stood by his bedside for a while making small talk, then gave him a hug and told him, "I truly hope that you get better again soon," and then quickly left the bedroom.

We both now stood in the kitchen. Martin hugged me and tears were rolling down his cheeks. "Please, Mom, please forgive me for leaving you here all alone. I did not want it that way." We hugged each other and I tried to be strong and told him, "Don't worry. If I can't no more, then

I will find a way out, but you have to do what you think is right for you and your family. You cannot live to make our dream come true. You have to live your own life."

One more kiss and he was gone. I was glad that he did not bring the children anymore. I said goodbye to them yesterday. I do not think that I could have handled to look at those happy faces that morning without breaking down.

Two days later I drove Henry to town to see the doctor. I had a very bad cold and was afraid I had pneumonia. But the doctor told me I just had a bad flu and should be on medicine, but could go home and work.

Henry, on the other hand, was put into the hospital immediately. He had a blood clot in his left leg, and they were worried that it would move and kill him. Come to find out later that was why he had the convulsions two days before. That was when some of the blood clots moved, and he really could have died. The doctor put him immediately on blood thinner intravenously, and Henry could not get out of bed for weeks. So I went home alone that afternoon.

Edith packed all the things they wanted to take along and had a moving sale with the rest of it. The movers came and loaded their belongings on a truck to be shipped overseas. Edith and Jessica stayed with me for the last three nights. We had it nice together, but did not talk too much about the future.

It was Wednesday morning and time for a final goodbye. Not knowing how Henry would take that, I called my Swiss friends, the Fuellemans, and asked them if they please would come visit Henry that afternoon. I know he needed some cheering up, and they were the only ones who could help him.

Edith, Jessica and I had our last breakfast together. I was not hungry at all. It felt like I had a lump in my throat and I was close to tears. If I could just say, "Please stay." But I knew there was no looking back. I had to go on and did not want to make it any harder on Edith than it already was.

They took their last suitcases, packed them into the trunk, and to the hospital we drove. We did not talk much on the way in, since we all dreaded that last goodbye. Yet Edith did not want to leave without seeing her dad one more time.

We sat by his bedside for awhile not knowing what to say. Then Mrs. Hoffman came. She volunteered to drive Edith and Jessica to the O'Hare Airport in Chicago. Now no longer could we hold our feelings back. All of us broke down. Henry sick, us not knowing if he ever would come home again — we all cried. The nurses, unaware of what was going on, came running. "Did someone just die?" they asked. We answered no, but were too emotional to go into details. And, yes, for me it was like part of me had just died. I felt so lonely.

I walked Edith and Jessica downstairs. One last desperate hug and kiss, the car door slammed, and they slowly drove away. My tears slowly rolling down my cheeks, and I said, "Please, God, help me to get through this."

I could not see them anymore when I finally got hold of myself, turned around, dried my tears and went upstairs to comfort Henry. And, as promised, Fullemanns came to see Henry and made him smile again. Thanks, guys, for being there when I needed you most.

It was four in the afternoon when I kissed Henry goodbye and went home to milk the cows. Those were the longest 10 miles in my life. I never felt lonelier. Heinz and Edith now in Switzerland, Lotti in Texas, and Reto in California. My eyes filled with tears; I could hardly see where I was going.

I drove slowly up Highway 64, turned onto CTH-E. One mile in on E is my dream house where Edith and her family lived, but the house was empty, and never again would I see my grandchildren play in the lawn. I could not leave it, I had to drive up the driveway and walk into the house. Deep down, I was hoping that this all was just a bad dream. I would wake up any minute and everything would be as it always was. But the house was cold and empty. I stood in the doorway for a while, then slowly turned around, locked the door behind me, and drove the last two miles to the farm.

Once back in the barn, there was no time to feel sorry for myself. There were animals to be fed and cows to be milked. It was almost 11 p.m. and I was dead tired when I lay down in bed, and it did not take long to fall asleep and get at least a couple of hours rest from all my pain.

Every afternoon I went to see Henry. Sometimes I dozed off through my whole visit, since his hospital room was so nice and warm, something I did not have at home, and the chair was so comfortable. More than once Henry took my hands and softly rubbed them, telling me, "Look how rough your hands are. I'm really, really sorry that I put you through all of this. You deserved better. I truly love you." I was too tired to hurt, so I smiled at him and told him, "It's okay. Just get better so that I can take you home again."

****

The farm economy was so bad that the government gave all of us farmers an option to participate in a buyout. Even though I was so busy and tired, I had to attend the meetings and figure out if that was an option for us. We would have to sell all our cows to the slaughter house, and then could not have any cows for five years. The government in turn would pay us part of the milk check we lost.

Many nights I sat at the kitchen table and put figures upon figures together. But with the money we would get, I could not even pay our loan off. And how could I pay the $8,000 in land tax, the insurance and the light bill? Yes, I could get a job and cash crop our land, but hay does not pay much either right now, and there is no job that I could get that would pay me the kind of money I needed.

There were very few farmers who could go along with the buyout. Only those farmers that did not have the debt load most of us had could. I came to the conclusion that the only option I had right now was to keep on farming.

Our house still had no furnace. I had a wood stove in the basement that I fired up before I went to the barn, but when I came back five to six hours later, the fire was out and the house cold again. Yes, I could restart the fire, but it takes a while to warm the house up, and by then I was asleep. Thank God Henry wanted a waterbed. At least that was always warm. I could cuddle up, and my head did no more hit the pillow and I was asleep.

****

My hired man was no good at all. One day he had to let silage down, but the silo unloader did not work. "Edith, I don't know what to do. There is no silage coming down," he came and told me. Here is this 240-pound, 23-year-old guy, and I have to take the crowbar, climb up into the silo, chop the ice from the silo door, and then try to center the silo unloader, while he stands there with his hands in his pocket, watching what I am doing.

One day I told him before he went to lunch, "Be back by 1:30, and please clean the calf pens. I will go to visit Henry." But when I came home, he was nowhere to be found. At 5:30 p.m. he walked into the barn.

"What about the calf pens," I asked.

"I was here earlier, but you were not here, so I went back home to watch TV," was his reply. I was too frustrated to answer, so I let it go.

Each of our cows always had the same stall. If I put them in the barn, I opened the door, let 12 or 15 cows in, closed the door, tied them on, and then let the next group in. But now matter what I said, my hired man opened the door and let all of them in. That sometimes was a disaster, especially if one was in heat (bullish).

One time he closed the door after he let the first couple of cows in. He looked down the aisle and said, "Oh, you're doing good," opened the door and let the rest in, too. Then all of a sudden I had an awful feeling. I ran to the back door and there he laid in a foot of stinky, wet mature, the bull pressing his nose onto his chest. God, did I get scared.

I chased the bull away and helped him to get up, but he sat right down again. I grabbed him and ripped him into the barn. "Do you want to wait till the bull attacks you again?" I screamed.

Once in the barn, I closed the door. He sat down again, his face white as a ghost. "Are you hurt?" I asked him once more. I was so scared my heart pounded 90 miles an hour.

"No," he said. "I just would like to sit for awhile."

I tied all the cows on, and then went back. "Are you sure you aren't hurt? Otherwise, I will call the ambulance," I asked.

He looked at me and whimpered, "No, I'm not hurt, but I would like to go home."

That's when my nerves gave in and I screamed at him, "Then get the hell out of here and never, ever show your face again."

He got up, walked out of the barn to his car, and drove off.

****

I did not realize until then that I'd injured my thumb when I ripped him into the barn, but now it hurt, and got really swollen. Yet I had no time to be sick. There was work that had to be done. I had to let the bull and the rest of the cows in and then milk those 90 cows. It was past midnight when I got done with my chores and walked up to my cold, lonely house. But I was even too tired to cry and feel sorry for myself this time of night. I soaked my hand in warm water for a while, put an elastic bandage on, crawled into my warm waterbed and was asleep in no time.

15

I HAD TO do my chores alone for weeks, but at least I could take Henry home, and that meant I did not have to go to town every day anymore. I was so glad and told the doctor, "Thank God that I can have Henry home again. He can be my housewife now and cook for me."

"No way," the doctor said. "He can't even wash dishes. Henry is on blood thinner medication, and if he would cut himself he could bleed to death." So I guess that does not work either.

But then I was lucky. Martin's sister and her boyfriend Peter came to stay for awhile. They stayed with us for three months, and I was very grateful. They must have been sent from heaven above. Theresa was my helper in the barn. She also cooked and baked and helped wherever she was needed. Peter helped with the field work.

Heinz and his girlfriend, Judith (Judith later became his wife) came to visit us that summer for two weeks. From here they went to see Reto in California and Lotti in Texas. It was so hard on Judith. She was amongst all those strangers, and the houses are so far apart. She could not believe that she could not see nor walk to the nearest town, but it was simply too far. Judith truly felt lost.

But in the time those two were with us, Heinz worked almost day and night to get everything fixed that had to be fixed. He was a big help to me. We certainly have great kids who did not ask what is in it for them. They just did what had to be done. Thank God for that.

Then I was alone again, but not for long. I found a young girl who wanted to help on a farm. She was handicapped, but good with cows. And through the newspaper I hired a guy to help with the field and barn work, but he was lazier than lazy, and I found out later that he had a dishonorable discharge from the Army because he got into trouble there, too. He lived with us, so I also had to cook and wash for him.

I got up a little after 5 a.m., got ready to go to the barn, and then woke up my hired man. Twice I hollered, "It is time to get up," and off to the barn I went. At 7 or 7:30 a.m. he'd walk into the barn and ask, "What can I do for you this morning?" I could have clobbered him I was so mad. But I had to keep quiet, since help was hard to come by.

It was three miles between the farm where Edith used to live and the main farm. I had all the heifers in the pasture over there. But the highway department made a new bridge on County Highway E that year, and because of that we had to make a 12-mile detour to get there. That was especially tough with the silo wagon. It took forever to get those loads home.

I told my two employees one day to go and check the fence so the heifers couldn't get out. Then hours later, when I went to check how far they got, they were sleeping in the shade of a tree. What a great help they were. I was just so frustrated.

I was still corporate area woman for AMPI, and for the last years, also a farm advocate for farmers in trouble. If a farmer is in financial trouble, he is mad and most of the time can't be reasonable anymore. On the other hand, the banker is frustrated, too. He doesn't want the loan to default. So they can't talk together anymore. Then I have to be the one who had to try to get the two to compromise.

It is monitored by the Department of Agriculture, but a job where one does not get paid. It is strictly voluntary. But I have first-hand experience. I know how much it hurts to know that you put the best years of your life into this farm, and now have to see your dream crumble. And I, out of all people, have enough troubles on my own. Yet, if I could help just one farm couple to have it easier, then it would be worth my effort.

The Department of Agriculture put on seminars with speakers from FMHA and Farm Credit Services. We Farm Advocates could ask questions pertaining to financial problems. But it got me upset that some of my fellow farmers felt that the bankers owe us a life on the farm. No matter how bad our financial situation is, I feel that we as farmers also have to make an effort and work hard to get out of our misery, and not just sit back and think the banker has to help us. No one owes me, as an independent human being, anything. I have to make the difference in my life, and even though it is sometimes hard, I can never stop trying.

Oh, boy, is it hard sometimes to get a farmer to see that. For example:

I helped one farm family. Dad had heart trouble and had to quit farming. The sons did not want to milk cows and sold out. They were debt-free after the auction. Then they planted sunflowers and bought a dryer to dry the sunflower seed, but since they had no experience, they did not know that sunflowers have a lot of oil, and drying them is almost a science. They burned up the dryer and the sunflowers, and later started a lawsuit against the company that sold them the dryer.

The following year they build two big silos and put all their cropland into corn. High moisture corn is the way to go, they thought. But the corn had more than 32% moisture when they combined it and put it into the silo, so it got moldy and no one would buy that moldy corn.

It took the sons three years and they were $500,000 in the hole, and the bank foreclosed. I went with them to talk to the banker, but I drove a Volvo with 130,000 miles on it, and they drove up to the bank in a new Cadillac. That is when I question myself, do I really want to give my precious time if they do not care?

Needless to say, they lost the farm. But I stayed with the program, since I learned a lot, and got an inside look at how the system worked.

I had to go to another one of those two-day seminars put on by the Department of Agriculture. I got up earlier that morning so that the barn work was done before I left. Like always, I had to hurry to make the 60-mile drive down to Plover on time. And, sure enough, just outside of Wausau I got a speeding ticket, so I was late to begin with. Then the speaker from FHA told us, there is a new law that just came into effect. If a farmer can't make the payments anymore, then FHA will foreclose. But then they had to rent the farm back to that same farmer who just lost it. The reasoning behind it was the farmer has the right to keep the lifestyle that he is used to.

But, if you as a farmer are financed through Farm Credit Services or any other bank, they will kick you off the farm, because they are not government regulated, yet you can only get an FHA loan if no other lending institution gives you a loan. I got up more than once and said that was unfair. "I feel no one owes me anything. I came to this country to work hard and support my family and myself. Yes, I'm glad if I can get help, but then it is up to me to make it work."

But there was really nothing I could change. Rules are rules.

The sessions were over at 4:30 p.m. Then we had supper and later open discussions. Before we sat down to eat, I called home to see if everything was okay. My hired man answered the phone and told me laughingly that the motor on the Allis Chalmers 210 just blew up.

That was all I had to hear that day. That was my final straw. Most everyone stayed overnight. I knew before already that I had to go home later to milk and then come back in the morning, but now I was really upset.

Yet I was hungry and the meal was ready, so I sat down and ate together with some Ag teachers from NCTI (North Central Technical Institute). They could feel that I was restless and asked what was wrong.

"I have to go home. My hired man just told me that the tractor motor blew up. This is at least a $5,000 repair. Yes, I know the bank would give us the money, but that means we are $5,000 more in the hole. I give the bank now already $7,200 a month out of my milk check, and that leaves me hardly any money to live on, and now this. I will drive home as soon as I'm done with my meal."

One of the Ag instructors asked me, "Since you drive my way anyway, could I ride along?" He came to the meeting with some of his fellow teachers.

"No problem," I answered. "I'm glad if I have someone to talk to. I'm too upset to keep my nerves calm and my eyes on the road."

Then the whole trip back we tried to figure out what my options were. We came to the conclusion that I had to give it up. He tried to cheer me up, and then told me to have an appraiser come out to the farm and then go from there.

I was so wound up when I got home I didn't know where to turn anymore. Henry, who now could walk again but could not work in the barn because he had farmer's lung, sat at the dining room table reading the paper. Without even saying "Hi," I asked him, "How bad is the tractor?"

"What tractor," he asked.

I told him what my hired man told me over the phone just hours before.

"That was just a joke he played on you," Henry told me. "The battery was dead so he had to get a new battery."

That sure was no joke in my eyes. I was so stressed out that I could not handle that kind of behavior. I knew I couldn't go on like this anymore, and I was determined to make an end to it. "I will call an appraiser tomorrow," I told Henry.

"But why," was his question. "We aren't behind in payments to the bank and can pay all our bills. What more do you want?"

"Yes, we aren't delinquent, but that does not mean we are making any money," I replied. "I will call tomorrow and when the appraiser comes, then I will go to town and you show him everything we have, and then we go from there."

And so I did. Two guys from the Wausau Sales Company showed up and appraised everything. Then we sat down and put the figures open on the table. Even though Henry saw it black-on-white, he was not convinced that we should abandon his dream. We were told that, because of the falling farm prices, if we had auction right now and sold everything, we would not even get what we owed the bank.

The banks were eager to lend money in the '70s when milk prices were high, especially to farmers who they knew worked as hard as we did, but land then went for $800-$900 an acre or more; now we would be glad if we get $250-$300. Cows went for $1,500 and up; now they are $500-$800. We bought a combine for $34,000 when Martin came to farm with us in 1981, and even though we kept it up and it was still in good condition, it is only worth $5,000. All the money that is lost is not the bank's money, it is our investment.

Dick, the loan officer from the PCA, sat at our dining room table in 1980 and told us we were worth $400,000 to $500,000, but then those are only figures on paper. Now, with the devaluation, we owe the bank more than we are worth. Yes, it is very tough to understand for an outsider, but it is reality.

Still, Henry could not see why we should abandon our dream (his dream). "Maybe times get better again," he tried to convince me.

If Henry would have been in good health and ten years younger, I might have given in, but not now. There has to be an easier way for me of making a living than here on the farm, working so hard all by myself. The guys from Wausau Sales agreed with me and told me to get in contact with Mr. Eberlein, a bankruptcy lawyer from Wausau.

I made an appointment, and one week later we sat in his office. He wanted to know our whole history. Then he looked at us and said, "I can see you both worked very hard and I will take you as my clients, but it will cost you $4,500 up front. I will get you out of your debt, but you will walk away without anything."

I was stunned, but then replied quickly, "We'll see. I worked too hard to do that. I will find a way to make it work for us." I did not know how I would do that, but I was determined not to walk away with empty pockets.

After a sleepless night, I came to the conclusion the best thing to do would be to start with the lenders. We went to the Credit Union first. There we had a little over a thousand dollars borrowed. "We will file bankruptcy," I told the loan officer. "We have to come up with $4,500 for the lawyer, and I do not know how. I don't have that kind of money."

And then I went on, "But don't worry, I will get a job and we will pay all the money we owe you, little by little, and you will get it all eventually."

"You aren't the first one, and the way the farm prices are going, sure will not be the last one who has to do that," he told us, and was very understanding. "Switch milk plants; then you get one full milk check without any deductions. The lender will catch up with you the following month, but that is okay. By then you got your $4,500 for your lawyer, and that is all you need. You will then be one payment behind, but since you are filing bankruptcy anyway, it does not matter." I was so thankful to that loan officer. Thank you, God. You opened a door for me again. You never let me down.

From there we went to the Lincoln County Bank where we had an $800 loan. That loan officer was the opposite.

"If one wants to get out the easy way and file bankruptcy, we bankers will have to stand together and never, ever lend money to this person again," he told us straight out.

"But my husband is sick, all my children are gone, and I just can't any more. It is too much work for me alone. The farm prices are bottomed out, so how could I sell our farm? Bankruptcy is our only way out of this. But if this is your attitude, you will wait to get your money. I will not pay you one more dime." Out the door we went, leaving him just standing there.

Everyone in town knew how hard I tried to make a go of it, and now this young guy can come and downgrade me for that. But I guess there will always be people like that.

Then we drove straight to Wausau to see Dick at the PCA and told him of our plans. That lending agency worked with us since 1968 and knew of all our heartache we had through all those years. He was very understanding. "What are your plans for the future?" he asked. He knew from before that Henry gets only $192 for his disability, and we sure could not live on this kind of money. Henry was 39 years old in 1968 when we immigrated to this country, and as a farmer, struggling through all those years we did not pay much Social Security, and in turn now did not get much.

"I will make you an offer. Go home and think about it before you file bankruptcy. You tell me how many cows and how much land you can handle; then that is what we will give you and reduce your loan accordingly. That way you at least have a roof over your head. Please think about it. I'm willing to help you every way I can."

I had tears in my eyes. Here Dick is a stranger, and yet has so much compassion. I promised to sleep on it.

Then it was time to hurry home, to do chores again. I had a lot of time to think while I was milking the 90 cows. But the more I repeated, "At least you have a roof over your head," the more determined I got. That is a handout again, and I won't take them. I want more out of life than just to work for the banker so that I have a roof over my head. Another sleepless night, and more followed. I wanted to make sure that I saw my future clear before I put my foot into my mouth.

On Sunday I sat down and wrote Dick a long letter. "I thank you so much for your offer, but I can't accept it. I'm too proud to live from handouts. But I thought about it and would like to make you an offer in return. We will file for a quick bankruptcy, no fighting whatsoever, if you give us the house where Edith used to live and eight acres of land debt-free. I will find me a job in town and you can have our farm and all the animals and machines tomorrow."

I sealed the letter and sent it off. What is going to be his answer, I asked myself over and over again.

Three days later I got a letter from PCA. My hands trembled as I opened it. I knew this letter would determine the destiny of my life. It was short and right to the point. I read it quickly, ran over to Henry and gave him a big kiss and a hug. "They accepted my offer," I screamed, laughing and crying both at the same time. Thank God! Thank God! I have a home and no more debt. Yes, that house has to be remodeled, too. The basement walls are in bad shape, but it still is a lot better than the one I'm living in now. At least we have a home.

But now I would have to find a job, which isn't easy either. What should I do? I farmed for the last 19 years and never worked for someone else in this country. Is my English good enough? What can I do? I'm not a nurse, and even though I like bookwork, I'm not an accountant, nor a secretary, nor did I ever work on a typewriter, let alone my terrible spelling in English. And I do not want to work for McDonald's or any other fast-food chain for minimum wages. The only thing I do know is how to run a store, and I'm determined to learn whatever is necessary to handle a job like that. Something will come my way. My Guardian Angel so far always watched over me, he has never let me down, and I hope and pray that he helps me now so that I find a way to get out of this.

Wednesday we had to bring our lawyer the letter from the PCA, and on the way there I stopped and ordered the local newspaper, since I had to look for job openings. Mr. Eberlein, our lawyer, could not believe his eyes as he read the letter. "No one ever could get a house and some land without a lawyer and some court costs," he said. My reply: "I was always honest and straightforward with the banker, and that is just what I did now. Honesty is the only thing that gets you somewhere." Mr. Eberlein was very pleased and promised to get it finalized through the bankruptcy court as soon as possible.

I was so busy with the cows that I did not have time until Saturday night to look at the papers. I read every ad — nurse, legal secretary, cooks — but I was none of them. To the next day's paper I went. There has to be something I could do.

Yes, there was one ad that caught my attention. "Want manager for convenience store at the Auto Stop in Merrill." Boy, that would be something; managing a store is something I know how to do. And the Auto Stop is on my side of town, only about five miles from here.

I was dead-tired that night, but I took pen and paper and wrote a resume. In Switzerland, if one applies for a job we have to write a short life story from the school one attended all the way through the last job one had, then add a recent picture to it and send it in. Since I never applied for a job here, I had no idea that that is not what one does. Anyway, I sat down, wrote my life story. I managed stores before but then came to this country to farm, and now have to quit, but have to support Henry and me; that is why I need this job. I looked for a decent picture, but could only find one with Henry and me together, so I put that one into the envelope.

But now what should I do? The application had to be sent to Abbotsford, and the ad was in on Thursday. My letter will not get there until Tuesday, but the ones who applied right away have to be there already; that could mean that I'm late. There is only one way to get around this, if I bring it there myself.

I lay down and slept for a couple of hours, got up early Sunday morning. I hurried up and got out of the barn a little after 10:30 a.m., took a shower and then told Henry, "Let's go. I take you for a Sunday drive."

We drove to Abbotsford, a little over 50 miles from our house. There I looked for the post office and threw my application into the mailbox right there. Then we found a nice local restaurant and together enjoyed a Sunday brunch. I was very happy and proud of myself. I think I did the right thing, I told myself.

Two long, sleepless nights followed, and I prayed, "Please God, help me. This would be a job I could do."

Tuesday, late afternoon, I got a phone call. "This is Phil," the person on the other end of the line said. "You applied for that manager's job. Would you please come in for an interview tomorrow at 3 p.m."

"Yes. I'll be there," was my answer.

There was no question at all. I will make it. I told Henry to come along. If I get the job, then maybe he could help me a little in the store, I thought.

Barn work was a breeze the next morning, and at noon, hours before I had to be there, I was all dressed up and ready for my first job interview. I had the butterflies, but I told myself, "Stand up straight, and make them understand that you can do the job."

Phil was a round, pleasant-looking guy. He gave us a tour of the little store and then took us in the small office in back. Phil told me what I would have to do and focused then on why I thought I was the person who should get the job.

"I need to work and I know I could do a great job for you. I have to quit farming, but since I worked so hard to get all the crops in I won't give the feed away. Even if I get the job, I will milk the cows until April of next year, and then have an auction. But to be able to get rid of the farm, we had to file bankruptcy. So I need to support us two. And I promise you, you will never regret it if you hire me," I told Phil.

He made some small talk, and then told me, "I have four more interviews this afternoon, but I will call you tonight if you got the job."

I was just so excited as we drove home. "Please God, help me. Please, I would like this job."

We grabbed a bite to eat, I changed clothes and went to the barn to milk the cows. We had a phone in the barn, too. Over and over again I ran to the phone, just to make sure it was not off the hook. I sure did not want to miss the call from Phil.

It was around seven o'clock when the phone rang, and yes, it was Phil. "You have the job," he told me. Tears in my eyes, I trembled as I asked, "When do I start?"

"Tomorrow morning at seven o'clock," was his reply.

I was speechless and had to gasp for air. At seven in the morning I have to milk 90 cows first, I thought to myself. But I need this job so, "At seven it will be," I answered.

I hung up the phone and ran to Henry, gave him a big hug and a kiss and screamed, "We did it. We did it. I'm going to make $12,000 a year now. That is $1,000 a month. That is just unbelievable. We're going to be rich someday after all."

I was so bubbly and ran around like a chicken with the head cut off. I had no idea how much energy I still had left. As soon as I was done in the barn, I went to bed, but I could hardly sleep. My alarm clock was set for 2 a.m., and it was not much before the alarm went off when I finally fell asleep. I was tired, but there was no getting around it. I had to get up.

I went to the barn, did the milking and the feeding. Henry had breakfast ready when I came in from the barn. I took a quick shower, and off to work I went.

Phil worked with me all day, but my heart was just pounding. The Auto Stop here in town had a manager and four employees, but all except one got fired a week before, so I had an almost brand-new crew and no one knew what to do.

This little old lady, walking on a cane, came into the store. She was one of my first customers. She looked at me with a smile and asked, "Are you the new manager?"

"Yes," I answered, "and I'm glad to have you as a customer."

"You won't last long. They change employees here like I change my clothes," she continued. She sure did know how to make me feel even worse than I already did. But I never, ever forgot her. She became a loyal customer for years to come.

Phil told me before he left that afternoon that he had to go to some meetings the next two days, "But a girl from Medford will be here in the morning and show you how to do the books. Have a good weekend. See you on Monday," and out the door he went.

It was just a little after three when I drove home. My tears were rolling, because I doubted myself. "I'm not smart enough to do this. I will never pull through this," I thought.

But as I made the last turn just a half-mile from the farm I stopped, dried my tears and straightened out my hair. Henry did not have to know that I was scared. He had enough on his mind. Yes, there were a lot more days like this one, days that I asked myself, "Why don't you just give up. You can't do it." And every time I had to tell myself, "Just take it one day at a time."

The one girl who did not get fired with the others made

it miserable for me. She told me straight out, "I was here before you, and I deserved the manager's job. You are new and should also start on the bottom and work your way up." She did everything in the book to work against me, so I had no choice. I had to let her go.

Phil told me months later that he almost didn't hire me for two reasons. First, when he read my letter he thought someone pulled a joke on him. No one would apply for a job the way I did. But then, as he put the envelope away, my photo fell out and made him curious. That was why he called me.

And, second of all, he said, "You tried to convince me that you could take care of your 90 cows and also do a good job here. I thought that you will never pull that one off. No one could do that. Yet you were so straightforward that I had to at least give you a chance. And you sure came through. You're doing a great job."

Henry was a big help, too. He kept the pumps clean for me, replaced the light bulbs if one was burned out, went to the bank for me, and just enjoyed talking to the customers.

Christmas was just around the corner, but I did not feel like decorating a tree. It hurt too much. No more children's eyes with the candlelight sparkle reflecting in their eyes. No more laughter and anticipation; Edith and Heinz in Switzerland, Lotti in Texas, and Reto in California. Henry's sister Martha still lived only miles away from us, but we had no contact. And all of that really, really hurt.

Yes, I had to keep it to myself, since once again I had to be the strong one. Henry was so homesick, and felt so worthless.

I went to a WWA (Wisconsin Women for Agriculture) meeting to get together with my old friends, even if it was just for a couple of hours. I told them that it was tough to keep my sanity, and for the first time in my life I would not celebrate Christmas. I just couldn't get into the Christmas spirit anymore. I would not even decorate a tree. I just didn't feel like it.

Martha Rusch called me days later and wanted to know if I was going to be home the following Saturday afternoon. She would like to come and show me something. "Yes, but I have to go to the barn no later than 3:30 p.m. I do not have to work in the store that day so I have a couple of hours free for you."

It was Saturday morning around 11:30 a.m. when her car pulled in, then another and another one. Here were all my friends from the WWA. Some of them opened their trunks. What the heck is going on now, I thought.

And then I could not believe my eyes. They brought a Christmas tree, the stand, the bulbs and even the tinsel. One of the women had apple cider and brandy along. She heated the apple cider and made a drink for everyone. They trimmed the tree and decorated it all the way, and even brought some presents for underneath.

It did not take long and I had the prettiest Christmas tree ever. The lights were glowing, and there was no doubt a little of that glow overshadowed the hurt deep in my heart. This tree was the most beautiful present I ever got. Martha, Rosemarie, Doreen, Mary Jo, Marie, Dennis and Barb, God bless you all. You will never fully understand what that gift meant to me.

Henry and I.

In 1988 we had to abandon our dream and put our farm on the auction block. That was one of the toughest decisions I had to make. It was heartbreaking.

Sadness was all around me the day we had to have the auction.

16

A NEW YEAR started. What will it have in store for us? One thing I knew for sure, that year will bring an end to Henry's dream. We had the auction date set for April 18th, the Saturday before Easter, and I didn't know yet how I would survive that day. But I guess for now all I can do is take one day at the time.

It was tough to work two jobs, but I only had to hang in there for a little longer. Henry helped me as much as he could, and that was not much. He could not stay in the barn anymore; his lungs would fill up with fluid, since he had farmer's lung, together with all the other troubles.

Henry never was sick before he had cancer surgery in 1978, and always told me there was no sickness that can't be overcome. You just have to tell yourself, "I'm okay." But now it got him. He was really sick, and one thing was for sure, this made up for all the years he missed, especially since the accident we had at Lotti's wedding. It is like his body said I don't want anymore.

He had all those dreams and big expectations, and now has to watch them crumble. I told him so often the children needed his love more than anything. His answer was always, "But they also will need my money. Watch them come home and ask me if I would help them. That will be my reward."

But they were all gone for years already, and none of them came home to ask for help. Our children got very independent and wanted to prove Dad wrong, show him that they can do it on their own. And without realizing what we were doing, teaching them independence might have been the greatest gift we could ever have given to our children. They all proved themselves and became outstanding citizens.

But whatever it was, Henry suffered tremendously. He missed the kids more than he would ever admit. I had a job and a responsibility, and through that, not too much time to feel sorry for myself. Henry had nothing to work for anymore, and he no longer felt a purpose in life. And that is very, very tough for a man who worked so hard all his life.

He did not read, nor know the Bible too well, but now always told me that even in the Bible it says, "The man is the head of the household." And that means he is the breadwinner.

But so what? Henry is sick. We can't live on air, so I have to go to work. Seeing me as the breadwinner was the toughest pill for Henry to swallow, and it slowly killed him.

Reto called a lot those days, asking how we are doing. But I did not know what really bothered him until I had a long talk with Brenda one day. "Reto is so depressed lately," she told me. "He feels so guilty."

Heinz was never a dairy farmer, but a good mechanic, and so that is what he should do. Reto, on the other hand, was always great with cows, and now felt that he had let us down. If he would not have left home, we would not have to sell out. It was high time to have a talk with Reto, and this time I called him.

"You do not have to feel guilty," I told him. "The farm economy is bad now. We aren't the only ones in trouble. You, Reto, have a great job. You are a #1 lineman now. You make good money. You get paid vacation. If you are sick, you just stay home. And if you guys have to work overtime, you get a dinner paid after the first nine hours, and every four hours after that.

"How many times do we farmers have to work from sun-up to sun-down, and then go home and cook our own meal. Health insurance for us is very expensive, but for you, everything is paid for. And then, when you are 55 years old, you can retire. Your dad is almost 60 years old and does not have the money to retire. Please, Reto, don't throw everything away just to keep Dad's dream alive. You have a great family, and that should be your number one priority. But, I think losing a farm is like having a family member die. So, if it would make you feel better, take vacation the week we have the auction and come home. I could really use your support. And that would also give you the opportunity to talk to other farmers and that might open your eyes."

Reto had to agree. "But it is just so hard, and I feel so guilty," he replied, but promised to bring his family home for the Easter weekend.

We finally filed bankruptcy as of April 1, 1987, and set the auction day for April 18th. For tax reasons, we had to file bankruptcy first, then after that it was the bank's loss if we did not get for the machines what they thought we should get.

The closer the final day came, the tougher it was emotionally. But it did not really hit me until I came home from work on Wednesday afternoon and the machines were lined up. It felt just as if I went through a cold shower.

I could see the sadness in Henry's eyes as I walked into the house. "It will be okay," I whispered in his ear. But my heart was heavy and I still did not know if I really did the right thing. But I could not let Henry know that I had such thoughts. Plus, there was no turning back; I made a decision and had to go on.

I still had to take care of the cows, but only for a couple more days. All through the winter we sold the calves as they were born, just to make my work a little easier. Yet, just milking and feeding the cows was hard work. But now I saw the end coming, and there were people everywhere. The auctioneer had a lot of help. Some of the guys sprayed the dust off the machines that had accumulated over winter and got all the small things together and itemized them. Some helped me shave the cows. It was a lot of work.

Thursday Reto, Brenda and their two girls flew in from California, and Henry and I picked them up at the airport. I warned Reto beforehand, but his eyes looked sad as we slowly drove into the yard and he saw the machines all lined up. He did not say anything, nor did I ask, but I could feel that it was just as hard on him as it was on us.

He helped me milk and also stepped in wherever he was needed. That also gave Reto the opportunity to talk to different farmers, and everyone told him that that was maybe not the easiest, but the best way out for us.

I took off work the Easter weekend. We had to milk the cows at 3 a.m. the morning of the auction so that their bags looked nice and full when they chased them through the ring later on.

Reto and I went to the barn at 2 a.m. We fed the cows and started milking. All along we two reminisced about all the things we went through the last 19 years. I did not feel too bad until I took the last milkers off, but then that was it; I fell to pieces. I truly loved those cows and now, after 19 years, I will never again milk my cows or help a calf to be born.

All the feelings that I stored deep down for so long broke through now. I just cried and cried. Plus, I was so tired from all the long hours I put in the last six and a half months, I just could no more.

Brenda had breakfast ready. I was not hungry, but she insisted I eat. She was just like a mother hen, and I was glad to have a shoulder to lean on, at least for a little while.

Slowly but surely the crowd moved in: some of our friends, Julius and his family, Fullemanns. Sturzeneggers, a young Swiss couple, brought their minister along. He prayed with us before the auction started. That helped a little, but one has to go through burying his most important dream, a dream he worked for so hard, to know how we felt that day.

Some people came just to be nosy. Hans, a countryman, said, "No wonder they went broke, building such a stupid, expensive Harvestore silo." But yet we paid $20,000 for ours. Hans built one a couple of years later and paid over $50,000 for it. But there will always be people like him who have something bad to say, no matter how hard one works.

But that didn't bother me much. What really got me, farmers standing around our machines bidding. "That machine is not worth much," they said. But to me every piece of equipment had some memory, which no money could ever pay for. My haybine, for example. I practically raised Jessica on it. It was my machine, and whenever I was on it, so was she. We laughed together, she sang to me as we were riding that machine cutting the grass. I took such good care of my haybine, always greased it before I used it, replaced a sickle as soon as one was missing, and now this one farmer looks at it and says, "What a piece of junk, not worth more than a couple hundred dollars."

I could not stand it anymore and went back into the house, crying. The haybine went for $1,600, but the combine we bought for $34,000 five years ago did not even bring $5,000. There just were not enough interested farmers around.

We had a very early spring, and most farmers were on the fields. We usually have around 50 degrees all through April, but this year was an extremely hot April. The day of the auction we had 92 degrees. The women walked around in tank tops, and everybody had a sunburn before the day was over. So the farmers that maybe would have paid more were not there. They planted their fields. And that maybe was part of the reason why the machines didn't bring much.

The last thing that was sold were the cows — my cows that I loved so much. And that to me was like someone turning a knife in my heart. I took very good care of my cows. They were well-fed and well-behaved. I never hit a cow. Talking to them got me a lot further than hitting them, but now with so many strange faces they got spooky. They got chased out of the barn and into the ring with pitchforks. All I could do was bawl, it hurt so much.

My friends from WWA had a stand and sold food and drinks, and they tried to cheer me up. It was a little after five when most of the people left.

Henry and I stood hand in hand on the steps by the back door looking at that empty barn and our tears were rolling, we felt so sad. Is this all that is left of our dream? What will the future have in store for us?

Reto and Julius took one look at us, and then they told us, "This is it. Go pack your belongings."

"What do you mean?" I asked.

"We will move you tonight," they answered.

"You can't do that," I replied.

They only said, "You want to bet," got the pickup truck and started loading our furniture.

"I want to paint some of the rooms at the house where Edith lived before I move in," I insisted.

But no luck. They were determined, and there were no ifs, ands or buts about it. Our bedroom was facing the barn, and so they were afraid of what could happen if we woke up in the morning and saw the empty barn. And they probably were right. It would have been devastating.

So, they moved us that evening. It was past midnight when they unloaded the last load. Brenda made something to eat, and we all sat down and talked. The biggest question was where do we go from here?

The sun came almost up when Julius and Erika finally went home, a sunny but sad Easter Sunday morning. It was good that Sierra, 2-1/2 years old, and Amanda,

4-1/2 months, Reto's girls, were here. Brenda colored Easter eggs and hid them outside, and we had to help Sierra find them. That left us no time to dwell on the past.

Reto and Henry tried Henry's new camcorder out, the one that I gave Henry last Christmas. He never used it before, but now was a good time to take a movie of the grandchildren so that we had a lasting memory of their smiles on one of the saddest weekends in our lives. Reto and his family returned two days later to California.

****

My job kept me busy, and it was a lot easier now that I could pay 100 % attention to it. Plus, we had a house we wanted to remodel. But first we needed to rake the lawn and get the outside cleaned up, since no one had lived there for the last year. Plus, our bankruptcy was not over yet. The worst was yet to come. Mr. Eberlein told us we had to appear in court the end of May. I was scared and still not sure if we really could keep the house we now lived in. I took off the day we had to go to court and went with Henry to Wausau, where we met our lawyer at the Federal building, since to preside over a bankruptcy one needs a federal judge.

We were the first ones to appear before the judge. Representatives from FMHA, PCA and the Federal Land Bank were there, too.

The hearing was supposed to start at 9 a.m. At 9:15 someone came and said they had trouble with the typewriter that keeps everything on records. "We will do our best to get rolling as soon as possible," they told us. The longer it took, the more time I had to think and the scareder I got. My heart was just pounding.

At 10 a.m. the judge proceeded. "We could not fix the typewriter, so we have to go with a tape recorder. Is that okay with all the parties involved?" he asked. Mr. Eberlein said, "That's okay with us." FMHA had no complaints either, but then the representative for PCA looked at Henry and me and said, "We will not accept a tape recorder, since we believe that the Grosses sold livestock that belonged to us, and that is a criminal act. We want that money."

Oh, no, not again. I went through that already when we left Switzerland, I thought to myself, and I could not understand. The loan officer from the PCA was the one who put it in writing that we could get the house and eight acres, because we were always honest. And now they don't trust us and think we cheated them? How can they do that to us?

Mr. Eberlein got mad, stood up and said, "Fine. Two people can play that game. We will not accept your offer for the house and eight acres of land. We will now not file for a quick bankruptcy the way you wanted, instead, drag this on, if it has to be five years. Grosses can live in that house without paying any rent whatsoever, and then after the five years are up, we'll see who gets the house. See you in court." And out the door he walked, leaving everybody behind. The judge told us that the court date would be postponed for four weeks. I knew for me that would be four nerve-wracking weeks.

We later met with Mr. Eberlein and I told him, "I don't want to drag it on for five years. I have to know where I am standing, otherwise I go crazy. I can't remodel the house, can't do anything if it isn't mine. But I will promise you to get this straightened out, no matter how long it will take me."

I could hardly wait to get home that afternoon, I was just so upset. It is humiliating enough to have to file bankruptcy, but then to be put down as if you were a thief in front of so many people is terrible.

Dick from PCA was at the farm two years before and took inventory, and that is where I started. I wrote every cow down, when she was bred, when she calved, and when we sold the calves, and where every penny went. Three cows died the last two years, and I even had a receipt form from the rendering service for that. It took me almost a week, besides working at the store, to get all my documents in order and everything straightened out, but I got it done. Then I sent it to our lawyer, who in turn sent a copy to all three lenders who were involved.

Four weeks later we went to court again. I was so nervous I could hardly sleep that night before, since none of the lenders contacted us or our lawyer.

We were way too early at the federal courthouse. The lady from FMHA walked up to us and said, "You really did your homework. Great bookkeeping job."

Mr. Eberlein came and together we were called to the judge's table. "Would the representatives from PCA and Federal Land Bank please come forward," the judge hollered into the audience; but silence. He asked again, but no one came forward.

"They're maybe a little late, so we will give them an extra 15 minutes, and get to the next case first."

We went back and took a seat by the rest of the people. The judge then called a young couple up to the bench. I could have listened to their discussion, but I was too nervous to care about their problems.

What does that mean for us? More bad news?

It did not take long and that young couple left. We were called up to the bench once again, yet there still were no representatives from PCA or FLB. The judge looked at us and smiled. "I guess you win your case. Congratulations. You just got a house and eight acres of land. Good luck! Case dismissed," and he pounded the little gravel on the table to finalize his decision.

I could not believe my ears, but Mr. Eberlein later told me that he heard PCA telling someone that they had no case against us so it was no use for them wasting their time in court.

I had tears in my eyes as we left the courthouse. "Thank you, God, for helping me get through this."

It was a completely different feeling walking into the house now that it is our home. About three months later all the paperwork was completed and the bankruptcy finalized. From the veterinary to the electric company to the feed store, not one company lost a penny. They all got what they had coming. I could hold my head up high and did not have to be ashamed at all.

After everything was finally done, I got one more letter from Mr. Eberlein, and enclosed was a check for almost $1,200. "Congratulations," he wrote. "After we paid all your debts, you had this much money left over. I never thought that you'd get a house out of it, let alone money. Edith, you did a great job. Keep up the good work."

Yes, I was very proud. We had a house and eight acres of land debt-free. That was the reward for all our hard work.

Henry already started dreaming again. "If I had a little bit more land, I could raise heifers and then sell them. But only eight acres is not enough."

I thought about it for a couple of days. We still have almost $9,000 stock at the feed store, and since we had to quit farming because of your illness, we could take that out. It does not bring much interest anyway. Let me investigate how much money they want for the 32 acres so that we would have a 40 again. You can go to the feed store and see how long it takes to get the money released."

Henry went right away and was told it only takes one week. I contacted the Federal Land Bank, and they told me I would have to put in a bid. As soon as we got the stock paid out, we drove to Wausau. "Here is a check of $9,500 for the 32 acres, take it or leave it," I told the loan officer.

"I can't decide by myself. Just wait a moment, I'll go ask my boss," she said.

It didn't take five minutes and she was back. "It's a deal," she said, "you sign the check over to us and you get the deed to the 32 acres of crop land."

Boy, that was easy, and I truly hoped Henry would be happy now.

Jessica came to visit us that summer. She spent two weeks with us, and two weeks with her dad. We took Jessica on a trip. We drove to Kewaunee and took the ferry across Lake Michigan. It was just gorgeous. The sun was setting in the west as they threw the anchor at Ludington, Michigan. We found us a nice motel right on the lake.

The next morning we drove north all the way to the Mackinac Bridge, stayed there overnight, and took Highway 2 along Lake Michigan to get back home. Henry and Jessica played on the sandy beach and got each other wet, and then we just sat there for awhile and watched the waves come in. It was so peaceful, and, all in all, a great weekend. Henry really perked up, but I knew very well he would fall to pieces again when Jessie left.

Jessie dreaded to go to her dad's house, and Henry did not want to let her go either, so those two lollygagged around all Monday morning, and when Henry finally brought her to Brian's house, he got screamed at by Brian's wife, Wendy. "Jessie should have been here three hours ago. You had no right to keep her so long. We paid half of her airfare and so we have the right to have her half of the time. You guys will never get her again."

Jessica was so disappointed that she started crying, went and locked herself into the bathroom. That got Henry even madder. I was at work, but from what I heard it was not a pretty sight.

But then Brian did not want to drive Jessie all the way to Chicago, so he brought her back the day before her departure and we drove her to Chicago and saw her off on the plane. Boy, why do goodbyes have to hurt so much. Neither of us said much on the long drive back to Merrill.

I went for a checkup and talked Henry into coming along, as I knew there definitely was something wrong with him. He himself told me more than once that he could not cook or do anything where he had to think anymore. "I just forget," he said so often. He imagined things, or yelled at me, and ten minutes later had it all forgotten already.

"Doctor, I think Henry has Alzheimer's disease, or something similar. He just is different," I said.

But the doctor's reply was, "I just talked to him and he seems all right to me." End of conversation. And like so many times before, I questioned myself. Maybe I'm losing it. Maybe there is something wrong with me.

But I'd lived with Henry so long now that I knew that he had changed drastically. Yet, there was no one who was so close to him as I was who could have noticed the changes.

****

We went for a visit to Switzerland in September of that year. Henry got an invitation to his class reunion. "I'm not going. My teacher was always mean to me and did not accept me at all," he insisted.

"Henry, you are now hurting so bad emotionally, and you are homesick. Maybe if you go there you can make peace with your past," I told him. I did not ask him anymore, I just went ahead and bought two tickets, and off to Switzerland we went.

It was great to be back home with the kids and grandkids, even if only for a short time. Then on the first Saturday Henry and I went to meet with some of his closest friends, and we had a good time together. On Sunday was the big day.

Henry went to a one-room school and only had three kids in his class. Yet this reunion was to honor the teacher. And because of that, all the students who went to school with Mr. Gantenbein were invited. On Sunday morning they met at 9:30 a.m. and went to the church service, from there to the restaurant where a delicious meal waited for them. The present children from that same one-room school had a skit and sang for entertainment. After that, the teacher, Mr. Gantenbein, an 82-year-old man by now, got up and welcomed them all. He went on.

"There is one student of mine amongst us that deserves an apology from me. I did not treat him decent because I thought he would never amount to anything, so he was not important to me. But he proved me wrong. He became a great, outstanding human being. So, please, Henry Gross, would you get up and accept my apology. I'm truly sorry for what I did to you."

Henry had tears in his eyes as he walked up to his teacher and shook his hand. What a great man his teacher was to acknowledge his mistakes.

****

Christmas came and went. I had to work in the morning of New Year's Eve. But then the clerk who was supposed to come to work at 2 p.m. and work until 10 p.m. did not show up at all, so I ended up working from 5 a.m. to 10 p.m. Around 7 p.m. I asked Henry, "Would you please go home and put the ham in the oven so we at least have supper when I get home."

I was tired and I had to open the store again at 6 a.m. the next morning. I thought if I work, at least I know I was sober on New Year's morning, and work for me is just like a medicine. That is the only thing that kept me going.

Henry went home, put the ham in the oven and got the beans ready, then came back to the store to help me finish up. I was so tired, but also glad at least we had a ham dinner, just as we did in the "good old days." But I could not believe my eyes when I tried to cut the ham. Henry put the chunk of dried beef in the oven. The ham was still in the refrigerator. The beef was so tough and salty that not even Henry could eat it.

"That's okay," I said. "I wasn't hungry anyway." But it proved once more that something definitely was wrong with Henry; yet no one wants to believe me.

Henry went the following spring to see his sister

Martha and asked her if she would like to rent our land to the north of the house and plow the piece to the south. He would help them make the hay, and in return we could have half of it, in case we got some heifers. We would put the fertilizer on; they would just have to use their machines. They thought that was a great idea. But on the way home Henry saw Dick Haas, our neighbor, and started talking to him.

"What are you doing with the land to the south? I would like to rent that so that I could plow it and put corn in," Dick asked.

Henry answered, "If you want it, you can have it." He already had forgotten that he also gave it to his sister.

When Albert, Henry's brother-in-law, came with the tractor a week later, the field was plowed and already planted. That got Martha and Albert really mad, but they still needed the hay on the north side.

The year 1988 was a really dry year, and since hay was scarce, Martha had to have it all and didn't want to give half to us. Henry called me one day at work. "Martha is here and she would like to know if they could have all the hay."

"It is your sister and since we have no animals yet, I can't see why they couldn't have it. But it is your decision," I told him. And so he let them rent everything. "But since we put all the fertilizer on it, I wanted $350 for the rent," I told them.

We were willing to wait until Christmas for the rent money to make it easier for them to pay us. Then, later, I found out that they went to the ASCS office and signed up for disaster money, since they did not get the crops off our land that they expected. That got me wild. We gave them the rent cheap because of that, and Henry even helped and cut the grass for them, now they turn around and make money on us.

I went to the ASCS office and found out that they would

get over $500 from our land. "That's not right," I told the clerk. "It should be split at least 50/50."

It was a good thing that Martha was busy or she would have had the money already. Everything got stopped, and since Martha thought it should be theirs, it came to a hearing where fellow farmers had to decide who gets that money.

To go there and fight against a sister was humiliating enough, but it did not get any better. The chairperson got up first and said, "No matter what the outcome of today's hearing will be, always remember, you are family and there is nothing more precious than the closeness of siblings."

And I had to agree, but that did not affect Martha one bit. She stood up and said, "I should get the money. Henry's life no longer depends on farming, but mine does. And, by the way, Henry was never good enough. He was bad news already as a child."

I looked at Henry and saw tears in his eyes. His face was pale and he hurt so bad that he couldn't even talk. I whispered in his ear, "Just go and get some fresh air. I will take care of this." He went out to the car and cried. Why can't they ever accept him as their brother and simply for the plain, hard-working person he is?

After Henry was out of the room I turned to Martha and asked Martha, "Do you really understand how much you just hurt Henry? We aren't here to talk about his childhood, which, in my opinion, was just terrible and left deep scars in his heart, we are here to talk about the disaster money. We paid the fertilizer and gave you a deal on the rent, so I think we should get half of that money."

The board took a vote. They all agreed with me and it was passed in no time. Yes, we had the money, but the scar in Henry's heart got even deeper. And I felt bad because there was nothing I could do to comfort him.

We got a letter from the FLB. Our next-door neighbor put a bid in on the remaining 40 acres where we are living now. That did not go over well at all with Henry. "I really would like that piece of land, and don't want him to have it," he said. "That would be good pasture if we buy heifers."

Here we go again, I thought to myself, but then answered, "I don't know. I would have to go and borrow the money, but I will think about it."

But the more I thought about it, the more I came to the conclusion that if that is what it takes to make Henry happy, it would be worth it. I went to the M&I Citizen's Bank the next day and asked them if I could borrow $9,000 to buy 40 acres of land. "Oh, yes," they said. "No problem."

If a lender gets farmland back because of a bankruptcy and then has someone who wants to buy the land, then they are obligated to let the former owner know about it, and if he can top the bid and come up with the money, they have to sell it back to the old owner.

Back to the FLB we went with the check in our hand. We topped the bid, and within a week the land was ours. Here we had 80 acres again and were right back into farming.

Henry bought barbwire and all new posts and made a fence all around the pasture, which was a quarter-mile long. It took him many, many of weeks to get it done, and he works so hard. Looking back, the only sad part is that we never had one animal in it. And Dick Haas later, after he bought that land from us, tore it all down again.

But even though we had all that land again, Henry was not happy. He had a nagging pain in his heart. It was just so hard for both of us. I did not know what to do anymore and could not help him.

One day I could not believe my eyes. I thought I was dreaming when Henry's sister Elsa from California came and walked into the store. We found out she was here on vacation and stayed with Martha. Elsa came in the store, but Martha stayed in the car, and like so many times before, Elsa cut us down. "Is that all you guys can do, run a little store like this," she asked Henry. He could not handle it, let her stand right there, walked out of the back door, sat in the car and cried. I couldn't believe it. Can't they ever leave him alone and stop hurting him?

I was busy in the store and could not get away right then. But after 3 p.m. when the next clerk came and took over, I drove Henry home and told him that I would go have a talk with his sisters.

Straight to Martha's house I went. Martha and Elsa were not home, but I had a long talk with Albert. "How can you do that to Henry?" I asked. "Do you really want to break him?"

"Oh, he promised us things and then did not follow through with it, and that got us mad," was his reply.

"Henry is sick, but no one wants to believe me, not even the doctor, not even you. I have to live with him. So, can't you just forgive him and accept him as he is? He was hurt enough in his life and doesn't need any more."

I was so mad that I cried; I hurt so bad for Henry. But I could not wait until those two came home. I had to get back and see how Henry was. I was scared that he would kill himself, like he threatened so many times before.

"Albert," I said before I left, "tell Martha and Elsa to cut it out, and if Elsa does not come to see Henry, then I will never, ever again talk to you guys."

Elsa did call later that afternoon, and she came to visit us for a couple of hours that evening. Thank God that made Henry feel a little better and he could smile again. And at least for a couple of days I did not have to be scared that he would kill himself. He had something else to think about, at least for a little while. It is unbelievable how much one can suffer and still go on.

****

May 3, 1988, 2 a.m. the phone rang. What now? What could that be? Did something happen to my mother? Half asleep I said, "Hello."

"Hi. Would you accept a personal call from Lotti Hess?" the operator asked.

"Of course," I answered, but what does Lotti want at this time of night. What she had to say woke me up in no time. "Mom, my baby is dying and I do not know what to do," she told me sobbing.

"What happened?" I asked.

"Cassy was fine when Larry came home for lunch on Monday at noon. She even tried to stand up on the coffee table. Then at 2 p.m. I gave her a bottle. That's when I saw that her pupils got big, small and big again. Something in me told me to hold onto that baby or you're going to lose her. I gave her a bath and put her to bed. She wasn't in bed for more than a couple of minutes when I went back to get her. I squished her in my arms and could not let go. I called the doctor, but then hung up before someone answered. What could they say, Cassy does not even have a fever. But I paced the floor with my beautiful little girl Cassy in my arms. At 3:30 p.m. I couldn't anymore. I called Larry and told him to pick Bobbi Jo and Tyler up from Kindergarten. I strapped my baby in the car-seat and drove her to the emergency room at the Ft. Worth Hospital.

"Cassy had a slight fever by then. The doctor said it was a chest cold, but they would do further tests. In no time Cassy's fever shot up and was at 106.5. They laid her on ice immediately, and the doctors knew then that that was more than just a chest cold. They took spinal fluid, but nothing showed. Just before midnight the fever broke and they thought Cassy was over the hill. The emergency room was very busy that night so the nurse asked me if I would give Cassy a bath, and I gladly agreed. I sang a lullaby to her while I sponged the sweat off her little body, and was so relieved that she pulled through.

Then, with no warning whatsoever, Cassy slipped into a coma. I started screaming. The doctors and nurses dropped everything, took Cassy and wheeled her into the trauma center where they hooked her up on all kinds of tubes. It looked terrible.

"Cassy got some black bumps. They were blood vessels that popped. That was when the doctors knew what Cassy's problem was. Little Cassy had monococcal meningitis."

Lotti swallowed some tears and then went on:

"Mom, they only give her a 30% chance. I don't think Cassy is going to make it. And if she makes it, she might be brain-damaged for life because of the high fever. Mom, what can I do? I'll lose my baby."

Oh how much I wished I could be with Lotti right at that moment, take her into my arms and tell her everything will be okay. But I'm 1,200 miles away.

"Lotti," I said, "your brother Reto was that far three times already. When he had a stroke, spinal meningitis, or the brain blockage, and he pulled through every time, and so will your baby. I sure will pray for her."

Lotti's reply, "I knew you could make me feel better. I just wish you could be here with me." Lotti promised to keep me informed, and we hung up.

I lay in bed for a while longer. "What can we do?" I asked Henry. But he had no answer either. I also knew Henry was no support to me, since if something really goes wrong he goes into his shell and will not talk anymore. But that is his way of coping with tough situations.

I got up, got dressed and told Henry, "I go to work now. That way I will have all my bookwork done before I open the store, and if something really goes wrong, we can leave immediately. Henry, please get the Winnebago ready. I will come later and pack a suitcase," and out the door I went. My hands were shaking as I drove to town, and I prayed all the way, "Please, God, please don't let Cassy die. Give her a second chance. Please help Lotti to get through this."

At 6 a.m. Lotti called me at work. "They lost Cassy 30

minutes ago, but got her back. I sure hope they can save her now."

"Keep on believing," I told her. "I got my bookwork done, and I called one of my clerks to come in and work for me. She will be here in one hour, so please, Lotti, hang in there."

I was busy like always that time of morning when everybody is rushing to work and stops to buy cigarettes, snacks, coffee or something else to get them through the day, but I had a hard time holding my tears back. How could I smile at my customers and tell them have "a good day" when my heart feels so heavy?

At 7 a.m. Lotti called again, and I could hear that she was crying. "Mom, Cassy is gone forever. We have no money for the funeral. Now I have to bury my baby way in the back of the cemetery where the grass is knee-high. Oh, how terrible. Only outcasts and street people that have no one get buried there. And now my baby will have to go there, too. How terrible," she sobbed.

"Don't worry, Lotti. I have a little bit of money saved. We will get Cassy a decent funeral." After everything Lotti went through, to worry about the funeral was not necessary.

I called Phil, my supervisor, and told him, "You have to come and help run the store. I will leave now. I just lost my granddaughter." That's all I could say before breaking down.

"Don't worry. I will be there. Just drive safe," he said. I rushed home, packed our suitcases. I knew Lotti was in no condition to let her siblings know what just happened, so I called first Reto, who said, "We will be there with you at the funeral. I will let my boss know, and then we will drive straight through to Texas. See you there."

I also called Edith and asked her to please tell Heinz and my mother. One more phone call to Patty, Julius' daughter. I asked her if she would please tell her parents when they called home what happened to our little Cassy.

Henry had the van ready, and on our long trip to Texas we went. Now that I finally could relax for awhile I could not stop sobbing. Why, God? Why did you take this precious little girl? I never saw her, never had her in my arms. Cassy was born on September 21st, the day before Henry and I went on vacation to Switzerland to participate at Henry's first and last class reunion. We planned on visiting Lotti and her family over Christmas, but I had employee problems right then and it was impossible to go. Then in February I tried again, but I just could not make it. I called Lotti. "We'll come for Easter," I told her. But she said, "Mom, why don't you wait just four more weeks. Then you can take Bobbi Jo and Tyler to Wisconsin for vacation, and then three weeks later we will come up there. We will baptize Cassy in the church where we got married and then take the kids back. Wouldn't that be nice?" I agreed and made plans to have the grandkids with us. That would have been a great boost for Henry. And now, only two weeks after Easter, Cassy is gone and I never, ever will be able to hold her in my arms. I know that is one thing I will never forget. That will hurt as long as I live.

We only stopped for diesel and coffee on the way, but I was not hungry. It was a nice, sunny day as we drove toward Texas, but the sun could not warm my heart. It did not make me feel any better. To me, everything looked gloomy. And Henry did not say one word. He pulled back into his own little world. I knew he felt bad, too, but he can't show his emotions, and a man sure does not cry.

We made it through Oklahoma and into Texas when Henry got tired. I never drove this van before and did not feel like driving it now. I was just like a zombie that goes through motions and just does not have the strength to go on.

We stopped at a rest area and lay down for awhile. I could not sleep, but Henry dozed off for a couple of hours and then was ready to drive on. I was glad that he was such a good driver and got us safely to our final destination.

It was 11 a.m. when we arrived at Lotti's house. She was just beside herself. "I just got a phone call from a guy at the hospital. He wanted to know if we had made any funeral arrangements yet."

""We can't wait any longer. We have to dispose of the body," he told Lotti.

How inconsiderate. What a thing to say to a mother who just lost her baby. I took Lotti in my arms and told her, "Don't worry. We'll take care of it," and said to myself, no more tears for me for now. I have to be strong. I have to help Lotti to get through this.

Boy, there are lots of things that have to be taken care of. One of Lotti's friends knew of a nice funeral home in Grapevine, just north of Keller where they lived, so we drove there.

The funeral director greeted us at the door, but before any decisions could be made, he said real cool: "You have to realize, we need the money up front."

This is what funeral homes are here for, to make money off someone else's sorrows, I thought to myself. But I told him not to worry, I would pay for it.

Then my first question was, "When can I see Cassy? Is this possible right now?"

The funeral director answered quickly, "No way. Her casket is sealed and I have strict orders from the doctor to keep it that way. What Cassy had is very contagious and she looks terrible, so no one is allowed to get close to her."

"But I'm her grandma. I never saw her. I won't touch her, I just would like to see her," I pleaded.

But no was no. There was no bending the rules.

Since she could not be shown, we decided to go to the graveside and have the service there. We picked a casket all padded with cloth, pink and white-checkered. The handles were white cords connected to little roses. It looked really pretty, if one can say pretty for a casket. Then we had to find a lot. Lotti wanted one by a tree where Cassy always could be in the shade. We found one that was available just a little up the hill, past a small pond where ducks swam between the sea lilies. It looked so peaceful, just right for our little Cassy.

We also picked a gravestone. It had to be plate, since the wind in Texas can be so very strong they won't allow anything that sticks out of the ground. The plate was in light green with a picture of an angel on it. As we were asked what they should engrave on that cold stone, Lotti came up with, "My baby is rocking in the arms of the angels." What a comforting thing to say. We had to pay the total bill before we could walk out the door, and it was not too bad, only a little over $900.

From there we had to order flowers. The lady at the flower shop did not know us at all, but she felt so bad for Lotti that she made a flower arrangement with a teddy bear on it for free, as a gift from her. Oh, how nice she was, and so generous. Thanks so much. It truly was appreciated.

It was late that afternoon when we got back home. Neighbors and friends were there with food. We sure did not have to go hungry. How thoughtful of them. For me, it was a long day. I was up almost 40 hours already. I went to bed early, but I could not sleep. I really could use a comforting hug. I wished Henry would take me in his arms and tell me it will get better again. But if Henry hurts, he gets cold. That is just the way it always was since Reto was real sick, and it is not any better now. I just lay in bed behind closed doors and cried myself to sleep.

Reto, Brenda and their two girls, Sierra and Amanda, arrived early the next morning. They were comforting to have around. We spent that afternoon shopping. Lotti needed a nice dress for her girl's funeral, and Larry a shirt and tie.

Brenda, Lotti, Bobbi Jo, Tyler, Sierra, Amanda and I

went to the mall. That kept Lotti busy and did not give her time to dwell. The kids were ready for bed by the time we got home and we adults could sit for awhile and talk.

Friday morning, May 6th, Lotti's 28th birthday. How can I say to my daughter "Happy Birthday" on the day where we bury her little girl? That is so sad, and a tough thing to do.

The funeral was set for two o'clock. It was around 10 a.m. when a big truck drove into the driveway. It was Julius and Erika. As soon as they knew what happened, they called their company and told them they would drop the trailer, and then high-tailed it all the way to Texas. No one could have more true friends than we have in Erika and Julius.

We all had a bite to eat, and then it was soon time to go to the cemetery. The little casket was at the graveside. Some of Lotti's friends stood by our side as the minister spoke the last goodbye words.

It was so hard. I had Lotti on one side and Henry on the other side, and I don't know who felt worse. If it would have been Henry or me lying in this casket, it would not have been that tough. We had lived our lives and fulfilled our tasks. I think God put us on this earth to have children and then raise them to become good adults, and we accomplished that, but this little girl had no chance. She had to go way too early.

After the "Our Father" and the blessings, we said one more goodbye and then left the graveside. Lotti went through the motions, a lot of handshakes and hugs, but I could see that she felt numb.

The first guests had left already when Lotti asked me if I would come once more with her to the graveside. Lotti was holding onto my arm as we walked back to the casket. We kneeled down, but then I got scared. She started touching up the casket to find a way to open it. Then she was so desperate and wanted to hold her baby just one more time in her arms. And over and over again she said, sobbing, "I love you so much, my baby. I love you so much."

There was no way Lotti could open that casket. It was sealed tight. I was relieved that she could not do what she intended to do, since I think she would have taken her baby home and would have never let go of her again.

We said one last prayer together, and then we got in the van and sat down, when Larry pulled on my arm and asked me if I could come with him to say goodbye to his little girl. Larry's mother was there, too, but he asked me and I could not say no to him.

I took his arm and towards the graveside we walked. There we kneeled down and prayed. Larry's hand glided over and over again over the pink checkered cover on the little casket, telling his little daughter, "I love you, Cassy. I promise I will never forget you. I love you so much."

It took quite some time till Larry was ready to let go. As we slowly walked towards the van I told him, "Some day we will be with your little girl again, and then we will never have to feel pain again."

"But it hurts so much now," he replied.

"Yes, I know how you feel. I'm hurting, too," I told Larry. And I thought, but I have no shoulder to lean on. For now, I just let him talk and hopefully that makes at least him feel a little better.

We got back to the van. I sat down and leaned back into the seat. My heart felt so heavy as Henry drove us back home. Lotti's friends and neighbors gathered at her house. The dining room table was full of food and drinks. One could take whatever their heart desired, all put on by them. That was just so nice of them.

Lotti was not hungry, not just because she was sad, also because of the medication they had to take. Everybody who was in contact with Cassy the last three weeks of her life had to be on real strong medication that they had flown in from somewhere else. It was very critical, since all of them could get it too.

They told Lotti at the hospital that they once had a young woman who was admitted with the same sickness Cassy had, and four hours later she was dead. Isn't it amazing, they can send men to the moon but they can't help a little girl? Isn't technology going the wrong direction? I would have given anything if I would be able to take the hurt away from Lotti, but there was nothing I could do.

Erika and Julius left later that night. They had to get back to work. But what friends they are. They could have lost their job over this, but they did not care, they just wanted to be with us in the hours of sorrow.

Reto, Brenda and their kids left early Saturday morning. Reto too had to get back to work. But before they left they gave me a present, since it was the day before Mother's Day. Their gift was a necklace. It had a little hanger and in small print it said, "We love you, Mom." I put it on my neck that day and never, ever took it off again. Whenever I felt blue in later years I looked at that necklace and thought my children will always love me and that is most important thing in my life.

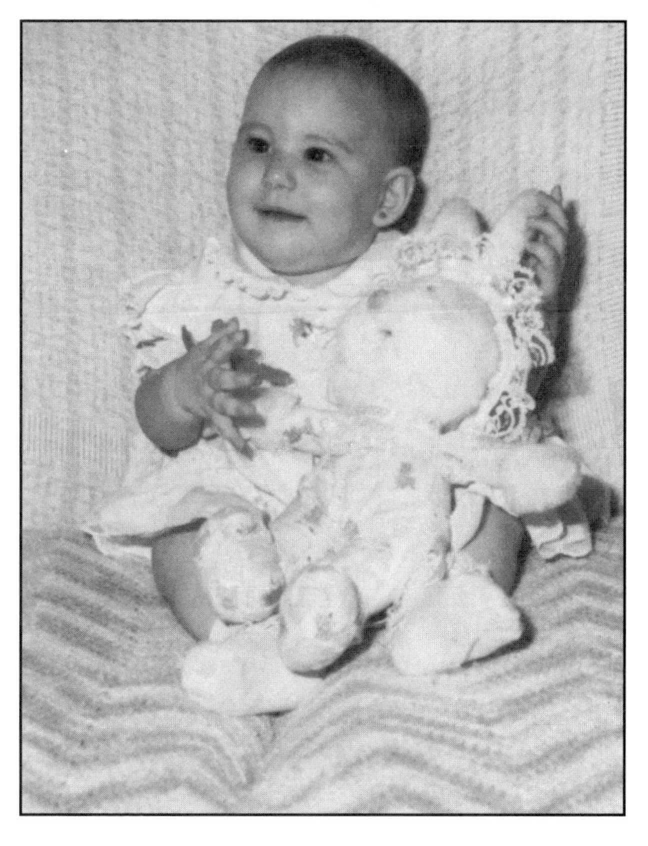

Grandaughter Cassandra,
September 21st, 1987 to May 3rd, 1988.
This picture was taken on Easter 1988 about three weeks before Cassy passed away.

THE CHILD GOD LENT

I'll lend you for a little time
A child of mine, God said,
For you to love the while she lives
And mourn for when she's dead.

It may be two or seven years,
Or twenty-two or three,
But will you till I call her back,
Take care of her for me?

She'll bring her charms to gladden you,
And should her stay be brief,
You'll have her lovely memories
As solace for your grief.

I cannot promise she will stay
Since all from earth return,
But there are lessons taught down there
I want this child to learn.

I've looked the wide world over
In my search for teachers true,
And from the throngs that crowd life's lanes
I have selected you.

Now will you give her all your love,
Nor think the labor vain,
Nor hate when I come to call
To take her back again.

I fancied that I heard them say,
"Dear Lord, Thy will be done,"
For all the joy thy child shall bring,
The risk of grief will run.

—Author unknown

17

WE STAYED ONE more day with Lotti. It was late Sunday, Mother's Day, and what a Mother's Day it was when we had to say goodbye and leave Lotti and her family alone with all their sorrows; but I, too, had a job and a home to take care. It was another one of those tough goodbyes that had to be overcome.

We had a dog, "Trixie," that we couldn't leave home alone, so we took her along to Texas. She was tied up in Lotti's back yard while Lotti's cocker spaniel could run free. As we drove home from Texas, I said to Henry, "I think Lotti's dog liked ours. I would not be surprised if ours was pregnant."

"No way," Henry said. What could she do, she was tied up all the time." But I was right. We got little puppies 12 weeks later.

Once back home the store kept me busy. Even though the girls did a good job while I was gone, I had a lot of catching up to do. Because of my manager's position, I also became a member of the Sixth Ward Business Association and took on the treasurer's job.

Crazy Days brings all kinds of customers out, and everyone looks for a bargain. Businesses have stands on the city streets and slash their prices as low as possible. We, as the Sixth Ward Business Association, had a stand, too, and sold brats, hot dogs, French fries, pop and beer, and we had a band for the evening. Part of the profit went to Santa Claus so that he could bring joy to the children in our part of town. And we did well that day. There were a lot of people who came out to enjoy an evening at the park, dance to some polkas and listen to rushing of the water in the background; the park is right on the Wisconsin River.

We closed our stand at 11 p.m., cleaned it up a little, and I took the money so that I could deposit it right away the next morning. A sheriff escorted me to the car so that no drunk could get the idea to rob me.

Henry started the car and homeward we drove, up Highway 64, and turned in to County Highway E. We did no more than take the turn when our car stalled. "What now?" Henry asked. But I didn't know what to do either. I'm not a mechanic.

After a couple of unsuccessful tries to start the car, Henry got out, opened the hood and tried to find the problem. A pickup truck stopped, two young men got out and asked if they could help.

"No, no," Henry answered. "We can take care of it ourselves." And off they drove. But we could not get the car going again. It was past midnight and we were about two miles from home. Henry gave up, closed the hood and, looking at me and said, "The only option we have is to push the car home." Then he sat behind the steering wheel.

"Now, what do you want?" I asked, since I did not understand what he meant.

"I will steer the car and you will push. You made most of the miles on this car so it's your car and you push."

I could not believe my ears, but without a question I went to the back of the car and started pushing. We had to go past Haas' and Koehler's house. I ducked down low so that they could not recognize me, since I felt like a thief.

I used to think that the road was slightly downhill, but, boy, did I look at it differently that night. It was a very tough job, but I made it all the way. The driveway is steep, so Henry got the tractor to pull the car up the hill. I was exhausted and breathing heavy. Henry looked at me and asked, "How come you're breathing so hard?"

"If you would have pushed, you would know," I answered, and hooked the chain to the car so that he could pull. Without another word we went to bed, but I was still tired when the alarm clock went off at 4:15 a.m., telling me it was time to go to work.

Henry fixed the car the next day. It had an electrical problem. But to this day, if I'm worried someone else's car stalls, I tell them, "You better make sure your car is running because I'm not pushing. I did not make those miles."

****

Henry kept busy that summer. He built a deck and reinforced the basement wall. I could see he was sick, not just physically, also emotionally, but I could not get him to a doctor, nor could I talk to anyone else about it. It was as if he were a completely different person in public than at home. Everybody liked him. He was so much fun and always had a joke ready. I know that was a cover-up, but I did not know how to change it.

Henry helped me a lot in the store, but the worst thing was he trusted me less now than he ever did before. He stood behind the office door watching every move I made, and if I talked with a man or smiled at one, then Henry would accuse me later of going out with him. It was like having a chain around my neck. I felt like suffocating. Henry left the store early one day, and I told him I will be home at 5 p.m. But then some vendor walked in just before I was ready to leave, so it took minutes longer. Henry called my employees to ask if they saw where I went and with whom. When I walked in the house, he screamed at me, demanding to know, "With whom did you go to bed today?" But there was no other man in my life.

The wife of one of my customers (he was about my age) had cancer, and she died that summer. Richard would talk to me, but just so he had someone to talk to, and I felt sorry for him, and there was always the counter between us. But Henry saw more behind it. He invited Richard for a Sunday dinner later on, just to see if one of us two would slip up. But Richard declined. He had a woman friend now. It was the nurse who took care of his dying wife. But that did not help Henry's suspicion.

Henry was so depressed. "If I just one more time could go with heifers up to the mountains, that would make me happy. This is my only wish," he told me ever so often.

My reply was, "That's no problem. Go home for a summer and then come back to me in fall. I have a job here, I can't just leave, but I will wait for you. Henry, do once in your lifetime what you want to do and not what everybody expects you to do."

"Oh, yes," was his quick answer, "you can't wait to get me out of here so that the next guy can move in."

But that was the last thing on my mind. "I would borrow money so that you could go, or do whatever you would like to do, just to finally find happiness. You are the only person who really matters to me," I told him over and over again, but no success.

So many times I thought Henry had to suffer from Alzheimer's disease. He had two personalities. He could yell and scream at me, accuse me of things I never did, and then walk out of the house ten minutes later, return and talk like nothing ever happened, not understanding what was wrong with me that I felt hurt. So many times I thought I was losing my mind, that I was imagining this. I felt I'm going crazy.

Henry also was suicidal. So often when I got up and got ready to go to work he cried. I could see it was not an act. He really felt bad and useless. "I'm no good anymore. I will kill myself and will not be here anymore when you come home," he told me so many times. Henry did really believe in the Bible, but said, "Even in the Bible it says the man is the head of the household. That means he supports his family, and I no longer can do that; that is why I end my life."

I sat by him on the bed, put my arm around him, kissed him and told him, "I love and need you. Even if you can't work, at least we are together."

I talked until I had to hurry to work, hoping that would ease his pain. Once I was at the store, I had to be friendly and smiling, telling my customers, "Have a good day." Yet my gut was just turning. How is Henry? I hope he does not keep his promises. Over and over again I tried to call home, but Henry would not answer. So often I was scared to go home, not knowing what he did to himself while I was at work.

It did not help matters that I did not feel like making love to Henry anymore. But how could I be screamed at one minute and feel loved the next? Henry couldn't understand that either, and said just turn your back toward me. I can see you don't want me anymore."

But that was not the case. He just was so different. Everything I did or said was turned against me. No doctor told me that a lot of male patients who had bladder cancer have that same feeling as Henry, because every time they get checked out, they get injured in their most important part of their manhood. But if we never could make love again, that would not bother me, since even without that we still could love each other and cuddle up. We shared so much together, went through so much hardship in our lives, we should be able to make it through this, too.

But I guess that is another thing I could not understand, that that is the most important thing for a man, and without that act he feels he no longer is a man. How could I know, I'm a woman.

So, slowly but surely we drifted farther and farther apart, and I became a nervous wreck, yet had no one to talk to. Plus, no one would have believed me. Maybe it is me that is crazy, I thought so many times.

****

Edith, with her children, Martin Junior and Heidi, came to visit us that November. Martin had to work and

Jessica had to go to school, so they could not come along. Reto and his family flew in from California for a long weekend. It was great to have at least two of my children and their families here. We celebrated Thanksgiving and Christmas all at once.

Edith, Reto, and Brenda bought us a Christmas tree and decorated the whole house. They baked some cookies. The smell was overwhelming and would bring anybody into the Christmas spirit.

It was really nice and well-meant, but I had a hard time getting into that Christmas feeling, knowing what was going on between Henry and me, but I put on a show for the grandchildren's sake.

I found out years later that that was the wrong thing to do, since because of that Reto never got to talk to his dad about Dad's problems, and never saw his dad for how much he suffered and what he was going through. But that is okay, too. At least Reto can hold onto his dream picture of his dad. And his dad was a good man, but also a man with a lot of problems and hurt emotions that haunted him all through his life.

For one weekend I forgot all my troubles and just enjoyed my grandchildren. And it was nice. Reto, Brenda, Sierra and Amanda flew back to California on Tuesday. It was hard for me to see them go, knowing how much I would like to say to them; but I kept quiet. They could see my tears, but did not know the feeling behind it.

That night after Heidi and little Martin were in bed, I no longer could hold back. I knew I had to talk to someone or I would lose it. And since Edith was here, with an open mind, I felt this was the right time.

I started talking, but then, to my surprise, Henry took over, telling Edith how tough he was with me through all those years, and how sorry he felt that he did not treat his children better. My tears were just rolling. I could not stop them anymore. Years of covering up pain finally broke open.

The alarm clock went off at 4 a.m. and we still sat at the kitchen table talking. I went to the bathroom, washed my red, swollen eyes, and got ready to go to work. I had to drive to Tomahawk that day to help Jim, the manager of Auto Stop. He had trouble with his bookwork.

I gave Henry a kiss and made him promise to never call my girls at work again and tell them what goes on between us. As I was ready to walk out the door, Edith told me she would like to go to Wausau later that afternoon and was I willing to go along.

It took longer in Tomahawk than I thought, so I called my store, telling my employee I would be late. She answered, "That's okay. I have everything under control. I heard you talked it out last night. Henry told me 'I can never again tell you when he calls and asks where you went, or if you are seeing someone else.' "

I had to do everything in my power to hold my tears back. Didn't I just ask Henry hours ago not to talk to my employees about our problems, and now he went and told Lori what was said? Boy, that hurts.

We went shopping that afternoon, but then talked again long into the night. Edith told her dad, "I can see that you two, after all, still love each other. Dad, if you think you do not need help, then you at least can see to it that Mom gets professional help. Please support her."

Henry agreed that support was needed, and so Edith called a psychiatrist the next day and made an appointment, but she was told there was no opening until March.

Edith flew out the following Saturday, since she wanted to spend some of her vacation days with Lotti and her family before it was time to go back to Switzerland. It was so very hard for me to see her go, since after all those years of covering up I finally could let at least one of my children know how life really was for me. Thank God I had a job, and that helped me cope with life. My job was for me like alcohol is for an alcoholic.

A new year started, but I felt it looked bleak for us. Henry did not get any better. Then in March, the day before our appointment with the psychiatrist, he said, "I will not come along tomorrow. If you think you need help, then go to your shrink, but I think that is stupid." Once again I gave in and canceled our appointment.

We had an early spring this year and Henry started making a new fence around our pasture. He spread three-row barbwires all around that piece of land, two 40-long and 1,000 feet wide. That kept him busy for weeks. We also planned a trip to California for July. Jessica, our granddaughter, was coming again.

Jessica's dad, Brian (Edith's ex-husband) lived in Merrill, too. In the divorce papers it said that Brian had to pay no child support if Edith went back to Switzerland, but he has to pay half the cost for the airfare if Jessica comes and visits.

Jessie was here two years ago, and she had trouble and was getting pulled between Brian and us. Now, Jessie is 13 and felt she wanted to put it right on the table. She wrote Brian a letter telling him she would stay with them the first two weeks, then come to us and fly with us to California to see Reto. Brian wrote Jessie a postcard and said whatever her plans were was okay with him.

So, Edith bought the ticket. But then later Brian sent Edith a letter, saying, "I would have to pay half of the airfare, yet since Jessica spends half her time with your parents, I will only pay one-quarter. Your mother can pay the rest."

Edith called me all upset. "What should I do? I can't afford that much, and I bought the ticket already." I told her not to worry about it. "I will pay for the whole airfare, but then I will let Jessie decide when she wants to see her dad," I told Edith.

But the closer it got to Jessie's vacation, the more scared I got. Brian is Jessie's dad and sure has more rights than I have as a grandma. What if he gets a police order and will not let her see us? What can he do to her?

After a couple of sleepless nights, I went to the District Attorney and asked him to settle this dispute in court, once and for all. He explained that we would have to see a mediator first, and then the mediator will make his recommendation to the court.

"Whatever it takes," I said. "The one who suffers is Jessica, and that is not right. She is not the one who got divorced." I told him what day Jessie would arrive, and he saw no problem putting her into my custody until the hearing two days after her arrival.

I picked Jessie up at the airport in Chicago, and we had a great weekend together. Then on Tuesday at 10:30 a.m. we had to see the mediator. Jessie was scared. "Just tell him honestly how you feel, that is all you can do," I told her.

Henry and I were questioned first, while they locked Brian and Jessie in a different room. The mediator wanted to know our side of the story, and then soon replied, "The typical hate for an ex-son-in-law."

But I answered, "No, I talk to Brian a lot. I was not married to him, so it is not my problem. But there is a girl out there who is scared and has suffered for years already. Listen to her and then make your decision." I didn't answer any more questions, since I felt it was useless.

Brian was on next, and then at last it was Jessie's turn. One long whole hour passed and Jessie was still in that room with the mediator. I felt so sorry for her; yet that was something she had to tackle by herself.

The door opened and the mediator called us back in. "There is no question in my mind what the outcome of the case should be," he told us. "I will take all the parental rights away from Brian. This girl suffered way too long.

"I called Brian about my decision," he went on, "and Brian in his own words said, 'I know I lost Jessica as a little baby already. I never was a real father to her.' And that strengthens my belief that this girl belongs in your custody," he said to me. "I will put it in writing, and will get it to you this afternoon. If Jessica wants to see her dad, then it is on her terms and her terms only."

Jessie was so happy she wanted to frame the letter.

I made arrangements for Jessie to spend one day with her dad and her new family anyway. It was on a Friday around noon when Brian picked her up.

But then I got scared when the clock went past nine and Jessie was not home. I told them to have her back by 7 p.m. My imagination ran wild. What if Brian skipped town with her? He could take her to Canada, or disappear somewhere else. What would I tell Edith?

What a sigh of relief when they pulled in at 9:30 p.m. and I could hold Jessie in my arms again.

Our house had four bedrooms, but Jessie was so scared that someone would come and take her while we were sleeping, she took her sleeping bag and put it on my side of the bed, and that's where she slept night after night. There was only three feet between the bed and the wall, but it did not bother her. At least she felt safe.

She came with me to the store and was a great help. Then for one week we flew to California to visit Reto. It was nice, but even amongst my loved ones I felt lonely. It felt as if I was no longer a part of Henry's life.

Reto had vacation, too, and took us everywhere. We went to the Water Park. Henry was just like a little kid. He was gone all day from one water slide to the other. He even injured one of his toes, but that did not stop him. On Saturday we went to see Henry's favorite sister, Elsa. They had their own business and gave us a tour through their shop. Elsa showed me the offices, but then when Henry walked in, she said, "That's nothing for you. You aren't smart enough to understand all of this."

How humiliating! How could she do that to the brother

who adored her so much? I could see in Henry's eyes that he was hurt, and I felt so sorry for him. But it was done and I could not change it.

We had a bite to eat at their house afterward. That's when they told us that the Swiss Club in town had a dance that night and asked, if we wanted to, we could go along. But we declined. "Thanks for asking, but the children have to get home," was our excuse.

I was worried that Elsa would keep humiliating Henry, even in front of their friends, and that is something he did not need. He worked hard all his life and tried to prove to his siblings that he is equal, yet it just will not go away. But Reto and Brenda were great and tried to take our worries away, and they helped us get over our disappointment.

On Sunday we had a picnic right on the ocean, and on Monday we flew back to Wisconsin. Jessie stayed with us for one more week, and then it was time to take her to Chicago so that she could fly back to Switzerland.

I had my children so close together, and then in later years would have loved to have another child. So often I suggested to Henry that we adopt one, but he didn't want to hear about it.

"We have enough troubles with the four kids we have, why do we want one more?" was his reply.

And then, when I was 36 years old, Jessie came along. Plus, Edith worked and Brian had something planned for every weekend. "Take Jessie to your mother," he used to say. And so Jessica became my little girl. She used to be with me every minute of the day. I loved her so much. All of that came to my mind as we waited for her departure. I had tears in my eyes, and my heart was heavy, but I had to smile and act strong since I knew that it was just as hard on Henry and Jessica as it was on me. We stayed until Jessie's plane was in the air, then had a long, silent drive back to Merrill.

****

Hilfikers, another Swiss family, needed help to bring their crops in, so Henry volunteered. He went there almost every day, and it felt like he was a different person. He never came home until late at night. Most of the time I was sleeping already, since I had to get up a little after 4 a.m. Henry never said why he liked helping them, and I did not want to ask. If this was what he needed, then so be it.

Then, before Labor Day, we got invited to a Garbage Pail Party. "What is a Garbage Pail Party?" I asked. But Henry didn't know either. I was kind of curious. Why would strangers invite us? Henry explained that Hilfikers were invited, too. That made me feel better. So we went. The meal was great. They took a metal garbage pail, filled it layer by layer with cabbage, carrots, potatoes, sweet corn and Polish sausage, and then cooked all of that over an open fire in the woods. It was delicious.

The owner of that 40 acres of woods had two daughters, 17 and 19 years old. Now I found out that they helped Henry unload the hay wagons and had a lot of fun together. They swung with a rope from one hay mow to the other to see who gets the farthest.

How come he could not tell me about this? Don't I matter to him anymore? He is so jealous of me and watches my every move, but that would not have bothered me at all, if he would have told me; now it kind of hurts. Was there more than just play that he had to keep it a secret? On the other hand, it made him feel good those last couple of months, and I guess that is all that counts.

****

Heinz, his wife Judith and their son Patrick came to visit us in October of 1989. It was great to have company. Heinz used to resent, sometimes even hate his dad, for what he did to his childhood. Now that Heinz is older, married and has a son of his own, he tries to understand his father. For many nights we talked way into the morning hours, and it was good they both could air their feelings. Henry told Heinz the same thing he told Edith the year before. Henry made Heinz understand that it was because of his own childhood that he punished me as his wife, but also especially Heinz as his first-born son. And then Heinz told his dad that he hated him for years for what he did, especially to us two.

But then Heinz went on, "Now I can forgive you for everything, since if it would not have been for my hard upbringing I would not have the job that I have now, nor the respect I get from my fellow co-workers and my boss. You, Dad, taught me that I always have to prove myself, and so I did."

Henry and Heinz hugged each other and cried together, and so finally, after all those years, came to peace with each other. Neither of them knew that it was the last time they would sit together at the same table.

We took one weekend during their vacation and drove all the way to Sault Ste. Marie to see the locks. Heinz could not believe how pretty the drive was and how interesting it was to watch those huge boats go through the locks. "I lived in Wisconsin for so many years and never knew how much beauty we had so close to us," was Heinz's comment.

We all were in tears when we had to say goodbye at the airport. Heinz and his family went on to Reto's and from there to Texas to see Lotti. I don't know why, but this time it hurt more than ever before, and it took me days to get out of my depressed mood.

Just weeks later, beginning of December, Lotti called. "Larry got a job offer in Wisconsin at his brother's company, so we'll move home again."

Yes, I was glad to have at least one of my children close, but I was also skeptical. John, Larry's brother, just started a new company. Those two worked together before for Rock & Water out of California, and now he wants to do the same work on his own. What if it does not work out?

But that was not for me to decide. It is their life. Larry had a drinking problem all along, and said so often, "If I could live back in Wisconsin by my friends, could fish and hunt again, I would quit drinking." And if this is what it takes, more power to him.

"We will rent a U-Haul, but could you come down with your Winnebago and help us move?" Lotti asked. Of course, we would help them.

The 15th of December we left Wisconsin and drove straight through to Keller, Texas, where Lotti lived since six months after Cassie's death. We helped them pack on Saturday and loaded the U-Haul truck on Sunday, then left Keller really early Monday morning, the 18th of December, my birthday.

It was cool in Texas and got colder the farther north we went. Our Winnebago was full-packed with plants that would have frozen otherwise, the aquarium with the fish in it, the two dogs, and then, of course, Bobbi Jo and Tyler were with us. Every couple of hours one of the kids had to blow into the fish tank to give the fish some oxygen.

We drove all the way to the Iowa border before we stopped and tried to sleep for a couple of hours. Larry kept his truck running, but slowly it froze up, and as we were ready to leave it did not run at all anymore.

We took Lotti and Larry along, drove to the next truck stop about 30 miles up the road, got a bite to eat and then some Heet to put into the gas tank and drove back to the stranded truck. Larry was worried that we would have to get a different U-Haul and unload everything, but Henry knew just what to do, and one hour later we were on our way, and it worked fine all the way home.

Larry fell off a roof a year before when he still worked in Texas and now got $10,000 from the workmen's comp.

for pain and suffering. That money could be used for the down payment on a house, they figured. So they stayed with us until they could find a house they liked.

I liked that, since this way they could spend Christmas with us, and it was nice to see the candlelight glow in children's eyes again and to see their excitement as they eagerly unwrapped their presents. That brought back memories from long, long ago, and I could not help it, I had to swallow a couple of tears.

Lotti and Larry found a house they liked in Schofield and moved out the beginning of February.

I still belonged to the Wisconsin Women of Agriculture. Then one Sunday in the middle of February they had a party at one of the member's homes. I had to work that Sunday morning, but was done at eleven and so we could have easily made it there for lunch, but Henry said, "We are not going. We are no longer farmers and only the laughing stock to them. I will not go there, and that is final."

We were not the only ones who lost their farm, and we did the best we could and did not have to be ashamed of our achievement. But there was no way I could talk Henry into going.

When he saw how disappointed I was, he suggested, "Let's go to Club Modern and have smorgasbord."

"No," I answered. "Everyone there is dressed up coming from church and I'm in my work clothes. I don't feel like going there. I just would like to be with our friends." But if Henry says NO, that is it. Neither of us said one word as we drove home.

Once at home I started crying and told Henry that I was not hungry and would not make lunch. If he wanted to eat, he had to make it himself.

Henry started yelling at me, and that was just too much for me. I could take no more. Something had to give. I was on the brink of having a nervous breakdown.

Henry watched every move I made, and it felt like I had a chain around my neck, and it was as if he slowly strangled me. He stood behind the office door at the store and watched if I smiled at a male customer, and always accused me of going to bed with some stranger.

In one way I could understand Henry. I was ten years younger than he was, still in good health, and had a job, and he was sickly. But there was nothing I could do about it. I had to, and thank God, could still work.

My nerves were at the end, and I don't even know how it happened, but there was a cup on the kitchen table; I took it and threw it in the corner. I never, ever did something like that before. Henry got angrier yet and started yelling, "A woman and a grandma at your age should never behave like this."

Now I really fell to pieces, but then, at the same minute, saw Lotti drive up our driveway. I ran into the bedroom. My grandchildren did not have to see me cry. Henry took the dustpan and swept all the pieces from the broken cup together and made a little pile on the kitchen table. Then, as Lotti walked in the door, he said, "Look what your mother just did. Fifty years old and does something so childish."

Lotti looked at her dad and said, "Dad, I can't say much. I've thrown a lot bigger things than that already." Then she turned around, told Larry to go to town and take the kids shopping. She and Henry came into the bedroom, and Lotti wanted to know what it was that triggered this.

"I can't anymore, I feel like someone is strangling me. I just can't go on anymore," I sobbed.

Lotti could see that I was desperate and tried to make Henry understand that we had a problem and it was high time we got professional help. Looking at her dad, she said, "If you think you don't need help, then at least help Mom before it is too late."

Lotti called Dr. Elmergreen's office on Monday, and he

had an opening the following Friday. I did not know what to expect, but I knew something had to give. I just could not go on like this anymore.

Then on Friday Henry and I went together to see the psychiatrist. “Henry has no will to live anymore, and he threatens almost daily to commit suicide, and that drives me crazy. I don’t know how to make him understand that even if he can’t work anymore, he still is important to me,” I told the doctor.

And then Henry started talking. I heard things I never knew before, things I could never imagine, but those things worked on Henry’s mind all those years. Henry said straight out, “I hated my mother for what she did to me. None of my siblings had to work away from home as a child like I had to. My mother never loved me and never had time to listen to me. So when I turned 18 I made a promise to myself never, ever in my entire life will a woman tell me what to do.”

Henry told Dr. Elmergreen that I told him before we got married that I was sexually abused as a child. Dr. Elmergreen asked Henry: “Edith was a young woman, a woman who loved you, so what did you think when she told you that?”

Henry replied quickly, “If her Uncle Henry could get his needs taken care of by his wife, then he would not have to go after Edith, so it isn’t his fault.”

I could not believe my ears. Could Henry really understand what I went through? I was only a little girl back then and had no way of defending myself. It hit me like a brick wall, and I could see the disbelief in Dr. Elmergreen’s eyes. Henry never felt sorry for me. He defended my uncle. And even though I believe Henry loved me, I think he also hated me because I was just another woman.

I asked myself, why did I try for the last 32 years to make Henry happy? How could I succeed if he hates women so much?

Dr. Elmergreen dug more into Henry's past. He could see how tired Henry was of living, and that he did not want to go on anymore. He asked if we had any guns in our house. Henry looked him straight in the eyes and replied, "I can kill myself without a gun, too."

As the one-hour session came to an end, Dr. Elmegreen came to the conclusion that Henry was a threat to himself, and because of that he felt he had to commit him to the Health Care Center.

"No, you can't do that to him," I begged. "That really would kill Henry. I will take him home and watch him very close. Henry finally could open up now, and that is a step in the right direction."

Dr. Elmergreen reluctantly gave in and let me take Henry home, but we had to make an appointment for the following Friday.

I was drained as I crawled into bed that night, but was hoping now that Henry could talk to someone about his problems it might get better. "Please, God, help him."

I had to train Cindy, a new manager at the Medford store. Medford is a neighboring town to the west of us and a little over 30 miles from my house. I had to teach her how to close and do the bookwork at night. I did not have to be there until 5 p.m. Before I walked out the door, I gave Henry a kiss and said, "See you a little past midnight."

I drove to Medford, and Cindy and I worked together all evening. We closed the store at 11 p.m. She then had to close out the cash register, count the money and then also the cigarettes. The cigarettes did not come out the first time around, and I made her recount them. I could have done it faster, but that would not have helped her.

It was a little past midnight when we locked the store door behind us. Cindy said, "Good night. Drive careful and watch out for deer."

"Have a good night," I replied, and slowly drove onto

Highway 64 thinking of all the things I heard and now would like to tell Henry.

I was halfway home when I saw a car come toward me on the wrong side of the road. The last minute the car moved over to his lane, but as soon as he was past me, swerved back into my lane. What an idiot, I said to myself. He could have killed me. He must be drunk. Oh, how stupid! My hands were shaky as I drove the rest of the way.

I slowly drove up the driveway and saw that the Volvo was gone. Maybe someone borrowed it, I thought to myself, and ran into the house. But Henry was not there. The house was empty.

I was so tired and my tears were slowly running down my cheek. Now what? Did Henry go through with his threat? Did he go and kill himself, or did he just leave me to start a new life somewhere else?

I paced the floor. I could not sit down. Where do I go and look for him? There are miles and miles of woods all around us. Do I go east, west, north or south? Please, God, please, God, bring him back alive, I prayed.

Two hours passed and nothing. No Henry and no phone call. I couldn't stand it anymore, I had to talk to someone, so I called Lotti. "Please forgive me for waking you up, but your dad is gone and I have no idea where he went. I don't know what to do anymore."

Just at that time I saw a car come up our driveway. I recognized the Volvo lights, and said to Lotti, "Your dad just drove up to the house." Before I could hang up the phone, he stormed into the house. "Where the hell were you? I drove all the way to Medford and thought you maybe drove into the ditch, but I could see you nowhere."

"Did you drive on the wrong side of the road?" I asked.

"Yes, I looked in the ditch for you. You said you close the store at 11 p.m. and were not home at 11:30. Then where were you so long? Did you meet a guy somewhere?"

Now I realized he was the one who almost drove me off the road. He must have mistrusted me again and thought I was with another man.

"I'm sorry, but I thought you were asleep. You know exactly that we have to count the money and the cigarettes. You helped me so many times already in my store, so you know how long it takes, especially if it does not come out. I did not think to call."

I gave Henry a kiss and went to bed. If I just could close my eyes for a little bit, since I knew the alarm clock would go off in 30 minutes, and that means it's time to go back to work.

Friday noon we had to see Dr. Elmergreen again. Henry did not feel well at all. I think the stress from two nights ago got to him. As we drove to Wausau, Henry said with tears in his eyes, "I'm a lot sicker than anybody thinks, but I will never again go to a doctor or to the hospital. I just want to die."

Henry talked for a whole hour to Dr. Elmergreen, and I said nothing. But my tears were rolling slowly down my cheeks as I could hear how much pain Henry went through. He could not live life. He just went through life with a hurt in his heart that choked him a little more each day. Oh, how sad! He had once everything going for him and could not even enjoy it because he hurt too much. He did not love himself. All through his life he thought he was a loser. This is what a mother can do to her child without even knowing it.

It hurt so much to see this once so strong and determined man fall to pieces. Henry and I had to dry our eyes as we walked to our car. I gave him a hug and a kiss as I opened the door for him. He was in no shape to drive. We stopped at Lotti's, and she and I together quickly went to a craft shop, then we got a bite to eat, but Henry would not come out of the car.

"Just go. I do not feel good. I'm not hungry," he said.

His eyes were surrounded by white stuff, and he looked pale. Lotti and I hurried up. I dropped her off at her house and then drove home. Henry lay down for awhile and then went outside to putz around. He was so depressed.

I had to work on Saturday morning, and Henry came along. He did not feel like helping me, but at least I knew where he was and did not have to worry about him. We stopped for lunch and then went home.

"That wood should be cut," Henry said, as we drove up the driveway.

"Just take it easy. The wood can wait until you feel better," I tried to convince him, but Henry took the chainsaw and started cutting some of the firewood that he bought the fall before. Then, after four or five pieces he was tired out, and neither of us had any idea that he would never have a chance to cut that wood himself.

I made supper. We watched some TV, but then went to bed early. We both were tired — tired emotionally and physically.

March 11, 1990. It is 4:15 a.m. My alarm clock started playing music, and that on a normal weekday means it was time to get up, but not today. It was Sunday, and I did not have to go to work. Henry woke up, too, and together we just lay there for awhile and listened to the country western songs coming from the radio.

Henry got up, went to the bathroom, and then crawled back in bed. He took me in his arms and kissed me. He was so gentle. It felt so good to be in his arms. He was so passionate, and he made love to me like he hadn't for many, many years. In fact, I think it was better than ever. I could not get enough of it. I felt like I was in love for the first time in my life. Nothing on this earth could make me feel warmer than the love I felt right then. There was no man on this planet that could love me more than Henry did in those early morning hours.

He was still on top of me as we both were winding

down. He looked me straight in my eyes and said so lovably: "Wasn't that nice?"

I smiled at him, nodded my head, and answered yes, that was better than ever."

He smiled back, but at the same moment jerked his head just a little, like someone pulled on his hair. Was it his Guardian Angel getting him, telling him, "Let's go. That is it. Your time on this earth is up."

What I saw then I will never forget. My eyes met Henry's, but his did not glow anymore. They were without any shine whatsoever. It hit me like lightning. Those are the eyes of death. I saw animals die on the farm, and there was no question, there is no difference.

I started screaming, "Not now! Not now! Please don't leave me now that we've found each other again. You can't do that to me."

I rolled Henry off of me and started pumping his chest, but he was hard like a rock. Naked as I was, I ran to the telephone and called the ambulance. I screamed in the phone, "Please come! Please come! My husband just passed away," and hung up. Back into the bedroom I ran, tried to pump his chest again, but no response. God, what do I do now?

To the phone I ran again and called Lotti in Wausau. I screamed at her, "Please meet me at the hospital. Your dad just passed away."

Sobbing, "Not now, not now," I kneeled down by him and hugged him. But he was stiff and cold.

I could hear the sirens come over the hill, and that brought me back to reality. Still naked, I ran, got my clothes and got dressed just in time for the rescue crew to knock on the door. I saw the ambulance in the yard, the red light still flashing, and the sheriff's car behind. He had his lights on, too.

I motioned them into the bedroom, and there lay Henry, naked, not even a blanket covering his body. How could I let him lay there like that; how inconsiderate of me. I could have at least covered him. I tried to sneak past the cot they wheeled in, but they pushed me out of their way and closed the bedroom door behind them.

The sheriff, I don't even remember his name, forced me gently down onto the sofa. I don't know what he said, but I remember him asking what happened. It felt just like pressing a button on a tape-recorder. I repeated the same thing I just said minutes ago to the ambulance crew. All I could think is, "I killed him; I killed him."

It must have been tough on the sheriff. He had his arms on my shoulder and tried to convince me, against my better judgment, that Henry is going to make it. "The rescue squad will do the best in their power to bring him back. You just can't lose hope," he said. But I was a farmer for too long, I knew there was no chance.

The sheriff got my coat and put it over my shoulders. He walked me to the squad car and drove me to the hospital. It was 6 a.m. Sunday morning. The first people were up and going to mass as we were driving through town with the red lights flashing, me repeating over and over again, "I killed him. I killed him, just as I did my Uncle Henry. Every time I don't know where to turn anymore, the person I have trouble with dies."

We made it to the hospital. Two nurses came out to greet me and walked me to the waiting room. They sat down by my side and rubbed my back. The ambulance was not there yet, but I was told that they called a priest, and that the doctors would do their best to save Henry. But just the way they talked to me I knew there was no hope.

Lotti and Larry arrived just as the ambulance drove in. I was like a zombie, just going through the motions and repeating the same thing over and over again. I do not know how much time passed, but the doctor came and told us that it was over and there was nothing they could do for Henry anymore.

A nurse then asked if I would like to sit by him for a little while. I nodded yes, and she walked me into the emergency room. There was Henry in this big, cold, empty room. His mouth was wide open, no teeth in his mouth, and his chest was just huge from all the oxygen they tried to pump into his lungs.

The nurse pushed a chair to his bed, and I sat down and my tears ran slowly down my cheeks. I grabbed his hand and apologized. "Please forgive me. I didn't want you dead."

Then I turned to the nurse and said, "See, that is what I do. I was abused as a child and when I did not know where to turn anymore, I asked God to please help me, and my Uncle Henry got killed in a motorcycle accident. And now Henry, he was so emotionally sick the last years, I prayed every night, God, please help me to get through this, and now he is dead, too. Now that we finally got help and saw a psychiatrist, this is what I do to men. How terrible of me."

The nurse just rubbed my back and said, "No, it is not your fault. Henry's time was up, and there is nothing anybody could do about it."

But I knew different. It was me that killed him. Slowly I got up, leaving Henry behind in that lonely room. Lotti hugged me and together we went to the chapel room where an older priest waited for us. I do not know if it was me being hysterical or what, but he did not know what to say or how to comfort me. We prayed together, but I was not with it. My thoughts were wandering in circles.

"I have to call my children. They have to know," I insisted. The nurses were so helpful and let us use the hospital phone. I could not remember any phone numbers, but Lotti took over and got them for me.

As Reto answered the phone, Lotti told him, "Mom has to tell you something," then handed me the phone. Then I insisted that I wanted to be the one that told him what had happened so that he knew I was okay, or at least acted like I was okay. Deep down I was hurting and I felt terrible, but there were a lot of things that had to be taken care of; I had to be strong.

We had to call Edith and Heinz in Switzerland, and Henry's siblings. Yes, his siblings did Henry wrong, but now all of that could maybe be laid to rest once and for all.

Lotti guided me out of the hospital and drove me home. She wanted me at her house, but I had to pick up some clothes first. I walked slowly back into the bedroom that Henry and I shared for years, and where he spent the last minutes of his life, proving to me that he truly loved me. But the bed was empty, the covers laid all over the floor. The only reminder was Henry's wristwatch on the dresser. I had a lump in my throat and my heart felt empty. It was as if part of me died with him.

Lotti got me a little suitcase and we packed some clothes. I tried to call Edith and Heinz in Switzerland, but neither of them was home. I locked the house up, crawled into the back seat and let my tears flow free, while Lotti and Larry drove me to Wausau to stay with them. From there I talked to Edith and later to Heinz, and then I had to call my mother, hoping that she would not worry too much about my state of mind.

Edith and Heinz were ready to get a plane ticket and come to be by my side, but I talked them out of it. Henry made a wish two years before, a wish that none of my children knew. He heard of a lady who immigrated from Great Britain. After she passed away, she got cremated and her daughter then brought her home to be laid to rest in her homeland. From that day on Henry said, "Should I ever go before you, then please bring me home. It would be so much cheaper, and I could be laid to rest where my heart was all along." I never thought I'd have to make that decision so soon. The more I thought about it, the more I knew that I did not want to go on that long trip by myself. "Lotti," I said, "it is your dad's wish to go home, and no matter what the cost, I would like to fulfill his wish, but would you please come with me?"

She was surprised, wanted to talk it over with Larry first, but could see no problem. Reto called later that day and told me that they were in Salt Lake City now. He got plane tickets for Brenda and him and they would arrive in Mosinee early Monday morning. I told him that his dad wanted to go home, and that I asked Lotti to come along.

Then I said, "Reto, please think about it, and if you want to come, too, then I would pay your airfare also." He promised to talk it over with Brenda. "I will call you later and give you the exact time we will arrive," he replied, and hung up.

Later that afternoon Lotti told me that Larry thought that was a good idea, but Larry felt that he was part of the family, too, and would like to be there when his father-in-law is laid to rest. I answered, "Okay, we'll see."

Reto called from Minneapolis where they had a five-hour layover. He told me that he would like to come along to Switzerland, but Brenda felt, since she is now part of the family, too, she would like to come with us.

I knew that would be very expensive, yet, on the other hand, that was once in my lifetime that I could have my whole family, my four children and their spouses together, and no money on this earth is worth more than that opportunity. What else could I do? I needed their support. So I said, "Yes, you can all come." But that meant a lot of planning in just a few short days.

There was one more phone call I had to make. Dr. Elmergreen had to know what happened. As I told him that Henry passed away this morning, his first question was, "How did he do it?"

"No," I answered, "it was not his doing. He made love to me and just like that was gone."

Dr. Elmergreen tried to comfort me, but before I hung the phone up made me promise that I would keep on seeing him.

I was very tired as I lay down that night, but I could not sleep, there was so much on my mind, and my heart felt so empty. I could still feel Henry's arms gently pulling me closer.

HENRY GROSS

Henry Gross was a strong man who had strong beliefs. He was hardworking and dependable and a very warm man. At the age of 61, Henry Gross died on Sunday, March 11, 1990 at the Good Samaritan Health Center. He was born on December 22, 1928 in Switzerland to Heinrich and Elsbeth (Wittenwiler) Gross. Henry proudly served in the Switzerland Army.

On October 26, 1957, Henry married Edith Zellweger in Switzerland. He and his wife came to the United States in 1968. He farmed in the Town of Harding until his retirement due to ill health.

Henry was active in numerous farming activities and was a member of the American Milk Producers Inc. (AMPI). Henry particularly enjoyed music and was adept at yodeling and had belonged to a number of yodeling clubs in Switzerland. He also belonged to the Swiss Alpine Club in his native land. Henry also enjoyed downhill skiing and jumping.

With a Swiss heritage, Gross was proud to be a Swiss. He had a great deal of respect for people and was very supportive. As a husband, Henry was upstanding and good for Edith. He was a devoted father and would have done anything for his children. He was also an exceptional grandfather, dearly loved by his grandchildren.

Henry Gross is survived by his wife, Edith, N2342 CTH E, Merrill; two daughters, Edith (Martin) Stillhart, Switzerland, and Lotti (Larry) Hess, Schofield, Wisconsin; two sons, Heinz (Judith) Gross, Switzerland, and Reto (Brenda) Gross, Elko, Nevada; four sisters, Elsbeth (Fritz) Hirsiger, Switzerland, Martha (Albert) Haltinner, Merrill, Elsie (Ernest) Boesch, Ripon, California, and Rosemarie (Hans) Boesch, Switzerland; one brother, Walter (Verena) Gross, Switzerland; and nine grandchildren. He is preceded in death by his parents and one granddaughter.

Local services were held this morning, Wednesday, March 14, 1990 at the Schram-Waid Funeral Home Chapel. Rev. Sherman Iverson officiated. The immediate family will travel to Switzerland where special services will be held and disposition will be in the Evangelical Cemetery in Kappel, Switzerland. Schram-Waid Funeral Home was in charge of the arrangements. FN

Thank You

Perhaps you sent a lovely card, or sat quietly in a chair. Perhaps you sent a funeral spray, if so we saw it there. Perhaps you spoke the kindest words, as any friend could say. Perhaps you were not there at all, just thought of us that day. Whatever you did to console our hearts, we thank you so much whatever the part.

Edith and family of Henry Gross

"Thy Will Be Done"

God did not promise "sun without rain,"
"light without darkness" or joy without pain"–
He only promised us "strength for the day"
when "the darkness" comes and we lose our way,
For only through sorrow do we grow more aware
that God is our refuge in times of despair . . .
For when we are happy and life's bright and fair,
we often forget to kneel down in prayer,
But God seems much closer and needed much more
when trouble and sorrow stand outside our door–
For then we seek shelter in His wondrous love
and we ask Him to send us help from above .
And that is the reason we know it is true
that bright shining hours and dark, sad ones, too,
Are part of the plan God made for each one,
and all we can pray is "Thy Will be done"!

18

MONDAY MORNING, A dreary, rainy day. We had to go to the funeral home and make all the arrangements. I asked Henry's sister Martha if she would like to come along and take part in making the final arrangements. We met her at the funeral home. I wanted to show Henry and have a service at the local funeral home and then cremate him and take him home.

There was so much that had to be taken care of in such a short time. A casket had to be picked out. I found one that resembled his personality. It was a pine casket, and in the corners was some wheat carved into the wood. I only leased the casket, since they put the corpse in a cardboard box to be cremated. The casket lease is 50% of the selling price, which was $4,400 (or $2,000 for me), and the cardboard box another $160. But someone who just went through the worst ordeal in their life is so vulnerable and can't comprehend dollar signs. It has to be done, and I would like it to be nice. That is the last thing I could do for Henry.

We had to decide what songs to be sung, and we needed a minister. My favorite songs are "Rock of Ages" and "The Old Rugged Cross." They would have been Henry's songs, too, but I was so scatterbrained that I forgot all about it.

Henry was not too fond of ministers, but Rev. Iverson from Grace Lutheran Church in Tomahawk was one that he believed in, so I called him and he was willing to have the sermon for Henry.

We also had to get 50 pictures of Henry's life. Lincoln Video made a 15-minute movie out of them for visitors to see as they came to the wake to say goodbye to

Henry for the last time.

We had to get clothes for Henry. He did not own a suit, so I took his favorite brown shirt and the sweater he got for Christmas from Edith. Henry did not like to dress up, so how could I change his image now?

Reto and Brenda flew into the Mosinee airport. We picked them up, and from there we went straight to the courthouse. I had a passport, but my children and in-laws had to have one, too. Lotti had one before and just had to renew hers. Larry had to get his birth certificate. That was no problem either. But Reto's naturalization papers were in Nevada, and so was Brenda's birth certificate. Brenda called her aunt and asked her if she please would go to their house and get those certificates out of the safe and send them out, overnight express.

Passport pictures had to be taken. The airplane tickets had to be purchased. Swiss Air had a special rate for bereaved families, and with proof of the death certificate it only cost me $560 per person, a total of $2,800.

Edith called again that night, since she had to make funeral arrangements in Switzerland and did not know where to start, and how long it would take us to get there.

Henry's favorite sister, Elsa, flew in from California and together with Martha came to see us.

It was almost midnight by the time I got to bed, but even though I was very tired I could hardly sleep. I could still feel Henry's arm around me and his warm body close to mine. I was also kind of scared, knowing that I would see Henry again the next day, but this time in a casket. It is still so unbelievable. How can someone be so active, lovable and happy one minute, and then just seconds later gone forever? How can that happen?

We went shopping on Tuesday morning. I needed a dress for the funeral here, and also in Switzerland. From the mall we went to the courthouse to get all the papers ready for the passports. Everything looked okay, but then the clerk said to Brenda, "Your birth certificate is a copy and will not be acceptable." What now? I got her ticket, but without a passport she can't come along.

Brenda has an aunt in Carson City, the capitol of Nevada, so she called her to go to the state capitol and get her an original birth certificate and send that overnight express, and hopefully we would get it in time. What a headache, but yet, I really would like to have Brenda go along, too.

At 3:30 p.m. we had to get to the funeral home. There were flowers everywhere. It took all my strength to walk up to the casket and say goodbye to someone I loved so much and lived with for over 32 years. I was surprised how good Henry looked. He still had the smile on his face, the same smile he left me with early Sunday morning. Goodbye, my love. Till we meet again someday.

Lotti and I saw Henry before, but it was very hard on Reto to see his dad lying there and not be able to talk to him anymore. He stayed in the back for a long time, but then with Brenda's support took that big step and walked up to the casket. I wish I could have helped him, but that was something he had to work out himself.

There were lots and lots of friends who came to pay their last respects. All I could say over and over again, "Doesn't he look good? He was so troubled and homesick the last 22 years, and now he smiles. It must be beautiful where he is now. He must be in heaven." It made me really feel good to see his smile. Maybe he finally found peace.

Most of our friends looked at the movie and got a little more insight into Henry's life. It was 8:30 in no time and, with that, time to say one last goodbye to Henry. Yes, I will see him once more the next morning, but I will never, ever be with him alone again.

We had heavy rain since Sunday, and as we walked into Lotti's house we could not believe our eyes. They had a family room and a bedroom in the basement. That is where Reto and Brenda had to sleep, and also Lottie's in-laws, who were to take care of Bobbi Jo and Tyler while we were in Switzerland. But the basement was flooded. The floor was covered with at least four inches of water. We ripped the carpet out, hung it up to dry and scooped the water out, bucket by bucket. It was 2 a.m. by the time we were done and it was possible for all of us to go to bed. They still got wet feet, but at least they could lie down and sleep for a couple of hours. How much more can go wrong?

Seven a.m. It was time to get up, since the sermon at the funeral home was set for 10:30 a.m., and we had to be there at least at 9 a.m. to visit with some of the friends who did not have time to come the evening before.

It was a beautiful spring morning. The sky deep blue, and not a cloud to be seen. It was as if the sun had a smile and at least could warm our outside, but my heart still felt so heavy and lonely. We also waited desperately for Brenda's birth certificate, which had not arrived yet.

I had not seen Julius and Erika since Henry was gone, my best friends who were always by my side when I needed them, but their daughter Patty called and said they dropped their trailer and were on the way home.

The casket was still open, and more friends came to see Henry. Willi Fuelleman, a good friend of ours, fell to pieces. But I know I had to be strong for everybody else's sake, and so I said to Willi, "Look at Henry's smile. He looks happier than he did for many years. We have to be glad that he finally found peace."

Just as Willi sat down, Erika and Julius walked in and that was hard for all of us. Erika and Henry had an argument the summer before and never talked it out. They both were mad at each other. Now it's too late. They can never again talk and tell each other they are sorry for whatever happened that day.

Grandma always said, "Never leave the house mad,

and never go to bed angry, since you never know if you see that person again, and then you would have to live with the unsaid words for the rest of your life." And I think she was right. I saw now how quickly it can go. But no matter what, it felt good to have Julius and Erika, and all my friends, by my side. I truly need their support.

Larry, the vice president of the company I worked for, and Phil, my supervisor, and also the managers from Antigo, Tomahawk, Medford and Abbotsford Auto Stop were there to support me. The Auto Stop in Merrill, the store I managed, was closed through the hour of services in Henry's honor. What a warm feeling, to have so much support from your employer. Thanks so much to all of you. That was really thoughtful.

The funeral home was packed. Every chair was taken and some of our friends had to stand. My heart felt heavy and my eyes were filled with tears as they locked the casket and Reverend Iverson started the sermon, His first remarks were that this casket symbolizes Henry's life to a T. He said Henry was rugged, like the pine tree that was needed to make the casket, and he was a nature person, symbolized by the wheat carved into that rugged wood. Reverend Iverson did not know Henry until Lotti got married, and then saw him only a few times after that, but he sure knew him well enough to understand his mentality.

More handshakes and hugs, but slowly, one after the other left. We packed the flowers into our van and then went to Les and Jim's for lunch, where our friends waited for us. We had beef and pork sandwiches, and our friends brought hot dishes and desserts. What would one do without friends? How comforting!

I gave some of the flower arrangements to our closest friends, but kept the plants for myself. We could not sit and visit with them too long since we had to get the passports taken care of and had to pick up Henry's ashes between 7:30 and 8 p.m. at the Peterson Funeral Home in

Wausau. Then we planned on leaving Wausau around midnight. We had to be in Chicago at 9 a.m. when they open the federal building where they make the passports or we wouldn't get them the same day.

It was 3:30 p.m. and Brenda's birth certificate still wasn't there, but the courthouse would close at 4 p.m. The lady clerk who took care of us was really helpful but told us in no uncertain terms that if we did not have that certificate within the next 30 minutes there was nothing she could do for us. She had to get all the information together in a certain order and then seal the envelope. Without that, we could not get the passports in Chicago.

Lotti started crying and explained what we went through so far and that all the arrangements were made overseas, and because of that we had to get on the plane as planned. The lady looked at me, saw the tears in my eyes and felt sorry for me. She took me into the back room and said, "I could be fired over this, but I will show you how to put all the forms together. They have to be in exact order or they will not be accepted in Chicago. I also will give you my stapler, since you can't use a regular stapler, and then you have to seal the big yellow envelope." I can't remember that lady's name, but I will be grateful to her as long as I live. "Thank you so much. You made Henry's last wish become a reality."

We went back to Lotti's house and had a bite to eat. At 6:30 p.m. we got a call from the Mosinee airport that the envelope for Brenda Gross just arrived. Reto and Larry made that 30-minute drive to pick it up. This time it was the right one. I put everything together just as that lady showed me. By then it was time to pick up Henry's ashes, plus, I had to go home and pack my suitcase.

Reto, Larry and I went alone, since Lotti and Brenda had to pack and get ready for our long trip. All three of us walked into the Peterson Funeral Home, not knowing what to expect. A man dressed in a dark suit greeted us, and we told him what we were there for. He went to the back room and then came back with a small box in his hand. It looked just like a shoe box, and he handed it to Larry. Larry didn't any more than get it in his hands when he started screaming hysterically, "That's my father-in-law. No, this is not Henry. What did they do to him?"

He handed the box to Reto. Reto could not say a word, he just stood there looking at the box in his hands and the tears were rolling silently down his cheeks, but he was like froze. I took the box out of his hands and understood in seconds what their problem was. The box was warm, and so Henry's ashes. It hit me, "What did I do? How could I do that to him? Now I really killed him. How could I do that?"

I did not say one word. My eyes filled with tears and my heart pounded like crazy. I took the box and walked back to the van. I still had the flowers in there, so I took that box and put it between the flower arrangements. That made me feel a little bit better.

None of us three said one word as we drove the 25 miles to Merrill. What could I do? I can't leave the box like this and take it on the plane. What could I do? As we got off the freeway and drove into Merrill, I told Reto to stop at the Wal-Mart Store. "I have to buy something," I said.

I went into the store and straight to the cosmetic cases. I found a nice blue one (Henry's favorite color). Yes, that looked just like a little suitcase. As I paid for it, the clerk said, "I got one of those, too, and I really like it. You can put a lot of things in it." I gave her a smile, since cosmetics was the last thing I had on my mind.

Back in the van I took the tray out and ripped the mirror off, then put the box with Henry's ashes into it. I took the ribbon — My Husband, Our Dad and Our Grandpa — and put it on top of the box, covering the box up. I broke off some carnations and laid them on each side of the box. Yes, that looked better. Now it was Henry's little casket.

On we went to my house. I packed my suitcase. Larry was still in shock, and there was not much said as we drove back to Lotti's house. We put all the suitcases in the van and got ready to leave around midnight.

It is about a five-hour drive to Chicago. I did not care if we got everything, but I did not let the four yellow envelopes, the plane tickets and the little blue cosmetic case out of my sight.

Reto volunteered to drive. I sat beside him so that I could talk to him and make sure he would not fall asleep. Brenda, Lotti and Larry made themselves comfortable in the back seats, and it did not take long and they dozed off. There was not much traffic that night and we made it past Madison and into Illinois when we heard a strange noise coming from the motor. Reto stopped the van. We took the flashlight to investigate, but we could not find anything wrong, so off we went again. It kept hammering for about 20 more miles, then all of a sudden it quit, but now we lost power. The van drove okay, but we could not drive faster than 50 miles an hour anymore, but every mile was one mile closer to Chicago.

A friend of ours, Frank Stauber, lives in Merrill but works in Chicago, and he volunteered to help us and show us where we could get the passports. He told us to call him as soon as we got through the last tollbooth.

Reto said, "Right over there is a telephone booth." But as we drove over to the telephone, a squad car turned his red lights on right behind us. What could be wrong now? We sure could not speed.

Reto and I got out to see what it was he did wrong. The policeman said, "You will not drive this van another mile. You left an oily trail behind you for miles, and rush hour will start in about 30 minutes. With you spraying everybody behind you with oil, we could have chaos and accident after accident." Now we knew what the noise was. The turbocharger blew.

I started crying, "How much more can go wrong?"

Reto told the policeman what happened, and where we were headed. The policeman called Frank and then said, "You have only four more miles to go, and because of those special circumstances I will let you drive the four miles. But I will escort you and make sure you get to your final destination without any more problems."

I do not know that policeman's name either, but he sure was sent from heaven. And I'm so thankful that he was so understanding.

Frank waited for us, and since it was only 5:30 a.m., took us to a restaurant to have breakfast. He worked at a salvage yard in Franklin Heights and was so eager to help us that he asked his boss for a couple of hours off. He did not know what he had gotten himself into.

Our van could not be driven anymore, so Frank volunteered to drive with his car. At 7:30 a.m. he told us that it was time to leave. "Make sure that each of you has their yellow envelope so that you can get your passport," I reminded them. And off they went, leaving me behind to guard the van and our luggage. It was not the best part of town, and I was scared. I locked the doors, but the wind was strong and rattled the loose metal on the junk cars and buses all around me. I saw two groggy-looking guys come out of an old bus in the next row. They must have slept in there. And here I sat, all by myself, with the ashes from my husband.

I brought something to read along, but I did not feel like reading. My hands would glide over and over again over that blue casket, my tears slowly running down my cheeks and dripping onto the cover. And, like a movie I saw, our life together passed in front of my eyes. What a lonely, lonely feeling that was!

It was almost 10 a.m. when someone knocked on my

door. I was scared, lifted the curtain just a little and saw it was Frank, but where were my kids? As I let Frank into the van, he looked at me and said, "When it rains it pours."

"What is it," I asked.

"The kids have all their papers, but they also have to have their airline tickets or they won't be able to get their passports on such short notice," he said, and then continued, "they were told that it was very likely they won't get them anymore today."

"But they have to. Our plane leaves at seven tonight and I can't go alone," was my reply.

He took the tickets. "It takes me three-quarters of an hour, if I speed, to get to the other side of Chicago where I left your children. They close the federal office at noon for their lunch hour, but I will do my best," and off he went, leaving me behind.

Here I sat, lonely and all by myself again, looking at that little casket, and I prayed. My tears were rolling, and I did not know how much more I could take.

It was Thursday already, and I had not had any sleep for the last 30 hours. It was so lonely and those hours went so slowly, it seemed the hands on my watch hardly moved at all. It was a little after three when I could hear some familiar voices. My children were finally back, but did they have their passports?

I quickly opened the door. They stormed in, gave me a hug and said, "Ma, we did it! We did it!" and then went on telling me that when Frank came back with the tickets, the clerk said, "No way can you get the passports today. You have to wait until tomorrow."

Lotti started crying and told her, "My mother is waiting for us on the other side of Chicago. She sits there all by herself with her husband's ashes. The funeral arrangements are made overseas, and then all of us have jobs and can only take one more week off to take care of all of this, so please help us. We have to fly out tonight."

The clerk was shook up and promised to do her best. "But we are closed from noon till 1:30 p.m., so stick around. We'll see what we can do," the clerk said.

They went on telling me that Frank went back to his job and told them to call him as soon as they're ready. Since they had no car, they went outside the federal building and waited. The wind was so strong it blew gravel into their hair. But no matter how bad they felt, they had to laugh. Just a little bit down the road from them was a portable potty. A guy sat on it when it blew over, but he just pulled his pants up as if nothing happened and went his merry way.

By now it was 1:30 p.m. and time to go back into the federal building. They called name after name off and one by one left, but their passports were not included. The clerk said, "This is it until tomorrow."

My kids were stunned and just looked at each other when another clerk walked in and said, "Wait. We have four last-minute passports here. They are for Brenda Gross, Reto Gross, Lotti Hess and Larry Hess."

Thank God, they made it. And all I would like to say is a big thank you to that clerk who cared enough to make this possible.

"We have been up since yesterday morning and only had time to change clothes, so let's go and take a shower before we go to the airport," I said. And they all agreed.

We could use Frank's car, went to a nearby motel and I rented a motel room for $40, even though we only used it for a little over one hour. We all took a shower and changed clothes, then grabbed a bite to eat at a nearby restaurant and off to the airport we went.

I would not let that little casket out of my hand. If nothing else, that had to be with me.

We went through check-in and boarded the plane. What a sigh of relief! I finally could quit worrying, at least for a couple of hours.

It takes eight and a half to nine hours, non-stop, to get to Zurich. I made myself as comfortable as possible and put the little casket under the seat. It is a long flight, and we were flying through the night, so maybe I could take a nap. I closed my eyes, but could not sleep. People all around me were talking about vacation and all kinds of fun things they had planned, but no one knew what I had under my seat.

There were the ashes of someone I loved and shared 32 years of my life with. It was Henry's wish to go back and he used to say that is the easiest way, but I know different now. I would never, ever put someone through as much as we had to go through the last five days, and more to come.

My eyes closed, my tears running slowly down my cheeks, and I saw once again my last 32 years pass by me.

Swiss time is seven hours ahead of Chicago time. It was 7 a.m. European time. They brought us breakfast and announced that in about two hours we will arrive in Zurich. It was Friday morning, March 16, 1990. Twenty-two years ago on March 18, 1968, we left Switzerland and emigrated to the United States, and now, exactly 22 years later, I am bringing Henry's ashes home and laying him to rest in his beloved Valley Toggenburg, by the church where he got confirmed. What a tough job to do!

Edith and Heinz were waiting for us at the airport, and in their eyes I could see how sad and scared they were. They still could not believe what happened and how to react.

We had no problem going through customs. They guy at the passport control, seeing that I was originally a Swiss citizen, said, "Welcome home."

I replied, "Thank you," but thought to myself, what a welcome. As Edith hugged me, Reto asked, "Do you have Dad?" For Edith and Heinz to hear that was like a cold shower, but we were so tired we could not even think straight anymore.

We stored our suitcases away, but I kept Henry's little casket on my lap, knowing well that that would be the last time I had him so close.

My mother waited at her apartment. We picked her up on the way through, and then went on to Edith's house. It had been hard for everyone. No one knew what to say or what to do. They all were worried that I would fall to pieces. But I knew it had to be done, and just went through the motions, but it was not easy.

After lunch we had to go to the courthouse, give them the box with the ashes and the death certificate. Edith, Heinz, Lotti, Reto and I went there, but before, I stopped at the flower shop and bought six fresh carnations to put on Henry's box with the ashes. The ribbons were still nice. Edith gave me a 5" x 8" picture of Henry, and we glued it where the mirror used to be. The clerk took us into her office, gave us each a chair, and then said, "I have to open that box in front of you as witnesses. Inside should be another box."

"Please no," I said, and explained what we went through at the funeral home. I told her, "I can never look at that plain box again, and I do not want to see you open it." I also asked her if she would have a nicer container to put the ashes in. When my dad passed away, he had a clay pot that looked like a vase.

She understood my pain and asked Heinz and Reto to go with her into the next room to open the box. When they returned, she explained, "That box looked that way because it had to be sealed by the funeral director. When I opened that box, there had to be a duplicate of the death certificate inside or you would not be able to bury Henry here. That is the only way to make it official."

And on she went. "I won't give you anything different for the ashes. It would only cost you money and your little casket is prettier than anything I ever saw before, so do not change it."

That made me feel a little bit better. We then had to take the casket and the authorized death certificate to the undertaker.

On the way back we had to stop at the minister's house. He was so helpful, too, and said since some of the guests did not speak German he would have part of the sermon in English. He said, "My English is not too good, but I will try."

It is unbelievable how many people touch one's life in such a short time, and how helpful everyone is.

It was supper time when we returned to Edith's, and I was drained. Sixty hours without sleep, and all that turmoil could make anybody tired. Brenda and Reto stayed at Edith's. My mother and I shared a room at Heinz's. Lotti and Larry got a room downstairs in Heinz's apartment building, a room that other renters gave voluntarily to Heinz. How nice and helpful everyone was.

It was good for my mother to be close to me, and she was glad to be there for her daughter when she needed her most.

We had a lot of things to do on Saturday. Flowers had to be ordered, and since my stay in Switzerland was short, the gravestone had to be picked out. I found a nice rugged stone that came from a nearby mountain. I had them carve Henry's name and favorite mountains, the "Churfirsten," and a little mountain house on it. The guy drew us a picture, and I thought it looked real nice. He told us that it would take about one year for the ground to settle, but promised to have if there by next Easter.

Henry thought it would be so much cheaper to get buried in Switzerland, but times there have changed, too. Most head stones were $5,000 and higher, but the one I picked was used once before and now ground down so the cost was only $2,700.

A grave in Switzerland is only used by one for 25 years. After that, the stone is removed and someone else will be buried at the same place. No one gets embalmed. In Switzerland one gets either plain buried, or cremated.

From there we stopped at the "Traube," a nearby restaurant. The meal had to be ordered for all the friends that would be with us for the last goodbye. Then we went back to Heinz's. It was Saturday evening by now, everything taken care of and I could finally relax.

Sunday we took it easy, went to church in the morning, and in the afternoon for a walk, just my daughter-in-law Judith, my mother and I. I could talk, and they just listened, and that felt so good.

Reto was six years old when we left Switzerland, and he was the only one who never went back for a visit, so Heinz took Brenda, Reto, Lotti and Larry, and drove them up to the mountain where Henry took care of his Grandpa's cows as a youngster, and where he was with hundreds of sheep when he was 17-18 years old. Heinz knew how his dad felt about his beloved mountains and wanted to make them understand why all of that was so important to their dad.

Monday morning the first guests came to say hi. The funeral was set for one o'clock. It was late morning when we heard some tires squishing. Heinz ran downstairs to see what happened, since just a short while before he let his dog out. The dog never had run into the road before, but today he did, and got run over by a car, that then just took off.

The dog was still alive. Heinz picked him up, put him into the car and drove him to the veterinarian, but there was nothing that could be done for him anymore, so they gave him a shot to get him out of his misery. It was hard for Heinz to tell his son Patrick that there would be two funerals today, one for Grandpa and one for his favorite dog. But Patrick just looked at Heinz and answered, "Grandpa did not want to go alone to wherever he is going, so he took my dog along. I can understand that."

Children make things a lot of times look a lot simpler than we as adults could ever do.

We all gathered at the cemetery where the little blue casket was at Henry's grave site. It was open, the ribbons, "My Husband, Our Dad, Our Grandpa" still there and fresh carnations on each side. The picture with his smiling face was surrounded by the white cloth that covered the top of the cosmetic box, and lots of flowers all around the casket. It looked really lovely.

The minister prayed with us, and from there we went into the church where the minister, who never knew Henry, had the sermon. He did a good job, and like promised, spoke in English. Every stranger who touched my life the last eight days went out of his or her way to help me, and I'm so thankful for that.

Even though we were gone for so many years, I always kept in contact through Christmas letters, and because of that we still had a lot of friends in our homeland. Henry went to a one-room school, so some of his classmates came to say their last goodbye. His brother Walter and sister Rosemarie and their families came; the only one who did not come was his oldest sister, Beth, the one who had not talked to Henry since 1973 when he was at his mother's funeral.

Henry's aunts and uncles were there, and then his friends that were confirmed with him. Some of the mountain climber colleagues came to pay their last respect. Not to forget that Walter, my best friend from my teen years, and his mother were present to morally support me, and also my godmother, my aunt and cousins.

All in all, I had over 80 people for supper at the nearby restaurant after church. It really made me feel good, after being gone for 22 years, that so many friends still remembered us. Isn't that what life is all about, to be with friends, especially in the tough hours?

But it was expensive. The meal cost me over $1,000.

Then the obituary and then the thank-you afterwards in the local paper was another $800. All in all, it was a lot more than Henry ever imagined. But I told the children, "If your dad and I would have gotten divorced, he would have gotten half of all our possessions. Now he took more than half along."

Yes, it was expensive, and I would never have anybody go through so much trouble for me, but I had to do it for Henry. It was his wish, and I can live with myself knowing that he is where he wanted to be, in the valley where he grew up, surrounded by his beloved mountains. He had a little smile on his face when he was shown the night of the wake. I think it had to be because he knew he finally could go back home, this time forever.

For me, it was another long, tough day. The guests slowly, one-by-one, said goodbye, and I could go back to Heinz's apartment and relax. We talked long into the night, but we had to. There was so little time left, and so much to be said.

We did not go home to enjoy ourselves. It was a sad reunion, but now that we were here we had to make the best out of it. So Tuesday morning I invited all my kids and in-laws to come on a trip with me.

Edith and Heinz took their cars. We went to Weite Wartau and stopped by the store where we lived just before we left Switzerland. Now it is made into an electric shop. Our old neighbors, Mr. and Mrs. Zogg, still lived there and we had a cup of coffee with them and reminisced for awhile.

Then we went on to Sargans where we boarded the train that took us to Chur where Reto was in the hospital when he had the stroke. We changed trains and drove on through the beautiful valleys over one of the highest viaducts in the world, and between the rugged mountains we loved so much.

The next stop was Bergun. We walked past the store where we once were such a happy family, stopped by

Priesig's, the local bakery, to say hi, then went past the schoolhouse and up the hill to the church where my children went to Sunday school. I think it was just as hard on my children as it was on me to look back through all those years.

Down that cobblestone street we walked where Edith, Heinz, Lotti and Reto once played with their friends. Boy, where did the years go?

We went to the restaurant "Piz Aela" to have lunch and old-fashioned "Bunthner" meal. Even there were some people who still knew us and came by to say hi and wanted to know how we were doing. It is unbelievable how many lives one touches as we walk the rugged road of life.

But enough of my reminiscing. It is time to go on. We walked back to the train station and boarded the next train going to St. Moritz. That is the most beautiful ride that one can take.

As we slowly left the train station, standing at the window we could see some cows looking for the first grass in the meadow. A farmer tried to spread some manure. Yes, life here goes on as usual, but how will the future be for me? I had to swallow some tears, since I truly loved this piece of land. I had some of my happiest hours here. Those days will always have a special place in my heart.

It is too steep for the train to go straight up over the Albula Pass, it has to make three loops, and every time you get out of the tunnel, you see Bergun from a little different angle. It is just so beautiful, that little town nestled between the huge, snow-covered mountains.

We passed the little lake called "Poponia See" where Henry and I sat for many hours holding hands. But gone are those good old days.

The train slowly climbed all the way to the top, and now we could see the ever so gorgeous Engadien Valley and our final destination, St. Moritz. We walked through town along the famous lake where they wind-surf on ice.

Big, fancy hotels are everywhere. The crown prince of England and monarchs from all over the world spend their vacation here. It is beautiful: mountain after mountain as far as your eye can see. But it was soon time to go back. One more time we went over the Albula Pass, and one more goodbye to my beloved little town Bergun. I will never forget your charm.

In Filisur we switched trains and took a detour to see Davos where we went to so many hockey games. From there it went to Chur and back to Sargans where we left the cars. It took us just a little over one hour and we were back home where Judith, Martin and my mother had supper ready for us.

Wednesday went fast. We had to pack and see to it that everything was taken care of. One last time I walked up to the cemetery to say goodbye to Henry. I sat on that small bench for awhile and watched the bumblebees take nourishment out of the flowers that covered his grave.

I guess that is our journey, just as it says in the Bible, "From ashes to ashes." I sure hope I did everything the way Henry would have wanted it.

As I was daydreaming, I could hear Henry say:

When I left my sweet homeland
So many, many years ago,
Oh how could I have known then,
That I will miss it so!

Henry, I sure hope you finally found your freedom.

****

It was hard to leave all of this behind, but I have a job to go to. And Henry had only $2,000 of life insurance. The total bill for the funeral was over $13,000, so I have to keep on working.

I'm 51 years old, now gone for 22 years. No one in Switzerland would give me a manager's job like I have in the States. The apartments here are so high, furniture and everything so expensive. I have no choice; I have to go back to the States.

It is even harder with two of my children and their families living in Switzerland and two in the States, so no matter where I live, we are far apart.

Edith, Martin and their children, Jessica, Heidi and Martin Junior, and then also Heinz, Judith and their son Patrick came to the airport, and so did my mother. It was a very tough goodbye for everyone involved, but it had to be.

I leaned back in my seat and reminisced for one more time as the plane lifted off the ground and made a big loop over the mountains, and then left Switzerland behind. My worries aren't over yet. Reto and Brenda have to get back to Nevada on Friday, but they fly out of Mosinee, yet how do we get there? Did Frank find someone to fix my van?

We made it safely back to Chicago, and Frank waited for us at the airport. But he told us that no one would touch that van. It is a small Winnebago with a four-cylinder diesel, a Renault engine that no one understands. "You have to go to a specialist to have it fixed," he said, "but you can leave it at the salvage yard until you know what to do with it."

I know Henry could have fixed it. He took it apart once before, but he is gone, and now what? We had to go home so the kids could get back to work before they lose their jobs. What else was there to do than to rent a big car that would bring us, plus our luggage, back to Wisconsin. Another $180, but it had to be done.

It was almost nine o'clock by the time we left Chicago and way past midnight when we arrived in Wausau at Lotti's house. We all spent the night there. Brenda and Reto got ready the next morning to fly back to Nevada, and Lotti and I had to take our rental car to Appleton. Tired from all the tension and traveling, I spent one more night at Lotti's.

19

IT IS SATURDAY morning, almost two weeks since Henry passed away, and it is time to face my future by myself. Lotti and Larry drove me to my house and stayed awhile.

My neighbors took care of my two dogs, "Trixi," a pure-bred "Appenzeller" dog from Switzerland (she was Henry's favorite), and then the little one I got from Bobbi Jo as we visited them when they still lived in Texas. His name was "Maxli." They both showed me how happy they were to have me back.

We always had dogs on the farm but never could one be in the house, but now I needed them. Little Maxli could even sleep in bed with me, the same bed where Henry and I spent our last hours together.

Yes, I changed the sheets, but it was still very hard for me. With Maxli beside me, at least I could hear someone breathing, and even though it was only a dog, it made me feel a little safer, since that first night by myself was a long and lonely one, and many of those nights followed. It is very hard after 32 years of marriage to suddenly be alone. This is the very first time in my entire life that I have lived alone. It scares me, but I know I will make it.

On Sunday I cleaned the house, did the laundry and just kept myself busy. Even though Larry and Phil, my bosses, told me not to worry about losing my job if I stayed away for awhile ... "Take all the time you need before you get back to work," they said ... but I thought that work might be my best therapy. I love my job and love to be with people, and being in the store does not give me the time to feel sorry for myself. Life goes on, and we all have to make the best out of it.

It was hard for everybody involved in the beginning. My customers didn't know, either, how to react. But it did not take long and everybody got over it. It is really amazing; most of us think that the job, our earthly possessions, how the neighbors think of us, all are so important. Then one day we are gone forever, and the world goes on as it always did, and it only takes a short couple of months and you're forgotten. If we could just take more time to show love and have time for each other instead of rushing through life, reaching for something we can never have.

My emotions were like roller-coasters. One day I was sad, the next day I was mad that Henry just went off and left me with all my problems. I had a lot of frustration to get out of my system.

Henry bought nine cords of pulp wood the fall of 1989, but never sawed one log until the Saturday before he passed away. I needed that wood to heat my house next winter, and it had to be cut and dried first.

One evening, as I was kind of angry at Henry for just letting me sit here, I went out to the garage, took the chain saw and tried to start it up, since I needed to cut some of the logs. I took the chain saw, checked the oil and filled the gas, pushed the little starting lever, then I tugged on the cord. But in no time, the saw went one direction and I went the other, falling on my butt. I just could not get that thing going. Henry always said there is no such thing as "I can't," but I just couldn't, so I asked Hoffmans, great neighbors of mine, if they would come and help me.

The following Saturday they brought some of their kids and some friends, and by evening the wood was cut. All it cost me was a case of beer. A big thank you for all your help. That was a great job.

Yes, the wood had to be split yet, but I still had the Allis Chalmers tractor and a wood-splitter. So, whenever I felt like it, I split wood all by myself. Sometimes I went to bed early but could not sleep. Then I got up again, got my tractor going and split wood for awhile. That got the frustration out of my system.

Other days I took the wheelbarrow, put split wood in it, wheeled it over to the basement window and threw it down the chute. With every piece I threw in, I said, "Henry, how could you leave me here all alone? That was not fair. It was your dream to come to the United States and farm, and now you just let me sit here."

That always helped. After an hour or two of hard work, I got it out of my system and did not feel that bad anymore.

But it was not just the wood. The Winnebago van was still in Chicago and had to be fixed yet. I knew Henry could have done it, but I sure couldn't. Fritz Hilfiker, a countryman and good mechanic, volunteered to help me. He ordered a rebuilt turbocharger for me, but you can't get one under $750 either. Then one day, middle of April, Fritz and I drove to Chicago and fixed it right there. It was a windy, cold day and we had to work outside. We tried gloves, but that did not work that well, plus Fritz did not even know if that turbocharger was the right one.

A good thing he knew what he was doing; I sure didn't. I could only hand him tools or screws, or get into tight places to put a nut on. Boy, it was cold, and I thought more than once about just leaving it there for whoever wanted it. It was around 5 p.m. when everything was back together. Fritz tried it, and it ran. Thank God, since we had a five-hour drive ahead of us.

We went to warm up and eat supper in a nearby restaurant, and then started our long journey back. I drove my car and Fritz drove the van. It was past midnight when we drove into my yard, and I was glad to be home. If it had not been for Fritz, I could never have done it.

Julius' daughter, Patty, got married end of April. Erika's parents and Julius' brother came all the way from Switzerland for that big day. Patty asked me around

Christmastime already if I would translate the sermon so that her grandparents, uncles and aunts would understand what the minister was saying. I kept my promise, since it was an honor for me to have been the one who could do something for the family that gave so much already to me.

It was a lovely day. After supper I was even asked to dance a couple of polkas, and it felt good. But when I walked out of the dance hall later that night and drove home, it was like someone hit me with a brick, and all I could do was let my tears free flow. That is how it's going to be from now on. No matter how happy the party is, I will go home alone to an empty house and a lonely, empty bed. That will be the hardest single thing for me to overcome.

There was something else I had to take care of. We bought our first new riding lawnmower in January but it was still in the crate, just the way Henry brought it home. It was time to mow my lawn, so I had to tackle that job. But it was not assembled, had no seat, the battery was not hooked up, nor did the battery have battery fluid. A couple hours later I had some scratches on my hands, since I slipped up with my wrench now and then, but my lawnmower was running, and I was proud of my achievement. Boy, what a person can do if they put their mind to it.

Henry had a lot of tools. He could have opened his own garage, but then he always fixed everything himself. He also had an old Jeep and the tractor that I did not really need anymore. I connected with a woman who had a farm but recently lost her husband. She was going to have an auction. I decided to bring everything I did not need anymore to her place to be sold at her auction, also.

Dennis and Mary came for days and helped me get all those things ready. They put tags on everything — what size drill, how long the chain, or how many horsepower on that motor. They also came along to the auction for moral support. I was so grateful to them. They did a super job.

But what really hurt was when I later was asked if Dennis tried to get close to me now that I'm "free game." What a way to put it. Aren't I an adult with a mind of my own? Dennis never even made a nasty remark, let alone tried something. And if he would have, I would have put him in his place. Mary and Dennis were for many years already my friends. How can I be called "free game" now that I lost my husband? But I talked to other widows and they had similar experiences, that best friends turned against them because they were afraid they would take their husbands away from them. So as a widow, a lot of times you do not just lose your spouse, you also lose your friends, and that at a time when you need them most hurts just as much.

I drove a lot to Wausau to see Lotti, since she was the only one of my children I could go to. I also kept on seeing Dr. Elmergreen. He tried to help me get through that rough time in my life and make me see the future in a different light. He heard so much from Henry in the two one-hour sessions he spent with him that he felt I needed to love me as me, and not always just live for someone else.

One time he put an empty chair by my side. "Close your eyes," he said, "and now imagine Henry sitting there. Tell him how much he hurt you through all those years. Yell at him, if it helps you."

I closed my eyes, but instead of talking to Henry, I cried. I could not be mad for long, and never yelled at Henry when he was alive, and now that he was gone, I felt so sorry for him. I truly loved Henry, and even though life was hard and not always fair, we had our good times, too.

I don't think I really mourned the first months. I kept my feelings hidden, something I was taught from little on. It helps me cope with life if I just do not think of my troubles, since then it won't hurt so much.

And Henry also still pulled the strings. One day after work I drove to the Dairy Queen to get an ice cream cone. I parked my car, got out and walked up to the counter, but then turned around without buying an ice cream and drove away. I could hear Henry say, "You're too fat the way it is, how come you eat those kinds of things?" and that made me leave.

I used to be around 130 pounds, but since we quit farming and I turned 50 my weight slowly went up to 165 pounds. Almost daily Henry told me, "You're getting too fat, and you get wrinkles. Do something about it." But after more than 30 years of marriage, the inside should count for more than the outside. And we all get older, and it will show in every one of us.

Another thing that really bothered me was driving to work early in the morning. I drove one mile south on E, and then east on Highway 64. If I looked straight ahead into the sky there was that big star that seemed to follow me all the way into town. So often I asked, "Henry, can't you leave me alone? How come you still have to watch my every move?"

It was not Henry that made me think that way, it was my grandson Tyler. About six months after he lost his baby sister Cassy they moved to a different town in Texas. Tyler was six years old at that time. It was late one evening when they got their old apartment cleaned and drove slowly towards their new home. Tyler was quiet for a while, and then said to Lotti, "Mommy, do you see that big star up there in the sky?"

Lotti answered, "Yes, what about it?"

"That is Cassy smiling. She is happy that we took her toys along, too," he replied.

What a painful feeling for such a small child. Now, two years later, I see the two stars, a big and a small one, close together. One had to be Henry, and beside him, little Cassy. It felt like he was watching every move I make. But I know I have to overcome that pain.

I learned years later that I can no longer pretend things don't hurt me, since that is living a lie. And as long as I do not face up to it, I cannot live life to its fullest.

The days got longer and the sun warmer. I could sit outside and read a book or do yard work, and that gave a good balance between work and pleasure.

I had company from Switzerland over the 4th of July. Hans Ueli, who worked for us on the farm in 1976, took two days out of his busy schedule and came to see me. That was really nice, and we could reminisce for awhile. It is great that someone like Hans Ueli, who only worked for us for four months, will never forget the time he spent with us.

Tom, who was our milkman almost all the years we farmed, stopped at the store at least twice a week. He came to get coffee and something to munch on, and then asked how I was doing. "It's very lonely," I answered.

He replied, "I feel the same way, but because of different circumstances."

I knew that he got divorced in the early '80s, but I did not know if he was remarried. He came around more and more often, even took me out to lunch. It made me feel good. Here I'm over 50 years old, fatter than I used to be and wrinkled, and there is still a guy interested in me. He took me to the plant's Christmas party, he opened the door for me, gave me compliments, and I was flattered. I still was kind of skeptical, because he didn't want his children to know about us; yet I had nothing to hide.

Then on New Year's Day, his whole family had a get-together at his farm. Since his farm is over 100 years in his family, they all liked to come home where they were raised. This time he wanted me to be there and to get to know his brother Ed and sisters, Mary Ann and Angi (Angi is my age), and their families. I was scared to meet them, not knowing if they would accept me, but it went better than I thought.

Tom and I started dating openly. I made a lot of miles to his house, and we even talked of maybe getting married sometime down the road. But that is not easy at our age, especially with the new Marital Property Reform Law Wisconsin adopted. Even though I testified against that law, it got through and now is a lawyer's nightmare.

Tom had his own business for 35 years already, and worked very hard to get where he is now. Plus, he lived on that farm all his life, had his shop there and could not move. On the other hand, it still bothers me to sleep in the same room where Henry passed away. Every time I walked into the bedroom, he was always there. So we decided I would move to Tom's house, but for right now not to get married. I felt it would not be right if he should pass away I could get half of his business. He worked hard all his life, and so it should go to his children. And, on the other hand, the little I have should go to mine.

It is easy to say we just moved together, which we did, but somehow it bothered me from day one on. For me it was a commitment when I moved into Tom's house. For me, it wasn't any different than if I had a marriage certificate. But there is no security, and it will never be our home. It will always be "HIS" home.

I kept working at the Auto Stop in Merrill, but now it was a 33-mile drive. I still opened the store at 5 a.m. I had to leave Tom's house at 4:15 a.m. And when I got home there was the normal household chores that had to be done: cleaning, washing, cooking. Tom's four beef cows and their calves had to be taken care of, and I loved every minute of it. If the cows were across the river, I would just holler for them and they would come, one by one. Yes, I loved the farm life.

There was lawn that had to be mowed, and lots of lawn,

about two acres of it. Tom has a beautiful place, 120 acres right on the Eau Claire River. He bought me a fishing rod one day. I got a fishing license and caught myself a trout the first time I went fishing. Tom sure knew how to cook those trout and made a great supper.

My co-manager and I worked great together as long as I lived in Merrill, but now that I had such a long drive, she played her cards to the fullest. There was always something. "I just looked at a different job, and they would give me health insurance," she said. So I talked to my boss and got her what she wanted. But it did not stop. I got her a wage increase, gave her half of my bonus, but nothing was good enough. Yet, I felt I was in love again, and did not want to sacrifice Tom for my job. So I looked around and found a manager's job at the Weinbrenner Shoe Store in Antigo, only eight miles from Tom's. Plus, I did not have to open the store until 9 a.m.

I wrote Larry a letter telling him that I appreciated working for them, but I found love again and also would like to take it easier. Larry understood and answered with a really nice goodbye letter.

It was on Thursday, August 22, 1991, when I unpacked the big weekly order. Vendors came to say goodbye and give me a hug. They said, "This store will never be the same." It made me feel good to be respected, and on the other hand, it hurt so bad to leave my store. But Pam would not say one word all morning. She just ignored me, and even though I had three more days on my job, she rearranged the office and everything already. She was now the manager.

Henry helped me a lot to get this store where it was, even though he was not an employee. He stocked shelves, fixed pumps for me and helped wherever he could. Letting this job go was the last tie I had to break, and it was hard.

My tears were slowly running down my cheeks as I stored away item after item. It was around eleven o'clock, and I was almost done when I just couldn't anymore. I walked into the store, handed Pam the keys and said, "I sure hope that brings you luck," then went into my car and drove off. It was hard to see with tears in my eyes, but I didn't care anymore where I was going. I felt so lonely.

I slowly drove through town. I passed the place on Highway 64 where Henry and I sat in April 1968, when we thought we lost everything. But there was no longer a bench, so I drove for a couple more miles and then drove into the woods, and just let my tears free flow.

Oh, how I missed Henry! Yes, I was in love with Tom now, but there was no tie. Henry was my husband, and we had four beautiful children together, something Tom and I will never have, and I think deep down I had doubts that it would work out.

Hours passed until I got hold of myself and dried my tears. It was Tom's birthday today, and I invited his siblings to celebrate with us, so I had better get going or I wouldn't be done when the guests arrived. I started my car up and slowly drove out of the woods, hopefully leaving my loneliness behind forever.

Tom did not have to drive truck that day and made fence for the cows. He was so busy that he could not see my pain, and I was glad.

It was Thanksgiving week, and Lotti wanted to drive to Texas to get Cassy's grave ready for the Christmas season. They asked if they could use my Winnebago, and I said yes, of course. That way it was easier for them to travel with two kids, or so I thought. Yet they only made it into Iowa when the alternator went out. I got a collect call: "Mom, what should we do?"

The mechanic told them they could get one from Forest City where the Winnebago headquarters are, but it would cost me $600-$700. Or he could try to use one from another motor that would bring the cost down to $250. Then I guess that was the way to go.

But now they had to stay overnight and they had no money, so I wired them $200 and charged the alternator on my credit card. "Please call me when you get to Texas," I told them.

The next night I got a collect call again. They made it into Oklahoma, but now the fan belt broke and they had to be towed again. Boy, how much more can go wrong with that stupid van? Thank God, the next day they made it all the way to Texas.

Saturday morning they called and told me, "The Winnebago runs good now and we are heading for home and should be back early Sunday afternoon." What a relief! But then Sunday morning I got a collect call again. They just drove into Minnesota when they broke down again and had to be towed one more time. The mechanic at the truck stop told them that they had to wait their turn, since it was very, very cold. A lot of semis had troubles and froze up and they would come first. For me, it was like sitting on needles. What if they can't fix it? Larry and Lotti had to go to work the next day.

At 4 p.m. Lotti called again and told me that they thought the head gasket blew, but they could not get one until at least the next day and would not get it fixed until Thursday. What now?

"I will come and get you," I said, and hung up.

I got some warm clothes and some blankets for the kids, and off I went. I had to drive all the way to Austin, Minnesota, over 300 miles. There was not too much traffic, it was so cold and the roads were icy. No one would even let a dog outside, let alone me.

It was almost 11 p.m. when I got there. We grabbed a bite to eat and then drove right back. I unloaded them at their house in Wausau. It was 6 a.m. when I got home, and at 9 a.m. I had to be at work. What a tough day that was! I could have slept standing up.

The Winnebago did not get fixed, and two weeks later

Lotti and Larry went with a U-Haul trailer and towed it back home. But no one here knew how to fix it either. All it did was cost me money. Several guys told me they knew what was wrong. I paid them another $300-$400 and it still wasn't fixed. So, after spending all that money, I ended up selling it years later for $300.

I never drove the Winnebago as long as Henry was alive. It was his baby. And now I felt he says, "This is my vehicle, and no one else can drive it." I was glad to get the Winnebago out of my hair, and I never, ever, no, never again want to get another collect call. That was enough to drive one crazy.

Larry, my son-in-law, lost his job, and they no longer could make the payment for their house in Wausau. When they lived in Texas, Larry had an alcohol problem, and those years said it was because he was homesick. If he could live in Wisconsin, by his friends, go hunting and fishing again, he would quit drinking. But now they lived here and it got worse, not better. He even threatened Lotti, shot in her car tires with the gun and got arrested for it. Lotti admitted him to the Health Care Center to get help, and she went to counseling. It was better for awhile, but then got worse again.

Larry had for the first time in his life a brand-new pickup truck, but in no time banged it all up. I was so scared that he would kill Lotti some day, but there was nothing I could do about it. If Lotti and I talked about it, she always said, "Ma, you did not leave Dad when he was ill, and alcoholism is an illness, too. If I help Larry, he will get over it."

Now Larry no longer had a job. My house was almost empty, and some of my furniture were still there, so I gave them my house to live in and hoped that would help them to get back on their feet. Lotti took a job and tried her best to support their family. If I heard on the radio that an accident happened or someone had gotten beaten in

Merrill, Lotti was always the first thing on my mind. Larry was the nicest guy when he was sober, but watch out after a couple of beers.

One day Larry beat Lotti's head against the car so badly that Tyler, their 10-year-old son, took the .22 cal. gun and shot into the air to get his dad scared. He was afraid that Larry would kill Lotti. That was when Lotti knew she had to do something.

She also said Larry would never go with another woman, but he did that, too, and got that woman pregnant. So Lotti filed for divorce. A good thing Lotti and the kids could live in my house. At least they had a roof over their heads, since Larry did not support them at all. His theme was, "Your mother works, she can support you."

Lotti also still suffered from losing her baby girl. I guess that is something a mother never gets over. There Cassy was, buried in Texas, 1,200 miles away, and no way for Lotti to go to her grave, a place where she could feel close to Cassy.

That Christmas I said to Lotti, "My Christmas gift to you is bringing Cassy home. I will buy two lots at a cemetery out in the country on Highway 107, one lot for Cassy and one lot for me," I said. "Through this I make sure I will never be forgotten. When you visit the grave of your baby girl, then if you want to or not, you have to come and see me, too," I said.

I really did not do it for that reason. I did it to have our little girl closer. I never had Cassy in my arms, never could hold her close to my heart, but this way I can at least lay beside her when I'm gone from here. What a good feeling!

I went to Waid's Funeral Home, the one that made all the arrangements for Henry, and they were willing to help me, but it took more than a year. Every time we turned around there were other forms that had to be filled out. But it finally got done. The little casket was dug out and

Mr. Waid's mother, who visited some friends in Texas, brought it up here. How nice of her.

It was on a warm, sunny Saturday afternoon when Rev. Iverson had the sermon for little Cassy and we laid her to rest right here in the soil that we call home now. Plus, I know where I will be laid to rest someday, and my children do not have to worry about it. What a relief.

For me it was another one of those lonely days. Lotti and Brian (who later became her husband), Larry and his new girlfriend, Larry's parents and brothers with their families, stood by Cassy's graveside. But I was alone. Tom had to drive his milk truck. To Tom, this funeral was nothing important; to me it meant everything in the world. This was when I had my first doubts. Will anything that is important to me ever matter to Tom? But I did not tell him how much it hurt. Like always, I just ignored my feelings.

Tom and I had it pretty good together. He drove his milk truck almost daily, but I could get his lunch box ready. Sometimes I put a little note in it, telling him how much I loved him. I had supper on the table when he came home. And if he had to work on the truck afterwards, I could help him and hand him the tools. So often he said, "I never in my life had it as good as I have it now."

****

In June of 1992 we went to Switzerland together. Edith and Heinz took off from work and drove us everywhere. We saw Switzerland from one end to the other, went to Germany, Austria and Italy. It was great, the first vacation Tom ever had, and I felt so good that I could be with him. Tom's grandparents came from Germany, and it was always his dream to go to Europe. And now I could make his dream come true. The two weeks went fast, and it was time to come back to reality. And that it was.

Tom was married with his first wife and had one son, Mark, but then got divorced. Looking back and knowing Tom the way I do now, I think it was because he is a workaholic who never had time to sit with someone and visit. His wife must have felt left out, just as I do now.

Tom then got remarried and had two kids with his second wife, Tom Junior and Rachel, but that marriage, too, ended in divorce. Tommy said often that he, as an 11-year-old boy, lay in bed and prayed every night, "God, please help my parents to stay together."

The parents were separated and Dad lived in the machine shop, but Mom would not allow Tommy to go and see his dad. And then when Tommy thought they had reconciled and everything will be okay, that was when the divorce was final.

The children hurt pretty bad, and even now, 12 years later, Tommy still can't understand why it had to be that way. Tommy, now 24 years old, did not live with us in the beginning, but now he just moved in, brought friends any day or nighttime, never asking if it was okay with us.

When I moved in with Tom, I made a deal. I said to Tom, "Since I still work, I will pay for the groceries and my long distance phone calls, and I will do all the work around here," and I had no problem with that. But now Tommy moved in and ate with us, used my shampoo, soap, etc., and I washed and cleaned for him, too. I did all the bookwork for Tom's business and also the paychecks. And since Tommy worked for Tom, I knew that he earned more money than I ever did, but he never paid one penny toward the household. I paid for my own gas that I used in my car to do mine and Tom's errands. Tommy even charged all the gas that he used to his dad.

After we came home from Switzerland, I could see that I was not welcome anymore. Tommy took over. Everything that was mine was pushed into a corner or closet. I wrote a long letter and put it in Tom's lunchbox asking him to please help me. I felt like Tom's ex was breathing down my neck. And, in fact, it was she who did it all. She told Tommy, "I just made a new will and you aren't included.

You got your dad's farm, and you better see to it that you get it." And in he waltzed. He showed no respect for his dad, and even less for me. I was just a low-life maid. He could say to his dad, "Go to hell," if something upset him. But that is something I would never allow my children to say to their dad. What if something happens to Tom that day, then Tommy would have to live with that for the rest of his life, that he wished his dad were in hell.

My grandma always said, never leave the house angry, and here fighting was an everyday thing, and no one thought anything of it.

If I said something to Tom, his answer was always the same. "You just feel that way because he is not your child. If he was yours, you would react different." But that is not true. I punished my children when they did something wrong. I kicked Lotti out of my house at the age of 17, and I took Reto to the police station when he did wrong. I could teach them right from wrong. They were my children.

Over and over again I begged Tom to please help me. Could he not see that he hurt me and we're drifting further and further apart? Yet his excuse was always the same; "You do not know how it feels when you lose the kids through a divorce." Yes, that is true. I am a widow. But now it is 12 years since his divorce, and Tommy is 24 years old and a young, good-looking man.

It got worse, not better. Tommy did anything in his power to hurt me, and when Dad questioned him, his answer was, "I don't know what her problem is. I didn't do anything wrong." And Dad believed him.

I cried a lot, but Tom could not, or would not, see my tears. Thank God I had a job. That was my refuge. I had an older woman, Annette, working for me and I could cry on her shoulder. She could understand and feel for me, and always tried to cheer me up. Thanks, Annette, for being my friend.

The Saturday before Easter I went and bought a nice

plant and made an Easter basket and then a card on my computer. Tom's teacher, an old lady who just lived across the river from us, is a widow, too, and has no children, so I thought it would be good for Tom and me to visit her after we had supper that night and take her the Easter basket.

Tom said, "Boy, that is nice of you to think of her. And, yes, I will come along. I just will talk to Tommy quickly and see why he is upset."

I watched them from the kitchen window and could see that they were arguing, but I did not understand a word they said, nor did I want to know. Then Tom came all mad into the house and said, "Go alone. I do not feel like coming along. Tommy just told me I had to change my will now. He wants me to put everything into his name to make sure that he gets it all." How could a child do that to his dad?

But it is not Tommy, it is Tom's ex. Tommy went to see his mother the day before, and I know now that it was because of me. How could Tom be so blind and not stand up for his rights?

I took my plant and went to see Tom's teacher all by myself. I was very sad and my heart was heavy, but had to pretend that everything was fine. What a lie we all lived!

One Saturday morning Tommy was just terrible. I went out to the shop to talk to him. "What did I do to deserve being treated like this? What did I do wrong?" I asked. His answer was plain and simple. He said, "I know you sleep with my dad, but there better not be anything going on between you two. And this place is all mine now, and you better get the hell out of here. You aren't good to me anyway, and do not deserve to live here."

I was stunned. "What do you mean not good to you? I cook, clean and wash for you, and I pay for all the groceries you eat, the soap and shampoo you use, isn't that good enough?"

"This is only a formality," he answered.

I went back to the house, lay on my bed and cried. I promised myself to talk it out as soon as Tom came home that night. But we got company, Tom's uncle and aunt came for a visit. I made supper for all of us and pretended nothing ever happened.

It was a little after 10 p.m. when they left. I told Tom to get Tommy, who disappeared five minutes before the company left. "I want to talk to both of you," I said to Tom. Tommy had to come downstairs again. I asked them, "What do you guys want from me? I work here as if I were your maid, but that is still not good enough," and repeated what was said that morning.

But Tommy quickly replied, "I do not have to listen to her lies," and stomped upstairs, Tom right behind him, asking him, "Then what did she do to you?"

I knew then that there was no future here for me. But, boy, did it hurt. I gave up all my friends I had in Merrill, gave up my job and moved over here, and for what? Tom didn't have to give up one single thing, but could not understand that I was hurting.

The pillow was wet from my tears when Tom came to bed and took me in his arms. He promised, "We will find a way out of this. You just have to be patient."

I hurt so bad and was so numb that I did not pull back, But I knew I had lost Tom forever, and something had to be done. Yet, I was scared. I reduced my salary by $5,000 a year leaving Auto Stop, and I knew it was expensive to rent an apartment all alone. Plus, I only had $4,000 in our joint savings account, and that would not get me far. I spent my whole paycheck for groceries, bought new curtains for the whole house. If Tom needed socks, shirts or underwear, I bought them. But all along I thought, that was it. We will be together for as long as we live, and someday when I can't work anymore Tom will take care of me. Oh, how wrong I was!

I cried on the way to work; I cried on the way back. What could I do, start all over again? How many times did I do that already? I felt so lonely, and I think that is when I really started mourning for Henry. It took all my power to not burst in tears when I talked to a customer at work. I was on the bottom, yet nobody to talk to except Annette, and she could not help me. Lotti had enough problems going through the divorce with Larry, and my other children were too far away.

Then one morning Phil, my former supervisor, walked into the store and asked me if I had time after work to have a bite to eat with him. He would not tell me why, since I had other customers in the store. But I could hardly wait. If nothing else, I could talk to a person who understood where I was coming from.

Phil stopped at 4:30 p.m. and we went and had supper together. I said without hesitation, "Boy, did I think often of you the last couple of weeks. If I just would have stayed in Merrill."

His answer surprised me. "That is what I would like to ask you. We have to let the manager here in town go, and so the company decided to come and ask you if you would be interested in coming back and working for us again."

I felt Phil was sent from heaven. We talked for awhile and he offered me $6,000 more than I make now. "Oh, thank you, God," now I can move without getting too much into financial trouble. Phil told me to sleep on it. He would call me the next morning. But there was no doubt in my mind, I had to say yes.

I told Tom that night that I would switch jobs, but did not tell him what my plans were, or he would have gotten mad. He wanted me there, but also let his son run all over him. Tom wanted the best of both worlds without giving anything up.

The next day Phil came with the contract, and I signed

it. On my lunch breaks I went to look at trailer homes. I found one I really liked, but then when I looked at the crowded, dirty trailer parks, I changed my mind, and I thought to myself, maybe that was not such a good idea after all. Back to the dealer I went and told him I changed my mind. I don't want the trailer, I told him. I do not want to live in a dump.

"Did you see my trailer park," he asked.

"Where," I asked.

"I got a nice lot right in front," he continued. "Go and look at it."

So I did, and I loved it.

From there I went straight to the Credit Union to see if they would give me a loan. Dan, a real nice loan officer who knew me, tried to talk me out of it. "Maybe you should rent an apartment first," he said, "just in case Tom and you get together again." But I knew better. That would never happen.

Three days later Dan called me and told me that I got the loan approved. The following week they hooked my trailer up.

It was on a Sunday morning, another one of those sad Sunday mornings, when I moved out of Tom's house. It was my bedroom we used, and some of my other furniture was stored in one of the spare bedrooms. I did not take everything along. How could I do that? Tom needed a bed, so I took the one from upstairs and put it into his bedroom downstairs. I made the bed for him, even left one of my nice, new quilts there to make it look nice, and put a thank you note on his pillow.

Tom's stove was old, so I brought my brand-new one along, but my trailer had a gas stove, and I left my stove for Tom. I also left the microwave oven, and some other things I knew Tom could use.

I took the last load out when Tom came home that night. His eyes were cold as he looked at me and said, "I guess the house is empty again, just as it was twice before." Since Tom got divorced twice, he must know the feeling. On the other hand, one would think he would try a little harder to keep a good thing going. But then I guess I will never understand. How could I? I was never divorced and I'm a woman.

Tom did not call or talk to me for weeks, and I thought it was all over. But then, slowly, he came around again. He asked if I would still do his bookwork, and I agreed. I felt sorry for him since he had no one. And I felt secure, now that I had my own place and nobody could kick me out again. Never would I have to feel so scared and so cheap again.

Tom eventually thought it was a good idea that I bought that trailer. He tried to talk me into moving the trailer in a corner of one of his forties. He even had the perk-test done and said, "We will move you as soon as the snow is gone." I thought this time he was sincere, but then Tommy saw a bulldozer he wanted, and Dad had to buy a flat-bed trailer to move it, and there went the money for the foundation for my (our) trailer.

Edith and her family came for a visit that summer and were impressed with my new home, even though it was not all decorated yet. They bought me a wooden bench and a chair for my deck, and even a little birdhouse that looked like a Swiss Chalet. Boy, my kids are just so good to me. They always give me things and tell me, "Mom, all we want is to see you happy!" What more can a parent want?

We truly enjoyed the short time we could spend with each other. Edith, Martin, Martin Junior and Heidi stayed ten days, and then went on to Nevada to see Reto and his family. Jessica stayed with me, and we had another great week together. But she had to go back to Switzerland, since she now has a job at a travel service. I sure miss her.

****

That fall I spent my vacation with Reto and his family in Elko, Nevada. Tom drove me to the airport. On the way there he said, "We will replant the pine tree this afternoon. You know, the one that sits in the middle of the lawn." He could have put a knife into my heart, it would not have hurt more.

There were five pine trees in Tom's lawn, but only the one that I decorated the last two years for Christmas had to go. That tree looked so pretty with little lights in red, blue, yellow and green, and it spread its joy all around us. I knew why it had to go. Tom's ex, Tommy and Rachel, belong to the Jehovah's Witnesses and they do not believe in Christmas. That is why the tree had to be moved. They were just worried that even though I did not live out there anymore, I would put lights up for Tom, who was raised Catholic.

Boy, what one does in the name of God. I do not care how anybody else sees God, that is each individual's choice, but please do not cut me down for my beliefs. There is only one God, and he takes care of us all, rich or poor.

I did not say much anymore and was glad that I could board the plane and leave all of that behind. Reto, Brenda and the children welcomed me as I stepped off the plane in Reno, Nevada, and that felt good.

It was great to be with them, even if it was only for four days. Reto has three beautiful children: Sierra, Amanda and Reto Junior. We played together and I could read stories to them.

Little Reto is just like his dad was, a dreamer. Cuddled up by me in the recliner, he listened to the stories I read, stories he knew a lot better than I did. Just for a couple of hours it was as if I had my son on my lap again. It felt like someone turned my clock back.

But those few days went fast, and it was time to get back to Wisconsin, back to my job and my own little world.

Again Tom promised as soon as the corn was off one of

his forties we would move my trailer and then could be together again. But the corn got chopped and the snow fell and I still lived in town. If he would have given me one acre of land and would have paid for the basement, then I would have signed the note for the money he owed me as paid in full, but I knew it would not work out, since Tom wanted to keep the land in his name and pay for the basement and then I should put my trailer onto that foundation.

But I would never do that. What if something happened to him? Tommy would kick me off that land in no time and my trailer would be lost. The sad part is, it does not even hurt anymore. I'm numb. So I guess I stay right where I am.

The first winter alone was lonely, and those were some long, sleepless nights. But I made it, and winter gave way to spring.

I went out to Tom's one Thursday evening to do bookwork, and there was the pine tree they replanted, blown over by the wind. When I lived with Tom, I was so proud and happy that I wanted the whole world to see it. I picked the pine tree closest to the kitchen window so that I could always see it, and decorated it with dozens of lights. I turned them on every night, and the little lights in red, blue, green, white and yellow would shine and tell the whole world how much love there could be if we let their glow into our hearts. And I could imagine how special that tree felt and how proud he was to carry the lights.

But Tommy had the tree dug out and replanted him on the other side of the driveway amongst other pine trees. But the tree was sad. He knew he would never, ever spread joy and be a Christmas tree again, so he lost his will to live. He felt if he could not spread happiness, he did not want to live anymore. Now, ten months later, he was nothing but a dried-up, brown, blown-over stem with branches that did not have one green needle on them.

And I feel just like that tree. If I can't spread love, life is not worth living. Only I looked at that now dead but once so beautiful pine tree today and told myself I would not give up like him. I will stand up straight and fight, and I will find love and happiness someday.

August 27, 1991

Edith Gross
N 6006 Rosedale Road
Deer Brook, WI 54424

Dear Edith:

We all will miss you greatly at SSG. You have been a most impressive, dedicated and honest employee of our company. I realize the frustrations you have had with us in our slow commitment to remodel your store and porsonal decisions that affect you, Tom and your family. We understand and respect that decision.

I cannot express enough how much I respect you as an individual and fellow employee. As a result of your contributions, the Merrill store developed into one of our most profitable stores. Your understanding of business is both rare and valuable. Your personality is sincere and your customers will miss you as well.

Edith, a gracious thank you to you for your hard years of success with us. I appreciate your ambition and an opportunity to know and work with someone like yourself. Your position will be difficult to replace and as for your future employer, they have a wonderful person to represent their company.

We would hope that you consider us down the road if the right situation arises. We all would be honored to have you back. All of us at SSG are saddened to see you go, but truly support you in your decision and your future.

Sincerely, Good Luck!

Larry

Larry Mitchell

715/386-8281 □ 612/436-7498
FAX 386-7421
P.O. BOX 287 512 SECOND STREET HUDSON, WI 54016

20

MY BROTHER HEINZ and his wife Lisa came to see me that spring. For the first time ever they visited the United States. They flew to California first and took part in a bus tour through Nevada, into Yellowstone Park, down to the Grand Canyon, Las Vegas, and back to San Francisco. And then they came to visit me for five days.

I took vacation days and drove them up to Lake Superior, then along the shore all the way to Sault Ste. Marie, Michigan. It was so pretty. We enjoyed it, and for the first time in my brother's and my life we could really talk together, talk about things that went on when we were kids. There is a lot my brother never knew about my childhood. But then I also got to see some happenings from his perspective. It felt so good, and I was never closer to my brother. Too bad it was just for such a short time.

Tom came and spent one day with Heinz and Lisa, since we stayed for a weekend at my brother's when Tom and I were in Switzerland together. We four took a whole day to look at double-wide homes. Tom even had a guy come out and appraise my trailer to see what they would pay me as a trade-in. "As soon as the corn is off the field, we will move," he said.

Lisa was impressed by Tom's determination and tried to convince me that this time it would work out between us two. "I think Tom really wants to be with you and will go through with it this time," she said. I had no hope and just answered, "Wait and see." And I was right. The corn was chopped, the snow fell and I still lived alone.

I know it is not just Tom's problem. It is just as much my fault, if not more. I would like to be good and help anybody, and especially the one I love, never asking what is in it for me, or do I get something in return.

I left my family and the friends I had in Switzerland behind to fulfill Henry's dream, yet he was never happy here. And now I did the same thing again. I gave all my friends and everything I had in Merrill up to be with Tom, and he did not have to make any changes whatsoever, but what did I get out of it? Another heartache.

I do not know how, but I have to get out of thinking that I just have to give and everybody else just takes. But it is hard to change, since that is what Grandma did and taught me from little on. That is what women have to do. They have to cater to their man. Their own feelings do not matter. I feel stronger now, and maybe someday will be able to find love without giving everything up that I believe in. We'll see!

Lotti kept me busy the following spring. She found a real nice guy, Bryan, and decided to get married again. She asked me if I would be her maid of honor. That really made me feel good. I was the one who kicked her out of the house before she even turned 17 because she did not want to follow our rules. And now to stand by her side when she says I do, that is something very special and few mothers can go through this great experience.

Lotti did not want a big wedding. No dance this time. Since Bryan was divorced also and had three children in California, she wanted to make it a family affair. But there was a lot that had to be done. She needed a wedding dress, and I had to have something special to wear. Everything was so expensive I decided to sew the dresses for the girls myself. And they turned out just great.

July 2nd was their wedding day. Since Lotti didn't have her dad, she made it very special and had her two children, Bobbi Jo and Tyler, walk her down the aisle and give her away. Bryan's oldest daughter, Jerica, gave him away, and the smaller two children, Michelle and Matthew, were flower girl and ring-bearer. Bryan's stepfather was the best man. All in all, it was a real nice day and I was pretty proud of my new family.

****

Work got hectic. Phil, my supervisor, had a hard time keeping all his stores in line, so I was asked if I would be his right-hand and help managers out if they had questions or trouble keeping the books straight.

I gladly accepted, since I knew most of the managers. Lori, who manages the store in Marshfield, expected a baby by the end of January, but had a hard time finding help. So I went there two afternoons a week. Those were long days. I opened my store at 5 a.m., worked till 10:30 a.m., then drove to Marshfield, which is about 96 miles from Antigo, worked there all afternoon till my replacement came in at 6 p.m., and then had a long ride home. I was tired, but happy that I could help Lori out, since she worked so hard, but had bad luck with some of her employees.

I stopped at Jim's in Tomahawk pretty regularly. He is like a big teddy bear, and I could chew him out, tell him: "Jim, why the heck did you do this?" But he never got mad at me. He knew that I only wanted to help him. I trained him already in 1988, the first year he worked for Auto Stop, and we became good friends.

I also did inventory in Waupaca and drove all the way to Neillsville to straighten out the books there. I really liked that, and it was easier for me, since I also was a manager and knew the frustration we have to go through.

And then, of course, I had to help out in Merrill. Pam had managed that store now for over two years, and still had problems. I cleaned the whole store for her and bent over backwards to help her, but she resented me now, just as much as the day I left there. Even though I told her that I was not interested in her store anymore, I only wanted to make it easier for her. Yet I could understand her feelings, too, since customers came in and asked me, "Why don't you come back to manage this store; we really miss you." If I would have been in Pam's shoes, that would have hurt me, too. But there was nothing I could do about it.

Then the first week of February 1994 I met Phil, and together we went to the Merrill store. I had to take over the store while Phil fired Pam. But it went from bad to worse. I trained two managers within three months. One did not work out, and the other one just quit after one month.

It was tough to run two stores, but it got done. I left my house at 4:15 a.m. one morning, so that I could open the store in Merrill at 5 a.m. I was tired and felt sorry for myself, working all those long, long hours. That is stupid, I thought. But I only got to the car and a little cottontail hopped by, looking at me as if it thought, what is she doing up so early? And then about eight miles from my house I had to stop to let a bear cross the highway. Deer and their fawns enjoyed the early morning hour and looked for some fresh grass along the ditches. That perked me up. With beauty like that all around me, how could I feel down and sorry for myself? Chin up. You went through so much already, and you will be able to handle this, too.

It was in June when two guys stopped at my store and asked if they could talk to me in private. My first thoughts, they had to be some vendors who wanted to sell me something, since I had never seen those two before.

But I was wrong. There was a new convenience store being built north of town with diesel and gas pumps, and a scale for semis. One of the two guys was the general manager for Farm Bureau, the co-op that would build that store. They came to ask me if I would consider managing their new store as soon as they were ready to open it.

"How come you want me," I asked. "You don't even know me."

But their answer was simple. "Farm Bureau is owned by the farmers, some of whom have known you for many, many years. They told us to come and ask you. They sure would be pleased to have you on board."

We talked for awhile, and I promised to think about it. But I was truly flattered that they came to offer me that job, me out of all people. I'm 55 years old and at that age one gets phased out at a lot of places. Three weeks later they had the ad in the paper, "Manager needed," and I applied.

I did that for two reasons: Number one, I know that Auto Stop wants to get rid of Phil, my supervisor, and they wanted me to replace him. Yes, Phil has his faults, just as we all do, but he gave me a job when I needed one, and now I can't just squeeze him out. If they let him go anyway, then so be it, but I would not be the one who did it to him. Number two, a brand-new store, arranged the way I want and run as if it were my own was a challenge by itself. I guess my life would be dull without challenges.

I got hired and would start my new job by September 15, but I had planned to fly to Switzerland later that fall, so I had to change my plans. I promised myself when I laid Henry to rest that I would visit his graveside every two years. And since I do not like to travel alone, I told my grandchildren that I would take a different one along every time I go so that they could see where their grandparents came from.

I went to the travel agent and asked how much they wanted for two plane tickets. Their answer: $2500. "No way," I told myself. I will not pay that much, and I left without making any reservations.

I could hardly sleep that night, since I knew with this new job I would have to wait at least one year until I could get vacation. My mother was 82 years old. If I didn't go now, I might never see her again, and no money could replace one more visit with her. Now that my children are gone, I can feel what she went through when I told her that I would leave my homeland, and sometimes I feel really guilty.

But I also know that we have to let go. We have to teach our children right and wrong and make responsible adults out of them, but then stand back and let them live their own lives. It hurts when we see them fall. We can be there to lend a helping hand, if they ask for it, but they have to find their own way.

With all of that on my mind, I went back the next day and bought the tickets. Thank God for credit cards.

Ten days later my granddaughter Bobbi Jo and I were on our way to Switzerland. It is great to see all my loved ones, and I especially enjoy chatting with my grandchildren. Bobbi Jo was queen amongst Jessica's friends — a 14-year-old, pretty girl from the United States. What guy would not fall for her?

This time I even had supper with Walter one Sunday evening. He is a widower and we could talk about the good old days, our teen years when we spent some happy times together. I promised him to keep in touch, but it is hard. We are worlds apart now. He never left the Toggenburg Valley, and he would be homesick in the United States, just as Henry was. Yet, I went through so much and my heart is in the States now. Plus, I do not want to start all over again. I'm getting too old for that.

But that is something my friends overseas will never understand. They think I could just pack up and come home. Yes, it was my homeland for the first 29 years of my life, but it isn't anymore. My home is where my heart is, and that is here now. The only ones that know where I'm coming from are my children. Then, even though they settled in Switzerland, they are still torn between the two countries.

I love my families there, and also have friends I would like to be with, yet my roots aren't there anymore. Here I enjoy my family, my friends, my home and my job. But I still talk different and have an accent, and because of that deep down sometimes still do not feel accepted. Like one lady said to me not too long ago, "Another one of those foreigners who takes our jobs away," and that hurt. Often I hate to open my mouth because I talk different, yet if I go to Switzerland, they too can hear an accent when I talk to them. Sometimes I feel like a little boat in the middle of the ocean, the wind pushing it in different directions, and I don't know how to steer.

The two weeks in Switzerland went fast, and it was time to come back. I do not like goodbyes because it hurts too much, yet it has to be. That is why I like to have a grandchild along. It gives me something to live for and I can't fall to pieces. Grandmas have to be tough.

This might be the last time ever that I can hug my mother. She is over 82 years old now. So I hung onto her just a little longer. A desperate hug and a last kiss and off we go.

The pilot got us safely back to Chicago, and then to Mosinee. I went right back to work, since there was a lot that had to get done before I changed jobs, and that left me no time to dwell on the past.

The new store was still empty, had no heat, no shelves, not even the coolers were installed when I started working for my new company. I hired five clerks, and together we scrubbed the store, stocked the shelves and got ready for our big day on October 14, 1994, when we finally opened the doors.

I was really proud of my achievements and very thankful to Don Albrecht for giving me the opportunity to take over this store and make it a success. I worked here now for one and a half years, and we did a lot better than anybody anticipated, but I didn't do it alone. I did it only with the help of all my dedicated employees. I'm really thankful for that.

Last fall I took a long weekend off and flew to Nevada. Brenda gave birth to a little boy, "Dustin." Now they have two girls and two boys; a great family. Dustin was only four weeks old, a cute little guy. I could spoil him, if only for a couple of days, but it made me feel good. I will never, ever let the opportunity slip by again to hold my grandchild in my arms, as I did with Cassy.

I was surprised how big Sierra, 10; Amanda, 8; and Reto Junior, 6 years old, were. They took me to their school, and all three are great students. What a reward to see your children having nice families like that.

I do not know what the future has in store for me, and that is good. But I hope and pray that I can stay healthy and work till I reach the age of 65. I have to do that to be able to have a decent retirement so that I can travel and visit my families here and overseas. I kind of dread getting old alone, since that is not how I dreamed it would be.

In Bergun lived an old couple next door from us. The Mrs. had a stroke and couldn't do anything anymore, but her husband kept the house clean, helped her getting dressed and made breakfast, and then every day at noon sharp he guided her on his arm to the nearby restaurant where they had a nice lunch together. It was just so neat to see all the love and passion those two had for each other, and I always hoped that Henry and I could enjoy our old age together like that. Yet, I had to learn the hard way that dreams do not always come through.

But no matter, alone or not, I can sit back in my rocking chair someday when I retire and be proud of my achievements. I will never be rich, money-wise, but I'm rich in memories.

And if I'm going to live to be a hundred, no one can ever take them away from me. I did not succeed in everything I tried, but I always did the best I could. And my biggest joys are my four children, who grew up to become great individual human beings. I'm proud of them and their families. There is only one big wish I have. I would like, once more in my lifetime, to get all my children and grandchildren together. That is something that might never happen, but at least I can dream about it.

****

I know this book might never be a success, but it helped me, emotionally, to let it all out. All I would like to do is help someone else who struggles through life and tell them, "Just hang in there and do the best you can do. That is all that anybody can expect of you."

I was in first grade when my mother gave me a wooden plaque, and now, 50 years later, that plaque still is with me and hangs in my hallway. It says:

Every time you think you can go no further,
There is a little light that shines from somewhere
Telling you to try one more time
And to sing of new hope and happiness.

Epilogue

IT IS A couple of years now since I ended my book in 1994, and a lot happened in that time, some good and some not so good, but I guess such is life.

The store that I took over did really well and went way beyond everybody's expectation. I worked hard and most of the time had a good crew. I had to be thankful for that, for I could never have done it alone. But I also had a lot of time to invest in my endeavor, since I did not like to live alone. And yes, the store really helped me to get over some pretty rough times.

And, like I promised myself after Henry passed away to go every two years, I went in 1996 to Switzerland again, and this time I took Tyler along. He was a great companion, and it gave me time to get to know him better. Once again I took my mom wherever I went, and she truly perked up. She didn't go out of the apartment much anymore, but she had no problem when I was there, and that was good for both of us. The highlight of the trip, besides seeing the kids and grandkids, was, like always, to get the friends and relatives together. It is unbelievable that, after all that time, I still have so many friends who come to see me. What a blessing that is. But the good times pass way too fast and I had to get back to work. It was a vacation neither Tyler or I will ever forget.

I got to know a guy, Willi, up north, and spent a lot of weekends there, just sitting outside, watching the wildlife and reading a book. During the week I stayed in Antigo and was busy taking care of the store.

I felt that my health was deteriorating. I had terrible headaches. I found out that was caused by an imbalance of my hormones and could be stabilized with medication, but I was more scared knowing that my head and left arm started shaking. Even though I got pretty good in covering it up, I knew it was there, and got worse. Yes, it scared me; what would I do if I could not work anymore? How would I pay my bills? Yes, since I'm a widow I could retire at 60 years old, but with no health insurance, where do I go then? So I went to social security office to see if that was a possibility. I could have done it on Henry's social security and would have gotten $192 a month, plus I could have worked to make another $9,500 a year, but a part-time job does not provide health insurance. With that little bit of money I could have hardly made a living, let alone visit my kids. So that idea was out the door.

Then one Saturday I got really sick and ended up in the emergency room. After they got me stabilized, the doctor asked if I was ever tested for Parkinson Disease. "No," I answered. But I thought to myself, "Oh, yes, I asked myself for quite some time if I had that, and now he finalizes it."

I had to see a specialist the following week. He made a couple of tests and then said quickly, "No, you do not have Parkinson's Disease. Your problem is ST, or Spasmodic Torticollis. Or, in plain English, ST is a neurological condition thought to originate in the basal ganglia portion of the brain. An overabundance of a chemical called Acetylcholine is going through the nerve pathway to certain muscles in the neck, where in turn spasms occur. The studies show that three women to one man have it, and it generally, but not always, will appear in people of Northern European heritage. There are only a very few medical people who understand ST, much less know how to treat it. Nobody knows for sure what causes ST. An accident or a trauma of some kind can trigger its onset. The accident we had after Lotti's wedding, or being kicked in the face by that cow could have done it for me.

But once again I had help from above; I was sent to Dr. Hiner in Marshfield, Wisconsin. A great guy. He looked at me and said then that 10-15 years ago they sent patients like me to a mental institution, but now they know better than that. "It might help if you get Botox shots; they have no proven side effects and there is really no internal medicine that could help you," he explained. Other methods of treatment would be learning how to relax, physical therapy, support groups and spiritual help. Positive thinking, but that should be done under the guidance of a person knowledgeable about ST.

There was no question about it, I had to try something, because I had to be able to keep on working. So I agreed, Botox it was. We started that treatment the same day. It takes a couple of weeks until it really works, then it has to relax the muscles that provoke the spasms. First I went every three months, then every six months, and now I'm able to wait 8-10 months. I don't want to overdo it so that it might help me in the long run. Boy, what a relief. It still is embarrassing if someone talks to you and then asks you how come you are shaking your head, saying no before I'm done asking the question, but so be it. I cannot explain to everyone what the problem is, but I know that I can control it, and I'm grateful that it will not take over my whole body. And the people around me got used to it.

****

Martin Junior got confirmed in June of 1998, which gave me a good reason to visit Switzerland once again. This time I took Sierra, my granddaughter from Nevada, along. Sierra flew in from Nevada all by herself and spent three days with me in the northwoods. We even celebrated her 14th birthday in Wisconsin, and the next day we flew overseas. It is always a long flight and one is dead tired getting off the plane, but half of the family is waiting, all excited, and that perks one up again.

I spent time at Edith's, then at Heinz's and, of course, I cannot forget my brother and his family. I had a great two weeks. Sunday will be Martin's confirmation, and then two days later we have to go back to the State's. My mom and I spent the Friday before confirmation at Edith's. Edith was so busy making all kinds of cakes. Why does she need that many, I ask myself, but it is none of my business so I do not ask questions. We sat around, talked and had a great evening. It was late already when we went upstairs and to bed. My mom and I shared Edith's bedroom, she and Martin slept on the couch. I was really tired and dozed off quickly, but my mom kept on talking and talking. It must have been almost 2 a.m. and she still was going on and on. Then she said that my cousin Peter also was invited to the party on Sunday, but he could not make it, but then he does not like to get together with some of his relatives that did not go on to high school.

"Who cares," I said, still half asleep. "If he does not like me because of that, then that is his problem. Why was he even invited, I asked myself. We aren't that close, and it was Martin's confirmation and I do not think he even knows him. Mom did not give up and went on, "But you could never have gone to high school anyway." Now I was awake! "Why could I not have gone on, I was not stupid," I asked, curious.

"Oh, no, you were not stupid at all," was her quick answer. But now I would not give up anymore. I wanted to know the whole story.

"Then why could I not have made it," I asked. I never in my entire life thought that I would ever hear the next couple of sentences. My mother said clearly, "Your 6th grade teacher came to our house, talked to your dad and me, and he said that you could not make it in high school because you were emotionally and physically too sick to go on."

"Mom, but why would he say something like that," I wanted to know.

"Oh, you know why," she went on, "because you were abused by your uncle." It was like if she slapped me! If the teacher, my dad, and she knew of my abuse, then why in the world would no one help me? Why would they just ignore it? I'm now almost 60 years old and never before had a clue that they knew. What a kick in the teeth!

I did not sleep much that night, and if I could I would have left Switzerland the next day. I was so disappointed and it hurt so much. I was pretty quiet all Saturday . I just could not understand how they could do that. Didn't they ever care about me? But Martin's great day, his confirmation, would come up tomorrow and I could not ruin it for everyone, so I kept quiet. And Sierra really looked forward to that day where she would meet more of her relation.

Everybody was busy getting ready on Sunday morning, then we had to be in church at 10 a.m. The church was packed. Sierra and I even took communion together and, yes, it was good that I had her along. After church we went to a nice local restaurant for lunch. The meal was good, and now it finally was time for dessert; we could sample all of Edith's cake. Then the door to the restaurant opened, and in walked my cousin Paula and her family. Then Walter, and close behind him Elisabeth and then Annekather, the girl who worked for me in 1964-65.

Now I know why we needed so many cakes. I'm going to be 60 years old in December, but I will not be here then, so they celebrated my birthday in summer. And now I also know why Peter was invited. But with or without him, it was a great afternoon, and I got lots of presents. From the kids and grandkids I got a clock out of wood in the shape of a cowbell, and they said that they hoped my life keeps on ticking and ticking, one beat at a time, just like this clock does.

On Monday I was busy with packing, then it was time to go back to the USA. Tuesday they all came to the airport to see us off. Yes, I gave Mom an extra hug, saying goodbye, but for some reason I felt distant. I still could not understand her. But, no matter what, it is never easy to leave them all behind, not knowing if we ever see each other again.

****

Back at the job, I was hoping that if I worked hard I would forget what my mom said that Friday night. But that was not so, it just turned and turned inside. So I sat down and wrote my mother a long letter, with lots and lots of questions. Why? Why didn't you help me? How could you do that to me? I know to be able to get my freedom back I had to send her this letter. But my mother was 86 by now, and I was afraid that she would get upset and have a heart attack over this. So I duplicated that letter, sent one to my brother and one to Edith, and attached a note to it. Should Mom get a heart attack over this, then it would be my fault. This is what I wrote her. But it did not take long and I had an answer from my mother, with all kinds of excuses. And she could not understand what my problem was. Other women had it so much worse, they got abused by more than one person.

No, it was not easy and it will always hurt, but life goes on and I too will get over it. And it wasn't all gloom; I had some happy events in my life, too.

It was on June 27, 1998, when my granddaughter Bobbi Jo, gave birth to a healthy, pretty little girl. They named her Cassandra, in memory of Bobbi Jo's little sister who passed away. Boy, I'm a great-grandma now. Where did those years go? And, yes, one has to grab onto the happy hours, as they pass away too quickly.

****

Another summer passed and fall will soon have to make room for Old Man Winter, and that reminds me of dead. Is dead ever lovable, and can we ever understand it? I don't really know. Even though I was with three of my closest relatives when they passed away, it felt so different each time. But then each is a different human being, with different lifestyles, different ideas and different backgrounds.

In 1980 I went back to Switzerland and took care of my dad the last three weeks of his life. He had liver cancer and was in terrible pain, but he was content and at peace when he finally could go home. And as for me, it felt good being able to help him those last weeks.

Then my husband. He passed away in my arms making love to me. It is still beyond me how one can be so happy one moment and gone the next. But he was troubled and homesick for so many, many years, and now he found peace. No more heartaches and no more sorrows, he finally was home.

And now to mother, she was the third person I watched dying, and that was completely different. My mother, still living in Switzerland, had a stroke on December 1st, 1998. She lay for over 24 hours on the floor in her apartment, deliberately not calling anyone, even though two years earlier I gave her a portable phone for that reason. She was hoping she would die before someone could find her. Then when she realized it wasn't as easy as she thought, she called my daughter Edith. Edith in turn called the police, because they had to break into her apartment. Ma was then transported to the hospital. Her left side was partly paralyzed; she needed help to get dressed and to go to the bathroom. She had some trouble swallowing, but could eat herself since she was right-handed, and she could talk. The doctors wanted her to get into physical therapy and said that would really help her, but she refused, because she knew that she could never go back into her apartment. She lived on the third floor and there are no elevators in that building, and for her to go into a nursing home was out of the question. She simply did not want to live anymore.

My mom called me the last five years at least once or

twice a week. She always told me to make sure to call EXIT if she could not make her own decisions anymore. She used to say, "I know your brother has trouble with this, but you will understand." My reply, "Don't worry, we will cross that bridge when we get there," never thinking that I would some day be the one that had a problem with EXIT.

EXIT is an organization in Switzerland of which anyone can become a member by paying 25 Swiss francs a year as dues. They will then step in, if one has a life-threatening injury, or is on life support and can't make their own decisions anymore. Someone from EXIT will come and turn the life support off. My parents belonged to this since the '70s, but about five years ago they made an amendment to their rules. Now it reads that they will also help if one has an incurable illness or an unreasonable handicap; they will then help you to commit suicide. And my mom was 100% for that.

I could not believe that my mother would give up so quickly. She was the one who went to every one of Dr. Kuebler-Ross' lectures, and she gave me her books. In there it says if one commits suicide he or she will have to come back to earth and learn to deal with the problems that he or she could not handle before. There are lessons to be learned all the way to the end, the end God sets for us, and my mother believed in all of that, but now my mother was 86 years old, had a stroke, and just did not want to go on anymore.

Edith went to see her four or five times a week and helped her every way possible. It was not easy for me, being so far away — they are seven hours ahead of our time — but I took a break in the morning, went to home to call her in the hospital and tried to talk her out of it, but no success.

So, at the end of December she called EXIT and told them to help her to die. She thought they would come right away and do it, but it does not go that fast. First a lady came to talk to her to see if she really meant it. Then she told Mom what it takes to do that, and gave her three weeks to think about it.

Three weeks later, on a Sunday afternoon, this lady invited my mom, my brother and my daughter Edith, and they talked, but there was no way anyone could change my mother's decision. She felt she was a cripple now and wanted to go. My brother, to whom she gave life, was born with only one leg and he had to live with being called a cripple all those years. I just could not understand her.

The next day when I talked to her, she told me that the day was set for February 4, 1999, at 2:30 p.m. I stopped my mother once before from committing suicide, why can't I do it now? I was so mad at her that I said, "Good luck. If you want to do that, do it alone. I'm not coming to watch you, even though I know that she had to have two witnesses, any witnesses. But why does it have to be that way? Nowadays everything is I want to; I want to. "Thy will be done" is gone. Life is so precious and she just throws it away.

I told my daughter Lotti about it and said, "I will not go home. I was more mother to her than she ever was to me. I went through a lot of hard times; she was never there for me, and now she wants to kill herself with the help of EXIT."

But Lotti, who knows me maybe better than I do, told me, "Ma, you should go. If you do not go, you will never forgive yourself. And if you want me to, I will come along." And yes, she was right. So she made all the reservations and we left the Mosinee airport on February 2nd, 1999. We had to wait a couple of hours in Chicago and then went on to Zurich. They showed a movie in the plane. Renee Zellweger (my maiden name was Zellweger) played the role of the daughter. The mother had cancer and asked her to help her to die, but she could not do it. And oh boy, could I feel her pain. Can I convince my mother to hang in there until God is willing to take her home?

It was 7:30 a.m., their time, when we landed in Zurich, and I was tired. Edith and Jessica were there to greet us and drove us straight to the hospital to see my mother. I was surprised how good she looked. Her left side of the mouth hung down a little, she could not use her left arm, and had very little control of her left leg, but she smiled and seemed happy to see us. We wheeled her downstairs and had coffee and cake with her. After lunch we let her take a nap and we went outside to get some fresh air.

Back upstairs sitting by her bedside, I was hoping we could talk. Talk about my childhood and how she saw it, from her perspective. But nothing, not a word. She talked about all kinds of women who did not have a good life. I interfered and said, "It wasn't always easy for me either, and I had to fight through it myself." She replied quickly, "No one has to feel sorry for you, you're one of those little wooden dolls that one can push down and it gets right back up again. You will always find a way to go on with your life." Now, was that a compliment or an insult? As the day went on, I felt like a flower that slowly dried up. My heart was aching for love and understanding, for a kind word, or anything to make me understand what went on in my mother's mind. Did she have to close up her heart and feelings to be able to go through with this? I guess I will never know.

I was exhausted as I lay in bed that night, but I could not find any sleep. What would the next day bring? I felt so numb, cold, unloved and empty inside.

My brother picked us up at 8:30 the next morning and together (daughter Edith, daughter Lotti, daughter-in-law Judith, my brother and I) we made that one-hour drive to Thalwil where my mother lived. None of us said much, each was in its own world. We stopped first at Mom's apartment and straightened it out a little. Then my brother,

Judith and I went to the hospital to pick my mother up. What the EXIT does cannot be done in the hospital, one has to be at home. Ma was already dressed and in the wheelchair waiting for us. The nurse wheeled her downstairs and gave her some flowers. I was so numb I just smiled. The head nurse helped getting Mom into my brother's car. After Ma was all situated, the nurse gave her a big hug and then fell to pieces. She ran crying back into the hospital and slammed the door behind her.

It was just a ten-minute drive to my mother's apartment building and none of us said a word; it was a very quiet drive. Edith and Lotti were waiting for us, and together with Judith pulled my mother in the wheelchair up to her apartment, a long five flights of stairs. My brother and I went shopping; we both had a hard time with this and were glad to get some fresh air. The girls put some sandwiches together after we got back. My ma even enjoyed a cup of hot milk and a roll. We sat around the small table, and for just a short time it felt like always. Mom laughed, told funny stories and seemed really relaxed.

At 1 p.m., my brother and I had to leave to pick Ms. Bomeranz up; she arrived by train. She was a short, stocky woman in the mid-forties. Looking at her, I asked myself how could she do that on voluntary basis, helping people commit suicide because one feels it is a person's choice when he or she wants to die? What kind of belief does she have? But I guess I have no more rights to question her beliefs than she has to question mine.

We returned to my mother's apartment and could hear them talking and laughing as we walked in. It sounded as if it were just another normal day. Then it got quiet. Ms. Bomeranz introduced herself and then asked my mother if she still felt the same way and was, out of her free will, ready to go through with this. “Yes,” my mom answered. “I do not want to go on like this.”

Ms. Bomeranz read the rules and regulations one more

time and then asked Mom to sign the document. "You have to press hard," she told her, "because it has to go down to the copy, which the police later will pick up." Then my mother signed her name for the last time.

At 2 p.m. the doctor rang the doorbell. And that was when the real task started. The doctor has to put the needle into Mom's arm and then hook up the salt solution, and Ms. Bomeranz has to do the rest.

"Where do you want to hang the bag," Ms. Bomeranz asked.

"Maybe we can put a nail in the wall," the doctor replied.

Then they took my dad's picture off the wall and used that nail. Those two went back and forth, and my mother just sat there in her wheelchair watching them. It was just like a rehearsal. When they finally agreed how to do it, they turned to Ma and asked her if she wanted to lie on the bed or stay in the wheelchair. Her reply, "Whatever is easier for you." So the bed it was.

The doctor put the needle into Ma's right forearm and hooked the salt solution up. He looped the hose through Ma's right hand and asked her if she could open the little valve. She could not, so they tried and tried again and made the loop bigger until it finally worked. Then the doctor said, "We will step outside to give you time alone. Call us when you are ready." And out the door those two went.

Again I was hoping that Ma would say some loving, caring words, or at least give me one last hug, but nothing. She just handed Edith, my brother, and me each a sealed envelope. No kiss, no hug, no goodbye, nothing. She said, "Tell them to come in. I want to go now."

The doctor sat by us while Ms. Bomeranz went to the kitchen. She took a glass, put the poison in it and then some water, then she took a spoon and mixed it. That sound made my hair on the neck stand up. I sat in the chair looking at my mother, thinking here is the witch in the kitchen mixing a witch's brew. Ms. Bomeranz came back, filled two syringes and then inserted them into the salt solution. Then she told my mother to open the valve. She took Ma's hand and said, "Goodbye. Mrs. Zellweger, have a good trip."

I was so furious. How could she say that, my mother is leaving us forever, this is not just a vacation. Edith got up and sat on the bed by Ma, and I reluctantly sat on the other side. And as I took my mother's hand, she smiled and wanted to say something, but she did not get it out anymore. Within five minutes she was gone. Gone forever, without saying goodbye, without a hug or a kiss, just gone. A body without life, stiff and cold, just an empty shell. Edith and I had to get off the bed and not touch my mother anymore because that could have left marks on her body, marks that could be used against us, Ms. Bomeranz told us. So back in the chair I sat.

The doctor left, his job was done, but Ms. Bomeranz had to stay. She had to call the police. Soon two policemen dropped in. They had to take pictures and asked all kinds of questions. Was it her free will or did you guys force her to do this? Her needle is in the right arm, then how could she open the valve with the right hand? Then they had to call the police chief. He came and took my mother's signed final statement along. Then the crime lab technician and his helper came to take pictures. They turned Ma every which way to see if we used force to get her to do that. Then he turned to us and said, "That is okay. It is a clean job." How could he say something like that? That is my mother he is talking about. I just can't understand.

Next was the district attorney's turn to investigate the scene. And he then released the body. It was almost 7 p.m. when they brought the casket and took her away. I still sat in the same chair, numb. I could not even shed a tear. It was so unbelievable; so cold.

I went to my brother's house that night, then the next

day we had to go and make all the funeral arrangements. We had to stop by the minister, and the first thing he asked us was how did she die. I was reluctant to tell him, but then I broke down and asked him in tears, "How could she do that to me? I loved her with all my heart." The minister replied, "Mothers have big responsibilities. Even if they feel sorry for themselves, there is a bigger picture a mother has to see. Sometimes she has to put her own feelings aside and be there for her children, no matter how old they are. But then you also have to understand that she was a very troubled woman who could not think straight anymore. She saw this as her only way out, and God will forgive her."

That night as I again lay in bed not being able to sleep, I opened Ma's letter. She wrote that letter in March of 1993, and now it was February 1999. Did she play with these thoughts for so many years? She apologized that they could not be the parents my brother and I deserved. She said thanks for coming home and taking care of Dad and making dying easier for him. Then she went on to say that she knew that I was abused but couldn't do anything for me. Her hands were tied and she kept quiet to avoid confrontation, just as I never spoke up to avoid troubles.

But did she ever understand, I was a child then and had no shoulder to lean on. She was an adult and could have tried to find a way to make a better life for us.

I have to tell myself now the past is the past and cannot be changed anymore, but it sure hurts like hell. And I questioned myself over and over again, did my mother finally find her freedom in heaven, or does she have to keep on suffering? What happens to the ones who end their lives, will they find God's forgiveness after all? Still so many questions and no answers. All I can do now is go on with my life and do the best I can for me and me alone. And I have to be happy to have great kids, in-laws and grandchildren. Thank God for that.

But I felt that I could not do it alone, I really needed a counselor. Where did that wooden doll go that my mother talked about? I guess she got lost in the shuffle. Sometimes we have to do things in life we never thought we would do, but I was on a crossroad; I needed help. And I found a great lady who helped me work through it and made me see a clearer picture.

And yes, I went back to work and tried to go on with my life, but it did not take long and I got another blow.

It was on April 18th, 1999 at 2 a.m. when my phone rang. I jumped out of bed. What could that be, what happened now? I answered the phone and there was Reto on the other end, and I could hear right away that he was crying. "Reto, what is wrong," I asked.

"Mom, the helicopter is leaving right now for California with Dustin and Brenda on board. We do not know if he is going to make it." Then he went on to tell me that Dustin was kind of tired all day, but Reto thought that it was the flu Dustin had just a couple of weeks ago. That night Reto wanted to give him a bath and put him to bed, but that is when he saw that Dustin had blue marks all over his body. He could not understand where that came from. They do not hit the kids. They called a friend who had a liver problem and asked her what they should do, if she knew what that could be. She had no clue, but said, "If you are that concerned, then bring him to the hospital right away and see what they have to say." And that's what they did.

The doctor took one look at Dustin, and his reaction showed Reto and Brenda that this was serious. The doctor knew right away what it was but would not tell them anything before the tests came back. Then he said, "I ordered a helicopter. Your son has leukemia and needs immediate attention."

"I could drive him to the University Hospital in Sacramento; it would take me only about three hours," Reto replied. But the doctor's response was, "He would not survive that trip over the Sierra Mountains, the air pressure in the helicopter is stable."

Yes, Dustin was deadly sick. God, please God, help us to get through this.

Boy, did I wish that I could be there for all of them and help them, even if it would just have been as quiet bystander. I couldn't even give Reto a hug that early Sunday morning; we were thousands of miles apart. I had a job, responsibilities and bills to pay and could not just leave. Life sure can be tough.

A friend of Reto's drove him to the hospital in Sacramento, and Brenda's dad, who lives in California, stayed there a lot. Their friends in Fallon took care of Sierra, Amanda and Reto Junior. It is unbelievable how people pull together in times of trouble. And even though they do not know me, I was so thankful to all of them.

Dustin was in intensive care for days, but then pulled through. Three weeks later he could go home already, but only because Brenda and Reto took over. Brenda wanted to know everything that had to be done to take care of a child with leukemia. The whole family pulled together and they did a super job.

Then four weeks later I flew out to Nevada to visit my family. It felt good to be with them and to be able to see first-hand what goes on. Brenda was a great "nurse" for Dustin. She even took me along to the hospital when Dustin had to have his chemo therapy and I could really be involved. It was tough on all the kids; they could not share food anymore nor drink out of the same glass, all things siblings do automatically. It does not just affect the one that is sick, no, the whole family has to change their lifestyle.

My week of vacation went way too fast, and I felt bad that I had to leave them again. I even played with the idea of leaving Wisconsin and moving to Nevada so that I could help them taking care of Sierra, Amanda and Reto Junior while Dustin and his parents had to go to the hospital; then this will not go away overnight, no, it will take years.

I'm 60 years old now and tired of starting over again. I have to have an income, and who would hire me out there at my age? There is really not much I can do. But I will always keep them in my prayers and I sure hope I could help them that way, too. I was so thankful that my kids in Nevada had so many friends who supported them one hundred percent. They had fundraisers, helped out with the kids, and the whole family could go to Disney World in Florida with the "Make a Wish" foundation. That was great.

Dustin was the first one of a whole cluster, who had leukemia. Four years later there were 17 kids in Fallon who had leukemia. Brenda and Reto fought then and now, years later, still do, to figure out why so many children in Fallon have to suffer. They went all the way to the capitol in Washington, D.C. to make sure that there is testing done so that no more children have to go through this difficult time.

****

Back home I had my work to help me go on, but I still was alone. If I just had a partner I could talk to and that would understand me. Yes, for years now I had a friend 25 miles north of Antigo. There I could sit outside, read a book, or go for a ride on the lake with the pontoon boat. Willi immigrated with his wife and four kids from Europe. He knew what it meant to start new, so we had something in common. He tried over and over again to talk me into moving in with him and selling my home. But he was seven years older than I, and I said every time, "I need security, and if I'm not good enough to be someone's wife, then I will not be his housekeeper either. And what would I do if something happens to you and your kids sell your house?"

"Oh, with the little you have, you could easy get a low-income housing apartment," he replied. Willi was a wealthy guy and said marrying me would be like throwing money out the window. I guess that does not say much for me. And I could not talk to him about my fears and pains. He would stop me and tell me put it behind you; forget it and go on with life. But that is easier said than done. So a friend he stays, and nothing more.

Lotti and I flew to Nevada again that Thanksgiving. Dustin is still on chemo. He lost all his hair, but now it is slowly growing back. It was so great to see that he is doing better. We could even take a ride up to Lake Tahoc, where they had snow already. How great to spend them four days with my kids and grandkids. Dustin, God be with you and protect you.

On January 31st, 2000, I became great-grandma again. Bobbi Jo gave birth to another little girl, and her name is McKayla. I wish them nothing but the best and hope that McKayla has a bright future that takes her wherever she wants to go.

In June of 2000 I took Amanda along to Switzerland, then now was Heidi's confirmation. We had, like always, a great time, but it was the first time without my mother, and that was different. Yet they kept us busy, like so many times before. We had breakfast on top of the Santis, a beautiful mountain. Jessica took a couple of days off work and drove us around. And all of us together even went to the monastery in Einsidelin, just a spectacular building. There I bought myself a doll in a Swiss costume, and she sings the song "Edelweiss." She has a special place on the dresser in my bedroom; she is my child within. Whenever I'm sad and do not know where to turn, I talk to her and hope she makes me see my future in a different light.

And as I still enjoyed my vacation in Switzerland, I became Great-grandma again. Grandson Tyler and Danielle had a little girl on June 17, 2000, Madison Marie.

A cute round-faced, curly- haired baby. Yes, the next generation is in full bloom. God bless you all!

Another year passed. I spent a week in Nevada and was happy to see that Dustin's health, even though he was still on chemo and lots and lots of medication, was improving. I hope and pray that God will help him to get better again soon.

Heidi came to see me in June 2001. She flew in from Switzerland, and I picked her up in Chicago. She is going to stay three weeks and will spend about half of the time with Lotti and the other half with me. I had to work but could squish a couple of vacation days in. We decided to go up north to Lake Superior. Willi volunteered to drive us. We went on Thursday from Antigo to Watersmeet, Michigan, stopped there at the Casino, then we went on to Ashland, Wisconsin, where we stayed at the casino overnight. And, of course, I lost some money. The next morning we drove along Lake Superior. We stopped at Bayfield and took a ferry to Madeleine Island. The ticket was $7 per person, and I thought that it would be great to walk around that pretty island. I was never there before. But we got off the boat, walked a couple of hundred feet, and Willis said, "This is all the same bullshit. What do we want to see here? I'm not walking around, my feet are hurting. Let's go back to the mainland." And disappointed, but without complaints, we boarded the ferry again. Then we drove without a stop all the way to Two-Harbors.

It was late Friday afternoon during school vacation and we had to look for a motel, and that was almost impossible. Finally we found a little motel that still had a room free for us. It was just a little room with a door and a small window. No air-conditioning and it was 95 degrees outside. Sure not sleeping weather. Heidi watched TV for awhile but, of course, not Willi's station. So she took a book and sat on the steps outside our door to read. But then I could not sleep. What if someone comes and grabs

Heidi. I know that was really stupid of me, but it made me think about my life and myself.

I made some decisions that night. First of all, we will drive straight home tomorrow, even though I had two more vacation days. Second, I will never ever travel with Willi again. In fact, I will never visit him again. I really do not like to be alone, but I'm also tired of being controlled. I cannot understand why it should be so hard to find a friend that takes me for who I am, the plain, simple woman without a lot of money.

Merrill had fly-in that Sunday, and Tyler, my grandson now being a pilot, invited us to come and fly with him. What a great experience! And Heidi thought that was just out of this world that she could fly with her cousin.

Yet the whole day Heidi was on my case and said over and over again, "Grandma, how can you let a man do that to you? Why don't you just say forget it. I do what I want to?" And yes, I know that she was right, but for me to change is easier said than done. All my life I was controlled, and it takes work to get out of that rut. But I promised myself to try it.

That night as I was ready to make us some supper the phone rang. This is Dennis Prigge, I heard a guy on the other side say. I could hardly believe my ears. Dennis and Mary were the ones who helped me get all my tools together after Henry died. But then after that Mary wrote me a letter and wanted to know if Dennis tried something with me, now that I was free game. They later moved to Missouri, but I never got in contact with them again. I felt it was not worth it. Mary wrote me a couple of times, but I ignored it and never answered her. I heard from some of my friends that Mary passed away. She had brain cancer. They even asked if I wanted Dennis' address to send him a condolence card.

"No way," I replied. "Then everybody will say, see, Mary was right. Edith was waiting for him." Yet, I can honestly say I never had any personal contact with him.

But now Dennis calls me. What made him do that? He started apologizing and said that when he cleaned some of Mary's stuff he stumbled across a copy of the letter that Mary wrote to me so many years ago. He felt that it was uncalled for and not fair towards me. I answered that that was in the past and not important anymore. I really did not want to talk. I had enough this weekend and just wanted to be left alone. But he was stubborn and would not hang up. He wanted to know why my name still was Gross and why I was not remarried yet.

I answered, "Who would marry an old bitch like me? At my age men want younger women, and I'm not rich either, so I'm out of luck."

He quickly replied, "I would marry you." Which I thought was funny, because he did not really know me. But we talked for almost an hour and I promised to write him and keep the communication open.

Then August 25th, 2001 was a big day in Merrill. Bobbi Jo got married to Jason Schulz, the father of her two girls. It was a beautiful wedding on a sunny summer day. Edith and Jessica flew in from Switzerland, and together we had a great week. But, like always, it goes way too fast. Lotti and I brought Edith and Jessica to Minneapolis and saw them off on their long flight to Switzerland. The four-hour drive home gave me time to talk to Lotti about Dennis, and I showed her some letters he wrote.

"Mom, it sounds to me like he wants to marry you. What would you say if he will ask you," was her question. "I do not know. Time will tell," I replied. A good question; what would I do?

Dennis called now weekly and we e-mailed daily. Then he took the weekend after Labor Day off and drove all the way up here to come and see me. I was scared; I did not know what to expect, and could I really live with him? But he was the same old Dennis. Friendly and polite, not pushy at all. We spent four nice days together, got to know each other better, and yes, he asked me the first weekend if I would marry him. He said he did not want to spend the rest of his life alone, but then neither do I. I could hardly sleep that night; I was just tossing and turning. What should I do; he is a nice guy, I have known him for years and, yes, I think I could spend the rest of my life with him. So the next morning at breakfast I said, "Yes, I will marry you, but I will stay right here in Antigo for now and will work until I'm 65. I can't just give everything up and move with you to Missouri."

Then on Saturday night we even took his three kids in Wausau out for supper, and there he introduced me as his fiance. None of the kids said a word as we ate. Then after the meal we sat in a cozy corner for an after-dinner drink.

That was when Joy, Dennis's oldest daughter, asked, "Did I hear that right, did you call Edith your fiance?" Dennis smiled and said yes. "Neither of us would like to spend the rest of our lives alone. Our spouses are gone and hopefully found their place in heaven. So we deserve some happiness down here, too." And I really think the kids understood where we came from.

It was that black day, September 11th, 2001, when Dennis left early in the morning and drove back to Missouri. So, I will never ever forget that day that brought so much sadness to our nation, yet a little spark of hope into my heart.

Now I had to get going and make wedding arrangements. We did not want to wait too long; neither of us knows how many years we have left on this earth. Dennis was 64 a couple of months ago, and I will soon be 63 years old. But I never thought that it would be so hard to make it all come together. Hall or church arrangements are made years in advance. If I had an open day in church, I could get no hall, or the other way around. I was pretty disgusted and thought to myself, why don't we just fly to Vegas and get married there, that would be a lot less complicated. But I kept those thoughts to myself and did not say a word to anyone. Lotti was a great help and would not let me sit around. One of those days when we went shopping for a wedding dress for me, we had lunch together. That was when she, out of the blue, said, "I think it is great that you two are getting married right here and all of us can be part of your big day. Going to Vegas, or any of those places to get married, is cheating family out of a very important part of your life." Boy, did she answer my question, without even knowing what my thoughts were.

I wrote Edith, Heinz and Reto and asked them to please be with me on that important day of my life. Edith answered quickly, "I thought that you might do that, but why so quickly?" All I could say was, "I do not have 30-40 years anymore. I want to be happy now, as long as I can enjoy it."

We set the wedding day for July 20th, 2002. It would be at the Calvary Lutheran Church in Antigo, and Pastor Kate would be our minister. I really, really like her; she always has a great message.

So that is taken care of, but what about the hall? There just wasn't anything available. Lotti again pulled through for me. Why don't you get a tent and have your reception right here in our back yard, and then have a pig roast, or something? I talked it over with Dennis, and it sounded great to us. So I ordered a tent and then also a caterer that would roast a whole pig and bring everything that goes with it.

We had to get invitations and make a list of all our guests. We both agreed that we would keep it small, but when it was all said and done we had 170 guests for supper.

To everything there is a season, a time and a purpose.

Because you have shared in our lives
By your friendship and love, we
Edith Gross
and
Dennis Prigge
Together with out children invite you to share
The beginning of our life together
When we exchange marriage vows
On Saturday, the twentieth of July
Two thousand and two
At two o'clock in the afternoon
Calvary Lutheran Church

The cake had to be ordered, and that became a wedding present from my brother. He could not join us, since he could not get vacation at that time, but he wanted to send us his sweet greetings with this beautiful cake. Thanks so much!

The flowers for the church were picked out and would be put together by a young woman who does that as a hobby, and she did a super job.

Bobbi Jo and Mary Jane made mine and Erika's bouquet, all the corsages and also decorated the tent. And Jessica was my personal attendant. A great job, guys.

Lotti ordered a band from Wausau to play for us that evening. And that band was very appropriate; they were all senior citizens, but they played just great. Everybody really enjoyed them.

The only thing that was missing was the music in church. I thought of a friend I have in Merrill; she too immigrated from Switzerland, and Susanna and her husband, Paul, make beautiful music. She sings and plays the violin, and he plays the guitar. Susanna even sang a song in Romanisch, the language that my kids spoke when we lived in Bergun. Yes, it brought tears to my eyes.

Now I think we have it together, and all we have to do

is to hope and pray that all our kids can come and it won't rain all day.

I do not know where the time went, but it was July already and in just a couple of weeks would be my wedding day. Is this really the right thing for me to do? Dennis retired in January of 2002 but still spends a lot of time in Missouri. There he has a remodeling project and a building to take care of. So will it work out for both of us when someday down the road we live together for good?

Yes, I think so. We respect each other's feelings and that, I think, counts for a lot already. Plus, slowly but surely, I really fell in love with Dennis.

Edith and her family flew in the beginning of July 2002 and we could spend some time with them before the wedding. Plus, they got to know Dennis a little better.

July 15th was Dennis's 65th birthday, so we invited all the kids and their families that were here for a party at a restaurant right at the Wolf River. It was a nice afternoon that gave all of us time to reminisce.

Heinz and his family flew in on Wednesday before the wedding. Reto and his family drove in on Friday with their camper and camped at Lotti's.

I had all my kids together on Henry's funeral more than 12 years ago, and even though I hoped and prayed to see that one more time, I never thought that it would happen as long as I'm alive. And now it became reality. What a great, great day! We had all our kids and in-laws, all our grandchildren here, except four. Martin Junior served in the Swiss Army at that time, and they would not give him time off, and Jerica, Michelle and Matthew live in California and could not be with us either. And, of course, we can't forget the fourth generation; our three great-grandkids were also with us. A lot of the in-laws and cousins did not know each other, so it was great for everybody involved.

It was Saturday now, my big day. The sun was smiling

and spread her golden sparkles deep into my heart. Everything was just perfect.

Reto and Paul (Dennis' son) were ushers and also helped with communion. Cassandra, my oldest great-grandchild, was my flower girl, and Dustin, who no longer is on chemo therapy, was my ring-bearer. Heinz walked me down the aisle. Edith baked the bread for communion and Joy, Lori and Christine gave us moral support.

Erika, my best friend for over 33 years who also immigrated from Switzerland, was my maid of honor, and George, Dennis' best friend, was our best man. Thanks, you two.

And Dennis' sister and two brothers with their families came to be with us. The church was packed. It's unbelievable, how much more can we ask for than to have all our families and so, so many friends with us on that important day.

And yes, important it was, especially for me. When months ago I said, "Yes, Dennis, I will marry you," I thought to myself this is not the love I hoped to find, but we have respect for each other. He is a nice guy and I'm sure he will be good to me, and I guess I can live with that. But now, almost one year later, as I walked down the aisle and saw Dennis waiting for me, I know that I really loved him with all my heart, and I could see in everything he did for me that he loved me just as much. And now today we can seal this love.

Pastor Kate asked one by one, Edith, Heinz, Lotti, Reto, Joy, Lori, Christine and Paul to stand up, and then wanted to know if they, in front of God and all our witnesses, would give us their blessing. They all said, "Yes, we do." This really sealed what we two felt for each other.

It was a beautiful day from the beginning to the end, and I will be forever thankful to all our kids who made such a sacrifice, especially financially, to be with us on that great day. I will always, always treasure the time we could spend together.

Edith and her family went back to Switzerland the following Tuesday, and Reto and his family headed back to Nevada with their camper. Heinz and his family stayed for two more weeks, and together we went to Missouri to see where Dennis lived the last seven years.

We realized that a lot of Dennis' friends in Missouri could not be with us to celebrate our wedding so we planned a reception for the following Saturday, July 27th, 2002, at Prince of Peace Lutheran Church in Springfield, Missouri, and we had a great turnout. So many friends, and the meal they cooked was super. Thanks so much!

Erika, my maid of honor, came along, too. She wanted to wear her pretty dark blue dress one more time, and that gave me a reason to wear my wedding dress again. Yes, memories that will linger on forever.

Jessica spent six more weeks, but then had to leave us, too. She cried the whole way to the airport in Minneapolis. She did not want to go back to Switzerland. She wished that the first five years of her life would come back. In her dreams she saw herself as my little girl again, but that time is gone and will never come back. Yes, in my heart she will always be my little girl, but she is 26 years old and a young woman now. A young woman who, no matter what, has to find her own life. I tried to convince her to try her best to make a life for herself, and she promised to do that. Jessica has settled down now; she lives in Switzerland, manages a travel office, is engaged and plans her own wedding. She too is now on the right track.

For Dennis and me life goes on. No more big parties. But we both do enjoy the calm and quiet times.

Over Labor Day 2002 we went to New Glarus, a Swiss town in the southwestern part of Wisconsin. Until then our plans were that I would eventually move to Missouri where Dennis had a church building that he wanted to make into a duplex. But now Dennis thought New Glarus would be nice, too. Not too far from the kids, I could keep up my Swiss language, and he could support his hobby, woodcarving. We looked for a house there, but this is too close to the big city of Madison and the prices were really out of our league.

Then one day in November 2002, I came home from work, and Dennis, like always, greeted me at the door. He had this funny grin on his face. Then he showed me this little ad and asked, "What would you say if we stay right here in the area?" He said I lit up like a Christmas tree. The same afternoon we went and checked that property out. It is a little 22' by 24' log cabin on 1.7 acres of land, woods all around it. It looks just like a little Swiss home. We fell in love with it, and within four weeks it was ours. Yes, we have to do some remodeling, but I will retire in February of 2004, and then we will have time to work together and make it our pretty, last home.

It was a busy 2003 for us. In March we went to Nevada and enjoyed the family we had there. Dustin is doing great now. Thank God for that! Brenda and Reto still fight for more testing and hope to find out why so many kids in their town had leukemia. They feel that it is worth the time they spend to fight if they could help to prevent another child from getting sick. Good luck, guys.

Then beginning of June we flew to Reno again to participate in Reto's 8th grade and Sierra's high school graduation. Sierra will now go on to college in Reno and eventually wants to be a children's doctor, because she was so involved with her brother Dustin's sickness. Good luck, Sierra, we love you.

Monday after graduation Dennis, Reto Junior and I left for Switzerland. I thought at first to wait until next year to go there and show Dennis my native land, but then I told myself, "No, I will do it now. At our age, who knows if we still would be able to do it next year." It was a long flight from Reno to Dallas and on to Zurich. There

Edith, Jessica and Heidi waited for us and then drove us to their home, which is in my favorite valley, the Toggenburg. The next morning we had breakfast on top of the Santis. It is just super the view one has from that mountain peak; and the food is great, too. The Santis is shown on the cover page.

That first Sunday we had a family reunion. Everybody wanted to get to know my new husband, and I was proud to show him off, because I love him. Even Annakather, a woman who worked for me in 1965 in Bergun, was with us. What a great friend she is.

My classmates from 7th and 8th grade made a special class reunion, just to see me and my new husband. This was the second time in 50 years that I got together with them. My brother drove us there, and it was fun to see that they all aged, too, not just me. A big "thanks" to all of them!

Some of our friends from overseas gave us a gift certificate as a wedding present. It was a trip with the Glacier Express, an eight-hour train ride from St. Moritz to Zermatt. I think that is the most impressive train ride in the world. My brother Heinz drove us to St. Moritz. We even stopped in Bergun and visited the store I managed in 1964-66. They still use the same desk I worked on almost 40 years ago. Yes, it has a couple more dents, but otherwise it is the same old desk, and it brought back a lot of memories. Then Heinz dropped us off in St. Moritz, where we stayed overnight and he drove back home.

The next day at 10 a.m. we boarded the train. The scenery was just spectacular. Castles, deep ravines, small towns surrounded by green meadows and, of course, the mountains. Dennis was so glued to the window that he got a blister on his elbow. Eight hours later we got off the train in the idyllic village of Zermatt, where we met up with Heinz and Lisa, my brother and sister-in-law. We stayed in a pretty motel all the way on the top floor, and from the balcony we could watch the clouds pull over the Matterhorn. It was just beautiful. The next day we went with the cog rail up to the Gornergrat. We could watch the wild mountain goats, the glaciers, and all those flowers; it was so pretty. We ate lunch at a nice restaurant, a little chapel close by, and a gorgeous view of the Matterhorn. Dennis took picture after picture. My favorite one is with the cross and the Matterhorn. On the cross it says:

Do you want to see God's love—look at this Cross
Do you want to see the Almighty God—
go to the mountains.

That evening we took a walk through that pretty tourist town Zermatt, where no cars are allowed. And we even stopped at the cemetery. There are a lot of graves from mountain climbers who tried to get to the top of the Matterhorn, but paid the price with their lives.

The next day we went with the cable car all the way up to the Little Matterhorn that is just around 12,000 feet over sea level. We had mountains and valleys all around us. We could see into Italy, and also the France mountains. There was a tunnel that they dug into the glacier, so we had to investigate that, too. The ice was deep blue and there were ice sculptures all along: cold, cold, cold, but what a sight. Yes, definitely a vacation to remember.

Then we boarded the train again, and it took us via Bern, the capitol, and Zurich, the biggest city of Switzerland, to my brother's house. His daughter, Irene, picked us up at the railroad station, took us to her home, and we enjoyed a nice evening with her family.

The last couple of days we shared with our kids, inlaws and grandkids.

But nothing will last forever and our vacation came to an end. I really do not like goodbyes, but now it is a lot easier, now that I have a guy with whom I can share my life. Dennis, thanks for loving me!

I pray to God that we can enjoy many, many more years together, years like the last two. From now on I will sit back and just enjoy my life.

There is no greater blessing than the love of family and friends.

May God bless all of you.

Reto, Dustin, Reto, Jr., Amanda, Lotti and Brittany.

Right: Dennis and me.

Below: George, Dennis, me, Erika, Cassy and Dustin.

Our eight children. Back: Heinz, Dennis, me, Reto, Paul. Front: Lotti, Christine, Lori, Edith, Joy.

Dennis and me with all my children, in-laws, grandchildren and great-grandchildren.